The Politics of Public Broadcasting in Britain and Japan

This book explores the remarkably similar national public broadcasters of Britain and Japan – the BBC and NHK. It considers the origins of both organizations in the 1920s, highlights how both have been major shapers of national life and national identity in their respective countries, how both have been significant innovators of broadcasting technology, and how both have high reputations for honest and balanced news reporting. It outlines how both have adapted to cope with successive major changes in the broadcasting landscape. The book also points out the major differences: the BBC's greater success at being commercial and entrepreneurial, the BBC's fierce protection of its editorial independence, often used to play a watchdog role in holding the powerful to account – which contrasts sharply with the approach of NHK, which cooperates with rather than confronts political elites, serving as an agent of social stability, whereas the BBC acts more as an agent of social change. As debates about the future of public broadcasting become more intense, this book provides useful evidence of how public broadcasting can be approached in different ways and how vital it is to democratic life.

Henry Laurence is Associate Professor at Bowdoin College, Maine, USA.

The aim of this series is to publish original, high-quality work by both new and established scholars in the West and the East, on all aspects of media, culture and social change in Asia.

For more information about this series, please visit: https://www.routledge.com/
Media-Culture-and-Social-Change-in-Asia-Series/book-series/SE0797

The Politics of Public Broadcasting in Britain and Japan

The BBC and NHK Compared

Henry Laurence

Routledge
Taylor & Francis Group

LONDON AND NEW YORK

First published 2023
by Routledge
4 Park Square, Milton Park, Abingdon, Oxon OX14 4RN

and by Routledge
605 Third Avenue, New York, NY 10158

Routledge is an imprint of the Taylor & Francis Group, an informa business

British Library Cataloguing-in-Publication Data
A catalogue record for this book is available from the British Library

Library of Congress Cataloging-in-Publication Data
A catalog record for this book has been requested

ISBN: 978-1-032-31038-1 (hbk)
ISBN: 978-1-032-31039-8 (pbk)
ISBN: 978-1-003-30775-4 (ebk)

DOI: 10.4324/b23015

Typeset in Times New Roman
by Apex CoVantage, LLC

Contents

Acknowledgments

I am deeply grateful for the support, encouragement, and input of so many friends and colleagues who have helped make this book possible. All have made it better: the remaining errors, omissions, and flaws are mine alone. My first thanks go to Susan Pharr for her unflagging encouragement and mentorship, and to her and Shin Fujihira for giving me invaluable opportunities to present and develop my ideas at Harvard University's US-Japan Relations Program. Victor Pickard, Paul Talcott, and Stewart Wood read earlier drafts and gave generous and insightful advice. The extended Bowdoin community was a constant source of support and intellectual camaraderie. Special shout-outs to Ericka Albaugh, Michael Arthur, Alison Cooper, Pete Coviello, Shelley Deane, Paul Franco, Barbara Elias-Klenner, Laura Henry, Marc Hetherington, Ann Kibbe, Aaron Kitch, Barry Mills, Steve Perkinson, Tom Porter, Clayton Rose, Andy Rudelevige, Jen Scanlon, Jeff and Vjaynthi Selinger, Maron Sorenson, Allen Springer, and Jonathan Weiler.

I'm indebted to Roger Goodman, Sho Konishi, Ian Neary, and Hugh Whittaker for being such welcoming hosts at the Nissan Institute of Japanese Studies at St. Anthony's College, Oxford, where it was a joy to research, write, and be inspired on two sabbaticals. While at Oxford, I also benefitted enormously from the unique community of scholars and journalists at the Reuters Institute for the Study of Journalism, including Pallavi Aiyar, Richard Danbury, John Kelly, David Levy, Henrik Ornebring, Ken Payne, Ruth Pritchard-Kelly, Meera Selva, and Michael Stark. It was my privilege, too, to discuss the challenges facing contemporary journalism with Josh Benton of the Nieman Lab, Lauren Elise Harris at the Columbia Journalism Review, and Lisa Bartfai.

In Japan, I received all manner of help, guidance, and great feedback from Rie Hayashi Takako Hikotani, Nobuhiro Hiwatari, Haruyuki Ishinohashi, Jin Nishikawa, Dave Leheny, Ai Nakagawa, David McNeil, Greg Noble, Miwako Ozawa, Ryuichi Kitano, Reiko Saisho, Toru Shinoda, Nobuko Shiraishi, and Mina Watanabe. My warmest thanks to James Minney, Safia Minney, and Toshio Ogahara for all their hospitality over so many visits, to Noko Seki for her support, and to Michiko Watanabe for her enduring friendship.

One of the greatest pleasures of academia is working with wonderfully engaged, smart undergraduate students. Liza Boles, Itza Bonilla Hernandez, Talia Cowen, Lousia Diaz, Kate Fendler, Gianni Jannke, Sara Jung, Liam Killon, Hari

Kondabolu, Yoonhyung Lee, Chris Rossi, Tung Trinh, and Qiao Wang all provided outstanding research assistance and help. Readers should be especially grateful for the phenomenal editorial assistance of Nora Biette-Timmons and Marika Josephson in improving earlier, uglier versions of the manuscript. Administrative support was provided with invariable professionalism and good cheer by Suzanne Astolfi, Lynne Atkinson, and Jane Baker. At Routledge, it has been a pleasure working with Peter Sowden, and my thanks to Andrew Schuller for introducing us, and for his keen interest in the project. I am also deeply grateful to the anonymous reader who gave such helpful and constructive suggestions. Research funding was generously provided by an Abe Fellowship from the Center for Global Partnership and the Social Science Research Council, as well as from Bowdoin College.

Lastly and most importantly, I would like to thank my family. Jessica and Neil Bett, Guy Bigland, Tony and Cynthia Lamport, Charlotte Laurence, Colin Laurence and Fabio, and Gabrielle Savoldelli, all have been unfailing in their patient enthusiasm for the project, encouragement, and advice. Gemma Laurence proved to be a wonderful proofreader when she had the misfortune to be pandemic-bound at home as I finished the final draft, and I truly appreciate the many occasions on which she implored me not to give way to despair. My biggest thanks go to my wife Sarah. She has always been a vital partner in this project, reading and rereading drafts, discussing ideas, giving wonderful advice, and providing constant emotional support.

Some of my fondest childhood memories are of our entire family gathering around the television on Sunday evenings: such moments are what public broadcasting is ultimately all about. So it is for this reason, among many far better ones, that I dedicate this book to the best parents ever: my father Tony Laurence and my late mother Nicola Laurence.

Abbreviations

BBC	British Broadcasting Corporation
BCC	Broadcasting Complaints Commission
BIPA	British Internet Publishers Association
BSC	Broadcasting Standards Commission
CBS	Broadcasting Inc. (formerly the Columbia Broadcasting System)
CPB	Corporation for Public Broadcasting
DTT	Digital Terrestrial Television
DTV	Digital Television
FCC	Federal Communications Commission
FM&T	Future Media and Technology Department of the BBC
FRC	Federal Radio Commission
GE	General Electric
ITN	Independent Television News
ITV	Independent Television
JEITIA	Japan Electronics and Information Technology Industry Association
JSP	Japan Socialist Party
Keidanren	Federation of Economic Organizations
LDP	Liberal Democratic Party
METI	Ministry of Economy, Trade and Industry
MIAC	Ministry of Internal Affairs and Communications
MITI	Ministry of International Trade and Industry
MP	Member of Parliament
MPM	Ministry of Public Management, Home Affairs, Posts and Telecommunications (sometimes referred to as MPMHT)
MPT	Ministry of Posts and Telecommunications
NAB	National Association of Broadcasters
NBC	National Broadcasting Company
NHK	*Nihon Hōsō Kōkai*
NPR	National Public Radio
Ofcom	Office of Communications
OMS	Organization for the Maintenance of Supplies
PBS	Public Broadcasting Service
PRI	Public Radio International
RCA	Radio Corporation of America
TUC	Trades Union Congress
UGC	User-generated Content

1 Introducing NHK and the BBC

On January 20, 2001, NHK, Japan's national public broadcaster, released details of what promised to be a groundbreaking documentary. *The Japanese Military's Wartime Sexual Violence* (*Nihongun Senji Seibōryoku*) concerned the redress movement for the so-called comfort women victims of the Imperial Army's system of sexual slavery. It focused on the International Women's War Crimes Tribunal, recently organized by Japanese and international activists to raise awareness of the issue. The penultimate draft of the documentary included testimony by Japanese veterans confessing to having raped women; testimony by Chinese rape victims; a statement by a leading human rights lawyer that Emperor Hirohito was guilty of crimes against humanity; opinion from an expert in international law that the Japanese government was liable to pay compensation to survivors; and a legal critique of the refusal of the ruling Liberal Democratic Party (LDP) to do so.

But a few days before the program was scheduled to air, senior LDP politicians, including future Prime Minister Shinzō Abe, paid a visit to NHK headquarters. What exactly was said is disputed, but immediately after the meeting, a senior NHK official ordered the documentary's producers to make major revisions. The version that eventually aired, retitled *Questioning Wartime Sexual Violence* (*Towareru senji seibōryoku*), differed dramatically from the earlier script. All the scenes mentioned earlier had been cut, while interviews critical of Japan's war crimes and related LDP policy had been misleadingly re-edited and diluted. New material included a hastily conducted interview with a conservative historian falsely introduced as having attended the Tribunal who was highly critical of the redress movement. Also added at the last minute was some seemingly irrelevant footage of a US bombing raid in Vietnam along with an assertion that the atomic bombings of Hiroshima and Nagasaki were war crimes. The documentary makers and other participants were incensed by the drastic change in message and tone. Many Japanese viewers were outraged but unsurprised because the episode seemed to confirm NHK's reputation for avoiding confrontation and presenting an unthreatening, conservative vision of the nation. Abe and NHK's President Ebisawa Katsuji denied any impropriety and carried on unscathed.

A quite different story played out at the BBC, the United Kingdom's public broadcaster, just a few months later. In the early hours of May 29, 2003, reporter Andrew Gilligan appeared on Radio 4's *Today* program to talk about the build-up

DOI: 10.4324/b23015-1

to the recent Iraq War. Gilligan quoted an anonymous source as saying that Tony Blair's Labour government had justified the invasion of Iraq using a report on Saddam Hussein's possession of weapons of mass destruction that they had "sexed up" with intelligence they "knew or probably knew" to be false. Blair furiously denied the allegation and demanded a retraction. The BBC's director-general Greg Dyke and chair of the Board of Governors Gavyn Davies refused, backing their journalist and defending the integrity of their reporting even after they discovered that Gilligan's allegations had gone beyond the evidence his source had shared. Dyke and Davies resigned when the official Hutton Inquiry found in Blair's favor, but their defense of editorial independence won widespread public sympathy. Their faith in the essential truth of Gilligan's reporting was validated years later, when the 2016 Chilcot Report concluded that Blair had indeed made claims about Iraq's military capabilities with unjustified certainty.

The difference in responses to political pressure could not have been starker. NHK's top managers instinctively jumped to present the LDP's narrative of national innocence, silencing the voices not only of their own staff but of the broader movement of Japanese citizens trying to uncover their country's darker and more complicated historical record. The BBC's top managers instinctively defended their reporter against government attack despite high personal costs. The contrasting responses are especially noteworthy considering that both broadcasters are regulated and funded along almost identical lines, with editorial independence legally required and guaranteed in both cases. The differing editorial attitudes are profoundly consequential, too, because these broadcasters are among the best-loved and most trusted media institutions in their respective countries.

This book tells the remarkable story of how the British Broadcasting Corporation (BBC) and the Japan Broadcasting Corporation (*Nihon Hōsō Kyōkai* or NHK) evolved from their shared origins as radio monopolies in the 1920s to their present form as vital national institutions and global multi-platform media organizations. Public broadcasting has many definitions and many variations, but here refers to two organizations that are publicly funded and universally available within their countries, whose stated purpose is to serve national interests by offering impartial news and a broad array of socially and culturally valuable content. Treating audiences as citizens as well as consumers, their mission is to inform and educate while they entertain. I argue that despite their many similarities, they serve quite different political, social, and economic roles. Their stories are worth telling for several reasons.

First, it is hard to exaggerate how important each broadcaster is to national life in just about every imaginable realm from politics to social values, culture, and national identity. They are the most trusted sources of news in an era of disinformation. They provide a rare platform for social unity in an era of polarization. They are perhaps their county's most prominent cultural institutions, both creating and curating national arts and letters. They celebrate national identity in an era of globalization and their countries' longest-serving ambassadors to the world. In the words of BBC historian Charlotte Higgins, they are "the national institution that most powerfully touches our inner lives – working its way into our sense of ourselves as individuals and as part of a community, our convictions, our imaginations."[1] Both, too, make vital economic contributions. The BBC is at the heart of the creative industries that make up one of the largest, fastest-growing, and internationally competitive sectors of the UK economy. NHK's communications technology research fuels Japan's mighty electronics industry. They are, in short, very worthy of study in their own right.

Second, to tell the story of NHK and the BBC is to tell the story of Japan and Britain over the past century, for these broadcasters are perhaps the single most important institutions in defining and shaping social values and national identity in a changing world. In the words of Maeda Yoshinori, one of NHK's greatest leaders: "The history of NHK in a narrower sense is a history of Japanese society and of Japan, and in a broader sense, a history of the changing international community since the end of World War II."[2] The book shows the different ways in which they reported, reflected, and interpreted the messy realities of war, imperial decline, the social turmoil of the 1960s, globalization and neoliberalism in the 1980s, the digital revolution in the 1990s, and the demands for gender equality and multiculturalism in the 2000s. Many themes reappear throughout the book: war, and how to report and remember it; citizenship, what it means and requires, and who it belongs to; national values, what they are, and who decides them. Anti-Americanism pops up across the decades as each broadcaster seeks to define and defend their national identity in the face of the US's seemingly boundless cultural and economic hegemony. I tell this story by exploring those critical moments when new media technologies – radio, television, cable and satellite TV, digital TV, and finally the internet – disrupted old practices and challenged old ways of thinking. Each new technology posed existential dangers to the public broadcasters, but they adapted successfully, turning threats into opportunities for reinvention.

The third reason for this comparative history is that the BBC and NHK present an intriguing puzzle to scholars of media and comparative politics. Superficially, they are remarkably similar institutions, sharing almost identical legal, organizational, and funding structures. Yet they often play strikingly different roles in their respective nation's political, social, and cultural life. I seek to shed light on this paradox by examining the ways that different organizational cultures have evolved over 100 years of conflict and challenge.

Finally, and most importantly, I argue that public broadcasting is needed more than ever in the era of misinformation, polarization, and the crisis in news journalism. Commercial media – including traditional newspapers, network and cable television, and social media platforms – has largely failed to address, and in many ways exacerbated, the erosion of civil discourse and informed engagement that are essential to a healthy democracy. The BBC and NHK can and must continue to play their vital roles in national democratic life.

Two Houses Alike?

The BBC and NHK are remarkably similar institutions. Both have dominated their nations' media markets since the 1920s, when they shared similar origins as consortia of commercial radio manufacturers and operators. Both were refashioned as publicly accountable but legally independent national broadcasting monopolies, which now coexist alongside powerful commercial media. Their institutional structures and funding mechanisms are almost identical, not coincidentally because the BBC served as a model for the Japanese founders of NHK in the 1920s, and again for the Allied occupiers who reinvented NHK in the postwar 1940s. Both enjoy legal autonomy, although their most senior officials and regulators are political appointees. Both are publicly funded by user fees. They share a similar remit to offer free, universally accessible, and socially valuable content to their respective populations.

Both take seriously their duty to "inform, educate and entertain." NHK and the BBC are consistently ranked among the most trusted sources of accurate, impartial news and information in their country. They also provide their country's most prominent public sphere, serving as the first place politicians, activists, and audiences go to discuss the great issues of the day. They offer extensive educational content, their value as sites of remote learning well-established long before the pandemic-era school lockdowns made such services indispensable to national education policy.

Yet their role as entertainers is far more important to most of their audiences than as providers of information or education. Both public broadcasters have created many, indeed probably most, of their nations' best-loved radio and television programs. In doing so, they have created some of the most important rituals of national life: the daily news, Sunday evening historical dramas, seasonal touchstones such as *The Morecambe and Wise Christmas Show* or NHK's New Year Song Contest *Kōhaku Uta Gassen*, and iconic sporting events such as the seasonal Sumo *bashō*, the FA cup final, or the Olympics. Both play outsize roles in shaping the public image of their Royal families as co-creators of spectacular national celebrations such as the enthronement of Emperor Reiwa or the fairy-tale wedding of Prince Charles and Lady Diana. The broadcasters also curate and celebrate national cultural traditions in art, music, and drama. In doing all this, the BBC and NHK have become vital to the creation and interpretation of national identity. To know the BBC is to understand a great deal about how the British see themselves: not just what entertains them, but how they see themselves, and how they would like to be seen. Similarly, understanding contemporary life in Japan would be impossible without soon encountering NHK. Dramas, comedies, even game shows, and cooking contests are constantly reflecting and shaping social values, permeating the collective national consciousness in deeper, broader ways than news reporting ever could.

Beyond programming, both broadcasters also serve as important tools of national economic policy. NHK's research laboratories play a vital role in developing the communications technologies that fuel the success of Japan's consumer electronics industry. The BBC has been used by successive governments as a central pillar of Britain's creative industries, training armies of actors, artists, and engineers and commissioning lucrative work for independent production companies. Both provided vital assistance to their governments in the vexed transition from analog to digital broadcasting. Finally, both serve as quasi-official ambassadors of their countries abroad – for example, as promoters of Cool Britannia and Cool Japan.

Yet, despite their manifest similarities, the BBC and NHK differ dramatically in their relationships to government, in the social and cultural roles their entertainment programming plays, and in their relationship to commercial media markets. As the country's premier news organization, the BBC is fiercely proud of its editorial independence, seeking to play a watchdog role in holding the powerful to account. NHK, by contrast, is much more likely to cooperate with rather than confront political elites. The broadcasters differ too in their approach to entertainment programming. The BBC is more likely to act as an agent of social change, willing to challenge prevailing social norms and appeal to diverse audiences. NHK acts more as an agent of social stability, preferring to reflect and reinforce status quo values and cultural traditions while avoiding controversial or contentious subjects. Finally, the broadcasters differ in how they relate to commercial media markets in which they operate. The BBC has proved more competitive and more entrepreneurial, for example, by leading the way in adopting new internet platforms. In doing so, it competes fiercely with hostile commercial rivals. NHK enjoys an easier coexistence with the commercial broadcasters, while providing vital technological research and development assistance to Japan's corporate sector, notably consumer electronics.

This book explains how and why the BBC and NHK evolved to be so similar in some respects and so different in others, showing how they successfully adapted to a century's worth of political and social upheaval and technological change. Following Paul Pierson's logic of path-dependent historical institutionalism, I argue that the broadcasters themselves were the primary agents of their own evolution, making editorial and programming choices strategically to generate support with political elites, audiences, rival commercial media, and other actors.[3] Drawing too on the insights of Lucy Küng-Shanklman, I argue that the two broadcasters offered distinctive responses to a succession of challenges. As the consequences of decisions made at one time shaped responses to subsequent challenges, the evolution of distinctive organizational cultures became self-reinforcing.[4]

I explore the process by which these broadcasters evolved by examining a series of critical junctures when new media technologies emerged in the context of different political and social challenges. At these moments, the broadcasters were forced to make far-reaching and ultimately self-reinforcing strategic choices about their overall editorial and programming philosophies. These episodes include the advent of radio and the birth of the broadcasters in the politically fraught world of the 1920s and 1930s; the rise of television amidst the social upheavals of the 1960s; the spread of multichannel cable and satellite broadcasting fueled by globalization and the triumph of Thatcherite neoliberalism in the 1980s; and the digital revolution, political polarization, and fracturing of trust in media during the 2000s. Over time, differences in organizational culture were reinforced rather than eroded by different strategic responses to successive waves of political, social, and technological change; technological convergence; and media globalization.

NHK and the BBC were created amidst the political and social upheavals of the 1920s as means to harness for public purposes the explosive popularity of radio. Chapter 4 shows how their organizational cultures were shaped by the circumstances of their founding and by different experiences of and responses to political challenges. The transformative new media technology took off in broadly similar political and social environments. Britain and Japan both were burgeoning but incomplete parliamentary democracies, each beset with deep class and regional divisions. Authorities in both countries were anxious to use the new technology to mold newly enfranchised electorates into responsible citizenry. Elites in both countries, too, saw in radio the possibility of unifying and legitimizing their sprawling empires. The BBC and NHK were, for these reasons, established along strikingly similar institutional lines. Much of their programming was also similar, tending to uphold and disseminate elite status quo values. The chapter examines the parallels in two of the first plays ever written specifically for radio. *Danger*, which the BBC commissioned in 1924, tells the story of a young couple and an old man trapped in a flooding mineshaft. Audiences saw in it a celebration of such British national virtues as stoicism, courage, and self-sacrifice. (Spoiler alert! The old man saves the young couple from drowning at the cost of his own life.) A few months later *Tankō No Naka* ("In a Mineshaft") aired in Tokyo, telling a remarkably similar story about an old man who saves a young couple from drowning when they are trapped in a flooding mineshaft. Japanese audiences also appreciated those same virtues of stoicism, courage, and self-sacrifice, which they saw as quintessentially Japanese. But the two broadcasters took different paths in the face of social upheaval and political division. The BBC's response to political pressure, most notably the 1926 General Strike, was vitally shaped by the first Director-General John Reith. His decision to assert the values of impartiality and editorial autonomy in the face of aggressive demands to toe the government line was to have a lasting influence on BBC practices. NHK, though, was eventually subordinated to serve the interests of an increasingly authoritarian state.

Chapter 5 tells the story of how the postwar Allied Occupation kept NHK intact, using it not only to help manage the Occupation, but also to promote democratic values. The wartime hierarchy of senior officials was purged, but many of the staff remained, relishing their new mandate to produce honest, provocative programming. Censorship remained a problem as the Occupiers refused to permit anything liable to undermine their authority, but for a brief period from 1945 to the mid-1950s, NHK took on the role of fearless, provocative truth-teller for the nation.

Chapter 6 looks at divergent responses to television, which blossomed amid the cultural turmoil of the 1960s and sparked borderline panic about its supposedly malignant influence. These fears, combined with broader anxieties in both countries about fraying social ties and American cultural hegemony, prompted major shifts in editorial philosophy within both organizations. At the BBC, creative staff fought to produce more outspoken, socially progressive programming. They wanted the new medium to reflect but also to lead the swirling currents of social change. Producers of documentaries such as *The War Game*, dramas such as *Cathy Come Home*, and even comedy shows such as *Monty Python* clashed with senior managers and often the government by tackling controversial issues such as nuclear weapons or taboo social problems such as homelessness or single motherhood. In the words of Jean Seaton, official historian of the BBC, "Somewhere in the sixties, Reithian conservatism had mutated into something like Reithian liberalism."[5] By contrast, NHK's management chose to retreat from the raging culture wars. They dropped the progressive programming that had flourished in the postwar period as well as supposedly antisocial content such as professional wrestling and anything American, including *Popeye* and *Lassie*. Instead, NHK turned to safer, more socially conservative fare such as sweeping big-budget historical dramas (*taiga*) and daytime soap operas (*asa dora*), each extolling traditional values and gender roles.

Chapter 7 discusses the broadcasters' responses to neoliberalism and the cable and satellite-led expansion of global media markets in the 1980s. The BBC was bitterly divided but forced by circumstances and outside pressure to adopt the logic and language of the market far more extensively than NHK. The BBC's resultant entrepreneurialism continues to differentiate the two. BBC's head-on clashes with Margaret Thatcher over issues such as Northern Ireland or the Falklands War marked another stage in the burgeoning of the Corporation's self-definition as an impartial and fiercely independent watchdog. The decade was one of great turmoil and danger for the BBC, but it emerged better adapted to the new media landscape. NHK had an easier ride. Japan's conservative political elites never embraced neoliberalism and appreciated the non-confrontational reporting and safe, reassuring entertainment. Moreover, NHK's research laboratories provided vital assistance to Japan's powerful consumer electronics industry in the development of new technologies. As a result, NHK had neither the external incentive nor the internal desire to change its bureaucratic organizational culture and staid programming.

Chapter 8 examines the internet and social media's challenges to traditional public broadcasting. NHK and the BBC faced similar legal constraints regarding how they could adapt to the new environment, but their responses differed markedly. The BBC was a proactive, innovative early adopter of new media platforms and content formats, while NHK accepted the restrictions on new media activity imposed upon it by regulators. The contrast reflects the BBC's culture of entrepreneurialism, forged in response to earlier neoliberal attacks, and NHK's more bureaucratic managerial culture that had served it well as a cooperative partner in Japan's state-led industrial policy.

Chapters 9 and 10 explore the broadcasters' relationships with both governments and audiences in the contemporary era, examining their different responses to cases of overt political interference, changing social norms and evolving understandings of national identity. Chapter 11 covers the BBC's assertion of editorial independence in its coverage of the British government's 2003 claims about Iraq's possession of weapons of mass destruction and its struggles to retain popular support in the era of multiculturalism, Brexit, and political polarization. Recent years have seen the governing Conservatives cut BBC funding, intervene in personnel issues, and threaten radical reforms. Many see the BBC as becoming meeker in response, more likely to engage in self-censorship or "both-sider-ism" than hitherto.

Yet the BBC's efforts to defend its autonomy from these attacks, incomplete and flawed as they are, still stand in contrast to NHK's acquiescent support of the politically dominant LDP over issues such as war memory and the 3.11 Fukushima nuclear disaster. NHK's broader programming, too, continues to uphold traditional representations of national identity, such as with the popular *Project X* documentary series. Meanwhile, NHK has become an important instrument in former Prime Minister Abe's increased use of public diplomacy and cultural boosterism to promote Japan's international image and soft power, not least in preparation for the delayed 2020 Olympics. Most recently, both broadcasters have been at the center of efforts to provide reliable information, and combat the flood of misinformation, about the COVID-19 pandemic, underlining their resilience and continued importance in national life.

Comparing the different models of public broadcasting represented by NHK and the BBC teaches us several lessons. First, the contrast between the organizational similarities and the cultural differences of NHK and the BBC challenges the assumption that institutional form determines media role. Mapping the divergent evolution of these two organizations across the past hundred years or so illuminates the deep roots of differences across national media systems.[6] The value of a comparative historical approach is that patterns of difference in outwardly similar phenomena are often best seen over a longer time frame, as I recently saw illustrated on the BBC Wildlife website comparing dog and fox tracks. Seen side-by-side, the paw-print of a fox can be almost indistinguishable from that of a dog. Viewed as a trail, though, they become easily distinguishable. Fox prints run arrow-straight because foxes are efficient predators who waste neither time nor energy. Dog prints veer all over the place, circling around and doubling back because dogs are, well, dogs.[7] In the same way, differences in organizational culture between the BBC and NHK reveal themselves more clearly over time than they might in a single snapshot.

Second, the book reaffirms the importance of NHK in Japanese political and cultural life. I cannot claim this book replaces Ellis Krauss's brilliant 2000 study *Broadcasting Politics in Japan*, but it updates the findings.[8] The book affirms that Krauss's characterization of NHK's cooperative relationship with the state remains pertinent in the internet age and suggests that this is unlikely to change any time soon. My focus is also broader, exploring the social and cultural significance of NHK's entertainment programming and the economic importance of its research laboratories.[9] Indeed, I show how both NHK and the BBC have relied on their entire range of programming (including such seemingly non-political content such as costume dramas, documentaries, or song contests) along with their technological and other contributions to national economic policies, to help secure the support of political elites, public opinion, or both.

Most importantly, the book demonstrates the continued resilience of both styles of public service broadcasting in the face of ideological assault, the internet and social media revolutions, and collapsing trust in traditional media. In the 1980s and 1990s, neoliberalism was seen as the greatest threat to public broadcasting. The idea of elite bureaucrats deciding what audiences should watch, then forcing them to pay for it, seems antithetical to the principles of individual choice and free markets.[10] James Murdoch, then a senior executive at his father Rupert's News International Corporation, even described what he called "state-controlled news media" as "Orwellian."[11] By the 2020s, the internet and social media have multiplied this threat beyond measure. Not least, the digital revolution swept away one of the core rationale for public broadcasting. When spectrum scarcity limited the number of possible broadcasters, public broadcasters were thought necessary to serve the broad social interests that the market would not cover. But in an era of limitless choice, many argue that it is neither necessary nor fair to force people to subsidize content they do not consume.[12]

In the wake of these threats, many scholars predicted the weakening of public broadcasting and the convergence of national media systems toward a commercial model. In 1998, Monroe Price argued that new technologies "will not turn America's stepchild of public television into a new and glorious BBC. If anything, the future of the world's public-service entities will become more like the present of its American exemplar."[13] Hallin and Mancini too saw diminishing influence for public broadcasters and "a convergence of world media towards forms that first evolved in the United States."[14] Daya Thussu argued:

> The commercial model of broadcasting – with its roots in the United States and largely dependent on advertising – as against the West European model of public service broadcasting – where the state (through grants and subsidies) or the citizens (through mechanisms such as a licence fee) has become the dominant model across the world.[15]

These arguments dovetail with a broader conventional wisdom holding that globalization entails convergence of national styles of capitalism toward a market-friendly US model. Some media scholars have taken the convergence argument further, predicting the imminent death of public service media.[16] Yet, while the tides of deregulation, commercialism, and technological change have fundamentally altered the environment for public broadcasters, I argue that both the BBC and NHK have demonstrated the resilience of national, public-interest institutions in the face of global marketization.[17] Their enduring popularity represents a standing rebuttal by both countries to the idea that free markets always know best.

As of 2021, though, the public broadcasters still face multiple challenges beginning with intense competition for audiences from ubiquitous social media such as Facebook and Twitter, and from massively better-funded streaming services such as Netflix and Amazon. In addition, political polarization and media fragmentation are destroying public faith in old ideas about the press and politics.

I argue here that both the BBC and NHK are not only surviving but are, in unexpected ways, flourishing in the new media environment. This somewhat rosy view admittedly stands in stark contrast with the generally downbeat, often apocalyptic expectations of the many journalists, producers, editors, and analysts I spoke with while researching the book, and I do not wish to disregard the very serious threats to both public broadcasters. Nonetheless, there are reasons for optimism. First, this is not the first new media revolution, and nor will it be the last. Successful adaptation to changed circumstances and new technologies is a central theme in the chapters that follow. In the 1920s, radio was the communications breakthrough predicted to change everything from family life to national politics and international relations. Next came commercial television, which Lord Reith compared to smallpox. Then came video, cable, and satellite television. Finally, of course, the internet and the digital revolution are well upon us. Yet the public broadcasters successfully adapted to each new challenge. Indeed, both have served as cutting-edge innovators in the key technologies and content formats of each new media revolution.

The second reason for faith in the future of public service broadcasting comes from overwhelming evidence that the shallowness, partisanship, and unreliability of the popular press and network television are being worsened rather than improved by the digital revolution. Commercial mass media have been caught in a well-documented spiral from commercialization to sensationalism, thence fragmentation, hyper partisanship, and an increasing stress on opinion over factual reporting.[18] Well before the explosion of outrage about fake news on Facebook, the phone-hacking scandal that engulfed News Corporation had undercut Rupert Murdoch's claims about the innate moral superiority of corporate media. The problem of dumbing-down can be exaggerated, especially in relation to an almost entirely mythical press "golden age" of some unspecified past.[19] As we will see, each new media revolution from the telegraph onward has prompted old-timers to complain that things were much better back in the day. However, the current journalism crisis is real, as new media destroy old business models for providing high-quality political journalism.[20]

Indeed, Victor Pickard argues that chronic misinformation has structural roots precisely in the for-profit media model.[21] Online sites and social media feeds have become sources for the rapid transmission of both misinformation (that which is inaccurate) and disinformation (i.e., that which is deliberately deceptive), although the relative amount of misleading content may be surprisingly small.[22] Everywhere, though, trust in media is collapsing.[23] With the collapse of the newspaper industry and the disintegration of traditional network news, funding sources to provide adequate replacements are not obvious. Public provision of content intended to serve rather than undermine informed democratic discourse is a practical solution to an urgent problem.

At heart, the book is about the idea that media can and sometimes should serve the common good. Publicly provided news reporting and other content, produced with integrity, can serve democracy in ways that commercial media are too often failing to do. Political polarization and media fragmentation are shredding the public sphere, destroying mutual trust and shared sense of a common identity vital to democratic life. Public broadcasters are among the few surviving institutions offering common ground. They enjoy, and deserve, among the highest levels of audience trust compared to commercial rivals. Furthermore, multiplatform globalization is making it easier than ever to serve broader audiences, as the trusted presence of the BBC in the United States and the growing popularity of NHK World attest.

The BBC and NHK are, in short, uniquely placed to meet new demands for well-funded civic journalism, non-partisan news, and culturally and educationally enriching content. The book therefore concludes, contrary to conventional wisdom, that the new media revolution will not doom the public broadcasters but give them new life.

Notes

1 Charlotte Higgins, *This New Noise: The Extraordinary Birth and Troubled Life of the BBC* (London: Guardian Books, 2015), 231.
2 Quoted in: Hirasawa Kazushige, "Broadcasting in Japan: 40 Turbulent Years," *Japan Times,* March 23, 1965.
3 Paul Pierson, *Politics in Time: History, Institutions, and Social Analysis* (Princeton: Princeton University Press, 2014).
4 Lucy Küng-Shankleman, *Inside the BBC and CNN* (London: Routledge, 2000).
5 Jean Seaton, *Pinkoes and Traitors: The BBC and the Nation, 1974–1987* (London: Profile Books, 2015), 247.
6 Peter Humphreys notes the value of historical institutionalism in mapping comparative media systems in "A Political Scientist's Contribution to the Comparative Study of Media Systems in Europe: A Response to Hallin and Mancini," in *Trends in Communications Policy Research*, eds. Natascha Just and Manuel Puppis (Bristol: Intellect, 2012), 159.
7 Steve Harris, "How to Identify Animal Tracks," *DiscoverWildlife.com*, accessed January 27, 2021, www.discoverwildlife.com/how-to/identify-wildlife/how-to-identify-animal-tracks-and-trails/.
8 Ellis Krauss, *Broadcasting Politics in Japan: NHK and Television News* (Ithaca, NY: Cornell University Press, 2000).
9 Many scholars of political communication stress the need for media system studies to look beyond the narrow confines of news production. See J. Hardy, "Comparing Media Systems," in *Handbook of Comparative Communication Research*, eds. F. Esser and T. Hanitzsch (London: Routledge, 2012), 196.
10 David Elstein et al., *Beyond the Charter: The BBC after 2006: Report of the Broadcasting Policy Group* (London: Premium Publishing, 2006). His and other critical views are well discussed in Higgins, *This New Noise.*
11 "Edinburgh TV Festival: James Murdoch's MacTaggart Lecture in Full," *The Guardian*, August 29, 2009, www.guardian.co.uk/media/video/2009/aug/29/james-murdoch-edinburgh-festival-mactaggart.
12 Barry Cox, *Free for All? Public Service Television in the Digital Age* (London: Demos, 2004); Elstein, *Beyond the Charter.*
13 Price, "Public Television and New Technologies," in *A Communications Cornucopia*, eds. Roger G. Noll and Monroe Price (Washington, D.C.: Brookings Institution Press, 1998), 144.
14 Daniel C. Hallin and Paolo Mancini, "Americanization, Globalization and Secularization: Understanding the Convergence of Media Systems and Political Communication," in *Comparing Political Communication: Theories, Cases and Challenges*, eds. Barbara Pfetsch and Frank Esser (Cambridge: Cambridge University Press, 2004), 26.
15 Daya Thussu, "The Murdochization of News," *Media Culture and Society* 29, no. 4 (July 2007): 593–611, 610.

16 In fairness, these works are uniformly more nuanced than their titles suggest, but the pessimism is palpable. Michael Leadman, *The Last Days of the Beeb* (London: Allen and Unwin, 1986); Thomas O'Malley, *Closedown: The BBC and Government Policy 1979–1992* (London: Pluto Press, 1994); James Day, *The Vanishing Vision: The Inside Story of Public Television* (Berkeley, CA: University of California Press, 1995); Michael Tracey, *The Decline and Fall of Public Broadcasting* (Oxford: Oxford University Press, 1998); David Barsamian, *The Decline and Fall of Public Broadcasting* (Cambridge, MA: South End Press, 2nd edition, 2002).
17 Peter Hall and Michelle Lamont, *Social Resilience in the Neoliberal Era* (Cambridge: Cambridge University Press, 2013). This concurs with the findings of others, including Mary Debrett, *Reinventing Public Service Television for the Digital Future* (Bristol: Intellect Press, 2010) and Mary Debrett, "Riding the Wave: Public Service Television in the Multiplatform Era," *Media, Culture and Society* 31, no. 5 (September 2009): 807–827.
18 Stephen Farnsworth and S. Robert Lichter, *The Nightly News Nightmare: Media Coverage of U.S. Presidential Elections 1988–2008* (Lanham, MD: Rowman and Littlefield, 3rd edition, 2010); Markus Prior, "News vs. Entertainment: How Increasing Media Choice Widens Gaps in Political Knowledge and Turnout," *American Journal of Political Science* 49, no. 3 (July 2005): 577–592; Suzanne Franks, "The World on the Box: International Issues in News and Factual Programmes," *Political Quarterly* 75, no. 2 (October–December 2004): 425–428.
19 The 2012 HBO series *The Newsroom* offered a liberal fantasy of a popular news anchor rejecting ratings-friendly sensationalism in favor of "hard" news. The premise that TV news used to be good but isn't now is ironically similar to that of the classic 1976 movie *Network*, set in what *Newshour* nostalgically viewed as the Golden Age of TV journalism.
20 Excellent treatments of the crisis in journalism include Victor Pickard and Robert McChesney, *Will the Last Reporter Please Turn Out the Lights? The Collapse of Journalism and What Can Be Done to Fix It* (New York: The New Press, 2013); Thomas Patterson, *Informing the News: The Need for Knowledge-Based Journalism* (New York: Vintage Books, 2013).
21 Victor Pickard, *Democracy without Journalism: Confronting the Misinformation Society* (Oxford: Oxford University Press, 2020).
22 Jennifer Allen et al., "Evaluating the Fake News Problem at the Scale of the Information Ecosystem," *Science Advances* 6, no. 14 (2020).
23 Nic Newman and Richard Fletcher, "Bias, Bullshit and Lies: Audience Perspectives on Low Trust in Media," Reuters Institute for the Study of Journalism's *Digital News Project* (2017).

References

Allen, Jennifer, et al., "Evaluating the Fake News Problem at the Scale of the Information Ecosystem," *Science Advances* 6, no. 14 (2020).
Barsamian, David, *The Decline and Fall of Public Broadcasting* (Cambridge, MA: South End Press, 2nd edition, 2002).
Cox, Barry, *Free for All? Public Service Television in the Digital Age* (London: Demos, 2004).
Day, James, *The Vanishing Vision: The Inside Story of Public Television* (Berkeley, CA: University of California Press, 1995).
Debrett, Mary, *Reinventing Public Service Television for the Digital Future* (Bristol: Intellect Press, 2010).

Debrett, Mary, "Riding the Wave: Public Service Television in the Multiplatform Era," *Media, Culture and Society* 31, no. 5 (September 2009): 807–827.

"Edinburgh TV Festival: James Murdoch's MacTaggart Lecture in Full," *The Guardian*, August 29, 2009, www.guardian.co.uk/media/video/2009/aug/29/james-murdoch-edinburgh-festival-mactaggart.

Elstein, David, et al., *Beyond the Charter: The BBC after 2006: Report of the Broadcasting Policy Group* (London: Premium Publishing, 2006).

Farnsworth, Stephen, and S. Robert Lichter, *The Nightly News Nightmare: Media Coverage of U.S. Presidential Elections 1988–2008* (Lanham, MD: Rowman and Littlefield, 3rd edition, 2010).

Franks, Suzanne, "The World on the Box: International Issues in News and Factual Programmes," *Political Quarterly* 75, no. 2 (October–December 2004): 425–428.

Hall, Peter, and Michelle Lamont, *Social Resilience in the Neoliberal Era* (Cambridge University Press, 2013).

Hallin, Daniel C., and Paolo Mancini, "Americanization, Globalization and Secularization: Understanding the Convergence of Media Systems and Political Communication," in *Comparing Political Communication: Theories, Cases and Challenges*, eds. Barbara Pfetsch and Frank Esser (Cambridge: Cambridge University Press, 2004).

Hardy, J., "Comparing Media Systems," in *Handbook of Comparative Communication Research*, eds. F. Esser and T. Hanitzsch (London: Routledge, 2012).

Harris, Steve, "How to Identify Animal Tracks," *DiscoverWildlife.com*, accessed January 27, 2021, www.discoverwildlife.com/how-to/identify-wildlife/how-to-identify-animal-tracks-and-trails/.

Higgins, Charlotte, *This New Noise: The Extraordinary Birth and Troubled Life of the BBC* (London: Guardian Books, 2015).

Hirasawa, Kazushige, "Broadcasting in Japan: 40 Turbulent Years," *Japan Times*, March 23, 1965.

Humphreys, Peter, "A Political Scientist's Contribution to the Comparative Study of Media Systems in Europe: A Response to Hallin and Mancini," in *Trends in Communications Policy Research*, eds. Natascha Just and Manuel Puppis (Bristol: Intellect, 2012).

Krauss, Ellis, *Broadcasting Politics in Japan: NHK and Television News* (Ithaca, NY: Cornell University Press, 2000).

Küng-Shankleman, Lucy, *Inside the BBC and CNN* (London: Routledge, 2000).

Leadman, Michael, *The Last Days of the Beeb* (London: Allen and Unwin, 1986).

Newman, Nic, and Richard Fletcher, "Bias, Bullshit and Lies: Audience Perspectives on Low Trust in Media," Reuters Institute for the Study of Journalism's *Digital News Project*, 2017.

O'Malley, Thomas, *Closedown: The BBC and Government Policy 1979–1992* (London: Pluto Press, 1994).

Patterson, Thomas, *Informing the News: The Need for Knowledge-Based Journalism* (New York: Vintage Books, 2013).

Pickard, Victor, *Democracy Without Journalism: Confronting the Misinformation Society* (Oxford: Oxford University Press, 2020).

Pickard, Victor, and Robert McChesney, *Will the Last Reporter Please Turn Out the Lights? The Collapse of Journalism and What Can be Done to Fix It* (New York: The New Press, 2013).

Pierson, Paul, *Politics in Time: History, Institutions, and Social Analysis* (Princeton: Princeton University Press, 2014).

Prior, Markus, "News Vs. Entertainment: How Increasing Media Choice Widens Gaps in Political Knowledge and Turnout," *American Journal of Political Science* 49, no. 3 (July 2005): 577–592.

Seaton, Jean, *Pinkoes and Traitors: The BBC and the Nation, 1974–1987* (London: Profile Books, 2015).

Tracey, Michael, *The Decline and Fall of Public Broadcasting* (Oxford: Oxford University Press, 1998).

2 Same Rules, Same Remits

What Is Public Broadcasting?

Public broadcasting and the closely related terms "public service broadcasting" and "public service media" mean different things in different countries. They typically, but by no means always, imply media sources that are publicly funded, non-profit, universally accessible to citizens, and that provide a public service component. For the sake of simplicity, I will use the term "public broadcasters" to refer to both the BBC and NHK, as this follows everyday English usage and is perhaps the term with which most readers are familiar. However, the ambiguities in terminology are worth noting at the outset because a major theme in this book is that understandings of what public broadcasting is, or should be, have varied widely across different times, people, and places.

Indeed, even the simple word "public" means different things in different national contexts. In Britain, public broadcasting refers to all free-to-air broadcasts, including those of commercial television networks, while the BBC is referred to as a "public service broadcaster." In Japan, the term *kōkyō hōsō* translates as "public broadcasting" and usually refers specifically to NHK. Communications scholar Kaori Hayashi notes, though, that the *kō* in *kōkyō* carries the more formal connotation of "public" as in "public official." In Britain, by contrast, "public" carries the connotation of open and freely available, as in "public beach." The Japanese term thus colors NHK as more bureaucratic. In contrast, the Japanese term for what is usually translated as commercial or private broadcasting is *minkan hōsō*, in which the character *min*, "people," is also used in *minshu shugi*, "democracy." This term thus translates more closely as "popular broadcasting" or even "people's broadcasting."[1] The starker contrast in Japan than Britain between "official" and "popular" broadcasting will be a recurrent theme.

Why have public broadcasting? Many see little justification for state-mandated funding of media beyond what the free market will provide. Neoliberal observers such as Barry Cox and David Elstein argue that media content should be treated like any other consumer good, with individuals deciding how much to consume and at what price.[2] They argue that public funding for state-controlled media distorts commercial markets, crowding out audiences and revenues for private enterprise. Other critics note that public broadcasting represents elitist paternalism at best and a blatant violation of press freedom at worst.[3] Such concerns are echoed

DOI: 10.4324/b23015-2

on the left by those suspicious of state power. Observers such as Matsuda Hiroshi and Tsuchiya Hideo argue that any form of government control over media invites abuse, undermining free speech rights and the independent watchdog role the press is supposed to play in democratic theory.[4]

In response, there are two broad rationales for government intervention in media markets. First, to address market failure problems; and second, to promote good citizenship. The market failure rationale sees public broadcasting as justified only to provide content likely to be undersupplied by the market. In the broadcast era of radio and television, spectrum scarcity meant that only a limited number of broadcasters could operate without degrading each other's signals.[5] Competition was therefore limited, and many countries instituted public monopolies instead.[6] Digitization and the internet have destroyed the spectrum scarcity rationale, but the language of market failure is still invoked to defend public broadcasting. Content such as reliable news or educational programming can be seen as public goods, conferring positive externalities on society but likely to be undersupplied by ratings-conscious commercial providers.[7] Critics of public broadcasting such as Nigel Farage might respond that the offerings of the BBC – and, to a lesser extent, of the NHK – go far beyond this narrow remit, citing programs such as *Top Gear* as having little public service rationale and plenty of commercial potential.[8]

The social responsibility approach takes a more expansive view of public broadcasting, seeing it as serving valuable social ends beyond mere profit. This view sees public broadcasters as an important democratic tool for informing and empowering citizens, providing meritorious content across all genres.[9] Such content may include thorough, independent news journalism that informs the electorate and holds the powerful to account. Indeed, public broadcasters are often seen as particularly well-suited to serve as watchdog on state or private interests, a role that commercial media, constrained by corporate ties and pressure from ratings and advertisers, may be unwilling or unable to perform.[10] Public broadcasters can also provide forums for democratic debate, or give voice to marginalized groups. They can educate and edify with cultural, artistic, and even entertainment programming. As media scholar Petros Iosifidis writes: "Public television can play an essential role in safeguarding a pluralist society and meeting its cultural and social needs and it is therefore at the center of the democratic systems."[11] In short, the social responsibility view sees media as treating audiences like citizens rather than consumers.

National Varieties of Public Broadcasting

A growing subfield within the comparative political communications literature studies the wide cross-national variation in the provision of public service media.[12] At one end of the spectrum are countries such as the United Kingdom, Japan, and much of Northern Europe where public broadcasting plays a central role in the media ecosystem and in national life. Then there are more regionally fragmented systems, such as the German federal model, or hybrid systems in which public service content is provided by private corporations, such as in France, or via the United Kingdom's Channel 4. At the far end of the spectrum is the US highly commercialized media system, where public broadcasting consists of a decentralized network of cash-strapped stations playing a marginal role, mostly filling niches left by corporate media.[13] Then, within each media system, individual broadcasters can vary from one another across dimensions, including organization; governance structures and accountability mechanisms; funding sources; editorial autonomy; and mission statement or programming remit.[14] In turn, media scholars invoke such institutional differences to help explain why public broadcasters can play such different roles in the political, social, and economic lives of their countries.[15]

The BBC and NHK, however, present a paradox for this literature. They are almost identical institutionally, yet they differ dramatically in their organizational cultures and in their understandings of the services they should perform. The remainder of this chapter will sketch out the similarities in their organizational structures, funding, governance mechanisms, and mission statements. The next chapter will elaborate on their different roles.

Similar Institutions, Similar Missions

The BBC and NHK both are relatively monolithic, highly centralized non-profit corporations coexisting with vibrant commercial media (see Table 2.1). They offer similar services and are funded almost identically. The BBC holds a central place in the United Kingdom's media landscape, with its two flagship TV channels (BBC 1 and BBC 2) as well as several specialized digital TV and radio channels and an extremely popular website.[16] Its share of the UK television audience is around one-third, larger than the approximately one-fifth share that watches the United Kingdom's commercial terrestrial television network Independent Television (ITV), and significantly larger than the 10% that watch the commercial public service broadcaster Channel 4 and News International's Sky TV.[17] The BBC's revenues in 2019 were approximately £5 billion, of which about three quarters (£3.7 billion) came from license fee income. The other principal source of income is generated by BBC Studios from the commercial use of BBC assets internationally, from content sales to franchising of programming formats or use of facilities. The BBC employs approximately 22,000 full-time staff.[18]

Table 2.1 Overview[19]

	BBC	*NHK*
Budget	£4.9 bn	£5.3 bn
of which, % license fee	75%	99%
Employees	22,000	10,000
TV channels (national)	8	6
Radio channels (domestic)	6	3
% of population that reports at least weekly news use (national ranking)	56% (1st)	48% (1st)
TV and radio/offline Website/online	45% (1st)	11% (2nd)
International radio channels (foreign language)	44 BBC World Service	17 NHK World-Japan

The license fee, currently £157 per household per year, was originally levied on all owners of radio sets and then TVs capable of receiving the BBC. The law was updated in the multiple-platform era to cover all devices capable of accessing BBC content, including TVs, computers, tablets, or phones. The fee is now payable by all UK households that watch any live TV; that watch or stream TV online; or that download or watch BBC content on the iPlayer streaming platform. Non-payment of the fee is a criminal offense carrying a maximum fine of £1,000 and possible (though extremely rare) imprisonment. Payment is enforced by roving vans capable of detecting TV signals and matching addresses against payment records. Despite this, the BBC estimates approximately 7% of households that should have licenses do not.[20]

The license fee was designed to ensure that income does not require regular political approval, which would be the case if the broadcaster were directly funded from general taxes, as with the US Corporation for Public Broadcasting (CPB). The mechanism thus offers some protection against political influence, although any increases in the license fee must be approved by Parliament. License fee revenues are also shielded from the influence of big business. In the United States, by contrast, the network of stations comprising the Public Broadcasting Service (PBS) and National Public Radio (NPR) receive approximately one-fifth of their revenues from underwriting, giving corporate sponsors editorial influence that can and has been abused.[21]

NHK is also a legally independent, non-profit public service broadcaster.[22] It offers two domestic terrestrial channels: the flagship General TV, offering a full range of news and entertainment programming; and educational TV. In addition, it offers two satellite TV channels, three radio channels, and international TV and radio channels, including NHK World Japan, an English-language showcase for Japan. With over 10,000 staff, it rivals Japan's four or five major commercial TV networks in terms of reach and budget, with comparable audience shares.[23] NHK has a substantial online presence, although, as we will see, management was slower and arguably less innovative in their adoption of the new platforms than the BBC.

NHK revenues, approximately ¥720 billion ($6.5 billion) in 2018, come almost entirely from viewer fees (*jushinryō*) in a mechanism similar to – because it was modeled on – the BBC's system.[24] The Broadcast Law of 1950 requires all owners of television sets capable of receiving NHK to enter a Broadcast Receiving Contract with NHK and pay a fee, currently about ¥14,000 ($124) annually for a terrestrial contract and more for satellite or on-demand services.

The collection method for viewer fees offers a minor but illustrative case in how near-identical institutional arrangements can be enacted subtly differently. In Japan, while it is illegal not to enter a contract with NHK, there were until very recently no penalties for non-payment of the fee. Instead, fees are still collected door-to-door by NHK representatives, usually subcontracted from private companies, who must try to persuade reluctant viewers to pay. For years, NHK officials I interviewed were proud that the Japanese collection method was voluntary, relying on a well-developed sense of social obligation and appreciation on the part of their viewers. In contrast, they implied, the British system relied on the brute force of law to coerce payment. The detector vans, one remarked, were too "dry" (*dorai*), meaning excessively business-like, as opposed to the "wet" (*uetto*) human touch brought by the Japanese collectors.[25] On the other hand, the absence of consequences for non-payment undoubtedly facilitated the popularity of payment boycotts by viewers unhappy with NHK for whatever reason. As described in later chapters, NHK has therefore begun to make strenuous efforts to strengthen the legal framework for collection in the face of increasing non-payment, legal challenges and a spate of creative ways for viewers to refuse the fee.[26]

The viewer fee model has long been under attack in both countries and from all sides. Left-wingers denounce it as regressive, while conservatives criticize it as unfair and anticompetitive. In 2020, British Prime Minister Boris Johnson described himself as "really strident" about wanting to reform BBC funding and his minister for culture suggested this might mean abolishing the license fee altogether.[27] In Japan, Tabana Takahashi, a disgruntled former NHK staffer, founded the "Protect the People from NHK Party" (*NHK kara kokumin o mamoru tō*) on the sole platform of replacing the mandatory fee with a voluntary subscription. The party proved surprisingly successful, winning over 1 million votes and an Upper House seat in the 2019 General Election.[28] Tachibana was to prove a highly controversial Diet member, not least due to his racist comments advocating genocide as a means of population control.[29] Less controversial critics of NHK's viewer fees include film director Beat Takeshi.[30] Meanwhile, the bogeyman of the "NHK collector" has become a popular cultural trope, cropping up as the recurring nightmare for the heroine of Haruki Murakami's novel *IQ84.*

The broadcasters' governance structures also resemble each other closely. The BBC is established by Royal Charter, which sets out purposes, governance, and regulatory arrangements, including the composition of the Governing Board. The BBC is required to be impartial and serve the public interest. The Charter guarantees editorial independence from government interference and must be renewed every ten years, following extensive review and Parliamentary approval.[31] The director-general, who serves as editor-in-chief, is appointed by the prime minister, who usually follows the recommendation of the governing body. Currently, this body is the BBC Board composed of 14 members, 4 of whom are political appointments representing the four nations of the United Kingdom (England, Scotland, Wales, and Northern Ireland). The chair and the members for each nation are chosen by the prime minister and the relevant national ministers. The rest of the board are chosen by the BBC. Current members are drawn heavily from broadcasting, the arts and academia, with a scattering of business executives and entrepreneurs. This structure, instituted in 2017, gives somewhat more insulation from political interference than previous incarnations of the governing body. The Board of Governors (1927–2007) and the BBC Trust (2007–2017) were entirely government-appointed. Changes to the funding structure – for example, raising the license fee, selling merchandise, or taking advertisements on foreign broadcasts – must be approved by Parliament.

The media environment in which the BBC operates is regulated by the Office of Communications (Ofcom), an independent regulatory body that is accountable to Parliament and whose chair is appointed by the Department of Culture, Media and Sport (DCMS). Ofcom was granted oversight of the BBC by the 2017

Digital Economy Act, prior to which direct regulatory authority was entrusted to the BBC Trust, a theoretically independent, stand-alone body. The switch of regulatory authority to Ofcom was undertaken to allay fears that relations between the BBC's management and the Trust were too close for the latter to exercise effective supervision over the former, and has had the effect of strengthening the BBC's claims of editorial independence.

NHK is governed by the terms of the 1950 Broadcast Law, which, like the BBC's Charter, stipulates that NHK must be editorially independent and non-partisan; government interference on editorial decisions is prohibited. Ultimate decision-making authority for all aspects of NHK's operations resides with a 12-member Board of Governors, although since 2008 the board has been forbidden from interfering with the content of individual programs. This decision followed incidents of partisan editorial interference to be discussed in later chapters. The governors, drawn principally from business and academia, are appointed by the prime minister and approved by the Diet. The governors appoint the chairman, who serves as editor-in-chief and has day-to-day authority over operations.[32] In addition, NHK's budget must be approved by the Diet every two years, usually a pro forma but occasionally contentious exercise. The broader media environment is regulated by the powerful Ministry of Internal Affairs and Communications (*sōmushō*). Prior to 2001, the media regulator was the Ministry of Posts and Telecommunications (*yūseishō*), and prior to that the Ministry of Communications, which was known at the time as the Ministry of Telecommunications.

In summary, the BBC and NHK have much in common, including universal accessibility for citizens, funding guaranteed from near-universally levied viewer fees, statutory impartiality, editorial independence, and a theoretically independent but politically appointed chief executive, editor-in-chief, and governing body. Their respective remits are correspondingly similar, as the following section discusses.

What Should Public Broadcasters Do?

What content, if any, should public media provide beyond what consumers demand and the market supplies? Is the public interest simply what interests the public, as the neoliberal chairman of the US Federal Communications Commission once suggested?[33] Or are there other considerations, such as nurturing citizenship, promoting inclusion for marginalized groups, or fostering healthy democratic discourse? Prescriptions for what public broadcasting should provide vary, but there is considerable overlap on the essentials. Karol Jakubowicz is representative of many observers who suggest that the purposes of public service media are to provide socially and culturally valuable programming; to provide a universally accessible public sphere for democratic debate and participation; and to act as a watchdog on the powerful, a point stressed also by Ellis Krauss.[34]

A more detailed remit, offered by the Committee of Ministers of the Council of Europe, stipulates that public service media should serve as (a) a reference point for all members of the public, offering universal access; (b) a factor for social cohesion and integration of all individuals, groups, and communities; (c) a source of impartial and independent information and comment, and of innovatory and varied content that complies with high ethical and quality standards; (d) a forum for pluralistic public discussion and a means of promoting broader democratic participation of individuals; and (e) an active contributor to audiovisual creation and production and greater appreciation and dissemination of the diversity of national and European cultural heritage.[35]

Both formulations, though, are subject to different interpretations. What sort of programming is innovatory, high quality, or socially and culturally valuable? Who should decide? Impartiality in the provision of information seems desirable but becomes problematic if used as an excuse for false balance or employed as a cudgel by partisans who equate critical reporting with bias.[36] In providing a public sphere, who should be included and who, if anyone, excluded? How should minority interests, marginalized groups, or extremists be represented?

Furthermore, the desiderata are frequently in tension with each other. For a media organization to serve as a factor for social cohesion, for example, it must presumably sustain a unifying national narrative, and cultivate and disseminate a common national culture. How can a single broadcaster do these things while simultaneously providing an inclusive public forum for democratic deliberation in which pluralism and diversity are promoted and, presumably, prevailing social norms are questioned? It is similarly difficult for broadcasters to provide culturally important content or act as a curator of national heritage without taking sides in deeply contested struggles over national identity. Director-General John Reith reasoned, for example, that because Britain was officially a Christian country, it would be inappropriate for the BBC, as the sole national broadcaster, to air Muslim or Jewish religious ceremonies. NHK caused fierce controversy, to be explored later, with a documentary about the Japanese army's system of sexual slavery during the Second World War. The program was intended to give a voice to hitherto marginalized victims, inform the public about a national war crime, and hold those responsible to account. As such, it was seen by many observers as admirably fulfilling the roles of inclusive public sphere and watchdog. But others, including senior politicians, saw the same documentary as violating impartiality and destroying social cohesion by promoting a divisive, unpatriotic view of history.

The book explores how the BBC and NHK came up with different ways of resolving these tensions and interpreting their roles. Over time, those decisions developed into an internal organizational logic that informs but does not predetermine responses to the next challenge. I explore these differences in the next chapter. Before that, we will examine each broadcaster's mission statement, seeing how closely they resemble each other in broad terms while noting subtle differences in emphasis that both reflect and inform their different managerial philosophies.

Comparing Mission Statements

Table 2.2 compares the Mission Statements of the BBC and NHK, illustrating considerable overlap between what they say they should be doing.[37] The first row articulates their primary mission, to provide reliable, impartial news and information.

Both have extensive news operations, dwarfing those of most commercial broadcasters in terms of resources such as numbers of reporters, hours of news content, and overseas bureaus. Both enjoy reputations for accuracy and impartiality even among journalists and editors at rival institutions.[38] Most importantly, both secure the highest levels of audience trust of any mainstream news sources in their countries. The Reuters Institute for Journalism survey on Digital News found BBC News to be the highest-used news source in the United Kingdom (67% used it at least weekly), the most trusted (70% ranked it most accurate), and the most likely to be placed in the middle of the political spectrum.[39] The same report found that NHK news was most trusted for accuracy by 59% of respondents. NHK was the most used source of television news (56% used it at least weekly), but considerably less popular online (23% used it weekly).[40] Dozens of different studies show that these high levels of trust relative to other news sources have been consistent for decades.[41] These enduringly high levels of trust in the public broadcasters are not always justified, as we will see, but they usually are. Surveys of media consumption and political knowledge by Christopher Collet and Gento Kato, Toril Aalberg and James Curran, Pippa Norris and Christina Holz-Bacha, and many others all find that a diet of public broadcasting news is positively associated with greater political knowledge and awareness of international events.[42]

Table 2.2 Mission Statements[43]

NHK	BBC
"The Work of Public Broadcasting"	*"Public Purposes"*
To answer "I want to know"	**To provide impartial news and information to help people understand and engage with the world around them**
Shiritai ni kotaeru	
To provide accurate, impartial, and fair information as well as rich, high-quality programming. Editorial autonomy is essential	The BBC will provide accurate and impartial news, current affairs, and factual programming of the highest editorial standards so that all audiences can engage fully with issues across the United Kingdom and the world
To take on culture	**To support learning for people of all ages**
Bunka o ninau	
Programs to improve general education; enhance social interest and deepen knowledge about life culture; develop rich emotions and a healthy spirit for children; preserve the excellent culture of the past and foster and disseminate new culture; preserve and nurture classical performing arts and nurture various arts; entertainment to brighten the home and enrich your life	Educational content will help support learning for children and teenagers across the United Kingdom, while audiences will be encouraged to explore inspiring and challenging new subjects and activities through a range of partnerships
	To show the most creative, highest-quality, and distinctive output and services
	Innovative content covering many different genres will be provided across a range of services and platforms, setting the standard in both the United Kingdom and globally

Regional support	**To reflect, represent, and serve the diverse communities of all of the United Kingdom's nations and regions and, in doing so, support the creative economy across the United Kingdom**
Chiki o ōen	
To make programs for the whole country. To respect regional diversity and help in the creation of regional culture	
	The lives of the people in the United Kingdom today will be accurately and authentically portrayed in the BBC's output and services to raise awareness of different cultures, contribute to social cohesion, and invest in the development of each nation's creative economy
Become more familiar	
Moto mijikai	
To gather all voices and listen to viewer opinions.	
Convey Japan to the world	**To reflect the United Kingdom, its culture and values to the world**
Nihon o sekai ni tsutaeru	
To conduct international broadcasting to deepen Japanese viewers' understanding of foreign countries, and contribute to the development of international cultural and economic exchange	High-quality, accurate, impartial news coverage will be delivered to international audiences, aiding understanding of the United Kingdom as a whole
Build a future for broadcasting	
Hōsō no mirai o tsukuru	
To conduct business necessary for the progress and development of broadcast and reception.	
Protect life and livelihoods	
Inochi to kurashi o mamoru	
Disaster prevention and disaster reporting. To convey accurate, prompt information during disasters	

The second row speaks to the common mission to educate. Both offer much conventional educational programming, from early childhood reading lessons to adult literacy and skills training, although only NHK has a TV channel (ETV) devoted exclusively to education. From 1971 to 2006, the BBC carried lectures and other content from the Open University, the United Kingdom's largest public, distance-learning university. More recently, in response to the school closures caused by the COVID-19 crisis, both broadcasters expanded content online and on TV, including children's programming to help ease anxiety and educational content in direct support of national curricula goals.[44] NHK also aired a national "Graduation Ceremony for Everyone" (*Minna No Sotsugyōshiki*) for those who lost their in-person events to the lockdown.

However, both broadcasters seek to educate indirectly as well, through broader programming content. To that end, entertainment programming has been considered essential since the 1920s when Reith observed that "you have to mix a little education with a lot of entertainment to carry people with you."[45] Reith believed that to entertain meant not simply to amuse or pass time away but to engage the critical faculties of the audience, and the ethos in both organizations is that entertainment should also edify. The challenge they have always faced is to provide content that is edifying enough to justify itself on public service grounds, while simultaneously being popular enough to warrant the public resources devoted to it.

Hence, while the BBC and NHK provide content in many genres that might not appear to warrant public provision, such as game shows or reality TV, producers aspire to create the best possible version of each genre in the belief that audience tastes can be shaped rather than simply pandered to.[46] Again, this philosophy dates back to Reith, who wrote:

> It is better to overestimate the mentality of the public than to underestimate it. . . . He who prides himself on giving the public what it wants is often creating a fictitious demand for low standards which he himself will then satisfy.[47]

Jean Seaton's description of BBC attitudes toward drama in the 1970s is thus apt for both broadcasters today: "Neither high-minded indifference to audiences nor ostensible vulgar audience-chasing were approved of."[48] The second row also underlines the central role both broadcasters are expected to play in national cultural production. This involves both producing culturally valuable programming, as Jakubowicz suggests, and appreciating and disseminating cultural heritage as the EU requires. Note, though, the nuanced differences in language that will be discussed in the next chapter.

The third row speaks broadly to the shared mission to provide what the EU called "a factor for social cohesion and integration of all individuals, groups and societies" and what Jakubowicz called providing a universally accessible public sphere. Both broadcasters have certainly had profound influences on social cohesion and national identity. Broadcasting came of age at a time of tremendous social and political turbulence as nations struggled with the demands of industrialization and the social, military, and economic challenges of the First World War and the Great Depression. Ernest Gellner theorizes that such strains put pressures on states to promote a homogenized national culture as a binding medium for disaffected and uprooted populations.[49] That both states were attempting to hold together culturally, ethnically, and linguistically disparate empires further intensified this need. In Benedict Anderson's account, too, mass media are vital in shaping a country's collective self-imagination.[50]

As the following chapters show, both the BBC and NHK have woven themselves tightly into their country's national consciousness from the earliest days when radio was used as an essential element in homogenizing national languages and marginalizing peripheral dialects.[51] At the most symbolically potent level, both became the primary heralds and chroniclers of their respective royal families. NHK's live broadcast of the enthronement of Emperor Hirohito in 1928 or the BBC's televised record of Queen Elizabeth II's coronation in 1952 became seminal national events, as have all subsequent royal weddings or funerals. One of the most iconic rituals in the UK calendar, the monarch's Christmas Speech, was the brainchild of Reith of the BBC who had to persuade a reluctant George VI to do it. Moreover, public expectations that royal events should be appropriately covered by public broadcasters remain strong, even in these less deferential times. In the summer of 2012, the BBC's coverage of the Queen's Silver Jubilee festivities was roundly criticized by media rivals, including the popular dailies *The Daily Mail* and *The Times*. The objection was not that the BBC was covering the event, which was generally taken as natural and appropriate, but that the BBC had failed to live up to the dignity and gravitas with which the broadcaster might traditionally have covered such a momentous event.[52] NHK enjoyed a rare scoop when it announced the stunning leaked news of Emperor Akihito's planned abdication.[53]

Beyond royalty, the national broadcasters contribute mightily to what Michael Billig calls the "banal daily rituals," which help sustain group identities long after the need for specific nation-building ideologies have faded.[54] Daily rituals include the news hours, the BBC shipping forecasts, or NHK's morning exercises. Both broadcasters help shape the longer rhythms of national life too, with their coverage of major sporting events (e.g., Wimbledon or the seasonal Sumo *bashō*) or their own seasonal rituals, such as NHK's New Year Song Contest (*Kōhaku Uta Gassen*).

Few activities short of war have the power to bind communities together and promote national pride as professional sports do, and the BBC and NHK have long histories of co-dependence with national sporting events. The Tokyo Olympics of 1964 was a major coming-of-age event for NHK television, while successful coverage of the 2012 Olympic was a big fillip for the BBC's national popularity.[55] NHK would certainly have been a major player relaying the pandemic-delayed 2020 Tokyo Olympics and Paralympics to the nation and the world. Both broadcasters have helped ingrain a "traditional" annual cycle of social and sporting events into the national consciousness with, for example, the BBC's coverage of the FA Cup, Wimbledon, Royal Ascot, and NHK's exclusive rights to the four national Sumo tournaments. When baseball sensation Ichiro Suzuki signed for the Seattle Mariners in 2000, NHK both reflected and encouraged national pride by announcing that they would air every single one of his first-season home games.[56] In doing all this, both broadcasters continue to provide what Karl Deutsch described as the "relatively coherent and stable structure of memories, habits and values" upon which national identities are centered.[57]

Both broadcasters are required to act as national ambassadors abroad, as shown in the fourth row of Table 2.2, and politicians in both countries have clear expectations that the global services are to promote "soft power" abroad. NHK World-Japan includes TV channels, radio in 17 different languages, and online services. It offers programming about Japan, including language lessons, documentaries, and informational material. Content typically extols the virtues of Japanese culture and highlights the many tourist, culinary, and other attractions of "Cool Japan."[58] NHK World was started in 1995 and expanded in 2009 specifically in order to cultivate a positive national image and "the correct view of Japan" to the international community.[59] The line between reflecting national culture and representing state interests is blurry, of course, and controversy surrounds the degree to which the real reason for NHK World's expansion was to help promote official government perspectives on international issues such as territorial disputes with Asian neighbors. The perceived importance of tying programming to Japanese-ness in the minds of the audience was perhaps unintentionally underlined when "NHK World" was quietly renamed "NHK World-Japan" in April 2018.[60] NHK World-Japan played a key role in promoting Japan ahead of the delayed 2020 Tokyo Olympics and Paralympics.[61]

The BBC World Service was established specifically in 1932, when it was known as the Empire Service. It offers news and other content across all platforms in over 40 different languages. Until 2014, it was paid for by the Foreign Office rather than the license fee, reflecting expectations that it would serve state interests abroad. And in 2015, it received a £289 million government grant specifically to help it promote the United Kingdom's soft power.[62] The World Service is not to be confused with BBC Worldwide, which was established in 1995 to sell BBC content abroad and has since been subsumed into BBC Studios, the highly entrepreneurial commercial arm of the corporation.

Both broadcasters also serve broader national economic goals such as assisting in the development of telecommunications technology. This purpose is explicit for NHK, as seen in the fifth row of Table 2.2. NHK has always been an important instrument in Japan's industrial policy, legally required to "conduct research and investigations necessary for the improvement and development of broadcasting and the reception thereof."[63] The generously funded NHK Science and Research Technology Laboratories are superb developers of media technology, working closely with government and consumer electronics manufacturers to develop technologies such as satellite broadcasts and high-definition TV.[64] As we will see, the BBC has also, at times, played an important role in developing the national media ecology. Chapter 7 shows how the BBC was essential to the fraught but vital transition from analog to digital broadcasting.[65] More recently, governments have leveraged the Corporation's resources to contribute to the United Kingdom's vibrant creative industries. For example, the requirement that the BBC outsource a certain proportion of programming has led to a boom in the number of independent British television production companies.[66]

Finally, both broadcasters act as central sources of information during natural disasters and other emergencies, a task made explicit for NHK in the sixth row. The remit reflects the great need for such a national media institution in Japan, vulnerable as it is to earthquakes, storms, and other natural disasters. NHK's coverage of the 3.11 triple disaster of tsunami, earthquake, and nuclear meltdown in 2011 was deeply flawed in certain respects, not least in its long-standing failure to question the corrupt ties between the government and the nuclear power industry. But there is also no doubt about the professionalism and bravery of its front-line news crews, or the essential, life-saving nature of its blanket reporting.[67] The BBC plays a similar role when disaster strikes in the United Kingdom. Both were the most trusted news organizations in their countries to provide information about the coronavirus.[68] NHK's provision of Chinese-language emergency information was one example of the kinds of service only a public broadcaster is likely to provide.

The Paradox: Same Structures, Different Roles

The BBC and NHK share much in common, especially in terms of institutional structure and stated missions. Yet, as Duncan McCargo notes, questions about what roles media organizations actually play in the lives of their countries are far more important than questions about their formal structures.[69] Charles Curran, director-general of the BBC in 1967, said something similar in describing how he interpreted the BBC's somewhat ambiguous legal remit: "Good broadcasting is a matter of practice, not a prescription. In my view, traditions are more important in this respect than written documents."[70] We can think about these traditions, these practical roles, as varying along political, social, and economic dimensions.

Much of the scholarly attention paid to both the BBC and NHK concerns their political role as major news organizations. To what extent do public broadcasters exercise impartiality and defend editorial independence from the government or other powerful actors, and to what extent do they tailor news coverage in accordance with government wishes or in anticipation of political pressure? Ellis Krauss argues that public broadcasters can act as a watchdog, monitoring the powerful and holding them to account. Alternatively, they can play a more cooperative role as a servant of the state, a guide dog to explain state policies to the public. Worse, they can act as a deferential lapdog, dutifully parroting the government's line.[71] This book follows Krauss and others in arguing that NHK is much more likely to act as a compliant guide dog for the authorities than the BBC, which is more confrontational and more likely to defend attacks on its editorial independence.

However, public broadcasters play an equally important role in the social and cultural lives of their nations. Indeed, entertainment is arguably far more influential than news and current events coverage. BBC biographer Charlotte Higgins' observation about the BBC applies equally to NHK: it is "the national institution that most powerfully touches our inner lives – working its way into our sense of ourselves as individuals and as part of a community, our convictions, our imaginations."[72] Dramas, comedies, documentaries, quiz shows, sports events, or even weather forecasts can reflect and reinforce traditional social values and beliefs about national identity. But such content can also challenge mainstream beliefs, champion marginalized groups, and reshape narratives of national identity. Using Duncan McCargo's terms, media organizations can act as agents of social stability or as catalysts for social change.[73] Along this dimension, the evidence in this book is that the BBC is more likely to act as an agent of social change, while NHK more likely serves as an agent of stability. The BBC is more likely to question traditional views about national culture and identity, and has become relatively more inclusive on issues such of ethnic and gender diversity.

Finally, public broadcasters may vary in their relationship to commercial media, acting either as rivals or as partners. They may act as a direct competitor, or they may cooperate in a formal or informal division of programming, with the public broadcaster providing content such as educational or children's television and commercial media providing more popular and profitable content. Public broadcasters may also vary in the degree to which they act collaboratively with the state, and sometimes with commercial media, in such activities as research and development of communications technology, or international broadcasting. While both the BBC and NHK make many important contributions to their national economies, the BBC demonstrates greater entrepreneurialism and competitiveness toward commercial media.

In other words, organizational culture at the BBC tends to be more independent, outspoken, socially progressive, and entrepreneurial, whereas NHK's organizational culture is more bureaucratic, non-confrontational, and culturally conservative, hewing to more traditional social norms and views of national identity. I am not arguing that any of these qualities are necessarily better or worse for any major media organization, especially not one charged with serving national goals at public expense. Reasonable people differ on which represents a more faithful or valuable version of public service broadcasting. My purpose here is to illuminate how, and help explain why, they differ. It is often assumed that differences in the roles broadcasters play are attributable to differences in factors such as legal status, institutional structures, or funding. Although the BBC and NHK are outwardly very similar organizations, the following chapters will show how they have developed quite distinct traditions over the decades, helping us understand why they now play such different political, societal, and economic roles. The following chapter elaborates these claims and situates them within broader academic discussions of media and politics.

Notes

1 Kaori Hayashi, "Reforming Japan's Broadcasting System," in *Television and Public Policy: Change and Continuity in an Era of Global Liberalization*, ed. David Ward (London: Taylor and Francis, 2008), 137–138, 145.
2 Barry Cox, *Free for All? Public Service Television in the Digital Age* (London: Demos, 2004); David Elstein et al., *Beyond the Charter: The BBC after 2006: Report of the Broadcasting Policy Group* (London: Premium Publishing, 2006).
3 Such views are common in the United States. See Pat Aufderheide, "Will Public Broadcasting Survive?" *The Progressive* 59, no. 3 (March 1995): 3.
4 Hiroshi Matsuda, *NHK- Towareru kōkyō hōsō* [NHK: Public Broadcasting Under Scrutiny] (Tokyo: Iwanami Shoten, 2005); Tsuchiya Hideo, *NHK Jūshinryo wa kyohi dekiruno ka* [Can't We Refuse the NHK Viewer Fee?] (Tokyo: Asahi Shoten, 2008).
5 In game theoretic terms, universal access and depletability meant spectrum was a collective good, subject to the same inefficiencies of overuse as common grazing pastures,

fisheries, and other "tragedies of the commons." Garret Hardin, "The Tragedy of the Commons," *Science* 162 (December 1968): 1243–1248.

6   The United States was an exception, with the federal government allocating spectrum to a wide variety of privately operated commercial and public-interest stations. Allan Brown, "Economics, Public Service Broadcasting, and Social Values," *Journal of Media Economics* 9, no. 1 (Spring 1996): 3–15.

7   Economist and one-time BBC Chairman Gavyn Davis argues clearly that public broadcasting is a classic non-rivalrous public good. Gavyn Davis, "The BBC and Social Market Value," *The Social Market Foundation*, November 2004, www.smf.co.uk/wp-content/uploads/2004/12/Publication-The-BBC-and-Public-Value.pdf.

8   Jon Stone, "Nigel Farage Wants the BBC to Stop Making 'Doctor Who', 'Strictly Come Dancing' and 'Top Gear'," *The Independent*, April 22, 2015.

9   Karol Jakubowicz, "Public Service Broadcasting and Public Policy," in *The Handbook of Global Media and Communication*, eds. Robin Mansell and Marc Raboy (Oxford: Blackwell Publishing, 2011), 210–229.

10 Herman and Chomsky argue that the corporate ownership of mass media in the United States leads to pro-corporate, pro-establishment bias irrespective of the political views of journalists or editors working at the bottom of the chain of command. Edward Herman and Noam Chomsky, *Manufacturing Consent: The Political Economy of Mass-Media* (New York: Pantheon Books, 1988). By contrast, notes Lars Nord, Sweden's public service broadcasters are legally required "to scrutinize authorities, organizations and private firms which exert influence over policy affecting the public," including the state that funds them. See: "Why Is Public Service Media as It Is? A Comparison of Principles and Practices in Six EU Countries," in *Public Service Media in Europe*, eds. Karen Arriaza Ibarra, Eva Nowak, and Raymond Kuhn (London and New York: Routledge, 2015).

11 Petros Iosifidis, *Public Television in the Digital Era: Technological Challenges and New Strategies for Europe* (London: Palgrave MacMillan, 2007), 5.

12 Daniel C. Hallin and Paolo Mancini, *Comparing Media Systems: Three Models of Media and Politics* (Cambridge: Cambridge University Press, 2004). Hallvard Moe and Trine Syvertsen, "Researching Public Broadcasting," in *The Handbook of Journalism Studies*, eds. Karin Wahl-Jorgensen and Thomas Hanitzsch (New York and London: Routledge, 2009). Michael Brüggemann et al., "Hallin and Mancini Revisited: Four Empirical Types of Western Media System," *Journal of Communication* 64 (2014). For a critical discussion of the subfield of comparative media policy, see Pippa Norris, "Comparative Political Communications: Common Frameworks or Babelian Confusion?" *Government and Opposition* 44, no. 3 (2009): 321–340.

13 Iosifidis, *Public Television in the Digital Era*, 5. See also Richard Gunther and Anthony Mughan, eds., *Democracy and the Media: A Comparative Perspective* (Cambridge: Cambridge University Press, 2000), 10.

14 Beata Klimkiewicz, "Between Autonomy and Dependency: Funding Mechanisms of Public Service Media in Selected European Countries," in *Public Service Media in Europe*, especially 118–122.

15 Iosifidis, *Public Television in the Digital Era*; Brüggemann et al., "Hallin and Mancini Revisited"; Arriaza Ibarra et al., eds., *Public Service Media in Europe*.

16 Ofcom, "Annual Report on the BBC," October 2019, www.ofcom.org.uk/__data/assets/pdf_file/0026/173735/second-bbc-annual-report.pdf.

17 Broadcasters Audience Research Board, "Viewing Report," April 2016, www.barb.co.uk/download/?file=/wp-content/uploads/2016/04/BARB-Viewing-Report-2016.pdf.

18 BBC, "Annual Report and Accounts 2018/19," http://downloads.bbc.co.uk/aboutthebbc/reports/annualreport/2018-19.pdf.

19 "Corporate Overview," NHK; BBC Annual Report, 2018–2019, http://downloads.bbc.co.uk/aboutthebbc/reports/annualreport/2018-19.pdf#page=6; Reuters Institute for the Study of Journalism Digital News Report 2021, accessed October 26, 2021, https://reutersinstitute.politics.ox.ac.uk/digital-news-report/2021.

20 BBC, accessed October 26, 2021, www.bbc.com/news/explainers-51376255.
21 Madhulika Sikka, "How Do Federal $$$ Get to Your Local Station?," accessed July 6, 2020, www.pbs.org/publiceditor/blogs/pbs-public-editor/how-do-federal-get-to-your-local-station/. James Ledbetter shows how content at various PBS stations was influenced to reflect the interests of corporate sponsors, including Archer Daniels Midland and Mobil Corporation. See James Ledbetter, *Made Possible by . . . the Death of Public Broadcasting in the United States* (New York: Verso Press, 1998).
22 Legally, NHK is a "corporate juridical person" (*Shadan hōjin*). On at least one occasion, though, NHK lawyers have argued in US court that it was a legal arm of the Japanese government.
23 Yoshiko Nakamura and Ritsu Yonekura, "Present Situation Regarding TV Viewing and Radio Listening," *Broadcasting Studies* (Tokyo: NHK Broadcast Culture Research Institute, March 2012), 128.
24 "Corporate Overview," NHK, accessed June 2019, www.nhk.or.jp/corporateinfo/english/corporate/index.html.
25 For a brief discussion of *dorai* and *uetto,* see Chalmers Johnson, "Omote (Explicit) and Ura (Implicit): Translating Japanese Political Terms," *Journal of Japanese Studies* 6, no. 1 (Winter 1980): 96.
26 "NHK dake utsuranai kiki setchi no dansei ni jushin-ryō 1310-en shiharai meirei [Man Who Installed Equipment Capable of Receiving Everything Except NHK Ordered to Pay ¥1,310]," *Sankei Shimbun,* July 20, 2016.
27 Jim Waterson, "TV Licence Could Be Abolished in 2027 Says Nicky Morgan," *The Guardian,* February 5, 2020, www.theguardian.com/media/2020/feb/05/tv-licence-could-be-abolished-from-2027-says-nicky-morgan.
28 "After Stunning Election Win, Anti-NHK Party Sets Higher Goal," *Asahi Shimbun,* July 25, 2019, www.asahi.com/ajw/articles/AJ201907250055.html.
29 "Anti-NHK Party Chief Goes Off the Rails Urging Genocide," *Asahi Shimbun,* September 29, 2019, www.asahi.com/ajw/articles/AJ201909290027.html.
30 Evie Lund, "Don't Want to Pay Your NHK Licence Fee? Beat Takeshi Agrees with You," *Japan Today,* March 2, 2015.
31 The most recent renewal was 2017. The next is due in 2027.
32 The Japanese word for the head of NHK, *kaichō,* is usually translated as "chairman," but the position is sometimes referred to as "president." Ellis Krauss, *Broadcasting Politics in Japan* (Ithaca, NY: Cornell University Press, 2000). Krauss notes that between 1950 and 2000, four of the ten NHK chairmen left office prematurely for political reasons.
33 Caroline Mayer and Elizabeth Tucker, "The FCC According to Mark Fowler," *Washington Post,* April 19, 1987.
34 Jakubowicz, "Public Service Broadcasting and Public Policy." There are almost as many slightly different lists of public service media roles as there are scholars of public service media. Krauss, *Broadcasting Politics in Japan.*
35 Council of Europe, "Recommendation CM/Rec (2007) of the Committee of Ministers to Member States on the Remit of Public Service Media in the Information Society," January 31, 2007, https://search.coe.int/cm/Pages/result_details.aspx?ObjectID=09000016805d6bc5.
36 Bruce Cunningham, "Objectivity Revisited," *Columbia Journalism Review* (July/August 2003).
37 These mission statements are adapted from the respective websites, closely following the language used in both.
38 According to various interviews conducted by the author with journalists in commercial news organizations.
39 Nic Newman, "Digital News Report: United Kingdom," Reuters Institute for the Study of Journalism at Oxford University, 2017, www.digitalnewsreport.org/survey/2017/united-kingdom-2017/.

40 Yasaomi Sawa, "Digital News Report: Japan," Reuters Institute for the Study of Journalism at Oxford University, 2017, www.digitalnewsreport.org/survey/2017/japan-2017/.

41 Daniel Marshall, "BBC Most Trusted News Source," *Ipsos MORI*, November 22, 2017, www.ipsos.com/ipsos-mori/en-uk/bbc-most-trusted-news-source; "Despite Everything, We Still Trust Auntie," *Ipsos MORI*, March 31, 2008, www.ipsos-mori.com/newsevents/ca/383/Despite-everything-we-still-trust-Auntie.aspx; Yokoyama Shigeru and Yonekura Ritsu, "Structure of Trust in the Mass Media," *NHK Hōsōkenkyū chōsa* [Broadcast Research Survey], (Tokyo: NHK Broadcasting Culture Research Institute, 2009), Mark Schilling, "NHK Up to Earthquake Challenge," *Variety*, April 2, 2011.

42 Christian Collett and Gento Kato, "Does NHK Make You Smarter (and Super News Make You 'Softer')? An Examination of Political Knowledge and the Potential Influence of TV News," *Japanese Journal of Political Science* 15, no. 1 (2014): 25–50. Toril Aalberg and James Curran, eds., *How Media Inform Democracy: A Comparative Approach* (New York: Routledge, 2012). James Curran et al., "Media System, Public Knowledge and Democracy," *European Journal of Communication* 24, no. 1 (2009): 5–26; Pippa Norris and Christina Holz-Bacha, "To Entertain, Inform and Educate: Still the Role of Public Television," *Political Communication* 18, no. 2 (April–June 2001): 123–140.

43 NHK *Keieikaikau* (Corporate Plan) 2015–2017, accessed October 26, 2021, www.nhk.or.jp/pr/keiei/plan/pdf/20150115comment.pdf (in English: www.nhk.or.jp/corporateinfo/english/publication/pdf/plan2015-2017.pdf); BBC website "About the BBC: Mission, Values and Public Purposes," accessed October 26, 2021, www.bbc.com/aboutthebbc/governance/mission.

44 Jim Waterson, "BBC Launches Daily Educational Shows to Keep Children Studying," *The Guardian*, April 3, 2020, www.theguardian.com/media/2020/apr/03/bbc-launches-daily-educational-shows-keep-children-studying; Jeremy Dickson, "Pubcasters Shift Programming, Schedules," *Kidscreen*, March 19, 2020, https://kidscreen.com/2020/03/19/pubcasters-shift-programming-schedules/; "BBC to Deliver Biggest Push on Education in Its History," *BBC*, April 3, 2020, www.bbc.co.uk/mediacentre/latestnews/2020/coronavirus-education.

45 John Reith, *Broadcast Over Britain* (London: Hodder and Staunton, 1924), 147–148.

46 As one producer remarked to me in June 2011 about "Top Gear," a BBC production extolling the virtues of fast cars and male bonding, "It may be just a car show, but it's the best car show."

47 Reith, *Broadcast Over Britain*, 34.

48 Jean Seaton, *Pinkoes and Traitors: The BBC and the Nation, 1974–1987* (London: Profile Books, 2015), 260.

49 Ernest Gellner, *Culture Identity and Politics* (Cambridge: Cambridge University Press, 1987), 15.

50 Benedict Anderson, *Imagined Communities: Reflections on the Origins and Spread of Nationalism* (London: Verso Books, 1983), 163.

51 Anderson, *Imagined Communities*, 78.

52 Katherine Faulkner and Mario Ledwith, "Diamond Jubilee: BBC Attacked for Inane and Celebrity-Driven Coverage of Queen's Thames Pageant," *Daily Mail*, June 4, 2012, www.dailymail.co.uk/news/article-2154424/Diamond-jubilee-BBC-attacked-inane-celebrity-driven-coverage-Queens-Thames-Pageant.html.

53 Reiji Yoshida, "Confidante Says Emperor Told Him He Wants Abdication Option Codified," *Japan Times*, January 21, 2017.

54 Michael Billig, *Banal Nationalism* (London: Sage Publications, 1995).

55 "Olympics Boosts Opinion of BBC, Royal Family and London," *Ipsos MORI*, August 15, 2012, www.ipsos-mori.com/researchpublications/researcharchive/3029/Olympics-boosts-opinion-of-BBC-Royal-Family-and-London.aspx.

56 David Shields, "Being Ichiro," *The New York Times*, September 6, 2016.
57 Karl Deutsch, *Nationalism and Social Communications: An Inquiry into the Foundations of Nationality* (Cambridge, MA: MIT Press, 1966), 75.
58 "Cool Japan," NHK World-Japan, accessed April 26, 2017, https://www3.nhk.or.jp/nhkworld/en/tv/cooljapan/.
59 NHK, *Keiei Keikaku 2015–2017* [NHK Corporate Plan 2015–2017], accessed August 15, 2018, www.nhk.or.jp/pr/keiei/plan/pdf/25-27keikaku.pdf.
60 "NHK World-Japan is New Name for International TV Service of NHK," *Global Newswire*, March 20, 2018.
61 Koichi Iwabuchi, "Pop Culture Diplomacy in Japan: Soft Power, Nation Branding and the Question of 'International Cultural Exchange'," *International Journal of Cultural Policy* 21, no. 4 (September 2015): 428.
62 Tara Conlan, "BBC World Service to Receive £289m from Government," *The Guardian*, November 23, 2015, www.theguardian.com/media/2015/nov/23/bbc-world-service-receive-289m-from-government.
63 Broadcast Law of Japan Article 9 (1) iii.
64 Roya Akhavan-Majid, "Public Service Broadcasting and the Challenge of New Technology: A Case Study of Japan's NHK," *International Communication Gazette* 50, no. 21 (1992). For an account of the development of high-definition television, see Jeffrey A. Hart, *Television, Technology and Competition: HDTV and Digital TV in the United States, Western Europe and Japan* (Cambridge: Cambridge University Press, 2004).
65 Michael Starks, *Switching to Digital Television: UK Public Policy and the Market* (London: Intellect, 2012); Henry Laurence, "Digital Television and Technology Diffusion," *International Journal of Digital Television* 2, no. 3 (September 2011): 359–366.
66 Department for Culture, Media and Sport, *Report of the BBC's Royal Charter: A Strong BBC, Independent of Government* (London: DCMS, 2005).
67 Schilling, "Earthquake Challenge."
68 "Shingata koronauirusukansenshō no kōdō jōkyō' to yūkōna media ni tsuite no chōsa [Survey on Behavioral Status of the New Coronavirus Infection and Effective Media]," *Nippon Research Center*, April 10, 2020, www.nrc.co.jp/report/200410.html; "Digital News Report 2020," Reuters Institute for the Study of Journalism at Oxford University, 2020, www.digitalnewsreport.org/survey/2020/country-and-market-data-2020/.
69 Duncan McCargo, *Media and Politics in Pacific Asia* (London: RoutledgeCurzon, 2003), 3–4.
70 Quoted in Seaton, *Pinkoes and Traitors*, 17.
71 Krauss, *Broadcasting Politics in Japan*. For discussion of the political roles of public broadcasters in other contexts, see Karol Jakubowicz and Mikloz Sukosds, eds. *Finding the Right Place on the Map: Central and East European Media Change in a Global Perspective* (Bristol: Intellect Books, 2008) and Hilde Van Den Bulck, "Public Service Media Accountability in Recent Decades: A Progressive Shift from State to Market," in Arriaza Ibarra et al., *Public Service Media in Europe*, 73–88.
72 Charlotte Higgins, *This New Noise: The Extraordinary Birth and Troubled Life of the BBC* (London: Guardian Books, 2015), 231.
73 McCargo, *Media and Politics in Pacific Asia*.

References

Aalberg, Toril, and James Curran, eds., *How Media Inform Democracy: A Comparative Approach* (New York: Routledge, 2012).
"After Stunning Election Win, Anti-NHK Party Sets Higher goal," *Asahi Shimbun*, July 25, 2019, www.asahi.com/ajw/articles/AJ201907250055.html.
Akhavan-Majid, Roya, "Public Service Broadcasting and the Challenge of New Technology: A Case Study of Japan's NHK," *International Communication Gazette* 50, no. 21 (1992).

Anderson, Benedict, *Imagined Communities: Reflections on the Origins and Spread of Nationalism* (London: Verso Books, 1983), 163.

"Anti-NHK Party Chief Goes Off the Rails Urging Genocide," *Asahi Shimbun*, September 29, 2019, www.asahi.com/ajw/articles/AJ201909290027.html.

Aufderheide, Pat, "Will Public Broadcasting Survive?" *The Progressive* 59, no. 3 (March 1995): 3.

"BBC to Deliver Biggest Push on Education in Its History," *BBC*, April 3, 2020, www.bbc.co.uk/mediacentre/latestnews/2020/coronavirus-education.

Billig, Michael, *Banal Nationalism* (London: Sage Publications, 1995).

Brown, Allan, "Economics, Public Service Broadcasting, and Social Values," *Journal of Media Economics* 9, no. 1 (Spring 1996): 3–15.

Brüggemann, Michael, et al., "Hallin and Mancini Revisited: Four Empirical Types of Western Media System," *Journal of Communication* 64 (2014).

Collett, Christian, and Gento Kato, "Does NHK Make You Smarter (and Super News Make You 'Softer')? An Examination of Political Knowledge and the Potential Influence of TV News," *Japanese Journal of Political Science* 15, no. 1 (2014): 25–50.

Conlan, Tara, "BBC World Service to Receive £289m from Government," *The Guardian*, November 23, 2015, www.theguardian.com/media/2015/nov/23/bbc-world-service-receive-289m-from-government.

"Cool Japan," *NHK World-Japan*, accessed April 26, 2017, https://www3.nhk.or.jp/nhkworld/en/tv/cooljapan/.

"Corporate Overview," NHK, accessed June 2019, www.nhk.or.jp/corporateinfo/english/corporate/index.html.

Cox, Barry, *Free for All? Public Service Television in the Digital Age* (London: Demos, 2004).

Cunningham, Bruce, "Objectivity Revisited," *Columbia Journalism Review* (July/August 2003).

Curran, James, et al., "Media System, Public Knowledge and Democracy," *European Journal of Communication* 24, no. 1 (2009).

Davis, Gavyn, "The BBC and Social Market Value," *The Social Market Foundation*, November 2004, www.smf.co.uk/wp-content/uploads/2004/12/Publication-The-BBC-and-Public-Value.pdf.

Department for Culture, Media and Sport, *Report of the BBC's Royal Charter: A Strong BBC, Independent of Government* (London: DCMS, 2005).

"Despite Everything, We Still Trust Auntie," *Ipsos MORI*, March 31, 2008, www.ipsos-mori.com/newsevents/ca/383/Despite-everything-we-still-trust-Auntie.aspx.

Deutsch, Karl, *Nationalism and Social Communications: An Inquiry into the Foundations of Nationality* (Cambridge, MA: MIT Press, 1966).

Dickson, Jeremy, "Pubcasters Shift Programming, Schedules," *Kidscreen*, March 19, 2020, https://kidscreen.com/2020/03/19/pubcasters-shift-programming-schedules/.

"Digital News Report 2020," Reuters Institute for the Study of Journalism at Oxford University, 2020, www.digitalnewsreport.org/survey/2020/country-and-market-data-2020/.

Elstein, David, et al., *Beyond the Charter: The BBC after 2006: Report of the Broadcasting Policy Group* (London: Premium Publishing, 2006).

Faulkner, Katherine, and Mario Ledwith, "Diamond Jubilee: BBC Attacked for Inane and Celebrity-Driven coverage of Queen's Thames Pageant," *Daily Mail*, June 4, 2012, www.dailymail.co.uk/news/article-2154424/Diamond-jubilee-BBC-attacked-inane-celebrity-driven-coverage-Queens-Thames-Pageant.html.

Gellner, Ernest, *Culture Identity and Politics* (Cambridge: Cambridge University Press, 1987), 15.

Gunther, Richard, and Anthony Mughan, eds., *Democracy and the Media: A Comparative Perspective* (Cambridge: Cambridge University Press, 2000).

Hallin, Daniel C., and Paolo Mancini, *Comparing Media Systems: Three Models of Media and Politics* (Cambridge: Cambridge University Press, 2004).

Hardin, Garret, "The Tragedy of the Commons," *Science* 162 (December 1968): 1243–1248.

Hart, Effrey A., *Television, Technology and Competition: HDTV and Digital TV in the United States, Western Europe and Japan* (Cambridge: Cambridge University Press, 2004).

Hayashi, Kaori, "Reforming Japan's Broadcasting System," in *Television and Public Policy: Change and Continuity in an Era of Global Liberalization*, ed. David Ward (London: Taylor and Francis, 2008), 137–138, 145.

Herman, Edward, and Noam Chomsky, *Manufacturing Consent: The Political Economy of Mass-Media* (New York: Pantheon Books, 1988).

Hideo, Tsuchiya, *NHK Jūshinryo wa kyohi dekiruno ka* [Can't We Refuse the NHK Viewer Fee?] (Tokyo: Asahi Shoten, 2008).

Higgins, Charlotte, *This New Noise: The Extraordinary Birth and Troubled Life of the BBC* (London: Guardian Books, 2015).

Iosifidis, Petros, *Public Television in the Digital Era: Technological Challenges and New Strategies for Europe* (London: Palgrave MacMillan, 2007).

Iwabuchi, Koichi, "Pop Culture Diplomacy in Japan: Soft Power, Nation Branding and the Question of 'International Cultural Exchange'," *International Journal of Cultural Policy* 21, no. 4 (September 2015).

Jakubowicz, Karol, "Public Service Broadcasting and Public Policy," in *The Handbook of Global Media and Communication*, eds. Robin Mansell and Marc Raboy (Oxford: Blackwell Publishing, 2011), 210–229.

Jakubowicz, Karol, and Mikloz Sukosds, eds., *Finding the Right Place on the Map: Central and East European Media Change in a Global Perspective* (Bristol: Intellect Books, 2008).

Johnson, Chalmers, "Omote (Explicit) and Ura (Implicit): Translating Japanese Political Terms," *Journal of Japanese Studies* 6, no. 1 (Winter 1980): 96.

Klimkiewicz, Beata, "Between Autonomy and Dependency: Funding Mechanisms of Public Service Media in Selected European Countries," in *Public Service Media in Europe*, eds. Karen Arriaza Ibarra et al. (London and New York: Routledge, 2015).

Krauss, Ellis, *Broadcasting Politics in Japan* (Ithaca, NY: Cornell University Press, 2000).

Laurence, Henry, "Digital Television and Technology Diffusion," *International Journal of Digital Television* 2, no. 3 (September 2011): 359–366.

Ledbetter, James, *Made Possible By . . . the Death of Public Broadcasting in the United States* (New York: Verso Press, 1998).

Lund, Evie, "Don't Want to Pay Your NHK Licence Fee? Beat Takeshi Agrees with You," *Japan Today*, March 2, 2015.

Marshall, Daniel, "BBC Most Trusted News Source," *Ipsos MORI*, November 22, 2017, www.ipsos.com/ipsos-mori/en-uk/bbc-most-trusted-news-source.

Matsuda, Hiroshi, *NHK- Towareru kōkyō hōsō* [NHK: Public Broadcasting Under Scrutiny] (Tokyo: Iwanami Shoten, 2005).

Mayer, Caroline, and Elizabeth Tucker, "The FCC According to Mark Fowler," *Washington Post*, April 19, 1987.

McCargo, Duncan, *Media and Politics in Pacific Asia* (London: RoutledgeCurzon, 2003).

Moe, Hallvard, and Trine Syvertsen, "Researching Public Broadcasting," in *Handbook of Journalism Studies*, eds. Karin Wahl-Jorgensen and Thomas Hanitzsch (New York and London: Routledge, 2009).

Nakamura, Yoshiko, and Ritsu Yonekura, "Present Situation Regarding TV Viewing and Radio Listening," in *Broadcasting Studies* (Tokyo: NHK Broadcast Culture Research Institute, March 2012),

Newman, Nic, "Digital News Report: United Kingdom," Reuters Institute for the Study of Journalism at Oxford University, 2017, www.digitalnewsreport.org/survey/2017/united-kingdom-2017/.

"NHK dake utsuranai kiki setchi no dansei ni jushin-ryō 1310-en shiharai meirei [Man Who Installed Equipment Capable of Receiving Everything Except NHK Ordered to Pay ¥1,310]," *Sankei Shimbun*, July 20, 2016.

NHK, *Keiei Keikaku 2015–2017* [NHK Corporate Plan 2015–2017], accessed August 15, 2018, www.nhk.or.jp/pr/keiei/plan/pdf/25-27keikaku.pdf.

"NHK World-Japan is New Name for International TV Service of NHK," *Global Newswire*, March 20, 2018.

Nord, Lars, "Why is Public Service Media as It Is? A Comparison of Principles and Practices in Six EU Countries," in *Public Service Media in Europe*, eds. Karen Arriaza Ibarra et al. (London and New York: Routledge, 2015).

Norris, Pippa, "Comparative Political Communications: Common Frameworks or Babelian Confusion?" *Government and Opposition* 44, no. 3 (2009): 321–340.

Norris, Pippa, and Christina Holz-Bacha, "To Entertain, Inform and Educate: Still the Role of Public Television," *Political Communication* 18, no. 2 (April–June 2001): 123–140.

Ofcom, "Annual Report on the BBC," October 2019, www.ofcom.org.uk/__data/assets/pdf_file/0026/173735/second-bbc-annual-report.pdf.

"Olympics Boosts Opinion of BBC, Royal Family and London," *Ipsos MORI*, August 15, 2012, www.ipsos-mori.com/researchpublications/researcharchive/3029/Olympics-boosts-opinion-of-BBC-Royal-Family-and-London.aspx.

Sawa, Yasaomi, "Digital News Report: Japan," Reuters Institute for the Study of Journalism at Oxford University, 2017, www.digitalnewsreport.org/survey/2017/japan-2017/.

Schilling, Mark, "NHK Up to Earthquake Challenge," *Variety*, April 2, 2011.

Seaton, Jean, *Pinkoes and Traitors: The BBC and the Nation, 1974–1987* (London: Profile Books, 2015).

Shields, David, "Being Ichiro," *The New York Times*, September 6, 2016.

Shigeru, Yokoyama, and Yonekura Ritsu, "Structure of Trust in the Mass Media," in *Hōsōkenkyū chōsa* [Broadcast Research Survey] (Tokyo: NHK Broadcasting Culture Research Institute, 2009).

"Shingata koronauirusukansenshō no kōdō jōkyō' to yūkōna media ni tsuite no chōsa [Survey on Behavioral Status of the New Coronavirus Infection and Effective Media]," *Nippon Research Center*, April 10, 2020, www.nrc.co.jp/report/200410.html.

Sikka, Madhulika, "How do Federal $$$ Get to Your Local Station?" accessed July 6, 2020, www.pbs.org/publiceditor/blogs/pbs-public-editor/how-do-federal-get-to-your-local-station/.

Starks, Michael, *Switching to Digital Television: UK Public Policy and the Market* (London: Intellect, 2012).

Stone, Jon, "Nigel Farage Wants the BBC to Stop Making 'Doctor Who', 'Strictly Come Dancing' and 'Top Gear'," *The Independent*, April 22, 2015.

Van Den Bulck, Hilde, "Public Service Media Accountability in Recent Decades: A Progressive Shift from State to Market," in in *Public Service Media in Europe*, eds. Karen Arriaza Ibarra et al. (London and New York: Routledge, 2015), 73–88.

Waterson, Jim, "BBC Launches Daily Educational Shows to Keep Children Studying," *The Guardian*, April 3, 2020, www.theguardian.com/media/2020/apr/03/bbc-launches-daily-educational-shows-keep-children-studying.

Waterson, Jim, "TV Licence Could be Abolished in 2027 Says Nicky Morgan," *The Guardian*, February 5, 2020, www.theguardian.com/media/2020/feb/05/tv-licence-could-be-abolished-from-2027-says-nicky-morgan.

Yoshida, Reiji, "Confidante Says Emperor Told Him He Wants Abdication Option Codified," *Japan Times*, January 21, 2017.

3 Different Roles

This chapter explores the different political, social, and economic roles that the BBC and NHK seek to play in national life. Drawing on the theoretical insights of Ellis Krauss, Duncan McCargo, Lucy Küng-Shankleman, and others, I argue that they differ in their relationships to the government, to their audiences, and to their commercial rivals. Each broadcaster has, since birth, interpreted their roles somewhat differently. Over time, in response to a succession of common technological and political challenges, the two have developed distinctive organizational cultures and editorial philosophies. These cultures have shaped, and in turn are shaped by, the ideas and interests of the other important actors. This chapter sketches these two broadcasting cultures: the BBC tends to be more protective of its independence, more confrontational toward authority, more proactive in embracing progressive social change, and displays greater economic entrepreneurialism. NHK tends to be more cooperative with state actors and commercial rivals, its programs more likely to embody traditional social values, and its relationship to the commercial broadcasting market more technocratic.

Political Roles: Watchdog or Guide Dog?

The BBC and NHK are their nation's premier news organizations in terms of audience share, resources, and access to political elites. Accordingly, much attention is paid to their editorial independence and journalistic impartiality. The two concepts are logically distinct but in practice, as Chris Hanretty points out, they mutually imply each other. In the words of Hugh Greene, former director-general of the BBC:

> Without true independence, therefore, it is difficult for any broadcaster to maintain the highest standards of truth, accuracy, and impartiality. Conversely, of course, without a reputation for these things – truth, accuracy, and impartiality – it is difficult for any broadcasting organization to be recognized as truly independent and to be generally trusted.[1]

Accordingly, both independence and impartiality must be considered when assessing the broadcasters' political roles.

DOI: 10.4324/b23015-3

Both the BBC and NHK enjoy legal guarantees of editorial independence and are required to provide accurate and impartial news and information. The 2016 Royal Charter states that, "The BBC must be independent in all matters concerning the fulfilment of its Mission and the promotion of the Public Purposes, particularly as regards editorial and creative decisions." Article 5 requires that "The Mission of the BBC is to act in the public interest, serving all audiences through the provision of impartial, high-quality and distinctive output and services which inform, educate and entertain." Article 6 states:

> The BBC should provide duly accurate and impartial news, current affairs and factual programming to build people's understanding of all parts of the United Kingdom and of the wider world. Its content should be provided to the highest editorial standards. It should offer a range and depth of analysis and content not widely available from other United Kingdom news providers.[2]

Article 3 of Japan's 1950 Broadcast Law pertains to "Editorial Freedom of Broadcast Programs" and states: "Broadcast programs shall not be interfered with or regulated by any person except in cases pursuant to the authority provided for in laws." Article 4 of the law requires:

> The broadcaster shall comply with the matters provided for in the following items when editing the broadcast programs: (i) It shall not harm public safety or good morals; (ii) It shall be politically fair; (iii) Its reporting shall not distort the facts; (iv) It shall clarify the points at issue from as many angles as possible where there are conflicting opinions concerning an issue.[3]

These legal strictures notwithstanding, however, the independence and impartiality of both broadcasters have always been matters of intense debate.

Hanretty defines independence for public service broadcasters, first, as the degree to which employees can make day-to-day editorial decisions without receiving inducements or threats from politicians, and second, as the degree to which such decisions are made without anticipating such pressure or considering politicians' interests.[4] Both the BBC and NHK generally enjoy a high degree of independence in the first sense: it is rare, though not unknown, for politicians to seek to exercise direct control over content. Neither now acts as a mere mouthpiece for whichever government is in power, and politicians usually do not exercise veto power over news items. That said, we will see that on the relatively few occasions where politicians do try to influence specific editorial decisions, the BBC has shown itself to be more likely to push back than NHK.

However, neither broadcaster is ever free from the *threat* of political interference. Governments in both countries and of all political stripes have shown themselves willing to attempt to influence coverage. Such political influence can easily be exercised through the governance structures the broadcasters have in common. Notably, prime ministers appoint key personnel, including members of the governing bodies as well as the director-general or president. In addition, although the viewer fee system insulates budgets from political bargaining in the short term, long-term financial arrangements such as fee increases are subject to parliamentary approval. Charter renewal provides regular occasions for intense negotiation between politicians and the BBC, while governments in both countries always have the "nuclear option" of changing – or not changing – relevant laws. For example, NHK's desire for the criminalization of non-payment of viewer fees required a revision of the Broadcast Law, which gave the ruling LDP increased leverage over the broadcaster. The question is not whether public broadcasters' editorial decisions are made in the shadow of political influence; they always are. The important question is how broadcasters shape their reporting in the face of that reality. In the second sense of independence, the degree to which content is produced (or not produced) in anticipation of political pressure or with political interests in mind, we see marked differences between the BBC and NHK. These differences are manifest, in part, in how each broadcaster interprets the requirement to be impartial.

Both broadcasters proudly claim accuracy and impartiality, which feature prominently in their respective editorial guidelines.[5] Employees in news departments are prohibited from publicly expressing support for political parties, current policy debates, or other controversial issues, although as we will see, there can be much debate over what constitutes partisanship or even controversy on sensitive issues such as climate change, nuclear power, Brexit, or the Black Lives Matter movement.[6]

But impartiality, along with the related concepts of non-partisanship, neutrality, and objectivity, is almost as hard to define as to achieve. Narrowly understood as something like neutrality, the term can be used as an excuse for lazy bothsidesism or "he said, she said" journalism in which reporters merely parrot opposing politicians without trying to establish which viewpoints are more truthful.[7] Similarly, factual accuracy is a necessary but not sufficient condition for good news reporting, which should also provide context. Flaws of narrowness can be avoided if impartiality is understood more broadly as something like objectivity, but that leads to other problems. Many media scholars note that protestations of objectivity mask the reality that all journalists have implicit biases of race, gender, class, education, nationality, and so on. The personal backgrounds of reporters and editors have been shown to influence every aspect of the news – which stories are covered; what sources are used; which questions are asked; what facts are showcased; and how the issues are framed. True impartiality, argue such scholars, is dangerous to claim and impossible to achieve.[8]

In response to those objections, others reply that journalistic impartiality should be understood as a process rather than as an endpoint. News organizations should be judged by how well they make good-faith efforts to uncover the whole truth of a story, represent all sides of controversial issues, provide appropriate context, and examine and broaden the background beliefs and assumptions of their staff. Service to telling the truth also means being unafraid to investigate and challenge the powerful: Impartiality should not mean simply avoiding confrontation or controversy.[9] Viewed in these terms, I argue that while both broadcasters can reasonably claim to be impartial in the narrow sense of being non-partisan, the BBC has been more successful than NHK in realizing editorial independence as well as impartiality in its broader and deeper sense.

NHK: Guide Dog

Ellis Krauss's classic study paints a clear picture of NHK as an organization more likely to take the "guide dog" role of explaining government policy than the "watchdog" role of questioning the state. NHK strictly interprets the letter of the law on accuracy (*seikaku*), fairness (*kōhei*), and impartiality (*kōsei*).[10] Airtime on news and current events programs is rationed to political parties in closely timed proportion to their strength in Japan's parliament, the Diet. Left-leaning politicians assured me that they appreciate NHK's serious tone and commitment to giving them appropriate airtime, at least relative to most other media outlets.[11] Facts are scrupulously checked, information comes mostly from official sources, which are presumed to be reliable, and news stories avoid airing rumors or speculation. The result, according to Krauss, is news coverage that is "factual, opinion-less, and dramatically anemic."[12] The desire to avoid controversy results in news coverage with only limited opportunities for voices outside of mainstream politics to be heard. Importantly, NHK's interpretation of impartiality has come to mean avoiding news coverage that might be construed as critical of the government. As Krauss concludes, "The most important consequence of the combination of formal and informal means of influence by the LDP on NHK has been a particularly effective self-censorship."[13]

Many critics go further, accusing NHK of often unsubtle bias toward the conservative LDP. In the words of one interviewee, NHK's editorial independence is merely *tatemae*, the official position. The true state of affairs (*hone*) is that the LDP intervenes so extensively that some staff quietly refer to the evening news as "The LDP Hour."[14] Comments made in 2014 by the then chairman Momii Katsuto about how NHK's international news should not contradict the government line on foreign policy confirmed for many the broadcaster's reputation as a lapdog.[15] This more critical assessment of NHK's independence and impartiality is stressed by scholars, including Hayashi Kayori, Matsuda Hiroshi, Philip Seaton, David McNeil, and Aurelia George Mulgan.[16]

Government pressure on NHK has been present since its birth, but the intensity of political interference, along with NHK's willingness to comply, has varied over time. State control was strong in the 1930s and the Second World War, when NHK became the mouthpiece for imperial propaganda. Even in the democratic euphoria of the allied occupation from 1945 to 1952, General Douglas MacArthur's use of NHK as an official mouthpiece, combined with widespread censorship, helped perpetuate a climate in which state influence on the media was seen as normal, if not always legitimate. Nonetheless, NHK underwent an outspoken progressive renaissance in the immediate postwar period, in part at the insistence of the occupation. The political turmoil of the 1960s and 1970s, though, pushed management back toward the comfort of neutral non-confrontation. Political intervention grew aggressive under hawkish Prime Minister Nakasone Yasuo in the 1980s and diminished during the early 1990s. The internal culture of self-censorship grew more oppressive again after 1997 with the appointment of Ebisawa Katsuji, a close political ally of conservative Prime Minister Hashimoto Ryutaro, as chairman. The decade or so following Ebisawa's forced resignation in 2005 was more editorially free, particularly during the rule of the progressive Democratic Party of Japan (DPJ) from 2009 to 2012. Thereafter, as Philip Seaton has documented, Abe Shinzō's aggressively confrontational approach to hostile media sources following his return as prime minister in 2012 reinforced NHK's conservative, pro-government tendencies.[17] Programming about the Second World War became more sympathetic to nationalist narratives about Japan's wartime past, and less likely to criticize LDP positions during Abe's second term. War documentaries reverted to focusing on decontextualized accounts of Japanese victimhood, with an uncontroversial "war is bad" moral.[18] By 2015, the derisory nickname *abechanneru* ("The Abe Channel") was so pervasive that NHK President Momii Katsuto was begging journalists not to use it.[19]

There is, though, much internal disagreement within NHK about how much news reporters should stand up to the government. Journalists and other staff clash with more senior management over the boundaries of what is appropriate to report, as routinely happens at all news organizations.[20] For example, we will later explore a particularly notorious episode when senior LDP officials demanded revisions to a documentary about Japan's wartime system of sexual slavery and NHK's management willingly acquiesced, to the fury of the program's writers and producers. Note too that although NHK is most frequently criticized from the left for being too conservative, there are those on the right who criticize it for not hewing closely enough to their version of Japanese values. The electoral success of the Anti-NHK party is a case in point. Finally, there are recent signs that NHK is beginning to take watchdog reporting more seriously.[21] As a partner in the International Consortium of Investigative Journalists, reporters from NHK, the Asahi Shimbun and Kyodo News contributed to investigations, including the Panama Papers and the failure of Olympus Corporation to report defective medical devices to Japan's Ministry of Health.[22] Nonetheless, the scholarly consensus remains that NHK's editorial culture is one shading toward editorial timidity and non-confrontation.

The BBC: Watchdog

The BBC has always been relatively more willing to resist political pressure, and has a reputation for operating independent of state influence.[23] In Hanretty's phrase, "The BBC is known for displaying the virtue of independence vis-à-vis the government."[24] At various times, too, countries, including German, Spain, and France, have sought to emulate the BBC's autonomy by adopting its institutional forms.[25] The reputation began with the BBC's refusal to toe Winston Churchill's government line during the 1926 General Strike. Churchill was livid but Conservative Prime Minister Stanley Baldwin accepted Director-General Reith's argument that an independent BBC would enjoy greater public trust, which would on balance benefit the government. The same argument prevailed during the Second World War, when the Corporation again had to tread a careful line between being supportive of the war effort and maintaining its independence. Even so, the BBC has had to defend its editorial independence in the face of government pressure repeatedly since, notably during the Suez Crisis of 1956, the Troubles in Northern Ireland in the 1970s, the Falklands War in 1983, and the 2003 Iraq War.

In peacetime, too, the BBC has developed a reputation as a confrontational adversary for politicians from all parties. Like NHK, the BBC prides itself on non-partisanship, but unlike NHK, it is more willing to dig into stories and speak truth to power, styling itself an equal opportunity watchdog on political misbehavior. Politicians can expect a serious grilling when they are interviewed by BBC reporters, although few reporters are as confrontational as Jeremy Paxman, the legendarily presenter of Newsnight who famously (or notoriously) asked an evasive cabinet minister the same question 12 times in under two minutes.[26] This organizational ethos is embodied in the statue of George Orwell to be found at the entrance to the BBC's Headquarters, accompanied by his quotation, "If liberty means anything at all it means the right to tell people what they do not want to hear."[27]

Impartiality is enshrined in concrete rules, in the form of editorial conduct and Producer Guidelines, which enforced norms within the organization. For example, BBC employees are prohibited from taking public positions on political matters. These internal rules were developed specifically to deflect criticism and reduce external pressure. In turn, the rules concerning BBC editorial standards and journalistic conduct were accepted by those in power as the appropriate frame with which to judge BBC content. Overall, the rules work. Ofcom, the independent regulator for the BBC since 2017, is charged with investigating complaints about the BBC. The regulator's 2019–2020 report found no cases where the BBC had violated its responsibilities to accuracy or impartiality.[28]

The struggle over editorial autonomy has always been fraught, however, and the BBC has never been entirely immune to political pressure. Later we explore various episodes of political intervention, including the shelving of *The War Game*, a docudrama highly critical of the United Kingdom's nuclear weapons policy. Now observers and staff suggest that fear of political retribution results in senior management suffering from a semipermanent "defensive crouch" toward government, more fearful of giving offense than the freer-spirited journalists and producers.[29] For other critics, the BBC's bias is more insidious, tending toward an implicit favoritism toward elite interests and the status quo. Sociologist Tom Mills argues that the central problem of the BBC is "the extent to which powerful interests have been able to influence its institutional culture and its output."[30] These interests, which he loosely labels "the neoliberal, business-dominated Establishment" include both major political parties and the Whitehall bureaucracy. The long-held perception that the BBC, based in London and staffed with Oxbridge graduates, was too preoccupied with southern middle-class issues eventually prompted the move to Manchester of a significant amount of production. Criticism of BBC elitism was certainly true in the early decades, when Reith's lofty vision of serving the nation rather than the government meant what Jean Seaton called "the denial of politics."[31] The BBC shrank from reporting controversy, while its reporting tended to ignore views and voices outside the Westminster establishment. Among other effects, this meant the BBC acquiesced with the Foreign Office's wishes to keep Winston Churchill off the air in the 1930s because his anti-Nazi rhetoric was undermining the national policy of appeasement.[32]

In addition to, and to some extent set against, accusations of pro-Establishment bias are regular accusations of partisanship, from both ends of the political spectrum. Conservatives in Britain regularly condemn the BBC for its supposedly left-wing partisanship and socially liberal worldview. The most recent iteration of that critique was that its Brexit coverage was marred by the implicit pro-Europe, pro-globalization biases of its cosmopolitan journalists and editorial staff.[33] Others see senior BBC management as trying too hard to assuage accusations of left-wing bias by overrepresenting conservative views. A 2017 study by Ivor Gaber of two of the BBC's flagship political programs found that in a seven-week period, conservative guests outnumbered progressives by two to one.[34] BBC journalists are among those who voiced fury at the regular prime-time appearances of unqualified climate change deniers such as former Chancellor Nigel Lawson in the interests of promoting "balance" in the climate change debate.[35] Ofcom ruled that the BBC had breached accuracy rules, first by failing to provide the necessary context that Lawson was unqualified as a scientist and represented a minority view, and second by allowing him to voice false assertions without challenge or correction.[36]

This is not to say that the BBC is free from bias or tendencies toward self-censorship. Politicians have always tried to influence the broadcaster, sometimes successfully, and the BBC has on many occasions failed to challenge authority. The Corporation's commitment to independence and impartiality has never been absolute and has evolved slowly over the decades. BBC journalists I spoke with reported feeling let down, even betrayed, by bosses who did too little to defend their autonomy. Instead, I argue only that the BBC has been relatively more successful in defending its editorial independence than NHK, relatively more willing to hold the political classes to account, and relatively more proactive in addressing its sociocultural biases. A similar story emerges when comparing the BBC and NHK's broader entertainment content. At an admittedly very broad level, they play quite different sociocultural roles.

Social Role: Agent for Stability or Agent of Change?

A growing literature identifies the influence of popular culture on political opinions. TV dramas, for example, help shape public opinion on overtly political issues such as trust in the criminal justice system. Avid watchers of US cop shows, in which the police are "good guys" and justice is served by the end of the episode, tend to be more supportive of the death penalty than non-watchers.[37] In a similar vein, Krauss argues that NHK's extensive and sympathetic coverage of government actors, often officials from the economic bureaucracy, surely served a legitimating function for the state.[38]

Pop culture can also influence broader social values such as tolerance and inclusivity.[39] John Street follows Antonio Gramsci in arguing that popular entertainment generates affinities, helps establish collective identities, and shapes norms.[40] Stereotyped characters, for example, help marginalize socially disadvantaged groups, as Saito and Ishiyama demonstrate in their study of how television dramas reinforce negative stereotypes about disabled people in Japan.[41] Yet pop culture also has the power to challenge prevailing norms. Diana Mutz provides evidence that Harry Potter fans are more likely than others to embrace values lauded in the series, such as greater tolerance for marginalized groups.[42] Measuring the precise degree to which the BBC and NHK have influenced national values over the decades would be impossible, but we should not underestimate the extraordinary hold that each broadcaster has had on social values and the national imagination. Of course, too, the relationship between national values and broadcaster's content is mutually dependent and self-perpetuating. Social values shape programming as much as they are shaped by it.

The book shows the degree to which the two broadcasters have differed in how they grapple with the tension between reflecting prevailing norms on one hand and reflecting and perhaps promoting changing values on the other hand, for example, concerning gender or racial diversity. I argue here that the BBC has become, over time, relatively more likely to challenge existing and traditional social norms, and to include a greater variety of different voices in its programming and personnel.

BBC: Agent of Change

In the early decades, the BBC's staff and programming mostly reflected the interests of Britain's overwhelmingly white, male, Christian, Oxbridge-educated elites. Much BBC content reinforces comforting narratives about national identity. *Dad's Army* (1968–1977), for example, looks back fondly at the Second World War as a time of national unity and common purpose, and became hugely popular during the economic malaise and national self-doubt of the 1970s.[43] The heroes are a bumbling Home Guard platoon of men too old or otherwise exempt from active duty who embody the plucky amateurism, which in British popular imagination defeated the professional killers of the Nazi Wermacht.[44] The series reflects Britishness in being charmingly self-deprecating – the main characters are comically inept, fitting into the BBC tradition that includes Basil Fawlty and Mr. Bean – but it is also entirely British in being self-satisfied about its charming self-deprecation. David Croft, one of the writers, wrote that "it gave people a taste of England and the English attitudes which had almost disappeared."[45] The series, argues Jeffrey Richardson, "has an ideal of national identity rooted in tradition, community, tolerance and good nature."[46] Such qualities are eagerly showcased in many other of the most popular BBC classics – *The Great British Bake-Off*, *All Creatures Great and Small*, and *The Archers*, to name but a few.

While these genteel, middle-class, and white frames persist to a degree many find alarming, the BBC had by the 1960s begun to broaden its outlook and challenge long-standing beliefs and values. Dramas began to tackle highly controversial social problems such as abortion (*Up the Junction*, 1965); race relations (*Fable*, 1965); unemployment (*Boys from the Black Stuff*, 1982); and poverty (*Cathy Come Home*, 1965; *When the Boat Comes In*, 1982). Docudramas such as *Culloden* (1964), *The War Game* (1965), and *Tumbledown* (1988) daringly questioned official narratives about national unity, nuclear weapons, and government attitudes toward the military. These and many other dramas were highly controversial, frequently attracting criticism for being, in the words of one group of Conservative MPs, "left-wing propaganda."[47] Indeed, they often raised difficult questions about whether and how the legal requirements for impartiality should be applied to entertainment.[48] More recently, the celebrity genealogy documentary *Who Do You Think You Are?* (first aired in 2004) used individual family histories to explore often uncomfortable historical issues such as slavery, immigration, and prejudice.[49]

The BBC has a mixed record for gender inclusivity, but one that has usually been somewhat more progressive than comparable media organizations or other bastions of the British establishment. Jean Seaton and Charlotte Higgins describe the enormous early influence of women in managerial positions such as Hilda Matheson, the first director of Talks, who established the first news service in 1926, and Grace Wyndham Goldie, who pioneered live television election coverage in the postwar era. In 1963, Verity Lambert became BBC Television's first woman producer, on *Dr. Who*. Ironically, the eponymous Doctor, an alien who regularly changes physical form, somehow morphed into another white man on 12 separate regenerations before finally taking female form in 2017.[50] In 2018, new regulations on transparency forced the BBC to reveal that it was paying senior male staff much more than equivalent female staff. China editor Carrie Gracie resigned in protest, sparking widespread criticism. The fact that the gender gap in pay was considerably lower at the BBC than at any other news organizations did little to lessen the outrage hypocritically expressed by their rivals. On average, men were paid almost 11% more than women at the BBC, compared to about 20% at ITN, 32% at the Economist, and 35% at the Telegraph Media Group.[51] However, internal recrimination and soul-searching resulted in the expansion of the 50–50 project, a Corporation-wide commitment to having at least half of people appearing on or contributing to on-air content be female. First impressions were that the initiative was making a positive difference in reducing gender inequity.[52]

Much BBC content, of course, has reflected problematic but widely held British attitudes toward race, with negative stereotypes abounding and underrepresentation of marginalized groups in all aspects of output. Shamefully, *The Black and White Minstrel Show*, in which white performers literally wore blackface to perform African-American song and dance routines, ran in prime time from 1957 until 1978 despite frequent entirely justified accusations of blatant racism.[53] However, the Corporation has also on occasion been active in challenging stereotypes. Darrell Newtown explores the complicated story of how the BBC encountered, reflected, and helped shape attitudes about race, racism, and race relations in Britain. In his telling, liberal producers and managers, always working within institutional constraints and alongside racist attitudes, pushed the BBC to address and reflect racial and ethnic diversity, especially as rising immigration coincided with the spread of television in the 1950s and 1960s:

> While networks such as ITV, Channel 4, and others surely featured Black people and race-related matters within selected programming, this study examines the BBC as a forerunner of these endeavours. No matter what the circumstances, or challenges to BBC management, television would play a highly significant role in how millions would perceive these hopeful citizens.[54]

Notable programs attempting to reflect and embrace diversity included Grace Windham Goldie's *Race and Colour: A Scientific Introduction to the Problem of Race Relations* (1952), the first British television program to address these issues; and dramas *A Man from the Sun* (1956), *Fable* (1965), and *Empire Road* (1978–1979), the first soap opera of Black British life. The BBC has been more conscious of the need to diversify its staff since Director-General Greg Dyke described the Corporation as "hideously white" in 2001.[55] Since then, the Corporation has made greater efforts toward inclusivity, with Ofcom stating in 2018 that the BBC is making progress in meeting its ambitious targets for greater workplace diversity, with a better record of hiring and promoting staff of color than all but one other UK broadcaster.[56] In summary, the BBC has, since at least the 1960s, styled itself as a proactive agent for social and cultural change, albeit with a mixed record.

NHK: Agent of Stability

NHK, by contrast, articulates its purpose as serving as an agent for social stability, a guardian and curator of national traditions and culture. In Anne Cooper-Chen's words, it sees itself as having "a mission of Japanifying its viewers rather than pulling them out of their cultural comfort zones."[57] In general, NHK devotes a significantly higher proportion of its programming to news, documentaries, educational, and other "worthy" content than Japan's commercial channels or the BBC. A survey showed 47% of NHK viewers found their programs "enjoyable and relaxing," compared with 82% of BBC viewers.[58] NHK also seems less willing than the BBC to deviate from accepted social values concerning, for example, gender roles or the portrayal of marginalized groups.[59] Entertainment programming – like the family-themed soap operas of the *asa dora* ('morning dramas') and the Sunday night, samurai-heavy historical *Taiga* dramas – tends to reflect and reinforce rather than challenge traditional norms.[60] Meanwhile, documentaries such as *Project X* display and encourage nostalgic national pride.[61]

Note how language about diversity differs in row three of the mission statements. NHK articulates universality as respecting differences in regional culture, while the BBC speaks of representing, and raising awareness of, diverse communities. Women and minorities are underrepresented in news reporter or managerial positions even compared to the generally unequal representation in Japan's commercial sector.[62] Of the 177 individuals showcased in the *Project X* documentary series, for example, just 3 are women.[63]

The two broadcasters differ also in how they conceive of their relationship to national culture, broadly defined, as the language in row two of the mission statements suggests. NHK speaks of "preserving" and "nurturing" traditional culture, portraying itself in a curatorial role.[64] Christine Yano, for example, notes that NHK more than anyone was responsible for preserving and nurturing *enka*, the uniquely Japanese folk music form.[65] The BBC, by contrast, stresses the "creativity" and "innovation" of new cultural production. Note the reference to "distinctiveness," the current buzzword used in British policy circles to distinguish public service content.[66] NHK speaks of "deepening" and "enhancing" social understandings of culture, while the BBC speaks of "inspiring" and "challenging" audiences. Overall, compared to the BBC, NHK's programming generally reflects Mari Miura's observation, made in the context of Japanese welfare policy, that "national interests are equated with the interests of the state, which are in turn defined by the conservative elite."[67]

Economic Role: Rival or Partner to Commercial Media?

Some public broadcasters coexist comfortably with commercial media. They remain in niches in the programming landscape, producing content that is socially valuable but commercially untenable, such as educational or arts programs. Often, commercial broadcasters are happy for them to exist in these niches as it relieves the commercial media of responsibility for producing such content themselves.[68] Others compete head-on with the commercial sector, producing popular content that battles for mass audiences and high ratings in what used to be called prime time. Whether a public broadcaster follows a strategy of coexistence or competition has important implications for its political support. Coexistence in niche sectors keeps commercial rivals happy but means small audiences and therefore narrower popular support.[69] Conversely, popular programming generates broad goodwill but incurs the wrath of well-funded, politically powerful commercial media.

The sheer size and centrality of both broadcasters inevitably cast them as rivals to the commercial sector, whose staff often speak enviously of the resources and protections the public broadcasters enjoy.[70] Yet as we will see, the BBC adopts a far more assertive approach in its relationship to the rest of the market. This entrepreneurialism, prompted in large part by pressure from Prime Minister Margaret Thatcher and her neoliberal successors, manifests itself in a number of ways. First, the BBC consciously competes directly with commercial rivals across a wider range of programming genres than NHK. Second, it has been more aggressive in expanding commercial operations overseas, capitalizing on its brand recognition and vast stock of content. The BBC's worldwide sales operation now accounts for a significant proportion – approximately one-quarter – of its annual revenue. By contrast, NHK's revenues are almost entirely from the viewer fee, and its most popular content – news, documentaries, and high-quality dramas – tends to be strongest in genres where the commercial stations have least interest. Third, the BBC has proved more innovative in adoption of digital media in all its forms. Indeed, the BBC's embrace of the internet and social media was so early and so aggressive that it prompted sustained criticism for crowding out private enterprise. The relatively slow development of the United Kingdom's independent podcasting sector, for example, has been attributed to the great difficulty commercial start-ups faced in encroaching on the huge audiences for BBC online content. The BBC had quickly retooled popular radio shows such as *The Archers* and aggressively created and marketed new content to build a huge stable of over 450 podcasts by 2016.[71] Such entrepreneurialism stands in marked contrast to NHK's slower and more cautious adoption of new media.

Why Do the BBC and NHK Behave Differently?

What explains NHK's greater deference to authority, social conservatism, and managerial caution compared to the BBC? Many scholars explain differences in the behavior of national broadcasters with reference to institutional factors such as funding mechanisms, charters, and political control over and governing bodies. As we have seen, though, these factors are almost identical at the BBC and NHK and are hence of limited value in explaining differences. In part, differences between the individual broadcasters reflect broader variations in each country's state–media relationships. Numerous scholars have argued that Japan's mainstream media tend to be deferential to authority. Structural causes for this timidity include the influence of corporate advertising, hierarchical patterns of employment within the big media organizations, and the institution of the press clubs (*kisha kurabu*) that allow elite actors to control media access to information.[72] Others cite cultural differences, such as Japan's supposedly more hierarchical and deferential culture.[73] However, as Susan Pharr notes, blanket generalizations about Japanese media deference do not fully capture the multiple, conflicting roles that media actually play in political and social life.[74] Building on this insight, I note that NHK's relationship to the state is more deferential and its broader programming more serious and conservative than that of the commercial networks. Indeed, much NHK content is more similar to that of the BBC than of the lighter fare of commercial stations, something which can't be explained with reference to national-level differences in culture or media system. Moreover, the relationship between NHK and the state varies over time, with political interference and editorial resistance waxing and waning.

In other words, the institutional and cultural factors usually cited to explain the alleged deference of Japan's press don't explain why NHK is so much more deferential than other media organizations. On the other hand, many of the factors used to explain NHK's particular timidity in the context of other Japanese media, such as its reliance on government approval of funding, and political control over senior appointments, don't explain why NHK is so much more timid than the BBC, which is subject to the same constraints.

I suggest that differences between the two organizations are better explained as a long series of strategic managerial choices each made, rather than being simply the result of institutional and structural forces beyond their control. The broadcasters themselves have played a major role in shaping their own destiny. This argument follows the logic of path-dependency, described by Paul Pierson and reiterated by Lucy Küng-Shankleman, in which a branching series of strategic decisions gradually creates a self-reinforcing organizational culture.[75]

Küng-Shankleman's study of the BBC and CNN argues for the importance of organizational culture in explaining why institutions with similar goals often go about achieving them in very different ways.[76] She defines organizational culture as follows:

> The accumulated learning shared by a set of members of an organization. This learning has been acquired as the group deals with the challenges posed by the environment and by the organization as it develops and matures. In the course of this problem-solving process a number of precepts emerge which repeatedly prove themselves effective. These represent a set of basic tacit assumptions about how the world is and ought to be, assumptions which determine perceptions, thoughts, feelings, and, to some degree, overt behavior.[77]

She notes that organizational cultures become self-reinforcing, echoing Pierson's argument about institutional evolution. Strategies and assumptions that worked to solve one set of problems become part of the intellectual toolkit for addressing new problems. The assumptions are passed on to new staff, and become embedded in institutional rules. These rules, in turn, reinforce the original thinking, not least by creating constituencies with a vested interest in the status quo. As the cycle goes on, "alternatives that were once quite plausible may become irretrievably lost."[78]

I once asked Greg Dyke where the BBC's fierce sense of independence came from. Dyke, director-general of the BBC during the ferocious battle between the BBC and the Labour Government over reporting on the 2003 Iraq invasion, gave a huge smile and an immediate one-word answer: "Reith!"[79] In answering thus, he was affirming, from a uniquely well-placed perspective, the conclusions of many more scholarly observers. Pierson stresses the predominant influence of decisions made in the initial period of an institution's history.[80] Küng-Shankleman finds that at both the BBC and CNN, organizational culture was to a large extent determined by the personal beliefs of their respective founders, John Reith and Ted Turner. This influence could be so strong, she noted, that in Reith's case it lived on even decades after his death.[81] Hanretty, too, notes that it was Reith who decided early on that political impartiality and independence would be vital to the BBC's survival during the existential crisis of the 1926 General Strike. The success of the strategy of confronting the Government rather than giving way ensured that those values were swiftly institutionalized and internalized by managers and staff alike.[82] Similar strategies were repeated on the numerous occasions thereafter when governments sought to exercise undue influence.

NHK, with no founding giant comparable to Reith, took a different path. Leadership at NHK's birth in the 1920s – and rebirth in the 1940s – was more bureaucratic, with top officials having very close ties to ruling elites. More importantly, at both times, political elites were eager to use NHK to serve state interests and gave themselves the power to influence programming much more closely than at the BBC. NHK's management felt they had little choice but to acquiesce. However, cooperation with the government also proved a successful survival strategy and one which senior managers have turned to repeatedly in the face of threat. Staff, in turn, had to internalize elite expectations for their reporting, as well as the limits of what was permissible. NHK journalists and producers rarely challenge the cautious corporate norms openly, though some grumble about them in private.

These two newsroom cultures – the BBC's practice of defending its independence and not backing down from confrontations, NHK's practice of not rocking the boat – have their corollaries in entertainment programming. Reith understood that being popular was essential for its survival, and the BBC has never since let popularity slip far from the center of its programming strategies. But it also discovered, over the course of the 1960s, that challenging prevailing norms and leading social change have also proved effective ways of keeping its audiences, especially younger audiences, as well as burnishing its reputation. NHK, by contrast, found that a reputation for staid, wholesome fare kept it in the good books of at least the conservatives in government.

Business cultures, too, reflect prior lessons learned about effective political survival strategies. The BBC's entrepreneurial culture was in large part forced upon it by the need to find some measure of financial independence from the governments they continually riled up, not least that of Margaret Thatcher. NHK's closeness to the ruling elites gave it a measure of financial security, which made entrepreneurialism less necessary. Moreover, NHK's position as a key component of Japan's industrial policy was a different but equally effective survival strategy, keeping it permanently in the good books of both politicians and commercial rivals. The evolution of these two distinctive approaches to public broadcasting are described in the following chapters. Before that, there are a few other points to make about organizational culture.

First, organizational cultures help inform managerial choices but they do not determine them. I follow Steven Reed in understanding culture as a widely shared "common sense" about what sorts of behavior might be appropriate for given contexts. There are, I believe, recurring patterns in the responses of the broadcaster to each new challenge and opportunity, but no iron laws. This is largely because of the second point: organizational cultures are never monolithic and are often hotly contested. As we will see at both broadcasters, outspoken journalists or creative producers have always fought with their more cautious editors and managers.

Third, the trade-offs required to balance conflicting goals are usually not resolved by formal debate as much as by day-to-day production decisions, informed by assumptions often but not always shared among the editors, writers, and producers. Neither the director-general of the BBC nor the chairman of NHK can rule as top-down autocrats. Both serve nominally as editor-in-chief, but in practice they are far removed from the day-to-day grind of pitching, planning, producing, and scheduling the thousands of hours of content their subordinates put out every day. This means that programming philosophies can bubble up from the program-makers as much as they can be strategized from above. For example, Jean Seaton describes how the BBC's association with environmental conservation and wildlife protection, most famously manifest in David Attenborough's documentaries such as *Blue Planet*, had its origins in the BBC Wildlife unit in the 1970s. Members of this team saw their role as to make the British public "more responsible custodians of nature" and made programs accordingly.[83] Similarly, the nostalgic conservatism of NHK's *Project X* was borne more of Chief Producer Imai Akira's worldview than any conscious managerial decision. In the same vein, I once asked a BBC current affairs producer how he managed the trade-offs between making news coverage comprehensive enough to be of public service while remaining accessible enough to be watchable. He replied somewhat tartly that he had to produce several hours of news accurate enough to not get him fired, with relentless deadlines and with too few resources day after bloody day, and never had time to think about philosophy. Even allowing for a high degree of modest British understatement, the remark illustrates how much corporate culture is shaped on the fly rather than on the drawing board.[84] In all three examples, decisions about content emerge from the usually unspoken assumptions of program-makers about what they ought to be doing rather than from any formal instruction or open debate.

The fourth point about organizational cultures is that they become self-reinforcing, as employees themselves can police prevailing values more effectively than written rules. In 2020, for example, legendary footballer and BBC commentator Gary Lineker tweeted against Brexit. He had used his private account and as a sports presenter was not bound by the BBC's ban on public partisanship, which applied only to staff in the News department. He was swiftly and predictably denounced by BBC critics in conservative media such as *The Sun*.[85] More tellingly, he was also roundly condemned by his fellow employees in BBC Sports. His bosses responded to the internal outrage by giving Lineker a pay cut and introducing stricter restrictions on social media use by all employees.[86]

Finally, note the profound influence that each broadcasting culture has had on the attitudes of other actors. Politicians, viewers, and commercial rivals interact with the public broadcasters on the basis of assumptions and expectations that the broadcasters themselves have played a large role in creating. Hanretty argues that the BBC's articulation of impartiality in the 1920s became the language adopted by the government in requiring it.[87] Japanese audiences became angry with NHK over ethics scandals because of disappointment with expectations about press trustworthiness that NHK itself had done much to shape. Conversely, Krauss cites former NHK Chairman Shima Keiji as arguing that the BBC's editorial independence is partly protected by the fact that government interference would be met by politically costly public outrage.[88] Yet it was in large part the BBC itself that

Table 3.1 Two Models of Public Broadcasting

	BBC	NHK
Political role Relationship to the State	Independent Confrontational *Watchdog*	Cooperative Non-confrontational *Guide dog/lap dog*
Social role Relationship to society	Broader entertainment content Challenges traditional values Greater emphasis on diversity *Agent of change*	More focused entertainment content Upholds traditional values Greater emphasis on social cohesion *Agent of stability*
Economic role Relationship to the private sector	Entrepreneurial Competitive *Rival*	Bureaucratic Cooperative *Partner*

shaped public opinion thusly. NHK's tendency to shrink in the face of political interference does little to strengthen public support for press freedom.

This chapter, in short, has sketched two distinctive approaches to public broadcasting, albeit at the cost of greatly oversimplifying two very complex organizations. The following chapters will attempt to flesh out these generalizations while illustrating and acknowledging the messy realities of their long, rich histories.

Notes

1 Quoted in Chris Hanretty, *Public Broadcasters and Political Independence* (London: Routledge, 2010), 94.
2 Department of Culture, Media and Sport, "Royal Charter for the Continuance of the British Broadcasting Corporation" (December 2016).
3 "The Broadcast Act as Amended Last by the Act for Partial Revision of the Broadcast Act and Other Related Acts" (Tokyo: Ministry of Internal Affairs and Communication, 2010), accessed April 3, 2022, https://www.soumu.go.jp/main_sosiki/joho_tsusin/eng/Resources/laws/pdf/090204_5.pdf.
4 Hanretty, *Public Broadcasters and Political Independence*.
5 "Guidance: Impartiality," *BBC*, accessed October 2020, www.bbc.com/editorialguidelines/guidance/impartiality. NHK *Hōsō gaidorain* 2020 (NHK Broadcasting Guidelines 2020), accessed October 26, 2021, www.nhk.or.jp/pr/keiei/bc-guideline/pdf/guideline2020.pdf.
6 "Gary Lineker Row: What Can BBC Presenters Say and Not Say?" *BBC*, December 14, 2018, www.bbc.com/news/uk-46566574.
7 Bruce Cunningham, "Objectivity Revisited," *Columbia Journalism Review* (July/August 2003).
8 John McManus, "Objectivity: Time to Say Goodbye," *Nieman Reports* (June 11, 2009); Regina Marchi, "With Facebook, Blogs, and Fake News, Teens Reject Journalistic 'Objectivity'," *Journal of Communication Inquiry* 36, no. 3 (2012): 246–262.
9 Bill Kovach and Tom Rosentiel, *The Elements of Journalism* (New York City: Three Rivers Press, 2007), 1–32; Thomas Patterson, "Political Roles of the Journalist," *The Politics of News*, eds. Doris Graber, Dennis McQuail, and Pippa Norris (Washington, D.C.: CQ Press, 1998).

10 NHK Hōsō gaidorain 2020 (NHK Broadcasting Guidelines 2020), accessed October 26, 2021, www.nhk.or.jp/pr/keiei/bc-guideline/pdf/guideline2020.pdf.
11 The point was made most clearly by Fukushima Mizoho, the then chair of the Social Democratic Party of Japan in an interview with the author in Tokyo in August 2005. The point was repeated by other Socialist and Communist Diet members even as many complained about NHK's general editorial conservatism.
12 Ellis Krauss, *Broadcasting Politics in Japan* (Ithaca, NY: Cornell University Press, 2000), 241.
13 Krauss, *Broadcasting Politics*, 256.
14 Interviews with NHK staff, Tokyo 2005. Krauss, *Broadcasting Politics*, 119–122.
15 Jonathan Soble, "Abe Accused of Blurring the Picture at Japan's NHK Broadcaster," *Financial Times*, February 4, 2014. Īmuro Katsuhiko quotes President Momii as saying *"Minshu shugi ni taisuru wareware no imeji de hōsō sureba seifu to mattaku gyaku ni naru koto wa ari enai"* ("With respect to democracy, we cannot as a broadcaster present an image totally different to that of the government"). *NHK to seiji shihai – jānarizumu wa dare no mono ka* (NHK and Political Rule: Who Does Journalism Belong To?) (Tokyo: Gendai Shokan, 2014), 13.
16 Hiroshi Matsuda, *NHK – Towareru kōkyō hōsō* [NHK: Public Broadcasting Under Scrutiny] (Tokyo: Iwanami Shoten, 2005); Kaoru Hayashi, "How NHK Lost Its Way," *Nippon.com*, July 23, 2014; Jeff Kingston, ed., *Press Freedom in Contemporary Japan* (London: Routledge, 2017).
17 Philip Seaton, "NHK, War Related Television and the Politics of Fairness," in Kingston, *Press Freedom in Contemporary Japan.*
18 Seaton, "NHK, War Related Television and the Politics of Fairness."
19 "NHK kaichō, anpo hōdō de 'kantei kara no atsuryoku ga nai' NHK no hōdō ga katayotte iru to omotte inai [NHK President: No Government Pressure in the Security Report, Does Not Think NHK News is Biased]," *Sankei Shimbun*, October 1, 2015.
20 Interviews with current and former NHK staff members conducted in Tokyo in August 2017.
21 Daisuke Nakai, "Japanese Media in Flux: Watchdog or Fake News" (forum report, Suntory Foundation Research Project's Reexamining Japan in Global Context, Tokyo, April 2, 2018).
22 Amy Wilson-Chapman, "Counting the Panama Papers Money," *International Consortium of Investigative Journalists*, July 15 2019, www.icij.org/investigations/panama-papers/counting-the-panama-papers-money-how-we-reached-1-28-billion/. *Japan Economic Newswire*, "Olympus Failed to Report over 800 Medical Device Defects," January 23, 2019.
23 See, for example: Chris Henretty, "Explaining the De Facto Independence of Public Broadcasters," *British Journal of Political Science* 40 (November 2009): 75–89; Chris Henretty, *Public Broadcasting and Political Interference* (Abingdon: Routledge, 2011); Jay Blumer, "To Be Independent or Not Independent, That Is the Question: BBC-UK Government Relations 2016," *Publizistik* 61 (July 2016): 305–320; Daniel C. Hallin and Paolo Mancini, *Comparing Media Systems: Three Models of Media and Politics* (Cambridge: Cambridge University Press, 2004). Carles Llorens and Isabel Ferández Alonso write that the BBC "has traditionally been considered a model for the quality of its programming and the independence of its professional staff and directors" in "The Reform of the Public Radio and Television System in the UK and in Spain (2004–2007)," in *Comparative Media Systems: European and Global Perspectives*, eds. Bogosława Dobek-Ostrows et al. (Budapest: Central European University Press, 2010).
24 Hanretty, *Public Broadcasting and Political Interference*, 124.
25 Mona Krewel, "Autonomy and Regulatory Frameworks of Public Service Media," in *Public Service Media in Europe: A Comparative Approach*, eds. Karen Arriaza Ibarra, Eva Nowak, and Raymond Kuhn (Abingdon: Routledge, 2015), 131. Karen Arriaza Ibarra, "Management and Organization of Public Service Media Companies," in *Public Service Media in Europe.*

26 BBC Studios, "Jeremy Paxman Interviews Michael Howard," accessed January 28, 2021, www.youtube.com/watch?v=Uwlsd8RAoqI.

27 Maev Kennedy, "George Orwell Returns to Loom over BBC," *The Guardian*, November 7, 2017.

28 Ofcom, "Annual Report on the BBC 2019/2020," November 25, 2020, www.ofcom. org.uk/__data/assets/pdf_file/0021/207228/third-bbc-annual-report.pdf.

29 Charlotte Higgins, *This New Noise: The Extraordinary Birth and Troubled Life of the BBC* (London: Guardian Books, 2015), 154.

30 Tom Mills, *The BBC: Myth of a Public Service* (London: Verso, 2016), 214.

31 Jean Seaton, "Reith and the Denial of Politics," in *Power without Responsibility: The Press and Broadcasting in Britain*, eds. James Curran and Jean Seaton (London: Routledge, 1997), 118.

32 Ronald Coase, "The Economics of Broadcasting and Government Policy," *American Economic Review* 56 (1966). See also Paddy Scannell and David Cardiff, *A Social History of British Broadcasting 1922–1939* (Oxford: Blackwell, 1991).

33 For example: Daniel Martin, "How the BBC Kept Brexiteers Off the Air for a Decade," *Daily Mail Online*, January 25, 2018.

34 Ivor Gaber, "The BBC Is Not Biased," *The Conversation*, July 24, 2017, https://theconversation.com/bbc-is-not-biased-but-its-idea-of-the-centre-is-now-tilting-to-the-right-when-the-uk-is-tilting-to-the-left-81409.

35 A House of Commons report found in 2014 that although the BBC's coverage of climate change was generally good and constituted the main source of information on climate change for most people in Britain, it was guilty of overincluding dissenting viewpoints for the sake of balance: "The lack of distinction within BBC News between proven scientific facts and opinions or beliefs is problematic." See House of Commons Select Committee on Science and Technology, "Report on Communicating Climate Science," *House of Commons*, April 2, 2014, https://publications.parliament.uk/pa/cm201314/cmselect/cmsctech/254/254.pdf.

36 Mark Sweney, "BBC Radio 4 Broke Accuracy Rules in Nigel Lawson Climate Change Interview," April 9, 2018, www.theguardian.com/environment/2018/apr/09/bbc-radio-4-broke-impartiality-rules-in-nigel-lawson-climate-change-interview. Ofcom, "Broadcast and On Demand Bulletin 351," April 9, 2018, www.ofcom.org.uk/__data/assets/pdf_file/0012/112701/issue-351-broadcast-on-demand-bulletin.pdf.

37 Lisa Kort-Butler and Kelly Sittner-Hartshorn, "Watching the Detectives: Crime Programming, Fear of Crime and Attitudes about the Criminal Justice System," *The Sociological Quarterly* 52, no. 1 (Winter 2011).

38 Krauss, *Broadcasting Politics*, 265–267.

39 Anthony Gierzynski, *The Political Effects of Entertainment Media: How Fictional Worlds Affect Real World Political Perspectives* (Lanham, MD: Lexington Books, 2018). See also Diana C. Mutz and Lilach Nir, "Not Necessarily the News: Does Fictional Television Influence Real-World Policy Preferences?" *Mass Communication and Society* 13 (2010): 197–217. Michale X. Delli Carpini and Bruce A. Williams, "Constructing Public Opinion: The Uses of Fictional and Nonfictional Television in Conversations about the Environment," in *The Psychology of Political Communication*, ed. Ann Crigler (Ann Arbor, MI: University of Michigan Press, 1996).

40 John Street, *Politics and Popular Culture* (Cambridge: Polity, 1997).

41 Shinichi Saito and Reiko Ishiyama, "The Invisible Minority: Underrepresentation of People with Disabilities in Prime Time Dramas in Japan," *Disability and Society* 20, no. 4 (2005): 437–451.

42 Diana Mutz, "Harry Potter and the Deathly Donald," *PS: Political Science and Politics* 50, no. 1 (October 2016): 722–729.

43 Jeffrey Richardson, *Films and British Identity from Dickens to Dad's Army* (Manchester: Manchester University Press, 1997), 135. See especially chapter 12, "Dad's Army

and the Politics of Nostalgia." A film version revived nostalgia during the Brexit-fueled angst of 2016.

44 The plucky amateur trope in Britain's collective war memory runs from JRR Tolkien's *Lord of the Rings* to Christopher Nolan's *Dunkirk*.

45 Corinna M. Peniston-Bird, "'I Wondered Who'd Be the First to Spot That': Dad's Army at War, in the Media and in Memory," *Media History* 13, no. 2–3 (2007): 183–202.

46 Richardson, *Films and British Identity*, 366.

47 Jean Seaton, *Pinkoes and Traitors: The BBC and the Nation, 1974–1987* (London: Profile Books, 2015), 268.

48 The debate continues unresolved, as demonstrated by the 2020 demands from senior Conservative politicians that Netflix add a warning to *The Crown* clarifying that it is fiction. Mark Landler, "'The Crown' Stokes an Uproar Over Fact vs. Fiction," *The New York Times*, November 26, 2020.

49 Ann-Marie Kramer, "Mediatizing Memory: History, Affect and Identity in 'Who Do You Think You Are'," *European Journal of Cultural Studies* 14, no. 1 (August 2011): 428–445.

50 Mark Lawson, "Dr Who: Why the New Time Lord Can and Must Be a Woman," *The Guardian*, January 31, 2017.

51 Rupert Neate, "Telegraph Media Group Reveals 35% Pay Gap," *The Guardian*, March 26, 2018.

52 Laura Hazard Owen, "The BBC's 50:50 Project Shows Equal Gender Representation in News Coverage Is Achievable – Even in Traditionally Male Areas," *Nieman Lab*, May 16, 2019, www.niemanlab.org/2019/05/the-bbcs-5050-project-shows-equal-gen-der-representation-in-news-coverage-is-achievable-even-in-traditionally-male-areas/.

53 Christine Grandy, "'The Show Is Not about Race': Custom, Screen Culture, and the Black and White Minstrel Show," *Journal of British Studies* 59, no. 4 (2020): 857–884.

54 Darrell M. Newton, *Paving the Empire Road: BBC Television and Black Britons* (Manchester: Manchester University Press, 2011).

55 "Dyke: BBC Is Hideously White," *The Observer*, January 7, 2001.

56 Ofcom, "Third Diversity in Television Broadcasting Report," September 18, 2019, www.ofcom.org.uk/__data/assets/pdf_file/0027/166806/diversity-in-tv-2019-in-focus.pdf.

57 Anne Cooper-Chen, *Mass Communication in Japan* (Hoboken, NJ: Wiley-Blackwell, 1991), 116.

58 Yoshiko Nakamura and Ritsu Yonekura, "How Public Service Broadcasting Is Talked About," *NHK Broadcast Research Institute Report*, (Tokyo: NHK Broadcasting Culture Research Institute, 2012), 134.

59 Carol Gluck, "The Past in the Present," in *Postwar Japan as History*, ed. Andrew Gordon (Berkeley, CA: University of California Press, 1993). Satoko Suzuki, "Multiculturalism or Cultural Nationalism? Representation of Ellie Kameyama as a Conduit and the Other in the NHK Morning Drama Massan," *Japanese Studies* 40, no. 2 (2020): 121–140. Iwona Merklejn, "Remembering the Oriental Witches: Sports, Gender and Shōwa Nostalgia in the NHK Narratives of the Tokyo Olympics," *Social Science Japan Journal* 16, no. 2 (2013): 235–250.

60 Shunya Yoshimi, "Television and Nationalism: Historical Change in the National Domestic TV Formation of Postwar Japan," *European Journal of Cultural Studies* 6, no. 4 (2003).

61 Hiraku Shimoda, "Memorializing the Spirit of Wit and Grit in Postindustrial Japan," in *Japan Since 1945: From Post-war to Post-Bubble*, eds. Christopher Gerteis and Timothy S. George (London: Bloomsbury, 2013), 23–56. David Leheny, *Empire of Hope: The Sentimental Politics of National Decline* (Ithaca: Cornell University Press, 2018), 18.

62 Makiko Hanami, "Minority Dynamics in Japan," in *Diversity in Japanese Culture and Language*, eds. John Maher and Gaynor Macdonald (London: Keegan Paul, 1995). Cooper-Chen, *Mass Communication in Japan*.

63 Shimoda, "Memorializing the Spirit of Wit and Grit in Postindustrial Japan."

64 Takashi Ogawa, "The Collection and Preservation of Japanese Folk Songs by the Japan Broadcasting Corporation (NHK)," *Journal of the International Folk Music Council* 13 (1961): 83–84.
65 Christine R. Yano, *Tears of Longing: Nostalgia and the Nation in Japanese Popular Song* (Cambridge, MA: Harvard University Press, 2002), 89.
66 In discussions of the BBC's 2017 Charter Review, the concept of "distinctiveness" was frequently invoked. The dubious value of this metric is well discussed in Peter Goddard, "Distinctiveness and the BBC: A New Battleground for Public Service Television," *Media, Culture and Society* 39, no. 7 (February 2017).
67 Mari Miura, *Welfare Through Work: Conservative Ideas, Partisan Dynamics and Social Welfare* (Ithaca: Cornell University Press, 2012), 6.
68 The US commercial networks were enthusiastic supporters of the founding of PBS and NPR in the early 1970s because the public broadcasters' mission to provide educational programming lifted intense political pressure on commercial networks to improve the "vast wasteland" of their own vapid offerings. Christopher Sterling, "United States of America: Continuity and Change," in *Television and Public Policy*, ed. David Ward (New York: Erlbaum Associates, 2008), 52.
69 Unless the niche audience is composed of highly influential people, as is arguably the case for PBS in America. But this approach raises other questions, such as why ordinary people should subsidize the provision of free high-end arts programming enjoyed mostly by wealthy, highly educated elites.
70 A point repeated to me numerous times in interviews and conversations with such staff.
71 Nicholas Quah, "Hot Pod: Is the BBC's Power to Blame for the U.K. Podcasting Scene's Underdevelopment?," *Nieman Lab*, June 28, 2016, www.niemanlab.org/2016/06/hot-pod-is-the-bbcs-power-to-blame-for-the-u-k-podcasting-scenes-underdevelopment/.
72 Most recent contributions include Kingston, *Press Freedom in Contemporary Japan* and Martin Fackler, "The Silencing of Japan's Free Press," *Foreign Policy*, May 27, 2016. Classics include Susan Pharr and Ellis Krauss, eds., *Media and Politics in Japan* (Honolulu: University of Hawai'i Press, 1996). Laurie Freeman, *Closing the Shop: Information Cartels and Japan's Mass Media* (Princeton: Princeton University Press, 2000). The literature is surveyed in David McNeil, "Japan's Contemporary Media," in *Critical Issues in Contemporary Japan*, ed. Jeff Kingston (London: Routledge, 2014), 64–76.
73 Karel van Wolferen, *The Enigma of Japanese Power* (New York: Knopf, 1990).
74 Susan Pharr, "Media as Trickster in Japan: A Comparative Perspective," in *Media and Politics in Japan*, 19–44.
75 Paul Pierson, *Politics in Time: History, Institutions, and Social Analysis* (Princeton: Princeton University Press, 2014).
76 Lucy Küng-Shankleman, *Inside the BBC and CNN* (London: Routledge, 2000).
77 Küng-Shankleman, *Inside the BBC and CNN*, 9.
78 Pierson, *Politics in Time*, 11.
79 Personal conversation with Greg Dyke, March 2008.
80 Pierson, *Politics in Time*, 66.
81 Küng-Shankleman, *Inside the BBC and CNN*, 205.
82 Hanretty, *Public Broadcasting and Political Interference*, 93–94.
83 Seaton, *Pinkoes and Traitors*, 113.
84 Interview conducted by the author in London on December 29, 2015.
85 Jonathan Reilly, "OH TWIT: Gary Linekar Laughs off BBC Boss's Threat after He Says He Could Ban Stars from Twitter for Political Views," *The Sun*, September 29, 2020, www.thesun.co.uk/news/politics/12797191/bbc-warns-stars-could-be-booted-off-twitter/.
86 Jim Waterson, "Gary Lineker Agrees £400,000 BBC Pay Cut and to Tweet More Carefully," *The Guardian*, September 15, 2020, www.theguardian.com/media/2020/sep/15/gary-lineker-takes-bbc-pay-cut-and-agrees-to-tweet-more-carefully.
87 Hanretty, *Public Broadcasting and Political Interference*, 93–94.
88 Krauss, *Broadcasting Politics in Japan*, 257.

References

BBC Studios, "Jeremy Paxman Interviews Michael Howard," accessed January 28, 2021, www.youtube.com/watch?v=Uwlsd8RAoqI.

Blumer, Jay, "To be Independent or Not Independent, That is the Question: BBC-UK Government Relations 2016," *Publizistik* 61 (July 2016): 305–320.

"The Broadcast Act as Amended Last by the Act for Partial Revision of the Broadcast Act and Other Related Acts" (Tokyo: Ministry of Internal Affairs and Communication, 2010), accessed April 3, 2022, https://www.soumu.go.jp/main_sosiki/joho_tsusin/eng/Resources/laws/pdf/090204_5.pdf

Coase, Ronald, "The Economics of Broadcasting and Government Policy," *American Economic Review* 56 (1966).

Cunningham, Bruce, "Objectivity Revisited," *Columbia Journalism Review* (July/August 2003).

Delli Carpini, Michale X., and Bruce A. Williams, "Constructing Public Opinion: The Uses of Fictional and Nonfictional Television in Conversations about the Environment," in *The Psychology of Political Communication*, ed. Ann Crigler (Ann Arbor, MI: University of Michigan Press, 1996).

Department of Culture, Media and Sport, *Royal Charter for the Continuance of the British Broadcasting Corporation* (December 2016).

Fackler, Martin, "The Silencing of Japan's Free Press," *Foreign Policy*, May 27, 2016.

Freeman, Laurie, *Closing the Shop: Information Cartels and Japan's Mass Media* (Princeton: Princeton University Press, 2000).

Gaber, Ivor, "The BBC is Not Biased," *The Conversation*, July 24, 2017, https://theconversation.com/bbc-is-not-biased-but-its-idea-of-the-centre-is-now-tilting-to-the-right-when-the-uk-is-tilting-to-the-left-81409.

"Gary Lineker Row: What can BBC Presenters Say and Not Say?" *BBC*, December 14, 2018, www.bbc.com/news/uk-46566574.

Gierzynski, Anthony, *The Political Effects of Entertainment Media: How Fictional Worlds Affect Real World Political Perspectives* (Lanham, MD: Lexington Books, 2018).

Gluck, Carol, "The Past in the Present," in *Postwar Japan as History*, ed. Andrew Gordon (Berkeley, CA: University of California Press, 1993).

Goddard, Peter, "Distinctiveness and the BBC: A New Battleground for Public Service Television," *Media, Culture and Society* 39, no. 7 (February 2017).

Grandy, Christine, "'The Show Is Not about Race': Custom, Screen Culture, and the Black and White Minstrel Show," *Journal of British Studies* 59, no. 4 (2020): 857–884.

"Guidance: Impartiality," *BBC*, accessed October 2020, www.bbc.com/editorialguidelines/guidance/impartiality.

Hallin, Daniel C., and Paolo Mancini, *Comparing Media Systems: Three Models of Media and Politics* (Cambridge: Cambridge University Press, 2004).

Hanami, Makiko, "Minority Dynamics in Japan," in *Diversity in Japanese Culture and Language*, eds. John Maher and Gaynor Macdonald (London: Keegan Paul, 1995).

Hanretty, Chris, *Public Broadcasters and Political Independence* (London: Routledge, 2010).

Hayashi, Kaoru, "How NHK Lost Its Way," *Nippon.com*, July 23, 2014.

Henretty, Chris, "Explaining the De Facto Independence of Public Broadcasters," *British Journal of Political Science* 40 (November 2009): 75–89.

Henretty, Chris, *Public Broadcasting and Political Interference* (Abingdon: Routledge, 2011).

Higgins, Charlotte, *This New Noise: The Extraordinary Birth and Troubled Life of the BBC* (London: Guardian Books, 2015), 154.

House of Commons Select Committee on Science and Technology, "Report on Communicating Climate Science," *House of Commons*, April 2, 2014, https://publications.parliament.uk/pa/cm201314/cmselect/cmsctech/254/254.pdf.

Ibarra, Karen Arriaza, "Management and Organization of Public Service Media Companies," in *Public Service Media in Europe: A Comparative Approach*, eds. Karen Arriaza Ibarra, Eva Nowak and Raymond Kuhn (Abingdon: Routledge, 2015).

Japan Economic Newswire, "Olympus Failed to Report over 800 Medical Device Defects," January 23, 2019.

Kennedy, Maev, "George Orwell Returns to Loom over BBC," *The Guardian*, November 7, 2017.

Kingston, Jeff, ed., *Press Freedom in Contemporary Japan* (London: Routledge, 2017).

Kort-Butler, Lisa, and Kelly Sittner-Hartshorn, "Watching the Detectives: Crime Programming, Fear of Crime and Attitudes about the Criminal Justice System," *The Sociological Quarterly* 52, no. 1 (Winter 2011).

Kovach, Bill, and Tom Rosentiel, *The Elements of Journalism* (New York City: Three Rivers Press, 2007), 1–32.

Kramer, Ann-Marie, "Mediatizing Memory: History, Affect and Identity in 'Who Do You Think You Are'," *European Journal of Cultural Studies* 14, no. 1 (August 2011): 428–445.

Krauss, Ellis, *Broadcasting Politics in Japan* (Ithaca, NY: Cornell University Press, 2000).

Krewel, Mona, "Autonomy and Regulatory Frameworks of Public Service Media," in *Public Service Media in Europe: A Comparative Approach*, eds. Karen Arriaza Ibarra, Eva Nowak and Raymond Kuhn (Abingdon: Routledge, 2015).

Küng-Shankleman, Lucy, *Inside the BBC and CNN* (London: Routledge, 2000).

Landler, Mark, "'The Crown' Stokes an Uproar Over Fact vs. Fiction," *The New York Times*, November 26, 2020.

Lawson, Mark, "Dr Who: Why the New Time Lord Can and Must Be a Woman," *The Guardian*, January 31, 2017.

Leheny, David, *Empire of Hope: The Sentimental Politics of National Decline* (Ithaca: Cornell University Press, 2018), 18.

Llorens, Carles, and Isabel Ferández Alonso, "The Reform of the Public Radio and Television System in the UK and in Spain (2004–2007)," in *Comparative Media Systems: European and Global Perspectives*, eds. Bogosława Dobek-Ostrows et al. (Budapest: Central European University Press, 2010).

Marchi, Regina, "With Facebook, Blogs, and Fake News, Teens Reject Journalistic 'Objectivity'," *Journal of Communication Inquiry* 36, no. 3 (2012): 246–262.

Martin, Daniel, "How the BBC Kept Brexiteers Off the Air for a Decade," *Daily Mail Online*, January 25, 2018.

Matsuda, Hiroshi, *NHK- Towareru kōkyō hōsō* [NHK: Public Broadcasting Under Scrutiny] (Tokyo: Iwanami Shoten, 2005).

McManus, John, "Objectivity: Time to say Goodbye," *Nieman Reports* (June 11, 2009).

McNeil, David, "Japan's Contemporary Media," in *Critical Issues in Contemporary Japan*, ed. Jeff Kingston (London: Routledge, 2014), 64–76.

Merklejn, Iwona, "Remembering the Oriental Witches: Sports, Gender and Shōwa Nostalgia in the NHK Narratives of the Tokyo Olympics," *Social Science Japan Journal* 16, no. 2 (2013): 235–250.

Mills, Tom, *The BBC: Myth of a Public Service* (London: Verso, 2016).

Miura, Mari, *Welfare Through Work: Conservative Ideas, Partisan Dynamics and Social Welfare* (Ithaca: Cornell University Press, 2012).

Mutz, Diana, "Harry Potter and the Deathly Donald," *PS: Political Science and Politics* 50, no. 1 (October 2016): 722–729.

Mutz, Iana C., and Lilach Nir, "Not Necessarily the News: Does Fictional Television Influence Real-World Policy Preferences?" *Mass Communication and Society* 13 (2010): 197–217.

Nakai, Daisuke, "Japanese Media in Flux: Watchdog or Fake News" (forum report, Suntory Foundation Research Project's Reexamining Japan in Global Context, Tokyo, April 2, 2018).

Neate, Rupert, "Telegraph Media Group Reveals 35% Pay Gap," *The Guardian*, March 26, 2018.

Newton, Darrell M., *Paving the Empire Road: BBC Television and Black Britons* (Manchester: Manchester University Press, 2011).

Ofcom, "Annual Report on the BBC 2019/2020," November 25, 2020, www.ofcom.org. uk/__data/assets/pdf_file/0021/207228/third-bbc-annual-report.pdf.

Ofcom, "Broadcast and on Demand Bulletin 351," April 9, 2018, www.ofcom.org.uk/__ data/assets/pdf_file/0012/112701/issue-351-broadcast-on-demand-bulletin.pdf.

Ogawa, Takashi, "The Collection and Preservation of Japanese Folk Songs by the Japan Broadcasting Corporation (NHK)," *Journal of the International Folk Music Council* 13 (1961): 83–84.

Owen, Laura Hazard, "The BBC's 50:50 Project Shows Equal Gender Representation in News Coverage is Achievable – Even in Traditionally Male Areas," *Nieman Lab*, May 16, 2019, www.niemanlab.org/2019/05/the-bbcs-5050-project-shows-equal-gender-representation-in-news-coverage-is-achievable-even-in-traditionally-male-areas/.

Patterson, Thomas, "Political Roles of the Journalist," in *The Politics of News*, eds. Doris Graber, Dennis McQuail, and Pippa Norris (Washington, D.C.: CQ Press, 1998).

Peniston-Bird, Corinna M., "'I Wondered Who'd be the First to Spot That': Dad's Army at War, in the Media and in Memory," *Media History* 13, no. 2–3 (2007): 183–202.

Pharr, Susan, "Media as Trickster in Japan: A Comparative Perspective," in *Media and Politics in Japan*, eds. Susan Pharr and Ellis Krauss (Honolulu: University of Hawai'i Press, 1996), 19–44.

Pharr, Susan, and Ellis Krauss, eds., *Media and Politics in Japan* (Honolulu: University of Hawai'i Press, 1996).

Pierson, Paul, *Politics in Time: History, Institutions, and Social Analysis* (Princeton: Princeton University Press, 2014).

Quah, Nicholas, "Hot Pod: Is the BBC's Power to Blame for the U.K. Podcasting Scene's Underdevelopment?" *Nieman Lab*, June 28, 2016, www.niemanlab.org/2016/06/hot-pod-is-the-bbcs-power-to-blame-for-the-u-k-podcasting-scenes-underdevelopment/.

Reilly, Jonathan, "OH TWIT: Gary Linekar Laughs Off BBC Boss's Threat after He Says He Could Ban Stars from Twitter for Political Views," *The Sun*, September 29, 2020, www.thesun.co.uk/news/politics/12797191/bbc-warns-stars-could-be-booted-off-twitter/.

Richardson, Jeffrey, *Films and British Identity from Dickens to Dad's Army* (Manchester: Manchester University Press, 1997).

Saito, Shinichi, and Reiko Ishiyama, "The Invisible Minority: Underrepresentation of People with Disabilities in Prime Time Dramas in Japan," *Disability and Society* 20, no. 4 (2005): 437–451.

Scannell, Paddy, and David Cardiff, *A Social History of British Broadcasting 1922–1939* (Oxford: Blackwell, 1991).

Seaton, Jean, *Pinkoes and Traitors: The BBC and the Nation, 1974–1987* (London: Profile Books, 2015).

Seaton, Jean, "Reith and the Denial of Politics," in *Power without Responsibility: The Press and Broadcasting in Britain*, eds. James Curran and Jean Seaton (London: Routledge, 1997), 118.

Shimoda, Hiraku, "Memorializing the Spirit of Wit and Grit in Postindustrial Japan," in *Japan Since 1945: From Post-war to Post-Bubble*, eds. Christopher Gerteis and Timothy S. George (London: Bloomsbury, 2013), 23–56.

Soble, Jonathan, "Abe Accused of Blurring the Picture at Japan's NHK Broadcaster," *Financial Times*, February 4, 2014.

Sterling, Christopher, "United States of America: Continuity and Change," in *Television and Public Policy*, ed. David Ward (New York: Erlbaum Associates, 2008), 52.

Street, John, *Politics and Popular Culture* (Cambridge: Polity, 1997).

Suzuki, Satoko, "Multiculturalism or Cultural Nationalism? Representation of Ellie Kameyama as a Conduit and the Other in the NHK Morning Drama Massan," *Japanese Studies* 40, no. 2 (2020): 121–140.

Sweney, Mark, "BBC Radio 4 Broke Accuracy Rules in Nigel Lawson Climate Change Interview," April 9, 2018, www.theguardian.com/environment/2018/apr/09/bbc-radio-4-broke-impartiality-rules-in-nigel-lawson-climate-change-interview.

Waterson, Jim, "Gary Lineker Agrees £400,000 BBC Pay Cut and to Tweet More Carefully," *The Guardian*, September 15, 2020, www.theguardian.com/media/2020/sep/15/gary-lineker-takes-bbc-pay-cut-and-agrees-to-tweet-more-carefully.

Wilson-Chapman, Amy, "Counting the Panama Papers Money," *International Consortium of Investigative Journalists*, July 15 2019, www.icij.org/investigations/panama-papers/counting-the-panama-papers-money-how-we-reached-1-28-billion/.

Yano, Christine R., *Tears of Longing: Nostalgia and the Nation in Japanese Popular Song* (Cambridge, MA: Harvard University Press, 2002), 89.

Yoshimi, Shunya, "Television and Nationalism: Historical Change in the National Domestic TV Formation of Postwar Japan," *European Journal of Cultural Studies* 6, no. 4 (2003).

4 Chaos of the Ether (Radio 1920s–1940s)

In June 1920, superstar opera singer Dame Nellie Melba took up a microphone in the Chelmsford factory of the Marconi Radio Company. She treated listeners to a medley of opera and popular songs before finishing with a rousing chorus of *God Save the King*.[1] The performance, one of the first to air nationally in Britain, was paid for by *The Daily Mail*. In 1922, Marconi would join a consortium of electronics manufacturers to form a private broadcasting monopoly, the British Broadcasting Company. In 1926, Stanley Baldwin's Conservative government refashioned it by Royal Charter as a non-profit, public interest monopoly: the British Broadcasting Corporation.

Japan's first radio broadcast, in March 1925, was a stirring performance of patriotic martial music by the Band of the Imperial Navy. Tokyo Broadcasting Station, which aired it, was one of three private consortia established by commercial interests, including Japan's feisty newspaper giants. By 1926, the Japanese government had declared broadcasting a matter of national interest, and forced the fractious consortia into the national monopoly, NHK. Radio soon showed its value to the state in nation-building: another early program was *Chushingura*, one of the most iconic texts in Japanese literature and national identity, telling of the loyalty and doomed courage of 47 samurai who die avenging the honor of their dead master.

The earliest programs, in short, foreshadowed national styles of media policy, which persist to this day. The British, with particularly English paternalism, combined popular entertainment with highbrow culture infused with mild, polite patriotism. The Japanese, meanwhile, harnessed the new technology to instill national values of pride and loyalty. But how were these different visions institutionalized?

Radio was to the 1900s what the internet was to the 1990s: a sensational new media platform raising fundamental questions about how to harness it for the common good. By the mid-1890s, the fledgling technology of "wireless" radio communication had developed sufficiently to offer commercial opportunities. Guglielmo Marconi patented the first wireless transmitter in London in 1896, and the use of radio waves to broadcast Morse code and, later, voice and music signals grew rapidly before and during the First World War. Private transmissions became wildly popular, to the point where there was not enough airwave space to accommodate them all. Governments across the globe became involved, striving

DOI: 10.4324/b23015-4

to balance the fiercely competing interests of entrepreneurs, admirals, educators, and civil society groups from labor unions to churches to individual amateur enthusiasts. Distinctive approaches to broadcasting became evident in the earliest programming choices.

British and Japanese authorities saw broadcasting as being too important to be left to the market and ruthlessly subordinated corporate to national interests. Governments in both countries forced private broadcasting consortia into national non-profit monopolies and prohibited political broadcasts while they debated how to harness the new technology to serve national goals. Much early programming had similar goals, often around the need to embed national values in newly enfranchised citizens. Both broadcasters took leading roles in defining and disseminating notions of what it meant to be British or Japanese, even to the extent of articulating the "languages of state," which Benedict Andersen argues are so important to state formation.[2] But the broadcasters took different paths on the vital issue of independence. The BBC fought to protect its autonomy and editorial independence from the government, while NHK quickly became a loyal servant of an increasingly authoritarian state.

There was nothing predetermined about either Britain or Japan's adoption of a state-controlled monopoly as a response to the exploding interest in radio. The United States, for example, had considered just such an option and rejected it in favor of a commercial system with spectrum space allocated by the state for commercial users.[3] Instead, the distinctive institutional structures and organizational cultures of both broadcasters emerged from the political battles fought over the earliest years of their existence. The persistence of these differences almost a century later is testament to the importance of path dependency in understanding today's media environment.

Birth of the BBC: "A Trustee for the National Interest"

On June 15, 1920, Britain's Marconi Company began regular musical broadcasts in order to stimulate demand for its radio receivers. Nellie Melba's songs were heard live from Europe to Canada, although reactions were mixed. Many listeners were ecstatic: "Art and Science joined hands," gushed the *Daily Mail*, proud sponsor of the event.[4] The military, on the other hand, were furious that the broadcasts interfered with important communications: they had sought their own monopoly on spectrum use. One source complained that a navy pilot "was crossing the Channel in a thick fog and was trying to obtain weather and landing reports from Lymne. All he could hear was a musical evening."[5] For such critics, light entertainment represented a frivolous misuse of an important national resource. Nevertheless, hundreds of small companies saw the appeal of popular entertainment broadcasting and applied to the Post Office for transmission patents.

The British authorities were anxious to avoid the US experience, where unrestricted broadcasting had caused grave problems of spectrum congestion and signal interference: the "chaos of the ether." Reith, his innate love of order clearly rattled, wrote;

In America broadcasting had been initiated more than a year earlier than in this country: with characteristic energy it had developed wholesale, largely on a commercial basis and without any method of control whatsoever. There is no coordination, no standard, no guiding policy.[6]

British policymakers concluded that for the time being broadcasting must be tightly regulated. In 1922, David Lloyd George's coalition government persuaded the largest radio manufacturers to pool their patents and provide the capital to form the British Broadcasting Company. This was to be a private limited company, owned and operated by commercial electronics manufacturers, with a monopoly on broadcasting for the primary purpose of selling radios sets. Thus, the BBC was at birth a commercial venture.

In 1923, Parliament charged the Sykes Committee with charting the future for radio broadcasting. Sykes accepted the idea of a broadcasting monopoly as a solution to spectrum congestion but opinions were sharply divided about how to pay for it. Advertising was an obvious solution, but many politicians were appalled by what they saw as the "vulgar and intrusive" advertisements that interrupted broadcasts in America.[7] In addition, the newspaper industry was lobbying hard against the threat to their profits if radio were allowed to compete for advertising revenues. Clustered along Fleet Street in the heart of the capital, the broadsheet dailies were well funded, enjoyed close social and political ties to Westminster, and were hugely politically influential. Under heavy lobbying, the Committee rejected commercial advertising, noting "We attach great importance to the maintenance of a high standard of broadcasting, and we think that advertisements would lower the standard."[8] The idea of BBC advertising was thus dropped, to be picked up and discarded again at regular intervals over the course of the next century.[9] Direct government funding was considered but rejected, most vehemently by the BBC. Reith, then General Manager, saw it as being too likely to invite political interference and otherwise compromise editorial independence. Instead, Parliament decided that the BBC would be funded by a license fee payable by all owners of radio receivers. Fees would be collected by the Post Office and go directly to the BBC.[10]

Sykes recommended a prohibition on all "controversial" material, reflecting both elite paternalism and the BBC's own reluctance to alienate audiences. Political broadcasting was expressly forbidden, in accordance with Fleet Street's forcefully expressed wishes. The Government also reserved for itself the power to require the BBC to broadcast what it chose, or to control it directly if circumstances warranted it.

In 1926, Parliament's Crawford Committee revisited the question of commercial sponsorship. Reith argued that in order to cater to the highest rather than the lowest standards, the BBC would require both a guaranteed income and protection from competition. This would require what he described as the brute force of monopoly.[11] Policymakers agreed that monopoly was necessary to prevent an American-style free-for-all, which in turn implied government control. However, the committee noted, within the monopoly, "Every effort should be made to raise the standard of style and performance."[12] Crawford's Committee accepted Reith's suggestion that the BBC be allowed to keep its monopoly but be recast as a public corporation to act as trustee for the national interest. The British Broadcasting Corporation would be established by Royal Charter, appointed by the Government, and would continue to be funded by the license fee.

Crawford also recommended easing the restrictions on broadcasting political news and other controversial material. The newspaper industry tried unsuccessfully to limit the threat to their business. Lord Riddell, vice-chairman of the Newspaper Proprietors Association, argued that racing, betting, and court news should not be broadcast, and that "nothing should be included in the programming that would be distasteful to any large section of the community."[13] Crawford disagreed: "A certain amount of controversial matter should be broadcast, provided that the material is of high quality and distributed with scrupulous fairness."[14] As a sop to the press, news broadcasts were limited to 20 minutes a day.

Parliament accepted Crawford's recommendations with little opposition. Conservatives liked the idea of national unity and paternalistic public service. The Labour Party, while suspicious of the elite nature of the new Corporation, liked anything that legitimized the concept of public ownership. A few Liberals admired what they saw as the freedoms of the US system, but they too liked the idea of public corporations. In contrast to the United States, the decision to merge the radio manufacturers into a national monopoly meant that there were no commercial broadcasters to lobby against BBC expansion. Absent any British equivalent of the First Amendment, few concerns were heard about press freedom outside Fleet Street. Politicians of all stripes complained of bias against them, but were mollified by the Postmaster General, who assured them that they were all getting equal treatment.[15] The British Broadcasting Corporation was founded by Royal Charter in January 1927. The Charter was to last ten years and spoke of "the great value of the Service as a means of education and entertainment."[16]

John Reith was the crucial driving force behind the BBC's early and lasting reinvention of itself as a public servant rather than a commercial enterprise. As the BBC's first General Manager, he played a hugely influential role in shaping the nascent broadcaster's broadcasting philosophy and organizational culture, and indeed his name has become synonymous with the idea public service broadcasting. As Küng-Shankleman puts it, "his vision of the role and responsibilities of public service broadcasting shaped not only the BBC but also its continental PSB peers from their inception to the present day."[17]

Born in 1889, the youngest son of a Minister in the Presbyterian Free Church of Scotland, Reith was a domineering character with a messianic faith in himself: fighting in the trenches during the First World War, he had regularly and disdainfully exposed himself to enemy sniper fire. Eventually shot in the face, he was invalided out of service in 1915 and spent two years in Philadelphia supervising British armaments contracts at the Remington Arms factories, a time he later described as the happiest of his life. After the war he returned to Glasgow to work for an engineering firm before moving to London to work as a political secretary. The overwhelming dynamism and organizational capacity Reith demonstrated in each job was so impressive that he was appointed General Manager of the BBC in 1922 at the age of just 33. The position was originally conceived as administrative rather than editorial, but Reith had no intention of quietly serving others. He had his own ideas for the new medium.

Reith's unabashedly paternalistic mission to use radio to "inform, educate, and entertain" quickly overwhelmed the commercial purposes for which the Company was originally established.[18] He believed that a national broadcaster with a monopoly on the airwaves had an obligation to contribute to the well-being of the entire nation. While entertainment may be the primary function for broadcasting, he wrote:

> I think it will be admitted by all, that to have exploited so great a scientific invention to the purpose and pursuit of "entertainment" alone would have been a prostitution of its powers and an insult to the character and intelligence of the people.[19]

Whatever public roles Reith had originally envisioned beyond entertainment, they had not included political reporting. However, circumstances soon forced politics onto the BBC. The challenges of covering the strike were to catalyze the development of an organizational culture of editorial independence and impartiality, which remain hallmarks of the Corporation.

Independence, Impartiality, and the General Strike

The General Strike, which lasted for ten days in May 1926, fell between the publication of the Crawford Report and the granting of the Royal Charter. The walkout by almost two million workers organized by the Trade Union Congress (TUC) was a nationwide protest against low wages and poor working conditions. Bitterly divisive, the strike was also a baptism by fire for the infant broadcaster, presenting one of the hardest challenges to editorial impartiality and independence that the BBC ever faced.

Regular newspaper production was halted by strike action, and the BBC became by default the nation's primary news source.[20] The only alternatives were the *British Gazette*, a daily newsletter of government propaganda inspired by Chancellor of the Exchequer Winston Churchill and published by the Treasury, and the TUC publication *The British Worker*. Each was the mouthpiece of its respective constituency, neither claiming impartiality nor inspiring trust. Churchill waved away criticism that the *British Gazette* was biased, retorting "I cannot undertake to be impartial as between the Fire Brigade and the fire."[21] He demanded that the government exercise its right to take direct control over BBC news broadcasts.

Reith fought hard to defend the BBC's impartiality. His attitude reflected in part the public service ideal that the BBC should serve the entire nation and not just one party. Perhaps too it was a reflection of what has been described by his daughter as his political naivety. Reith hated "the horrid technique of politics" and did not associate himself personally with any party.[22] His Church of Scotland values were more closely aligned with the Labour Party, but his strong sense of patriotism, order, and traditional family values were deeply conservative. Reith could also let his strong personal prejudices influence his judgment, even keeping a regularly updated list of the people he hated most. Winston Churchill was usually at the top.

Primarily, Reith saw impartiality as the best practical strategy to navigate dangerous and ever-shifting political currents and so ensure the BBC's continued existence. He expressed himself in terms that read eerily like an early articulation of the Fox News slogan: "We report, you decide." The following passage, written in 1924, is worth quoting at length because it foreshadows the BBC's editorial evolution from simply avoiding controversial issues to attempting to cover them impartially. As we will see, the near-impossible challenge of reporting on politically sensitive issues while avoiding accusations of bias continues.

> People are no doubt very glad to have advice given to them, and usually need it badly. What they want still more is to have all the facts of the case presented to them, in such a way that it is possible for them to make up their own minds on the subject, guided no doubt by the advice which is appended to the presentation of the facts. . . . It has been considered wise policy up to the present to refrain from controversies as a general principle . . . it is necessary to be cautious. It will not be easy to persuade the general public of an absolute impartiality, but impartiality is essential.[23]

Reith persuaded Prime Minister Stanley Baldwin that it was in the government's interests to respect the BBC's editorial impartiality, and broadcasts sought to reflect independence. The BBC aired statements by strikers as well as government officials, to Churchill's fury. However, the BBC refused airtime to Labour Party politicians, including leader Ramsay MacDonald. Even more controversially, they denied the Archbishop of Canterbury his request to broadcast a message of conciliation. Reith seems to have wanted to allow both to broadcast, but was dissuaded by strongly expressed disapproval from the Government. Reith later wrote, "We were not exactly a free agent."[24] One Cabinet member told Reith that MacDonald should be kept off the air because "it would set Churchill off again" and both Baldwin and Reith feared that Churchill would insist on more draconian measures against the BBC.[25]

The strike raised bigger questions about the appropriate role of, and conflicting pressures on, any national broadcaster during a time of national emergency. Is its primary responsibility to report the often uncomfortable truth, to maintain national morale, or to assist in any way possible the democratically elected government in its handling of the crisis? Such questions were to recur in later crises such as Japan's 3.11 disaster or the COVID-19 pandemic. Reith felt the dilemma keenly because he believed the strike had been declared illegal by the High Court, although this interpretation was hotly contested. In a memorandum to staff, he later wrote:

> There could be no question about our supporting the Government in general, particularly since the General Strike had been declared illegal in the High Court. This being so, we were unable to permit anything which was contrary to the spirit of that judgment, and might have prolonged or sought to justify the strike. . . . The broadcasting of official communiqués by the Government

would have been expected and demanded irrespective of its political complexion. But as it was we were able to give listeners authentic impartial news of the situation to the best of our ability.[26]

Later he added:

Since the BBC was a national institution and since the Government in this crisis were acting for the people, apart from any Emergency Powers or clause in our License, the BBC was for the Government in the crisis too; and that we had to assist in maintaining the essential services of the country, the preservation of law and order, and of the life and liberty of the individual and of the community.[27]

Perhaps more significant than what the BBC did broadcast was what it did not: there was no discussion of why the unionists were striking. Inaccurate reports of strikers going back to work were frequent, but the BBC never broadcast corrections when the Unions informed them of inaccuracies.[28] Provincial Station Directors were instructed "When in doubt about any particular item . . . delete it. You are not, however, to exclude items from TUC sources provided they are objective and you are convinced of their truth."[29] However, "nothing calculated to extend the area of the strike should be broadcast."[30] In the meantime, government sources, which the BBC treated as inherently trustworthy, comprised the vast majority of broadcast material.[31] Ramsay MacDonald later complained of the "hopelessly one-sided" nature of what was broadcast.[32]

Many aspects of strike coverage seemed to give overt support to the Government. Stanley Baldwin's first message to the nation was transmitted from Reith's own house, with Reith rewriting the Prime Minister's speech and coaching him through the broadcast. Broadcasts took on a wartime tone, trying to spread good cheer while making no attempt to depict the harsh realities of working-class life.[33] As the strike wore on, Reith even took to reading broadcasts himself in response to accusations that some announcers were sounding worried.[34] He personally announced the end of the strike, playing the rousing, nationalistic hymn "Jerusalem" as he did so. Prime Minister Baldwin made a point of thanking Reith at a public dinner to mark the transition from Company to Corporation: "When the whole country might have been panic-stricken by the dissemination of false news people listened to and trusted that service of news from 2LO [i.e. the BBC]."[35]

A decade later, the Ullswater Committee, debating the Corporation's future, were divided on the BBC's coverage. The committee officially endorsed Reith's claims of impartiality: "It has been the avowed policy of the BBC to hold the scales even between the various political parties and in this . . . it has on the whole been successful."[36] But some in the committee, including Labour MP and future Prime Minister Clement Attlee, disagreed:

The BBC should have sufficient independence to resist being made the instrument of one side in a national controversy . . . while I agree that on the whole the BBC has endeavored to hold the scales even between the various political parties, there have been outstanding instances to the contrary.[37]

Later historians are similarly divided.[38] Most see in Reith's framing and agenda-setting a barely veiled bias in favor of the Establishment. Seaton and Curran argue that the strike marked "the end of propaganda based on lies and the start of a more subtle tradition of selection and presentation."[39] On the other hand, the crisis catalyzed Reith's decision to champion independence and impartiality. As Symons puts it: "The BBC performed its difficult task well and conscientiously. It became, inevitably, a Government information agency but . . . the attempt to maintain impartiality was genuine."[40] Looking ahead, it's tempting to draw parallels to NHK's coverage of the 3.11 disaster. Unquestionably, the provision of reliable information was vital during the crisis. *The Times*' praise for the BBC could easily be applied to NHK 85 years later: "It killed rumours, broke down the isolation threatened by restricted transport and kept every listener in close touch with the steps that were being taken to maintain order and facilitate the distribution of supplies."[41] On the other hand, these valuable services came in both cases with a refusal to dig deeper into the murky underlying politics.

Overall, as *The Times* wrote in the immediate aftermath, "the general strike brought only good to wireless broadcasting."[42] The BBC had emerged with its independence intact, its reputation greatly enhanced, and its immediate future secured. The broadcaster had earned a reputation for being the place to find out what was really happening. Socialist writer Beatrice Webb wrote that "The sensation of a general strike . . . centres round the headphones of a wireless set."[43] Partly as a result, the strike effectively ended the restrictions on BBC news coverage, which had increased from a single evening slot to at least five bulletins a day. Proposals to make this expansion permanent met with some resistance, articulated by one MP thus:

> The more a government-controlled broadcasting monopoly supersedes the daily press for purposes outside entertainment and the dissemination of unbiased news, the greater is the danger of insidious one-sided propaganda and the curtailment of liberty in the expression of different points of view . . . this really is the beginning of an attack upon what is known as the freedom of the press.[44]

Within weeks of the end of the strike, though, Parliament gave the BBC ringing endorsements and extended its monopoly with a ten-year license.

Reith's lasting insight was that it would be impossible to educate and inform without being entertaining. Mass audiences had to be drawn in and hooked, and programming thus needed to be popular as well as uplifting. Crucially, Reith believed that the two were not incompatible, arguing that real entertainment should engage and not simply pass the time. He was confident that his audience would agree: "It is better to overestimate the mentality of the public, than to underestimate it."[45] Furthermore, he had a high opinion of the capacity of the broadcaster to raise the tastes of its audience rather than merely catering to them, declaring that BBC's job was "to make the good popular, and the popular good."[46] To that end, early programming included a lot of highbrow entertainment and music as well as news and information. Artistic creativity and innovation were encouraged from the outset, illustrated by what has been claimed as the world's first foray into an entirely new art form: radio drama.

In 1923, the BBC approached popular novelist Richard Hughes to produce something unheard of: a play with sound but no vision. Hughes came up with what he called a "listening play." *A Comedy of Danger* is a short drama set in a collapsed and flooding mineshaft in which three characters, an older man and a young couple, are trapped and forced to contemplate death as well as their rela- tionships to each other.[47] The play, first aired in January 1924, was prefaced by an instruction for listeners to turn off their lights, and the action begins with the words: "The lights have gone out!" The sound effects team had fun producing the various bangs, crashes, and running water that alerted the audience (and the characters) to the danger of collapse and flooding. To simulate the echo effect of being in a tunnel, the actors wore metal buckets over their heads. Needing a distant, unseen rescue party, Hughes went onto the streets of London to round up a group of Welsh miners, visiting to busk Christmas carols during the holiday season. Unable to get them either to stop or start singing on cue, Hughes had them caroling continuously in the corridor just outside the recording studio, opening and shutting the door as needed to modulate the volume, and hence convey the approach of the rescue party.[48] The play proved a sensation when it first aired. Local broadcasting stations and theater companies were inundated by "very many requests" for repeat transmission of "the mine play."[49] It was promptly adapted for Japanese radio, as well as being reproduced at CBS studios in the United States.[50]

The 1930s saw the BBC consolidate its position as a central feature of Brit- ish life as well as a self-appointed arbiter of national culture. Reith moral val- ues reflected his strict religious upbringing, and he fervently believed that "the broadcasting system of a nation is a mirror of that nation's conscience."[51] Hence, high standards and educational, morally uplifting programs were seen as essen- tial. Reith's paternalism was undisguised, but so too was his faith in his audience:

> Our responsibility is to carry into the greatest number of homes everything
> that is best in every department of human knowledge, endeavor and achieve-
> ment, and to avoid things which are, or may be, hurtful. It is occasionally
> indicated to us that we are apparently setting out to give the public what we
> think they want – and not what they need, but few know what they want, and
> very few what they need. There is often no difference.[52]

To this end, early broadcasts featured a lot of uplifting classical music, and talks by learned experts. Listenership grew rapidly and the news, concerts, and talks became popular features of public discourse.[53] The humor magazine *Punch* joked that "The BBC claim to have discovered a new type, the 'middlebrow.' It consists of people who are hoping that someday they will get used to the stuff they ought to like."[54]

The BBC's role as perhaps the premier interpreter of British national iden- tity was cemented at this time. Reith believed that the BBC should have truly national appeal, and serve "the general audience" rather than any particular group or groups. He saw radio as a means of binding the nation together, reinforcing a collective sense of Britishness. Shaping a more uniform national language from the hundreds of local dialects still spoken in the early 1990s was just one part of the nation-building.[55] The Advisory Committee on Spoken English, including George Bernard Shaw and Rudyard Kipling, established correct pronunciation of what was later known across the globe as "BBC English."[56] The BBC Empire Service, forerunner to today's World Service, was launched in 1932 with the express intention of helping bind together the disparate British Empire.[57]

The evolving organizational culture was complex mix of often contradictory impulses – at times stuffy, paternalistic, and conservative, but also too progressive and sometimes anarchically creative. Reith unapologetically used the BBC to serve his religious beliefs, declaring that "Christianity happens to be the stated and official religion of the country."[58] The BBC broadcast Christian services and observed the Sabbath. No jazz was allowed on Sundays, only appropriately serious, often religious programs. Critics of Christianity were denied airtime. An inadvertent mention of birth control during a talk on science produced howls of protest and a groveling apology from the BBC.[59] On the other hand, women succeeded in leadership roles in numbers far greater than elsewhere in the United Kingdom's highly sexist establishment. Hilda Matheson, as the first Head of Talks, was responsible for establishing the news service during the general strike while Margery Wace started and edited *The Week in Parliament*.[60]

The advent of television in the 1930s prompted another debate about the public and private uses of broadcasting. There were many demands to allow commercial television broadcasting on the new platform. On the other hand, much of the commercial entertainment sector, including the film industry, music halls, theaters, football, boxing, and other sports associations, feared competition from television and demanded it be restricted. Many imposed their own broadcasting boycotts.[61] Reith himself was deeply suspicious of television, comparing its introduction to that of the bubonic plague. His daughter, Marista Leisham, suggests that this reflects his religious upbringing.[62] In the austere Free Church of Scotland tradition, music and the spoken word were central to the mission of spreading the Lord's message. Visual finery and embellishment were frowned upon as frivolous distraction at best and a violation of the Second Commandment prohibition on graven images at worst. However, Reith's tenure was nearing an end. Despite the enormous success and prestige of the organization he had built, Reith's brooding paranoia and massive ego left him profoundly dissatisfied and he was to quit the BBC in 1938. "Reithian values," however, remained.

The National government, a cross-party coalition led by Prime Minister Ramsay MacDonald, chose not only to reaffirm public service broadcasting but to expand it onto the new medium. In 1934, the Selsdon Committee recommended the BBC take a monopoly on television broadcasting, paid for by an increased license fee. The committee even suggested that the Treasury assist paying for the service, indicating how important they believed public broadcasting was. In

1935, the BBC made the first television broadcast. In 1936, the Royal Charter was renewed for another ten years.

The Second World War saw the BBC's reputation greatly enhanced at home and abroad. Jonathan Dimbleby even argues that the War "made" the BBC. First, the obvious challenges reinforced the BBC's determination to uphold its independence and impartiality in news reporting. A small prewar news operation of just two political journalists had to be greatly expanded to keep the public abreast of the global conflict. Forced to balance editorial credibility with national loyalty during the vicious conflict, the BBC slowly and often painfully learned how to report as truthfully as possible within the constraints of necessary and often unnecessary censorship. As during the General Strike, many politicians and generals wanted the BBC under official control or even shut down. Wiser heads prevailed, and the BBC's willingness to broadcast bad news reaffirmed its editorial independence from the Government, making it an increasingly trusted news source across the world.[63]

Second, the war forced the BBC to reconsider its previous high-mindedness with regard to entertainment. To boost sagging public morale, the BBC greatly expanded its popular entertainment, often to the horror of the older management. The Board of Governors initially banned Count Bassie's Big Band sound, and they "deplored" the beloved Vera Lynne.[64] Persuaded by staff to reconsider, the Corporation adapted its programming in response to dire circumstance. Finally, the war elevated the BBC's role as a symbol of national unity. The central London location of the Corporation's headquarters put it in the front lines during the Blitz, and the newscasters' stoicism and eternally upbeat tone worked wonders for national morale, most memorably when news broadcasts continued almost immediately after a direct bomb hit on Broadcasting House killed several employees.

NHK: "An Affair of State"

Radio broadcasting policy developed during a pivotal moment in Japan's political history, as the struggles between liberalism and authoritarianism peaked in the mid-1920s. The Meiji Restoration of 1868 had replaced the feudal Shogunate with a modernizing but authoritarian oligarchy. The new oligarchs encouraged newspapers, even subsidizing them, as a means of keeping the citizenry well-informed about the immense project of national industrialized modernization. However, press content was tightly controlled. The first newspaper regulations (*Shimbun Jōrei*) were enacted in 1872, stating that the purpose of the press was "the enlightenment and expansion of knowledge of the general public."[65] The Ministry of Home Affairs (*Jichishō*) was given the right to pre-censor papers, and many editors and journalists were imprisoned for criticizing the government.[66]

Japanese liberalism flowered briefly in the period of "Taishō Democracy" (1912–1926). Progressives gained ground politically, and civilian political parties won control of the Diet. A lively, independent press emerged alongside an active popular rights movement, although press controls remained on the books.[67] Several decades of state-led modernization, industrialization, and mass education, all driven by a desire to catch up with the Western imperial powers, had generated demands for political liberalization but also strengthened a powerful, highly centralized state.[68] The Universal Male Suffrage Law of 1925 marked the high point for prewar democracy. In the same year, however, the Peace Preservation Law, passed in response to fears of the spread of communism from the newly formed Union of Soviet Socialist Republics, restricted liberties, including freedom of expression. This proved a major step on the road toward the totalitarianism of the 1930s.

Broadcasting policy reflected the political confusion created by these cross-currents of liberalism and authoritarianism. In the aftermath of the First World War, although the government retained the *de jure* right to censor, the press enjoyed unprecedented political freedom, and the newspaper industry flourished.[69] Private companies, led by the great national newspapers *Asahi Shimbun*, *Yomiuri Shimbun*, and *Mainichi Shimbun*, had been experimenting with radio broadcasts since the early 1900s, and by the 1920s were investing heavily in transmitting equipment imported mostly from the United States. In 1921, the Ministry of Communications (*Teishinshō*) began to receive applications for public broadcasting licenses, and in 1922 the Ministry set up a study group to discuss regulation of the new medium.

The Ministry of Communications made two vital but seemingly contradictory decisions. First, they concluded that broadcasting was to be governed by the 1915 Wireless Telegraphy Law, the first line of which was "The Government will manage wireless communications," thus mandating state control.[70] The law granted the Ministry of Communications considerable autonomy to exercise such control. However, the bureaucrats also acquiesced to the demands of the newspapers and electronics manufacturers that broadcasting would be privately operated for commercial purposes. These decisions reflected deep divisions within the Ministry. Many wanted state control over broadcasting at the outset, but Minister for Communications Inukai Tsuyoshi was, initially at least, a strong supporter of commercial radio.[71] His decision to allow civilian ownership was taken in part because, while the authorities deemed radio to be a public matter, they did not yet believe it to be essential to the national interest. In addition, public finances were severely strained and state management was not considered feasible.[72] Foreign precedent also influenced the decision: commercial broadcasting was then the norm in Europe and the United States, from whence the head of the Ministry study group had recently returned from a fact-finding mission.[73]

The Ministry of Communications issued the first Regulations on Private Radio Telephone Broadcasting Facilities in 1923.[74] These regulations allowed commercial broadcasting but forbade advertising, and followed the British example of financing by a license fee on radio sets. Regulations on content issued in 1924 stipulated that all programs would be inspected before transmission, monitored during transmission, and would always be subject to government approval or alteration. In this respect, broadcasting was subject to the same laws on public morals as applied to the newspaper industry, although the authorities were to assume greater supervisory powers over radio than the press.[75] The Press Law of 1909 and the Publication Law of 1893 both allowed for state inspection and approval of newspapers and periodicals before or after publication, although, as noted earlier, the authorities did not always wield those powers actively. The Government retained the right to require broadcast of any transmission they wanted. Finally, the broadcasting of music and entertainment was to be restricted on the grounds that the workforce should not be distracted.[76] Despite these restrictions, over a hundred organizations flooded the Ministry with applications for broadcasting licenses. The economy was booming and newspapers, electronics manufacturers, and other entrepreneurs were anxious to cash in on the ballooning profits to be made from the new medium.[77]

The bureaucrats at the Ministry of Communications had permitted commercial broadcasting, but they were no more committed to laissez-faire principles than their British counterparts. The Ministry restricted broadcasting to just one station in each of the three big urban areas (Tokyo, Osaka, and Nagoya) and exercised considerable *gyōsei shidō* ('administrative guidance,' otherwise known as arm-twisting) on leading applicants to collaborate in regional joint ventures. The not-so-friendly persuasion succeeded in Tokyo and Nagoya, despite vociferous complaints from the private companies who argued for free competition between stations.[78] However, rival applicants in Osaka were unable to work together. Communications Minister Inukai did not like the competitive bickering in Osaka, and concluded that his difficulties were caused by too many applicants. He was troubled too by reports of bribery and corruption among the earliest broadcasters. Finally, many of his colleagues were still arguing for complete state control of broadcasting.[79] Inukai therefore abandoned the experiment in commercial broadcasting, forcing broadcasters to pay attention to the national interest by turning the stations from for-profit joint-stock companies (*kabushiki gaisha*) into non-profit public-benefit corporations (*shadan hōjin*). Tokyo Broadcasting Station (*Tokyo Hōsō Kyoku, TBS*) began broadcasting in March 1925 under the call-sign JOAK (Tokyo Central Broadcasting Bureau).[80] The Osaka and Nagoya Broadcasting Corporations quickly followed.

Inukai's own strong moral sensibility and patriotism dovetailed with the government's burgeoning conviction that radio should be used for state ends.[81] To that end, he appointed Gotō Shinpei as first governor of TBS. Viscount Gotō could not have been a more entrenched member of the political establishment. The son of a samurai, he had served as a military doctor before becoming a colonial administrator in Taiwan, first head of the South Manchuria Railway Company and Mayor of Tokyo. He had held high-ranking cabinet positions, including Minister of Communications, Home Minister, and Foreign Minister. Like Inukai and Reith, he believed that radio should be used for the improvement of national welfare and the refinement of public taste.[82] He promised that under his leadership, radio would revolutionize the quality of family life, promote public education, and "invigorate the economy."[83]

Early programming on these stations was intended to edify and educate as well as inform. One of the earliest programs from TBS was *Chūshingura*, a national legend extolling the loyalty and courage of 47 samurai who died avenging the honor of their dead master.[84] However, as Kerim Yasar argues, the early days also saw the brief flourishing of an extraordinarily creative and productive group of playwrights and intellectuals in the Radio Drama Research Group (*Rajio Dorama Kenkyūkai*).[85] Much of their prolific output was original, but from this group also came *Tankō no Naka* ('In a Mineshaft'), first aired August 1925. This was TBS's adaption of the BBC drama *A Comedy of Danger* discussed earlier. Broadcasters at TBS were impressed by the BBC's innovation in *rajio dorama* (radio drama) and rushed to remake it before their rivals at the Osaka and Nagoya stations.[86] Modernist playwright Osanai Kaoru, a founding member of the Radio Drama Research Group, followed Hughes' original closely: two lovers and an older man are trapped in a mineshaft, hoping for rescue but believing themselves close to death. Ultimately, as well, the old man sacrifices himself to save the young couple. As in Britain, the play was prefaced with an instruction to listeners to turn off lights.[87] The challenges of sound effects were similar, although the Japanese version used giant taiko drums to simulate underground echoes.[88]

Critic Oyama Katsumi argues that despite its foreign origins, *Tankō no Naka* resonated deeply in Japan, where listeners appreciated the stark simplicity of the setting and the suspense as the characters prepared for what appeared to be their imminent demise. The human relationships (*ningenkankei*) between the characters involved love, loyalty, sacrifice, and betrayal, and were also said to have struck a particular national chord.[89] The play was an immediate hit: Yasar quotes contemporary reports of the tension in Tokyo during the broadcast, the houses all shrouded in darkness.[90] Tankō became a model for Japanese writers and was later adapted as a novel by Kubata Mantaro and an NHK television play in 1956.[91] *Tankō no Naka*'s plot, themes, and tone are also strikingly echoed in Uno Nobuo's *shinsaku* ('New Kabuki') play *Fubuki Tōge* ("The Snowbound Pass"), first performed in 1935 and regularly revived.[92]

Entertainment programming in the brief commercial era was strikingly cosmopolitan. This reflected Japan's broader engagement with the Western world at that time as well as the artistic sensibilities of the broadcasters themselves. One of the first dramas specifically written for Japanese radio was an adaptation of Alexander Pushkin's *The Captain's Daughter*. However, the broadcasters' tastes proved more cosmopolitan than those of their audiences. An early survey reported that listeners wanted fewer broadcasts of Western music and more children's songs and traditional Japanese *naniwa-bushi*.[93]

Before long, bureaucrats and politicians awoke to the power of the new medium to serve state goals. In the first place, radio proved much more popular than most had expected. TBS estimated that it had anywhere from 20,000 to 100,000 listeners, and there was a boom in the number of amateurs making their own receivers. By 1945, almost half of Japanese households owned a radio.[94]

The authorities were also impressed by the influence of the BBC during the General Strike of 1926.[95] Communications Minister Adachi Kenzō, a conservative former journalist who served as Communications Minister from 1925–1927, stated:

It goes without saying that the broadcasting business exerts an enormous influence on the nation's general culture. Further, when necessary for the state, namely when the state confronts an emergency, broadcasting is a great, unrivaled communications medium that can be used for state duties . . . this undertaking for the most part is to be treated as an affair of state.[96]

This view came against a background of already-tightening restrictions on the press. The Ministry of Communications was already active in censoring the content of private broadcasts, having established local offices to preapprove scripts and monitor broadcasts. In May 1925, the Ministry had issued a list of subjects that could not be broadcast, reserving the right to prohibit any content, and forbidding anything likely to disturb the public peace or corrupt public morals, any matters about government not made public by official sources, any items under investigation, and any diplomatic or military secrets.[97] By late 1925, the authorities decided to go further, in order to secure a national public network that could be kept under closer political scrutiny.

In August 1926, the Ministry of Communications invoked the Wireless Telegraphy Law to force the three private commercial broadcasters to form a single national broadcasting monopoly, *Nippon Hōsō Kyōkai*. The commercial broadcasters fought hard to maintain their independence, but in vain.[98] NHK was required to "execute business for the government as an outpost agency of the Ministry of Communications."[99] While much of NHKs production and transmission were centralized around the gigantic facilities of JOAK in Tokyo, programs were relayed via regional operations.

NHK was nominally independent, but state control was pervasive from the start. To placate the angry members of the old commercial stations, the first President, Iwamura Kenzo, was a prominent businessman not formerly affiliated with the government.[100] Thereafter, officials from the Ministry of Communications were appointed to serve as directors and in nearly all other important management positions. Representatives of the Army, the Navy, and the Ministry of Foreign Affairs also sat on the program council.[101] All broadcasts had to be reported in advance to the Ministry of Communications. Where that was not possible, for example, during live broadcasts of baseball games, a Ministry official was stationed close by to intervene if necessary.[102] Censorship was often informal at first, reflecting mutual trust and understanding between senior management, political elites, and state officials.[103] Indeed, a popular joke had it that the ideal NHK executive was a "three-*tei*" man: a graduate of *Teikkoku Daigaku* (the Imperial University); associated with *Teishinsō* (Ministry of Communications), and a *teino* (an idiot).[104]

NHK immediately began to serve national, state-designated ends by creating a national network of regional stations and the smaller relay circuits that were essential in mountainous Japan. The network was to be hurriedly completed in time for the enthronement of Emperor Hirohito in November 1928 and, as in Britain, the fortunes of the Royal family and the national broadcaster were to become closely intertwined. Indeed, among NHK's first news broadcasts were hourly reports on the deteriorating health of the Emperor Taishō in August 1926.[105] Coverage of the Enthronement ceremony boosted radio listenership dramatically and firmly established NHK's place at the center of national life.[106] Sandra Wilson notes that radio allowed, for the first time, the simultaneity of national political action, which David I. Kertzer identifies as "essential to political communion."[107] Wilson describes, for example, how NHK was essential in the military-inspired attempt to have the entire population shout "Banzai! Banzai! Banzai!" at the moment of Coronation.[108] Recordings of the naval band's funeral march for Emperor Taisho had been aired earlier in the year.[109] The Imperial ceremony was also the occasion of the first live broadcast by a Japanese Prime Minister, when Wakatsuki Reijiro gave his impressions of the ceremony of Hirohito's first formal audience in late 1927.[110]

NHK broadcasting, as at the BBC, included much entertainment. As well as drama, Kabuki was very popular, along with a wide variety of music. There was also much foreign programming, from Western music recitals to talks delivered by visiting dignitaries and entertainers. NHK and the BBC developed a close working relationship despite increasing political tension between the two countries. For example, NHK technicians were sent to train at the BBC.[111] Even during the relatively liberal 1920s, though, state interference in programming was not uncommon. Hiromu Nagahara recounts how the Ministry of Communications banned radio performance of the popular song "Tokyo March" (*Tokyo Kōshinkyu*) in 1929 on the grounds that its theme of runaway lovers encouraged juvenile delinquency.[112] The fact that the song also critical of the era's economic inequality may also have factored into the Ministry's decision.

Sports coverage grew quickly, beginning in 1927 with live coverage of a Sumo tournament in the Korean colony, followed by a middle school baseball championship game in Osaka.[113] As in Britain and the United States, professional sports organizations initially feared the new media. Japan's Sumo Association, for example, initially refused to allow radio coverage of *bashō* for fear it would erode their live audiences. After they relented, NHK broadcasts were responsible for a marked revival in Sumo's popularity.[114] Live baseball coverage, even of high school games, also became tremendously popular. As in the United Kingdom, such events contributed to the sense of both national ritual and cultural identity. Coverage of the 1932 Olympic Games in Los Angeles and the Berlin Games of 1936 was every bit as nationalistic as any modern-era US network's coverage.

Daily radio calisthenics (*rajio taiso*) began in 1928 to celebrate the Emperor's enthronement, and quickly became a literal exercise in national unity.[115] Kampo, the Postal Life Insurance business established by the Ministry of Communications, copied a similar program run by Metropolitan Life Insurance in the United States to improve population health. Postmen distributed millions of exercise cards to elementary school children who won prizes for completed schedules. The exercises were dropped during the Occupation for being too militaristic, but were revived in 1950 and remain extremely popular.[116]

Government control over broadcasting, as on press freedoms more generally, tightened as the political climate grew more authoritarian, notably after the Manchuria crises of the early 1930s.[117] Rules were tightened to require advance reporting of all news broadcasts at least one hour ahead of scheduled airtime.[118] The government asserted the right to present and explain policy decisions. The 1938 National Mobilization Law banned reports that contradicted government policy. Criticism of the state, even implicit rebuke such as the reporting of suspensions of telephone services due to thunderstorms, was also forbidden. Expressions of political opinion were banned and announcers were instructed to maintain neutral voice tones.[119] By the late 1930s, even listening to foreign broadcasts was made illegal, as was ownership of all-frequency receivers that could receive such broadcasts. Kasza notes, however, that restrictions on political reporting were increasingly common across the world in the 1930s. Most democracies, including the United States, did not allow broadcasting of legislative hearings, and political neutrality was more typically defined as the exclusion of politics rather than as the appropriate balancing of competing views.[120]

The government's active mobilization of NHK radio for state purposes began in earnest after the 1931 Manchurian crisis. Like the BBC, NHK had by then firmly established itself as a central pillar of national society, its entertainment programming by then a central part of daily life. Often listening was a semi-public event, as *izakaya* bars and tea shops bought radio sets to attract customers.[121] More than in Britain, though, authorities engaged in conscious attempts to shape public opinion and social values. Mandated coverage would eventually include lectures and positive reports from the war fronts, and broadcasts of memorial services and meetings of patriotic societies.

Educational programming began on a national scale in 1935, despite the resistance of some educationalists who feared it would make teachers redundant.[122] Most NHK staff had been very enthusiastic about the idea, specifically admiring what the BBC had accomplished in terms of mass education. They had been preparing a second channel devoted to education since 1929, but the start was delayed for years by bureaucratic in-fighting between the Ministry of Education (*Monbushō*), which demanded authority over the venture, and the Ministry of Communications, which exercised effective control over NHK and feared that surrendering sovereignty on this issue might lead to similar demands, for example, from the Home Ministry to control news programming.[123] At the same time, rivalry between the regional stations was prompting local experimentation with programs such as Radio Gymnastics for Schools, Kindergarten Hour, and Teachers' Hour, all innovations from the Osaka regional station.[124]

Political elites lost little time in using the educational programming to advance their agenda. In the weekly "Morning Address," for example, a prominent public figure gave a lecture directed at elementary school children. Subjects, intended to inspire loyalty and national pride, included "Send-off for the Emperor of Manchuko," "Why Our Military Force Is Strong," "On Being a Loyal Japanese," and "The Strength of the Japanese."[125] NHK established special departments to craft edifying programming for children, women, and teachers, among others.[126] In 1934, for example, the broadcaster played a central role in popularizing the story of Hachiko, the dog who patiently waited for his master to return to Shibuya Station every evening for nine years after the man died. The story was presented as epitomizing Japanese values of absolute loyalty and deference to authority.[127] Children's programs more generally began to reflect what NHK's prewar Program Controller would later describe as "a completely one-sided devotion to militarism."[128] These included stories of heroic exploits by children and military animals.[129] The title of the "Children's Time" (*kodomo jikan*) program was changed to "Little Subjects Time" (*shōkokumin jikan*) in reflection of the martial nature of the era.

NHK, like the BBC, was also active in shaping the national language, for example, but in 1934, on instruction from the Ministry of Education, NHK helped establish the National Language Commission specifically to root out foreign words and phrases from broadcasts, an act which seems to have no counterpart by the BBC.[130] The broader point is that, perhaps even more than at the BBC, entertainment programming was at least as important a component of NHK's mission and social influence as its fledgling news services.

By the late 1930s, the state had assumed direct control over NHK following the declaration of the Sino-Japanese War and the passage of the 1938 National Mobilization Act. The broadcaster became an explicit tool for the dissemination of state propaganda and national policy under the slogan "*Ikkani Ichidai Sonaeyo Rajio*" ("One household, one radio").[131] The government used NHK to broadcast the Emperor's order for surrender to the rebel troops during the February 26, 1936, mutiny.[132] The authorities used NHK overseas broadcasts extensively to communicate with the colonies and engender loyalty to the homeland. The BBC, it should be noted, was doing exactly the same. After Japan withdrew from the League of Nations, the government turned increasingly to overseas broadcasts to present Japan's case to the world, as during the Manchuria Incident in 1931.[133] Jazz and foreign language music and programming, with the exception of German and Italian, were banned.[134] The amount of entertainment dropped dramatically after 1937 in deference to the gravity of the international situation, but rose later as the state sought to improve national morale with broadcasts of traditional music and arts, culminating in the 1940 campaign for patriotic *kokumin ongaku*: National Music.[135]

By 1941, NHK had become a tool for wartime propaganda. Announcers were ordered to change from a "disinterested tone" (*tantan chō*) to a "war-cry tone" (*otakebi chō*). Recording crews were embedded with Kamikaze units. Recordings of Shintō enshrinement ceremonies for war dead at Yasukuni Shrine were played continually.[136] News announcements, accompanied by martial music, were designed to serve national interests while appearing to be objective.[137]

Historian Jane Robbins notes that in seeking to maintain the appearance of objectivity, NHK's propaganda was more often a matter of selective presentation rather than the blatant lying of the Nazis. In this sense, she argues, it had more of the character of wartime BBC reporting.[138] However, NHK had to carry increasingly fictitious reports from the Imperial General Headquarters, for example, by deliberately underreporting battle losses.[139] In the later years of the war, as the devastation grew, NHK broadcast edifying and entertaining programming in an attempt to boost sinking morale.[140] Broadcasts continued, despite considerable bomb damage and scant resources, until the bitter end. In one sense NHK ended the war, broadcasting Emperor Hirohito's message of surrender to his subjects. After the surrender, NHK relayed appeals for order from Prime Minister Higashikuni Naruhiko as well as emergency information about food rationing, etc. Weather forecasts, daily exercises, and children's programs were resumed almost immediately.[141] But no sooner had the Imperial Government relinquished control at NHK than another set of authorities picked up the reins. NHK was to become a mouthpiece again, but this time for democracy.

In both Britain and Japan, then, the explosive popularity of radio generated intense political conflict over its regulation. Corporate powers, including electronics manufacturers and fledgling private broadcasters, fought with each other and with military and other state interests for the best terms. At first, policymakers in both countries adopted strikingly similar approaches to governing the amazing new technology. British authorities, determined to avoid "chaos of the ether" they saw in the United States caused by unregulated broadcasting, formed the competing commercial broadcasters into a single British Broadcasting Company (later Corporation) as a non-profit, public service monopoly. A listener fee system was fashioned to guarantee public funding, which was nonetheless one step removed from direct political control, thereby shielding the broadcaster from outside influence over its creative and editorial decisions from either governments or advertisers. In Japan, too, policymakers quickly strong-armed a consortium of squabbling private broadcasters into a quasi-independent monopoly, the *Nippon Hōsō Kyōkai* (NHK). It, too, was funded by listener fees and enjoyed notional editorial independence. Both broadcasters quickly established themselves at the heart of national life, informing, educating, and entertaining their respective populations with programming, which often reflected fruitful creative and cultural exchange between the two countries. Director-General John Reith's paternalism and insistence that programs respect traditional values were shared by the Ministry of Communications bureaucrats who influenced much of early NHK broadcasting.

However, differences between the two broadcasters soon took shape. Reith's stubborn defense of editorial autonomy during the 1926 General Strike forged a legacy of editorial independence, which is still revered within the BBC. In Japan, increasingly authoritarian elites established a level of dominance over the national broadcaster that British politicians, including Winston Churchill, had tried and failed to achieve. With the steady shift from liberal to authoritarian politics in the 1930s, NHK surrendered its editorial independence to become a loyal mouthpiece of a militarized state.

Notes

1 The splendid-looking microphone itself is on display at the Museum of the History of Science in Oxford.
2 Benedict Anderson, *Imagined Communities: Reflections on the Origin and Spread of Nationalism* (London: Verso Books, Revised edition, 1991), 78. Tessa Carroll, "NHK and Japanese Language Policy," *Language Problems and Language Planning* 19, no. 3 (Fall 1995): 271–293.

3 This story is excellently told in Victor Pickard, *America's Battle for Media Democracy: The Triumph of Corporate Libertarianism and the Future of Media Reform* (Cambridge: Cambridge University Press, 2014).

4 "Melba's 1000 Mile Song," *The Daily Mail*, June 15, 1920.

5 *The Financier*, August 25, 1920, quoted in Briggs, *The History of British Broadcasting in the United Kingdom Vol. 1 The Birth of Broadcasting* (Oxford: Oxford University Press, 1961), 49.

6 J.C.W. Reith, *Broadcast over Britain* (London: Hodder and Staunton, 1924), 17.

7 John Cain, *The BBC: Seventy Years of Broadcasting* (London: BBC Publications, 1992), 9.

8 *Broadcasting Committee Report* (Sykes Committee), Cmmd. 1951 (London: HMSO), para 41.

9 Advertising was eventually accepted for international programming, but remains forbidden on UK domestic services.

10 Initially, the revenues were split between the BBC and the Treasury.

11 John Reith, "Memorandum" to *Report of the Broadcasting Committee* (Beveridge Report) Cmmd. 8117, appendix H, paper 62, (London: HMSO) 1949.

12 *Report of the Broadcasting Committee* (Crawford Committee) Cmnd. 2599 (London: HMSO), 1925.

13 "The Broadcasting Inquiry: The Attitude of the Press," *The Times*, December 18, 1925.

14 *Report of the Broadcasting Committee* (Crawford Committee).

15 Briggs, *The Birth of Broadcasting*, 352.

16 Briggs, *The Birth of Broadcasting*, 357.

17 Lucy Küng-Shankleman, *Inside the BBC and CNN* (London: Routledge, 2000), 70.

18 The ordering in Reith's phrase contrasts tellingly with an earlier articulation by US broadcasting pioneer David Sarnoff who wrote in 1922 that "the principal elements of broadcasting are entertainment, information and education." David Sarnoff, *Looking Ahead: The Papers of David Sarnoff* (New York: McGraw Hill, 1968), 41.

19 Reith, *Broadcast over Britain*, 81.

20 "The BBC and the Strike," *The Times*, May 19, 1926.

21 Julian Symons, *The General Strike: A Historical Portrait* (London: Cresset Press, 1959), 162.

22 According to a diary entry from November 29, 1936, quoted in Jean Seaton and James Curran, *Power without Responsibility: The Press, Broadcasting and New Media in Britain* (Oxon, UK: Taylor & Francis, 2003), 118.

23 Reith, *Broadcast over Britain*, 112.

24 According to a diary entry from May 10, 1926, as quoted in Briggs, *The Birth of Broadcasting*, 376.

25 Symons, *The General Strike*, 182.

26 Reith to BBC senior staff on May 15, 1926, as quoted in Briggs, *The Birth of Broadcasting*, 365.

27 Briggs, *The Birth of Broadcasting*, 365.

28 Symons, *The General Strike*, 181.

29 Briggs, *The Birth of Broadcasting*, 373.

30 Briggs, *The Birth of Broadcasting*, 373.

31 "BBC and the Strike," *The Times*.

32 Briggs, *The Birth of Broadcasting*, 374.

33 Briggs, *The Birth of Broadcasting*, 374.

34 Richard Havers, *Here Is the News: The BBC in the Second World War* (Stroud, UK: Sutton Publishing, 2008), 3.

35 "New Broadcast Era: Mr Baldwin on the Changes," *The Times*, December 17, 1926.

36 *Report of the Broadcasting Committee 1935*, Cmnd 5091, (London: HMSO, 1935–36), para. 87.

37 *Report of the Broadcasting Committee 1935*.

38 The debate is reviewed in Laura Beers, "Is This Man an Anarchist? Industrial Action and the Battle for Public Opinion in Interwar Britain," *Journal of Modern History* 82, no. 1 (March 2010): 30–60.

39 Curran and Seaton, *Power without Responsibility*, 119.

40 Symons, *The General Strike*, 181.

41 "The BBC and the Strike," *The Times*.

42 "The BBC and the Strike," *The Times*.

43 Symons, *The General Strike*, 183.

44 Patrick Ford, MP, Letter to the Editor, *The Times*, June 2, 1926.

45 Reith, *Broadcast over Britain*, 34.

46 Reith, *Broadcast over Britain*, 35.

47 Richard Hughes, *A Rabbit and a Leg: Collected Plays* (London: Alfred Knopf, 1924), 142–159. A partial clip can be heard at https://audioboom.com/posts/2751698-a-comedy-of-danger-1st-play-written-for-radio-1924.

48 Interview with Richard Hughes' grandson conducted by the author in Tokyo in November 2017.

49 "Broadcasting," *Nottingham Evening Post*, January 28, 1925.

50 Dedwydd Jones, "Mining the Scenes of Radio History: Richard Hughes and 'A Comedy of Danger'," *The Stage*, May 9, 2005; Robert Landry, "One Who Loved Radio for Its Own Sake," *Variety*, January 5, 1955.

51 John Reith, "Notes for a Blattnerphone Record on Broadcasting," (1931), quoted in Asa Briggs, *Golden Age of Wireless* (Oxford: Oxford University Press, 1965), 414–415.

52 Reith, *Broadcast over Britain*, 34.

53 "Popularity of Talks," *The Times*, January 9, 1926, 18.

54 *Punch* 169, no. 4437 (December 3, 1925).

55 Briggs, *The Birth of Broadcasting*, 242–243.

56 Shaw's contribution to the language committee and to radio drama in general is discussed in L.W. Conolly, "GBS and the BBC: In the Beginning (1923–1928)," *Shaw* 23 (2003): 75–116. See also Vivian Ducat, "Bernard Shaw and the King's English," *The Atlantic*, September 1986.

57 Briggs, *The Birth of Broadcasting*, 323.

58 Reith, *Broadcast over Britain*, 272.

59 "The BBC Broadcasting Birth Control," *The Times*, November 19, 1926, 15.

60 Jean Seaton, *Pinkoes and Traitors: The BBC and the Nation, 1974–1987* (London: Profile Books, 2015), 210. Matheson's story is engagingly told in Charlotte Higgins, *This New Noise* (London: Guardian Faber Publishing, 2015), 16–36.

61 Andrew Crisell, *An Introductory History of British Broadcasting* (Abingdon: Routledge, 2002), 79.

62 Marista Leisham, *My Father: Reith of the BBC* (Edinburgh: St. Andrew Press, 2006), 112.

63 Richard Havers, *Here Is the News: The BBC and the Second World War* (London: The History Press, 2007), 4.

64 Jonathan Dimbleby, "The BBC and the Second World War," *BBC Radio 4*, aired June 2015.

65 Hidetoshi Kato, *Communications Policies in Japan* (Belgium: UNESCO, 1978), 14.

66 Mikiso Hane, *Modern Japan: A Historical Survey* (Boulder, CO: Westview Press, 1986), 120.

67 Gregory J. Kasza, *The State and Mass Media in Japan, 1918–1945* (Berkeley, CA: University of California Press, 1988).

68 Chalmers Johnson, *MITI and the Japanese Miracle: The Growth of Industrial Policy 1925–1975* (Stanford, CA: Stanford University Press, 1982).

69 Laurie Freeman, *Closing the Shop: Information Cartels and Japan's Mass Media* (Princeton: Princeton University Press, 2000), 38–50. See also Ch. 4 in William de

Lange, *A History of Japanese Journalism: Japan's Press Club as the Last Obstacle to a Mature Press* (Richmond: Curzon Press, 1998).
70 NHK, *Fifty Years of Japanese Broadcasting* (Tokyo: NHK Broadcasting Research Institute, 1977), 34.
71 Kato Motonori, "Hōsō Seido no Seiritsu to Inukai Tsuyoshi" [Inukai Tsuyoshi and the Founding of the Broadcasting System], *NHK Hōsō Kenkyū Chosa* (Broadcast Research Survey, April 2011): 58–69.
72 NHK, *Broadcasting in Japan*, 29.
73 Gregory J. Kasza, "Democracy and the Founding of Japanese Public Radio," *Journal of Asian Studies* 45, no. 4 (August 1986): 745–767.
74 "Way Is Set for Radio Broadcasting," *The Japan Times and Mail*, December 20, 1923.
75 NHK, *Broadcasting in Japan*, 34.
76 Kasza, "Democracy," 750.
77 Maruis Jansen, *The Making of Modern Japan* (Cambridge, MA: Harvard University Press, 2000), 569.
78 Kasza, "Democracy," 751.
79 Kato, "Inukai Tsuyoshi," 66.
80 "Broadcasting in Tokyo to Start Definitely in March," *The Japan Times and Mail*, December 27, 1924.
81 Kato, "Inukai Tsuyoshi," 68.
82 "JOAK Celebrates First Anniversary," *Japan Times*, March 23, 1926.
83 Sachiko Kodaira and Seiji Watanabe, "Utilization of Educational Media in Japanese Schools," NHK *Broadcast Research Institute Reports* 6, no. 6 (2008).
84 The play's cultural significance and postwar censorship are discussed in Donald Keene *Chūshingura, The Treasury of Loyal Retainers* (New York: Columbia University Press, 1971).
85 Kerim Yasar, *Electrified Voices: How the Telephone, Phonograph and Radio Shaped Modern Japan 1868–1945* (New York: Columbia University Press, 2018), 154–191.
86 Oyama Katsumi, *Shisetsu hōsōshi: kyodai mediya no ishizue o kizuta no netsujō* [Personal Broadcasters: The Passion of the Founders of Giant Media] (Tokyo: Kodansha, 2007), 38–39.
87 Aoyama Sugisaku, "Saisho no rajio dorama 'Tanko No Naka' ['The First Radio Drama: In a Pit'],*" NHK *Hōsō Bunka Chosa* [Broadcasting Culture Survey] 6, no. 5 (May 1951): 29–31.
88 Yasar, *Electrified Voices*, 181.
89 Oyama, *Shisetsu Hōsōshi*, 39.
90 Yasar, *Electrified Voices*, 155.
91 Masunori Sata and Hideo Hirahara, eds., *A History of Japanese Television Drama* (Tokyo: Japan Association of Broadcasting Art, 1991), 31.
92 In the play, a young couple and an older man find themselves trapped in an isolated hut in the midst of a life-threatening snowstorm. Suspense builds as the storm worsens and the characters struggle with fear, love, and betrayal before the old man dramatically sacrifices himself to save the lovers. I have, admittedly, absolutely no hard evidence beyond circumstantial similarities to link Fubuki Tōge to Tankō no Naka or Comedy of Danger, but Leitner writes that adaptions, including from popular radio dramas, were the "meat and potatoes" of new kabuki writing and that Uno, a highly prolific and successful dramatist of the genre, was something of a specialist at adaptations. Samuel L. Leiter, *Kabuki at the Crossroads: Years of Crisis 1952–1965* (Leiden: Brill, 2014), 210, 454.
93 NHK, *Broadcasting in Japan*, 39–41. See also: Yasar, *Electrified Voices*, 144–147.
94 Yuzo Takahashi, "A Network of Tinkerers: The Advent of the Radio and Television Receiver Industry in Japan," *Technology and Culture* 41, no. 3 (July 2000): 462.
95 Krauss, *Broadcasting Politics*, 89. Kasza, "Democracy," 87.
96 Quoted in Kasza, "Democracy," 87.
97 NHK, *Broadcasting in Japan*, 34.

98 "Radio Feud Ends after Long Battle," *Japan Times*, August 22, 1926.
99 Yukio Omori, "Broadcasting Legislation in Japan: Its Historical Process, Current Status and Future Tasks," *NHK Studies of Broadcasting* 29 (1989): 7–40.
100 NHK, *Broadcasting in Japan*, 36.
101 Kasza, "Democracy," 88.
102 Yasar, *Electrified Voices*, 128.
103 Kasza, "Democracy," 97.
104 Eric Johnston, "Truth Hurts: Censorship in the Media," *Japan Times*, August 8, 2015.
105 Yasar, *Electrified Voices*, 116.
106 Over 1 million households subscribed by early 1932. *Far Eastern Economic Review* 28, no. 8 (August 1932): 386.
107 David I. Kertzer, *Ritual, Politics and Power* (New Haven: Yale University Press, 1988), 23; Sandra Wilson, "Enthroning Hirohito: Culture and Nation in 1920s," *Japan Journal of Japanese Studies* 37, no. 2 (Summer 2011): 289–323, 297.
108 Wilson, "Enthroning Hirohito," 309.
109 "Burial at Asakawa Takes Place at Dawn," *Japan Times and Mail*, February 9, 1927.
110 "Prime Minister Wakatsuki to Speak over Radio," *Japan Times and Mail*, January 9, 1927.
111 Gordon Daniels and Philip Charrier, "Nation Shall Speak Peace Unto Nation: The BBC and Japan 1929–1939," in *History of Anglo-Japanese Relations, 1600–2000, Volume V: Social and Cultural Perspectives*, eds. Gordon Daniels and Chushichi Tsuzuki (Basingstoke: Palgrave MacMillan, 2002).
112 Nagahara also notes the editorial pressures on NHK exercised both externally by the Home Ministry, which claimed the rights to radio censorship, and internally by Japan's traditionally minded musical establishment. Hiromu Nagahara, *Tokyo Boogie-Woogie: Japan's Pop Era and Its Discontents* (Cambridge, MA: Harvard University Press, 2017), 41, 74.
113 Yasar, *Electrified Voices*, 127.
114 NHK, *Broadcasting in Japan*, 45.
115 NHK, *Broadcasting in Japan*, 41.
116 Natsuko Fukue, "Wake Up, Hike Out, Tune In," *Japan Times*, July 22, 2009.
117 Laurie Anne Freeman, *Closing the Shop: Information Cartels and Japan's Mass Media* (Princeton, NJ: Princeton University Press, 2000), 52–53.
118 Yujiro Chiba, "Broadcast Law and Self-Control in the Broadcasting Industry," *International Communication Gazette* 6, no. 1 (February 1960): 23–33.
119 NHK *Fifty Years of Japanese Broadcasting* (Tokyo: NHK Broadcasting Research Institute, 1977), 190 quoted in Kasza, "Democracy," 92.
120 Kasza, "Democracy," 94.
121 Akiko Takeyama, *Rajio no Jidai: Rajio wa chanoma no shuyakudatta* [The Radio Era: Radio Was the Main Character in the Tea Room] (Tokyo: Seikai Shisosha, 2002).
122 Mitoji Nishimoto, *The Development of Educational Broadcasting in Japan* (Tokyo: Charles Tuttle, 1969), 14–15.
123 Nishimoto, *Development of Educational Broadcasting*, 14–16.
124 Nishimoto, *Development of Educational Broadcasting*, 19.
125 Nishimoto, *Development of Educational Broadcasting*, 37–38.
126 Gordon Daniels, "Japanese Broadcasting in the Pacific War," in *The Routledge History of Modern Japan: Shōwa Japan*, vol. II, ed. Stephen Large (Abingdon: Routledge, 1999), 272.
127 Aaron Skabelund, "Fascism's Furry Friends," in *The Culture of Japanese Fascism*, ed. Alan Tansman (Durham: Duke University Press, 2009), 173. The Hachiko Statue outside Shibuya Station remains an iconic meeting point, and the story received a Richard Gere update in 2009's *Hachi: A Dog Tale*.
128 Nishimoto, *Development of Educational Broadcasting*, 38.
129 Kasza, "Democracy," 95–96.
130 A. Morgan Young, *Imperial Japan 1926–1936* (Westport: Greenwood Press, 1974).

131 Takahashi, "A Network of Tinkerers," 464.
132 Masami Ito, *Broadcasting in Japan* (London: Routledge, 1978), 13.
133 Jane Robbins, "Presenting Japan: Overseas Broadcasting by Japan during the Manchurian Incident 1931–1937," *Japan Forum* 13, no. 1 (April 2001): 41–54.
134 This included a ban on NHK's traditional rendition of Auld Lang Syne every New Year's Eve. See Nishimoto, *Development of Educational Broadcasting*, 50.
135 Kasza, "Democracy," 256–257.
136 Ellen Schattschneider, "The Work of Sacrifice in the Age of Mechanical Reproduction," in *The Culture of Japanese Fascism*, 300.
137 Kasza, "Democracy," 262–263 quoting NHK, ed., *Nihon Hōsō Shi* [History of Japanese Broadcasting], vol. 1 (Tokyo: NHK), 495.
138 Jane Robbins, *Tokyo Calling: Japanese Overseas Radio Broadcasting 1937–1945* (Florence: European Press Academic Publishing, 2001).
139 NHK, *History of Broadcasting*, 66–67.
140 Daniels, "Japanese Broadcasting in the Pacific War," 279.
141 Daniels, "Japanese Broadcasting in the Pacific War," 277–278.

References

Beers, Laura, "Is this Man an Anarchist? Industrial Action and the Battle for Public Opinion in Interwar Britain," *Journal of Modern History* 82, no. 1 (March 2010): 30–60.
"The BBC and the Strike," *The Times*, May 19, 1926.
Briggs, Asa, *Golden Age of Wireless* (Oxford: Oxford University Press, 1965).
Broadcasting Committee Report (Sykes Committee), Cmmd. 1951 (London: HMSO), para. 41.
"The Broadcasting Inquiry: The Attitude of the Press," *The Times*, December 18, 1925.
"Broadcasting," *Nottingham Evening Post*, January 28, 1925.
"Broadcasting in Tokyo to Start Definitely in March," *The Japan Times and Mail*, December 27, 1924.
"Burial at Asakawa Takes Place at Dawn," Japan Times and Mail, February 9, 1927.
Carroll, Tessa, "NHK and Japanese Language Policy," *Language Problems and Language Planning* 19, no. 3 (Fall 1995): 271–293.
Chiba, Yujiro, "Broadcast Law and Self-Control in the Broadcasting Industry," *International Communication Gazette* 6, no. 1 (February 1960): 23–33.
Chūshingura, Donald Keene, *The Treasury of Loyal Retainers* (New York: Columbia University Press, 1971).
Conolly, L.W., "GBS and the BBC: In the Beginning (1923–1928)," *Shaw* 23 (2003): 75–116.
Daniels, Gordon, "Japanese Broadcasting in the Pacific War," in *The Routledge History of Modern Japan: Shōwa Japan*, vol. II, ed. Stephen Large (Abingdon: Routledge, 1999), 272.
Daniels, Gordon, and Philip Charrier, "Nation Shall Speak Peace Unto Nation: The BBC and Japan 1929–1939," in *History of Anglo-Japanese Relations, 1600–2000, Volume V: Social and Cultural Perspectives*, eds. Ian Nish and Kibata Yoichi (London: Palgrave-Macmillan, 2002).
de Lange, William, *A History of Japanese Journalism: Japan's Press Club as the Last Obstacle to a Mature Press* (Richmond: Curzon Press, 1998).
Dimbleby, Jonathan, "The BBC and the Second World War," *BBC Radio 4*, aired June 2015.
Ducat, Vivian, "Bernard Shaw and the King's English," *The Atlantic*, September 1986.

Far Eastern Economic Review 28, no. 8 (August 1932): 386.

Ford, Patrick, "MP, Letter to the Editor," *The Times*, June 2, 1926.

Fukue, Natsuko, "Wake Up, Hike Out, Tune In," *Japan Times*, July 22, 2009.

Hane, Mikiso, *Modern Japan: A Historical Survey* (Boulder, CO: Westview Press, 1986), 120.

Havers, Richard, *Here is the News: The BBC in the Second World War* (Stroud: Sutton Publishing, 2008).

Higgins, Charlotte, *This New Noise* (London: Guardian Faber Publishing, 2015).

Hughes, Richard, *A Rabbit and a Leg: Collected Plays* (London: Alfred Knopf, 1924), 142–159.

Ito, Masami, *Broadcasting in Japan* (London: Routledge, 1978).

Jansen, Maruis, *The Making of Modern Japan* (Cambridge, MA: Harvard University Press, 2000).

"JOAK Celebrates First Anniversary," *Japan Times*, March 23, 1926.

Johnson, Chalmers, *MITI and the Japanese Miracle: The Growth of Industrial Policy 1925–1975* (Stanford, CA: Stanford University Press, 1982).

Johnston, Eric, "Truth Hurts: Censorship in the Media," *Japan Times*, August 8, 2015.

Jones, Dedwydd, "Mining the Scenes of Radio History: Richard Hughes and 'A Comedy of Danger,'" *The Stage*, May 9, 2005.

Kasza, Gregory J., "Democracy and the Founding of Japanese Public Radio," *Journal of Asian Studies* 45, no. 4 (August 1986): 745–767.

Kasza, Gregory J., *The State and Mass Media in Japan, 1918–1945* (Berkeley, CA: University of California Press, 1988).

Kato, Hidetoshi, *Communications Policies in Japan* (Belgium: UNESCO, 1978), 14.

Katsumi, Oyama, *Shisetsu hōsōshi: kyodai mediya no ishizue o kizuta no netsujō* [Personal Broadcasters: The Passion of the Founders of Giant Media] (Tokyo: Kodansha, 2007), 38–39.

Kertzer, David I., *Ritual, Politics and Power* (New Haven: Yale University Press, 1988).

Kodaira, Sachiko, and Seiji Watanabe, "Utilization of Educational Media in Japanese Schools," NHK *Broadcast Research Institute Reports* 6, no. 6 (2008).

Küng-Shankleman, Lucy, *Inside the BBC and CNN* (London: Routledge, 2000).

Landry, Robert, "One Who Loved Radio for Its Own Sake," *Variety*, January 5, 1955.

Leiter, Samuel L., *Kabuki at the Crossroads: Years of Crisis 1952–1965* (Leiden: Brill, 2014).

"Melba's 1000 Mile Song," *The Daily Mail*, June 15, 1920.

Motonori, Kato, "Hōsō Seido no Seiritsu to Inukai Tsuyoshi [Inukai Tsuyoshi and the Founding of the Broadcasting System]," *NHK Hōsō Kenkyū Chosa* (Broadcast Research Survey, April 2011): 58–69.

Nagahara, Hiromu, *Tokyo Boogie-Woogie: Japan's Pop Era and its Discontents* (Cambridge: Harvard University Press, 2017).

"New Broadcast Era: Mr Baldwin on the Changes," *The Times*, December 17, 1926.

Nishimoto, Mitoji, *The Development of Educational Broadcasting in Japan* (Tokyo: Charles Tuttle, 1969).

Omori, Yukio, "Broadcasting Legislation in Japan: Its Historical Process, Current Status and Future Tasks," *NHK Studies of Broadcasting* 29 (1989): 7–40.

Pickard, Victor, *America's Battle for Media Democracy: The Triumph of Corporate Libertarianism and the Future of Media Reform* (Cambridge: Cambridge University Press, 2014).

"Prime Minister Wakatsuki to Speak Over Radio," *Japan Times and Mail*, January 9, 1927.

"Radio Feud Ends After Long Battle," *Japan Times*, August 22, 1926.

Reith, John, *Broadcast Over Britain* (London: Hodder and Staunton, 1924).

Reith, John, "Memorandum," to *Report of the Broadcasting Committee* (Beveridge Report) Cmmd. 8117, appendix H, paper 62, (London: HMSO) 1949.

Report of the Broadcasting Committee (Crawford Committee) Cmnd. 2599 (London: HMSO), 1925.

Report of the Broadcasting Committee 1935, Cmnd 5091 (London: HMSO, 1935–36), para. 87.

Robbins, Jane, "Presenting Japan: Overseas Broadcasting by Japan during the Manchurian Incident 1931–1937," *Japan Forum* 13, no. 1 (April 2001) 41–54.

Robbins, Jane, *Tokyo Calling: Japanese Overseas Radio Broadcasting 1937–1945* (Florence: European Press Academic Publishing, 2001).

Sarnoff, David, *Looking Ahead: The Papers of David Sarnoff* (New York: McGraw Hill, 1968).

Sata, Masunori, and Hideo Hirahara, eds., *A History of Japanese Television Drama* (Tokyo: Japan Association of Broadcasting Art, 1991), 31.

Schattschneider, Ellen, "The Work of Sacrifice in the Age of Mechanical Reproduction," in *The Culture of Japanese Fascism*, ed. Alan Tansman (Durham: Duke University Press, 2009), 300.

Seaton, Jean, *Pinkoes and Traitors: The BBC and the Nation, 1974–1987* (London: Profile Books, 2015).

Seaton, Jean, and James Curran, *Power Without Responsibility The Press, Broadcasting and New Media in Britain* (Oxon: Taylor & Francis, 2003).

Skabelund, Aaron, "Fascism's Furry Friends," in *The Culture of Japanese Fascism*, ed. Alan Tansman (Durham: Duke University Press, 2009), 173.

Sugisaku, Aoyama, "Saisho no rajio dorama 'Tanko No Naka' ['The First Radio Drama: In a Pit']," NHK *Hōsō Bunka Chosa* [Broadcasting Culture Survey] 6, no. 5 (May 1951): 29–31.

Symons, Julian, *The General Strike: A Historical Portrait* (London: Cresset Press, 1959).

Takahashi, Yuzo, "A Network of Tinkerers: The Advent of the Radio and Television Receiver Industry in Japan," *Technology and Culture* 41, no. 3 (July 2000): 462.

Takeyama, Akiko, *Rajio no Jidai: Rajio wa chanoma no shuyakudatta* [The Radio Era: Radio Was the Main Character in the Tea Room] (Tokyo: Seikai Shisosha, 2002).

"Way is Set for Radio Broadcasting," *The Japan Times and Mail*, December 20, 1923.

Wilson, Sandra, "Enthroning Hirohito: Culture and Nation in 1920s," *Japan Journal of Japanese Studies* 37, no. 2 (Summer 2011).

Yasar, Kerim, *Electrified Voices: How the Telephone, Phonograph and Radio Shaped Modern Japan 1868–1945* (New York: Columbia University Press, 2018).

Young, A. Morgan, *Imperial Japan 1926–1936* (Westport: Greenwood Press, 1974).

5 NHK Remade (1945–1952)

The Allied Occupation had the twin goals of demilitarizing and democratizing Japan. SCAP, as the authorities led by Supreme Commander Allied Powers Douglas MacArthur were known, pursued sweeping social, economic, and political reforms with the revival of press freedom a central part of their mission. The Broadcast Law of 1950 was the centerpiece of the regulatory framework for broadcast media for the next half-century, establishing NHK as a publicly funded, politically independent national public broadcaster coexisting with a vibrant commercial sector. However, there were deep disagreements between and among Japanese and American interests over the future of Japan's media and NHK's place within it. Accordingly, the Broadcast Law, like so much of the Occupation's legacy, was the result of often-messy compromises between these competing constituencies.[1] This chapter examines how these political battles came to shape the form NHK has today.

The long-term Allied goal was democracy for Japan, including freedom of speech and a free press. In the short term, however, the authorities faced immense humanitarian and economic crises, and ruled autocratically. SCAP accordingly and paradoxically employed widespread censorship to stifle dissent and resistance to their democratizing mission.[2] In addition, they actively used all forms of mass media from radio to movies to disseminate liberal values, with NHK central to these efforts.[3]

Practical disagreements over how to manage the competing demands of long-term liberty versus short-term stability and security mapped, to some extent, onto existing ideological divisions between progressives and conservatives within both the Japanese and American camps. These fights resulted in a series of political compromises, reflected in, for example, the 1947 Constitution.[4] Freedom of Speech was guaranteed in Article 21 which states:

> Freedom of assembly and association as well as speech, press and all other forms of expression are guaranteed. No censorship shall be maintained, nor shall the secrecy of any means of communication be violated.[5]

DOI: 10.4324/b23015-5

However, as a result of disagreements among the various constituencies involved in drafting the document, there was, and remains, a constitutional loophole to these protections. Article 12 states:

> The freedom and rights guaranteed to the people by this Constitution shall be maintained by the constant endeavor of the people, *who shall refrain from any abuse of these freedoms and rights and shall always be responsible for utilizing them for the public welfare.*

(Emphasis added)

While generally unused, the "public welfare" provision remains an avenue by which authorities have on occasion justified infringements on speech.[6]

Ideological and interest-group battles played out in negotiations over broadcasting policies, including NHK's status, the extent of regulatory control, and the future of commercial broadcasters. The central debate was whether to follow the British model, with NHK continuing as a public service monopoly, or adopt a dual system with NHK and commercial broadcasters. Japanese interests were divided. The national newspapers, former commercial broadcasters, and other corporate interests were quick to demand the right to resume their long-curtailed commercial broadcasting operations, with the Mainichi Shimbun submitting a request for a commercial broadcasting license in September 1945, just weeks after the war ended. Left-wingers, labor unions, and intellectuals also demanded free speech and a free press. On the other side, conservative elites in the Diet and the bureaucrats of the Ministry of Communications favored greater political control over the press in the defense, as they saw it, of stability against threats such as communism.

Within SCAP, progressives and New Dealers argued for a free press, commercial broadcasting, and an end to the government-controlled media that NHK had become during the war. According to an early memorandum:

> In order further to encourage liberal tendencies in Japan and establish free access to the news sources of the world, steps will be taken by the Japanese government forthwith to eliminate government-created barriers to dissemination of news and to remove itself from direct or indirect control of newspapers and news agencies.[7]

One of the loudest voices in CIE's media policy was Frank Shozo Baba, a Japanese-American who had worked for the Voice of America during the War.[8] Baba had been the inspiration behind the *Shinsō no ko da*, discussed subsequently, but believed that edifying documentaries such as this were not enough to retain mass audiences. He had, for example, insisted that the language used in all NHK broadcasts should be simplified so that it could be easily understood by 14 year olds.[9] Moreover, he feared that unless commercial broadcasting were introduced, NHK could easily slip back into authoritarian ways. Accordingly, he pushed for popular programming, first at NHK and then in the commercial sector he helped revive. Stating that "the basis of broadcasting is to be for the public," Baba argued that the long-term health of democracy in Japan could be best served by a flourishing commercial sector.[10]

However, the more conservative SCAP leadership were the ones calling the shots, and they believed that neither the political nor the economic environment was ready for press freedom. In the first place, they doubted that Japan's devastated economy could sustain a dual system. In addition, they were angered that Japanese news sources were reporting stories hostile to the Occupation, such as rapes committed by US servicemen.[11] Most importantly, according to historians Catherine Luther and Douglas Boyd, they saw in NHK an important tool to help control the country.[12] Accordingly:

> The present system of distribution of news . . . will be permitted under strict censorship until such time as private enterprise creates acceptable substitutes for the present monopoly.[13]

Specifically, SCAP continued, "The Supreme Commander will suspend any publication or radio station which publishes information that fails to adhere to the truth or disturbs public tranquility."[14] Memoranda for the Press Code and for the Radio Code included the strictures that "newscasts must be factual and completely devoid of editorial opinion" and that "there shall be no false or destructive criticism of the Allied Powers."[15]

To that end, censorship was practiced by the Civil Censorship Detachment (CCD), whose blacklist of impermissible content included discussion of the food shortages. *Kimigayo*, the national anthem that had played nightly during the war, was promptly banned. The Occupiers were, understandably, particularly wary of traditional Japanese folk stories in which loyal troops of defeated masters meted out bloody revenge on their conquering foes, and favorites, including *Chūshingara*, were barred from stage and microphone.[16] Censorship of broadcasting was lifted only in 1949.[17] Even then, SCAP blocked commercial broadcasting until 1951 in order to better control public discourse.[18] The Japanese simply had to live with the inconsistency between the SCAP's insistence that the press be free and independent and their equally vehement insistence that the same press must behave responsibly, as they saw it, and actively support Occupation goals.[19]

SCAP saw two valuable roles for NHK. First, General MacArthur saw the broadcaster's national reach and monopoly power as valuable tools for managing the day-to-day administration of the Occupation, for example, by relaying instructions to distant officials. NHK's second role was to serve SCAP's self-appointed task of reeducating the Japanese about democratic values and civic responsibility. Conventional wisdom among the Allies was that Japan's turn to fascism had been facilitated by underdeveloped popular sense of civic duty, and that their role was therefore

> [t]o help change the present cynical, and therefore, passive attitude towards government to one of more positive participation, and to awaken the people to the fact that it is their responsibility to maintain a government which they can trust.[20]

SCAP officials quickly realized that a government-controlled radio monopoly was perfectly suited to that task.[21] NHK would enjoy far greater freedom than before, but programming would have to serve SCAP's goals.

SCAP's Civil Information and Education Section (CIE) was charged with educating the Japanese citizenry in the ways of democracy.[22] Appropriately, it was located directly in the NHK building.[23] NHK itself came under the direction of the CIE Radio Branch, headed first by two US experts in psychological warfare, and later by two former NBC staffers.[24] Senior managers with ties to the old regime were purged. Takano Iwasaburō, a socialist academic, was appointed new president. Furukaki Tetsurō, a cosmopolitan graduate of Lyons University and long-time foreign correspondent for the progressive *Asahi Shimbun*, served as his general manager and successor as president.[25] Most junior staff were retained, old broadcasting frequencies restored, and SCAP instructed that radio set production should be stepped up to facilitate audience growth. Information essential for democracy to function, such as that pertaining to elections was, naturally, required. In April 1946, over 2,000 candidates for the national Diet elections were given airtime, and large numbers of voters chose their candidates based on those broadcasts.[26] But SCAP also demanded that NHK programs helped disseminate democratic values.

CIE first demanded programs tackling the painful realities of the war. *Hōsō Toronkai* ("Open Forum") allowed all manner of discussion, including Communists questioning the Emperor system. *Shinsō wa ko da* ('Now, it can be Told') and *Shinsō Bako* ("Truth Box"), written and produced by Baba and his staff at CIE, raised ugly issues from the recent past, including the Nanking massacre and the Bataan "Death March."[27] "Those Who Defended Freedom" examined the lives of resisters to the authoritarian regime. But these programs proved highly controversial and were soon withdrawn following fierce backlash from listeners, and even death threats to NHK staff.[28]

A more palatable means of spreading democratic values were *Vox pop* programs such as *Watashitachi no Kotoba* ("In our Own Words") and *Gaito Rokuon* ("Street Recordings"), which gave ordinary citizens a chance to complain about problems such as food shortages. The latter broke extraordinary new ground in the field of broadcast documentary-making: an early, highly controversial episode included interviews with sex workers in the red light district of Tokyo.[29] In 1946, NHK even aired conversations recorded between Emperor Hirohito and ordinary citizens he met on official visits.

Informational programs for workers, teachers, and miners were all encouraged too: each had their own "Hour."[30] Most popular of all was *Nodo Jiman* (literally "pride in my voice" but more often referred to in English as "Amateur Singing Contest"). As Dower points out, all of these programs represented a strikingly egalitarian departure from prewar days when ordinary people would never have been heard on the airwaves.[31] CIE believed that programming for women was particularly important, and was actively involved in all aspects of producing the first few editions of *Fuji no Jikan* ('Women's Hour') as well as "Family Hour" and "Baby Hour."[32] The Americans even saw to it that a woman, Fuji Eguchi, was appointed head of women's programming, thus becoming the first woman to hold a policymaking position within NHK.[33] However, NHK tended to either avoid religious programming altogether or, if that were unavoidable, to include all religious viewpoints in the segment. Managers believed they were bound by Article 20 of the new Constitution that decreed the separation of church and state.[34] Educational broadcasting was revived almost immediately, in October 1945. CIE worked closely with NHK and the Ministry of Education (*Monbushō*) to produce school broadcasts. English lessons were also very popular, and *Come, Come English*, hosted daily by Hirakawa Tada'ichi and exuding cheerful optimism about democracy and the Occupation, became wildly successful. Hirakawa, a Christian progressive, was voted the most popular public figure in Japan behind only the Emperor and MacArthur.[35]

Entertainment broadcasts began within a month of the war's end, with musical shows, quizzes, talent contests, and dramas. Takemae Eiji argues for the importance of such programs in generating goodwill for the American occupiers in a form of what he describes as democratization from below.[36] New shows were often modeled on US originals, but traditional *rakugo* and *manzai* comedy and *naniwa-bushi* performances were also popular. The New Year's Eve Singing Contest *Kōhaku Uta Gassen*, originally intended as a professional counterpart to *Nodo Jiman*, was to become wildly popular. Production was delayed because SCAP interpreted *gassen* as "battle" and insisted on a less militaristic title. For a few years the word *shiai* ('match') was used, before the show began in its present form with its original title in 1951. Both singing contests have remained immensely popular. Shelley Brunt argues that by celebrating a common, if diverse, national musical tradition at the culturally significant moment of New Year's Eve, *Kōhaku* "serves to regenerate the national community by confirming its people's cultural identity." This role, she notes, was never more important than in the confusion of the postwar period.[37]

Many of NHK's journalists and creative staff were delighted with the environment. They appreciated that they had vastly more freedom than in the war or even prewar era, although they also chafed at what one senior official described as "interference from the CIE in the name of guidance."[38] An early casualty of SCAP censorship was the satirical sketch show *Uta no Shimbun* ("Song Newspaper" 1946). Conceived by NHK Music Director Maruyama Tetsuo, the show used music and stories to air social and political commentary. Individual sketches had often been banned by CIE for seeming too controversial or subversive to Occupation goals, and the program itself was canceled within months. Following a change to a more relaxed leadership at CIE, Murayama was allowed to produce a similar show, *Nichiyo Gorakuban* (Sunday Entertainment Edition), which became *Yumoa Gekijo* (Comedy Theatre, 1952–1954).

NHK's new freedom was by no means absolute, however. In September 1946, the Japanese Congress of Industrial Unions (*Sanbetsu Kaigi*) called a strike in support of labor disputes at the *Yomiuri* newspaper.[39] NHK employees, members of the affiliated All Japan News and Radio Workers Union, came out in solidarity.

Officials from the Ministry of Communications, backed by SCAP, promptly took direct control of NHK, managing broadcasting for a two-week period in October 1946.[40]

The intense debate over commercial broadcasting was resolved in 1950, when the Diet passed laws establishing the regulatory framework for Japan's postwar media environment.[41] The Broadcast Law (*Hōsō Hō*) reestablished NHK as a special public corporation (*tokushu hōjin*).[42] The law was intended to give NHK freedom from the political control of the prewar era.[43] To that end, the law established a 12-seat Board of Governors who would choose the president and set management policy independent of political interference. The governors would be appointed by the Prime Minister, but only with the approval of both Houses of the Diet. They were to be drawn from the fields of education, culture, science, and industry, and eight would represent different regions of Japan. Not more than four could belong to the same political party.

NHK was forbidden from commercial activities. Funding would come from receiver fees (*jushinryō*) in an arrangement that was similar to the BBC but went even further in providing insulation from political interference. Owners of radios and televisions would be required to enter a contract with NHK, who would collect the fees from contract holders directly. This gave NHK complete control over its revenues, unlike in the United Kingdom where the Post Office collected fees and passed them along to the BBC. Another major difference to the BBC system was that there were no penalties for those individual receiver owners who didn't sign a contract or pay the fees. Such a requirement was regarded as being too unpopular to be politically viable. The Broadcast Law also required that NHK conduct research into broadcasting technologies, regularizing the central role that NHK was already playing in Japan's industrial policy.

The laws also laid out the broadcasting environment in which NHK would operate according to three broad principles.[44] First, commercial radio (and soon television) would be permitted, so NHK lost the broadcasting monopoly that the BBC retained for another decade. This represented a win for Frank Baba and for the newspaper companies, represented by the NSK (Nihon Shimbun Kyōkai), which had raised fears of censorship in their lobbying against too much state control.[45] According to the compromise worked out, they would be allowed to own stakes in commercial radio stations and hence came to represent well-funded competition to NHK.[46] Many Americans had also supported the speedy introduction of commercial broadcasting, most notably in SCAP's Legal Section, which was highly influenced by the First Amendment in the American Constitution.[47] However, both NHK and the Ministry of Telecommunications had sought to delay or even prevent commercialization, in order to protect NHK's dominance.[48] Their efforts resulted in legal restrictions on commercial broadcaster ownership, which had the effect of preventing the sort of large, centralized networks found in the United States.[49]

The second principle of the Broadcast Law was that freedom of broadcasting was guaranteed only if it were in the public interest. The law articulated four requirements for programming to govern NHK, as well as the commercial

stations. Broadcasts of news and information were required to follow the following stipulations: (i) to not disturb public security and good morals; (ii) to
be politically impartial; (iii) to broadcast news without distorting facts; and (iv)
regarding controversial issues, to clarify the points of issue from as many angles
as possible.[50]

The requirements of impartiality and the airing of multiple views on controversial issues reflected US influence. They closely resembled the Fairness Doctrine,
which was being debated concurrently in the United States and which the FCC
adopted in 1949. That year, two senior officials at the Ministry of Telecommunications had visited the United States to study broadcasting and particularly the role
of the FCC. The requirement that broadcasting "shall not disturb public security
and good morals" had for years been a bone of contention between conservatives
in the Diet and the Ministry of Communications on the one hand and the Japanese
press and American free speech advocates on the other. The stipulation had been
debated, accepted, and then abandoned in earlier drafts, and hastily reinserted just
before the final Diet vote.[51]

The third pillar of Japan's new broadcasting landscape was the Radio Regulatory Commission Law, which established an independent regulatory authority
for broadcasting, the *Denpa Kanri Iinkai* (Radio Regulatory Commission). This
reform, proposed by SCAP, was comparable to the US Federal Communications
Commission (FCC). The intention had been to create a regulatory authority for
media that would be independent of the sort of direct press control the state had
exercised prewar. But it had been fiercely resisted by an odd coalition of Japanese interests. Progressives and the newspaper industry demanded an entirely
free press, fearing any institutionalization of state control. By contrast, the
Ministry of Telecommunications wanted to keep direct press control for itself.
Ultimately, the law was passed, thanks to the personal intervention of General
MacArthur, who wrote directly to Prime Minister Yoshida Shigeru insisting on
its passage.[52]

With the new regulatory framework for broadcasting in place, attention turned
to television. NHK had established a research laboratory for communications
technology in 1930 and, working with the state and the electronics industry, had
been test-broadcasting television ever since. In 1951, the Diet passed a resolution to promote television sales in order to aid the fledgling consumer electronics
industry.[53] Television had not originally been part of MITI's plan for strategic
promotion but took off because of the extraordinarily high public demand.[54] The
political debate was over who would be awarded the rights to television broadcasting. In 1952, four commercial broadcasters and NHK applied to the RCC for
television licenses, but technological constraints meant the RRC could award one
or at most two.

The most prominent commercial applicant was Nippon Television (NTV)
established by Shoriki Matsutaro, owner of the Yomiuri and backed by the Asahi
and Mainichi newspapers. NTV also received support from various religious
groups, including Buddhists and Protestants who were upset at NHK's reluctance
to cover religious issues.[55] Shoriki was a larger-than-life character, a former chief

of the Tokyo secret police turned right-wing media mogul who pioneered the use of baseball to first sell newspapers and then television advertising.[56] He would later become a Cabinet Minister in the first LDP government, but immediately after the war he had been imprisoned, accused of war crimes. In 1951, Shoriki persuaded SCAP to drop their blacklisting of his business activities if he founded a commercial television station to spread anti-communism.[57]

NHK argued that it should keep its monopoly. Setting the tone for future patterns of programming, NHK explicitly distanced itself from NTV and the other by deciding to concentrate on information and education and leaving entertainment to the despised commercial rival. President Furugaki Tetsuro argued that "NHK is better situated to carry on its high quality programs than private stations."[58] The Tokyo Shimbun agreed, noting that "telecast by a commercial enterprise may result in lower quality of program, as the program makeup will be greatly influenced by the commercialism of sponsors. But we cannot expect NHK to give good entertainment."[59]

The major newspapers all backed commercial broadcasting. Their arguments invoked press freedom, free speech, and "broadcasting democracy."[60] The Yomiuri Shimbun, backer of NTV, argued:

> Operation of telecast by a public corporation will hamper growth of democracy. Domination of a means of mass communication by bureaucrats will pave the way for dictatorship. . . . Collection of TV fees will make television the possession of only a privileged few . . . [and] might constitute a violation of the Constitution.[61]

Commercial broadcasting won. The RRC awarded the sole provisional television broadcast license to NTV in August 1952.[62] This turned out to be the last act of the RCC, which was abolished immediately as soon as the Occupation ended. Regulatory authority was transferred to the MPT who awarded NHK a television license a few months later. NHK began television broadcasts in 1953, a few months ahead of NTV.

Soon after the passage of the three laws, however, the Occupation undertook the "Reverse Course." Deepening tensions with the USSR, the outbreak of the Korean War, a growing fear of communist-influenced union power, and Republican success in American congressional elections in 1952 prompted SCAP to step away from its more progressive goals in favor of anti-Communist measures. SCAP launched a national purge of suspected Communists, and approximately 120 NHK staff, the largest number of any media organization in Japan, were summarily dismissed on suspicion of harboring leftist sympathies.[63] Legal challenges by the sacked staff were dismissed, and while they won some compensation, they were not rehired.

Legacies

The Occupation's legacy on NHK is mixed and contradictory, as it was in so many other aspects of Japanese life.[64] In some ways, the explosion of vibrant, highly progressive output marked a decisive break with the past. At the very least, the period revealed that there were many talented, creative, and independent-minded people at NHK – editors, producers and educators, biting satirists, and unflinching documentary filmmakers – who might have given postwar NHK a very different vibe if given the right encouragement and support. On the other hand, the patterns of top-down managerial control and close attention from government authorities were never fully lifted. In Katō Etsurō's famous contemporary cartoon, a Japanese person revels in new-found freedom, his shackles sundered by a pair of gigantic American scissors.[65] But the passive voice of the caption says it all: "Chains were cut." Many of the freedoms granted by SCAP, from regulatory protection to editorial autonomy, came up for grabs again.

The Occupation ended in April 1952, with NHK broadcasting General MacArthur's final departure live as *Auld Lang Syne* played in the background.[66] Nightly renditions of *Kimigayo* resumed immediately. More significantly, the Diet scrapped the Radio Regulatory Authority and put broadcasting back under the jurisdiction of the Ministry of Posts and Telecommunications.[67] NHK promptly began reevaluating all programming with SCAP origins, rooting out ones deemed too radical.

Notes

1 Seiichi Murakami, "Stipulations on Programming in the Broadcast Law: The Intersection of Japanese and GHQ Agendas," *NHK Broadcasting Studies* (2009): 133–156.

2 For a contemporary account of MacArthur's contentious relationship with the Japanese press, see William Coughlin, *Conquered Press: The MacArthur Era in Japanese Journalism* (Berkeley, CA: Pacific Books, 1952).

3 Hidetoshi Kato, *Communications Policies in Japan* (Belgium: UNESCO, 1978), 15.

4 Available on the Prime Minister's Office website: http://japan.kantei.go.jp/constitution_ and_government_of_japan/constitution_e.html.

5 Constitution of Japan, Article 21. Kyoko Inoue notes the ambiguity in this articulation of press freedom, which fails to specify agency, making it unclear exactly who cannot censor. This contrasts with the First Amendment in the US Constitution, which clearly specifies who is being protected from whom. See Kyoko Inoue, *MacArthur's Japanese Constitution* (Chicago: University of Chicago Press, 1991), 73–81.

6 For example, the Supreme Court of Japan invoked Article 12 while upholding the obscenity conviction of the Japanese publisher of *Lady Chatterley's Lover*. See: Kato, *Communications Policies in Japan*, 10.

7 Government Section, Supreme Commander of the Allied Powers *Political Reorientation of Japan September 1945 to September 1948: Report*, vol. 2, SCAPIN 51, 24th September 1945 (Washington, DC: US Government Printing Office, 1949), 461.

8 Kiyoshi Ishii, *Nihon no Hōsō o Tsukutta Otoko: Furanuku Baba no Monogatari* [The Man Who Made Japanese Broadcasting: The Frank Baba Story] (Tokyo: Mainichi Shimbunsha, 1998).

9 Eiji Takemae, *Inside GHQ: The Allied Occupation of Japan and Its Legacy* (New York: Continuum Press, 2003), 398.

10 Ishii, *Baba no Monogatari*, 149–150.

11 Coughlin, *Conquered Press*, 16, 32–33.

12 Caroline Luther and Douglas Boyd, "American Occupation Control over Broadcasting in Japan, 1945–1952," *Journal of Communication* 47, no. 2 (June 1997): 39–59.

13 Government Section, Supreme Commander of the Allied Powers *Political Reorientation of Japan September 1945 to September 1948: Report*, vol. 2, SCAPIN 51, 24th September 1945 (Washington, DC: US Government Printing Office, 1949), 461.

14 Government Section, Supreme Commander of the Allied Powers *Political Reorientation of Japan September 1945–September 1948: Report*, vol. 2 Appendix B 2a (Memorandum on Civil Liberties SCAPIN 16, September 10, 1945) (Washington, DC: US Government Printing Office, 1949), 195.

15 NHK, *Broadcasting in Japan: The Twentieth Century Journey from Radio to Multimedia* (Tokyo: NHK Publications, 2002), 80.

16 For more on the conflicted attitudes of SCAP officials toward the need to censor great Japanese art, see James Brandon, "Myth and Reality: A Story of 'Kabuki' during American Censorship, 1945–1949," *Asian Theatre Journal* 23, no. 1 (2006): 1–110.

17 NHK, *Broadcasting in Japan*, 100.

18 John Dower, *Embracing Defeat: Japan in the Wake of World War Two* (New York: W.W. Norton, 1999), 206.

19 Coughlin, *Conquered Press*, 33–34.

20 Government Section, Supreme Commander for the Allied Powers *Political Reorientation of Japan: September 1945 to September 1948* (Washington, DC: Government Printing Office, 1950), vol. 1 Section XII Political Education, 365.

21 Government Section, Supreme Commander for the Allied Powers *Political Reorientation of Japan September 1945 to September 1948* (Washington, DC: Government Printing Office, 1949), vol. 1 Section XII Political Education, 367–368.

22 Peter Duus, ed., *Cambridge History of Japan*, vol. 6 (Cambridge: Cambridge University Press, 1989), 168.

23 John Dower, *Embracing Defeat Japan in the Wake of World War II* (New York: W.W. Norton & Company, 2000), 206.

24 Takemae, *Inside GHQ*, 398.

25 Takamae, *Inside GHQ*, 398.

26 Dower, *Embracing Defeat*, 244.

27 NHK, *Broadcasting in Japan*, 88–89.

28 Takemae, *Inside GHQ*, 399.

29 Akira Miyata, "Rokuon Kosei no Hassei [Birth of Radio Programs Composed of Recorded Voices]," *NHK Hōsō Bunka Kenkyūshitu Nenpō* [NHK Broadcast Culture Institute Yearbook] 60 (2016): 102. Nanako Ota's analysis of the *Gaitō Rokuon* episode in question, "How to Prevent Juvenile Delinquency Part 2: Girls under the Railroad Track" concludes that the program was a less effort at democratization than often claimed. Nanako Ota, "The Voiceful Voiceless: Rethinking the Inclusion of the Public Voice in Radio Interview Programs in Occupied Japan," *Historical Journal of Film, Radio and Television* 39, no. 3 (July 2019).

30 Takemae, *Inside GHQ*, 399.

31 Dower, *Embracing Defeat*, 244.

32 Seiichi Murakami, "GHQ no Bangumi Shidō to 'Fujin no Jikan' [GHQ's Instructions on Program-making and 'Women's Hour']," *NHK Hōsō Bunka* Monthly Report, January 2016.

33 Luther and Boyd, "American Control over Broadcasting in Japan 1945–1952," 48.

34 Yoshiya Abe, "Media and Religion under a Church-State Separation Scheme: The Japanese Case," *Social Compass* 37, no. 1 (1990): 172. Later, religious programs such as the radio show *Shūkyō no Jikan* ("The Religion Hour") or *Kokoro no Jidai* ("Age of Humanity"), which invited religious leaders and scholars to discuss current issues, were broadcast as education.

35 Takemae, *Inside GHQ*, 402.

36 Takemae, *Inside GHQ*, 402.

37 Shelley D. Brunt, "The Infinite Power of Song: Uniting Japan at the 60th Annual Kōhaku Song Contest," in *Made in Japan: Studies in Popular Music*, ed. Tōru Mitsui (New York: Routledge, 2014), 37–51.

38 Nitoji Nishimoto, *Development of Educational Broadcasting in Japan* (Tokyo: Tuttle Publishing Ltd. 1969), 78.

39 Takemae, *Inside GHQ*, 318.

40 NHK, *Broadcasting in Japan*, 85.

41 The Radio Law was concerned with the technical aspects of spectrum management. Seiichi Murakami, "Stipulations on Programming in the Broadcast Law: The Intersection of Japanese and GHQ Agendas," *NHK Broadcasting Studies*, no. 7 (2009). See also Chapter 7, "The Making of an Institution: The Rebirth of NHK" in Michael Tracey, *The Decline and Fall of Public Broadcasting* (Oxford: Oxford University Press, 1998).

42 Available on the website of the Ministry of Internal Affairs and Communications (Sōmushō) www.soumu.go.jp/main_sosiki/joho_tsusin/eng/Resources/laws/pdf/090204_5.pdf.

43 Discussed in Ellis Krauss, *Broadcasting Politics in Japan: NHK and Television News* (Ithaca, NY: Cornell University Press, 2000), 102–103.

44 NHK, *Broadcasting in Japan*, 98–103.

45 Murakami, "Stipulations on Broadcasting," 152.

46 "Commercial Firms Plan for Free Broadcasting," *Japan Times and Mail*, July 18, 1948, 1.

47 Murakami, "Stipulations on Broadcasting," 146.

48 The Ministry of Communications was broken up in 1949 into the Ministry of Postal Affairs and the Ministry of Telecommunications before reforming as the Ministry of Posts and Telecommunications in 1952. Koichi Nakano, "Becoming a Policy Ministry: The Organization and Amakudari of the Ministry of Posts and Telecommunications," *Journal of Japanese Studies* 24, no. 1 (Winter 1998): 98–100.

49 James D. White, *Global Media: The TV Revolution in Asia* (London: Routledge, 2005), 87.

50 The Broadcast Law, Ch. II, Article 44, quoted in Murakami, "Stipulations," 151.

51 Murakami, "Stipulations," 150–151.

52 "Denpa Kanri Iinkai o Meguru Giron no Kiseki [How the Debate on the Radio Regulatory Commission Developed]," *NHK Hōsō Bunka Kenkyūjo*, March 2010.

53 Yoshioka Hitoshi, "The Advent of the TV Age," quoted in Nakayama Shigeru and Gotō Kunio, eds., *A Social History of Science and Technology in Contemporary Japan* (Baldwyn North, Australia: Trans Pacific Press, November 2001).

54 Yoshioka, "The Advent of the TV Age."

55 "Protestants Support TV," *Japan Times*, December 17, 1951.

56 Jayson Makoto Chun, *A Nation of a Hundred Million Idiots: A Social History of Japanese Television 1953–1973* (New York: Routledge, 2007).

57 "Matsutaro Shoriki: Japan's Citizen Kane," *The Economist*, December 22, 2012.

58 Kiyoaki Murata, "NHK on the Air," *Japan Times*, September 12, 1952.

59 Tokyo Shimbun, "Television in Japan," quoted in *Japan Times*, May 27, 1952.

60 "Commercial Broadcasters Need Cooperation of Newspapers," *Japan Times*, May 12, 1966.

61 Yomiuri Shimbun, "Telecast in Japan," quoted in *Japan Times*, June 25, 1952.

62 "Nippon TV Given Video License," *Japan Times*, August 2, 1952.

63 NHK, *Broadcasting in Japan*, 100.

64 See, for example: Edwin O. Reischauer et al., "The Allied Occupation: How Significant Was It?" in *Japan Examined: Perspectives on Modern Japanese History*, eds. Harry Wray and Hilary Conroy (Honolulu: University of Hawaii Press, 1983).

65 Reproduced and discussed in Dower, *Embracing Defeat*, 70–71.

66 Dower, *Embracing Defeat*, 549.

67 Nakano, "Becoming a Policy Ministry," 99–100.

References

Abe, Yoshiya, "Media and Religion under a Church-State Separation Scheme: The Japanese Case," *Social Compass* 37, no. 1 (1990): 172.

Brandon, James, "Myth and Reality: A Story of 'Kabuki' during American Censorship, 1945–1949," *Asian Theatre Journal* 23, no. 1 (2006): 1–110.

Chun, Jayson Makoto, *A Nation of a Hundred Million Idiots: A Social History of Japanese Television 1953–1973* (New York: Routledge, 2007).

"Commercial Broadcasters Need Cooperation of Newspapers," *Japan Times*, May 12, 1966.

"Commercial Firms Plan for Free Broadcasting," *Japan Times and Mail*, July 18, 1948.

Coughlin, William, *Conquered Press: The MacArthur Era in Japanese Journalism* (Berkeley CA: Pacific Press, 1952).

"Denpa Kanri Iinkai o Meguru Giron no Kiseki [How the Debate on the Radio Regulatory Commission Developed]," NHK *Hōsō Bunka Kenkyūjo*, March 2010.

Dower, John, *Embracing Defeat Japan in the Wake of World War II* (New York: W.W. Norton & Company, 2000), 206.

Duus, Peter, ed., *Cambridge History of Japan*, vol. 6 (Cambridge: Cambridge University Press, 1989).

Inoue, Kyoko, *MacArthur's Japanese Constitution* (Chicago: University of Chicago Press, 1991). Const. of Japan.

Ishii, Kiyoshi, *Nihon no Hōsō o Tsukutta Otoko: Furanuku Baba no Monogatari* [The Man Who Made Japanese Broadcasting: The Frank Baba Story] (Tokyo: Mainichi Shimbunsha, 1998).

Kato, Hidetoshi, *Communications Policies in Japan* (Belgium: UNESCO, 1978).

Luther, Caroline, and Douglas Boyd, "American Occupation Control over Broadcasting in Japan, 1945–1952," *Journal of Communication* 47, no. 2 (June 1997): 39–59.

"Matsutaro Shoriki: Japan's Citizen Kane," *The Economist*, December 22, 2012.

Miyata, Akira, "Rokuon Kosei no Hassei [Birth of Radio Programs Composed of Recorded Voices]," *NHK Hōsō Bunka Kenkyūshitu Nenpō* [NHK Broadcast Culture Institute Yearbook] 60 (2016).

Murakami, Seiichi, "GHQ no Bangumi Shidō to 'Fujin no Jikan' [GHQ's Instructions on Program-making and 'Women's Hour']," *NHK Hōsō Bunka*, Monthly Report, January 2016.

Murakami, Seiichi, "Stipulations on Programming in the Broadcast Law: The Intersection of Japanese and GHQ Agendas," *NHK Broadcasting Studies*, no. 7 (2009): 133–156.

Murata, Kiyoaki, "NHK on the Air," *Japan Times*, September 12, 1952.

Nakano, Koichi, "Becoming a Policy Ministry: The Organization and Amakudari of the Ministry of Posts and Telecommunications," *Journal of Japanese Studies* 24, no. 1 (Winter 1998): 98–100.

"Nippon TV Given Video License," *Japan Times*, August 2, 1952.

Ota, Nanako, "The Voiceful Voiceless: Rethinking the Inclusion of the Public Voice in Radio Interview Programs in Occupied Japan," *Historical Journal of Film, Radio and Television* 39, no. 3 (July 2019).

"Protestants Support TV," *Japan Times*, December 17, 1951.

Reischauer, Edwin O., et al., "The Allied Occupation: How Significant Was It?" in *Japan Examined: Perspectives on Modern Japanese History*, eds. Harry Wray and Hilary Conroy (Honolulu: University of Hawaii Press, 1983).

Shigeru, Nakayama, and Gotō Kunio, eds., *A Social History of Science and Technology in Contemporary Japan* (Baldwyn North, Australia: Trans Pacific Press, November 2001).

Shimbun, Tokyo, "Television in Japan," quoted in *Japan Times*, May 27, 1952.

Shimbun, Yomiuri, "Telecast in Japan," quoted in *Japan Times*, June 25, 1952.

Takemae, Eiji, *Inside GHQ: The Allied Occupation of Japan and its Legacy* (New York: Continuum Press, 2003).

Tracey, Michael, *The Decline and Fall of Public Broadcasting* (Oxford: Oxford University Press, 1998).

White, James D., *Global Media: The TV Revolution in Asia* (London: Routledge, 2005).

6   Sex and Violence (Television 1950s–1970s)

"Television is sure to exert a revolutionary influence on all our lives," announced President Furukaki Tetsurō as NHK's first national TV broadcast began in February 1953.[1] Sure enough, television soon replaced radio at the heart of daily life and so became the central battleground for the immense social and political upheavals of the 1960s and 1970s. In the United States, elite fears about commercial television's malign cultural influence, famously described by US FCC Chairman Newton Minnow as a "vast wasteland" were sufficiently grave as to catalyze the founding of PBS and NPR. Similar anxieties in Britain and Japan intertwined with elite fears that television would serve as a Trojan Horse for the Americanization of their national cultures, a prospect made more toxic by broader national angst about American hegemony and, in Britain's case, imperial decline. NHK and the BBC became central actors in intense struggles over social values and national culture, serving as both agents and subjects of television's expanding social influence. Meanwhile, the vast potential for advertising profits sparked intense struggles between the public broadcasters and their commercial rivals.

In Britain, the BBC lost its broadcasting monopoly in both radio and TV. But rather than accommodating independent television, the BBC chose to tackle its commercial rivals head-on, attempting to match them in all programming genres. Not unrelatedly, the Corporation undertook a profound shift in programming philosophy, seeking to lead rather than merely reflect the many of the profound progressive changes in social attitudes that the 1960s wrought. In doing so, the BBC made a sharp break with the generally sympathetic reflections of elite establishment values that its programs had hitherto displayed. In the words of Jean Seaton, "Somewhere in the sixties, Reithian conservatism had mutated into something like Reithian liberalism."[2]

In Japan, by contrast, NHK's response to social upheaval was to retreat from controversy as it sought to uphold and promote a more traditional, conservative set of national values. In so doing, NHK and the commercial stations came to an implicit division of labor, with NHK sticking to news, information, education, and high-culture content, while commercial television programming focused more heavily on popular mass entertainment.

DOI: 10.4324/b23015-6

Breaking the BBC Monopoly

The BBC's prominence during the Second World War had an unexpected down-side: its monopoly became the subject of intense debate. Reith had always argued that "it was the brute force of monopoly that enabled the BBC to become what it did . . . that made it possible for a policy of moral responsibility to be followed."[3]

> The present system [i.e. BBC monopoly] is best suited to the circumstances of the United Kingdom. Where only a limited number of suitable wavelengths is available to cover a comparatively small and densely populated area, an inte-grated broadcasting system is . . . the only satisfactory means of ensuring that the wavelengths available are used in the best interests of the community[4]

Prime Minister Clement Attlee's Labour Government, which had won a sur-prisingly handsome victory over Winston Churchill's Conservatives in 1945, was sympathetic to the BBC. Attlee was pursuing an ambitious program of social reform that included the introduction of public welfare and pensions; the found-ing of the National Health Service; and the nationalization of the coal, steel, and railway industries. Public broadcasting fitted the agenda perfectly.

But the authorities were aware that times were changing. Listeners were demanding greater choice, while airwaves were being transformed by the success of offshore commercial radio stations such as Radio Caroline, broadcasting from ships off the English coast, and Radio Luxembourg, based on the European con-tinent.[5] Both were heard all over Britain and supported by British advertisers but were beyond the reach of UK authorities.[6] Radio Luxembourg's audience of up to one million in 1949 was less than the seven million listeners to the BBC's Light Program, but Luxembourg's popularity among the young, women, and the work-ing classes gave cause for concern to the old establishment. Many policymak-ers, sensitive to Britain's declining international prestige, feared that powerful US broadcasters would set up in Europe and dominate the airwaves.[7] Thus, while the Government renewed the BBC Charter in 1946, it did so for only a five-year term to allow full debate on the future of postwar broadcasting.

Criticism of the BBC monopoly came from diverse sources. Backbenchers in the Conservative Party opposed monopoly on both ideological and commercial grounds. They were joined by economic interests such as the Incorporated Soci-ety of British Advertisers. *The Economist* magazine wanted competition and was sympathetic to the Conservative backbenchers sending out "private enterprise skirmishers to harry the flanks" of a nationalized industry.[8] Progressives such as the Liberal Research Group saw monopoly as an infringement on democratic free expression, while fascism had demonstrated the dangers of state-controlled pro-paganda. Scottish nationalists disliked the BBC's Southern bias and the "emascu-lated voices" of its usually English announcers.[9] They were not alone in arguing that regional interests would be better represented by private enterprise than by the BBC's London-based Oxbridge elites. Many even within the BBC believed that competition would strengthen the organization. Fredrick Ogilvie, Director-General of the BBC from 1938 to 1942, wrote:

> Freedom is choice. And monopoly in broadcasting is inevitably the negation of freedom, no matter how efficiently it is run, or how wise and kindly the boards of committees in charge of it. . . . The BBC, good as it is, would gain vastly by the abolition of monopoly and the introduction of competition.[10]

Despite such internal dissent, BBC management defended the monopoly on paternalistic grounds. The Corporation argued that competition would "submerge" the aim of using broadcasting constructively in the general social interest, and that monopoly was necessary for impartiality and for

> [t]he preservation of standards and the re-establishing on a broader basis of a regard for values, for the use of broadcasting as an educational medium and a means to raise the public taste.[11]

Against the criticism that competitive broadcasting would better represent minority interests, the BBC made the intriguing defense that while the *claims* of some minorities would increase and of others decrease, "the *rights* of all minorities would disappear."[12]

The BBC monopoly was more broadly championed by establishment elitists, including many patrician Conservatives from the House of Lords, who feared the quality of commercial programming. They were joined by senior members of the Church of England fretting about what they called the cultural crisis occasioned by too much Marxism and Scientific Humanism and "an all-round decline in serious listening."[13] The philosopher Maurice Cranston warned that freedom from the BBC could lead instead to "bondage to makers of razor-blades, deodorant, malted milks, and tonic wines."[14] From his position in the House of Lords, John Reith thundered that competition "will be of cheapness, not of goodness."[15] He later likened the prospect of commercial television to dog racing, smallpox, and the Black Death, all introduced to Britain unwelcome.

More broadly, support for the BBC drew on two pervasive if amorphous fears. First was the belief that the rise of fascism in the 1930s had been facilitated by a failure of democratic engagement, and that there was therefore more need than ever for public broadcasting to promote engaged citizenship.[16] Second, many Britons, especially among those in the paternalistic, class-conscious establishment, feared American-style commercialism.[17] This anxiety, part of the broader postwar malaise of imperial decline, was captured in almost allegorical perfection by the 1953 Coronation of Queen Elizabeth II. The BBC's live coverage of the Westminster Abbey Service was widely regarded as a triumph of dignity, doing much to popularize television ownership. The loyal British public were horrified to learn that when rebroadcast in America, the service had been interrupted by adverts for deodorants and chimpanzees selling tea.[18] These outrages and other instances of what the *Economist* called "the most frightful breaches of good form by the commercialized American networks" engendered a strong desire to protect Britain's identity and perceived cultural superiority.[19] Such fears of American cultural hegemony were to be found within the BBC's creative staff as well as among policymakers. *The Quatermass Experiment* (1953) and *The Hitchhiker's Guide to the Galaxy* (1978) have been seen as conscious attempts to shape a specifically British science-fiction genre in opposition to the all-conquering US model.[20] Media historian Su Holmes notes that the BBC was quick to play the role of protector of national culture for strategic purposes, and made a point of stressing to policymakers the supposed quality and distinctive Britishness of its output.[21] However, Holmes adds that the Corporation's editors and producers were also quietly but ruthlessly adopting American formats in their quest for popular programming.[22]

The Labour Party had mixed feelings about the BBC. The working-class party saw the broadcaster, with considerable justification, as championing political and social values much closer to those of their upper-class Conservative rivals. Labour complained that BBC news reporters seemed to regard Socialist politicians as dangerously political, while those with anti-Labour views were "somehow non-political."[23] The result was that "anti-Labour bias appears in programmes as a matter of course."[24] Their biggest complaint, though, was the class bias in variety shows, drama, and light entertainment, which almost exclusively catered to southern, educated, middle- and upper-class audiences. On the other hand, Labour liked public corporations, and had no wish to echo Conservative demands for a more pro-business system. Labour certainly had no love for the generally pro-Conservative newspapers. "One of the most valuable functions which the BBC can perform is the objective presentation of the news, without the biases and distortions which are only too common in the popular press."[25] The Labour Party linked the BBC's perceived superiority to its non-commercial status, making an explicit comparison to America's system of sponsored radio:

> One undesirable consequence of sponsored radio would be that the vast majority of listeners who would naturally prefer to be entertained rather than educated, would no longer receive the talks, features, discussions, news and news commentaries which the BBC has so effectively infused into its programmes. . . . We do not want that [American] kind of broadcasting here. The BBC has given us higher standards which sponsored radio would inevitably dilute. Sponsored radio is undesirable in the public interest.[26]

Ultimately, Labour came down on the side of the BBC monopoly, reflecting what one Labour politician described as "a mixture of socialist doctrine and Puritanism."[27]

William Beveridge, architect of that other beloved British institution the NHS, chaired the Parliamentary Committee that recommended the BBC retain its monopoly. Beveridge's report disliked "obtrusive and objectionable" adverts in America and feared commercials or sponsorship would "sooner or later endanger the traditions of public service, high standards and quality" established over the previous 25 years.[28] "The right of access to the domestic sound and television receivers of millions of people carries with it such great propaganda power that it cannot be trusted to any person or bodies other than a public corporation."[29] However, the Committee carried a powerful minority opinion written by Conservative MP Selwyn Lloyd, who described it as "intolerable . . . that there should be any single body of people deciding what is to be put over on the air."[30] Even so, while Lloyd recommended the introduction of a commercial network, he argued that such a network should be regulated by a body with "considerably more powers than has the FCC in the United States of America" to control content.[31]

Winston Churchill's Conservative Party regained power in the 1951, and although they accepted Beveridge's recommendations, the monopoly question was reopened by a vociferous group of backbench Tory MPs.[32] At first, Conservative leaders such as Antony Eden were not at all enthusiastic about commercialization.[33] Churchill himself had no love of popular television, demanding "Why do we need this peep-show?"[34] On the other hand, his dislike of the BBC stretched back to the General Strike, and he blamed them for his electoral defeat in 1945.[35]

The Conservative's 1952 White Paper on Broadcasting called for commercial competition. However, the White Paper stressed that any commercial television would be strictly regulated for content, and would be financed by advertisements and not by sponsorship. The insistence on advertising rather than "American-style" sponsorship was intended to prevent companies from hiring their own airtime and controlling their own programs, thereby ensuring that responsibility for content stayed with the broadcasters rather than the sponsors. Lord Reith called the conclusions a "betrayal and surrender."[36] But the tide of both public and elite opinion was turning in favor of at least some competition.

Conservative leaders withdrew their opposition to commercial television once they had been persuaded that it was possible to compromise between monopoly and the "pure commercialism of America."[37] Conservative leader Lord Salisbury had assured the House of Lords in November 1953 that "the new system would be totally different from the American."[38] The Party began to emphasize its political liberalism over its cultural conservatism, demanding "There's Free Speech, Why Not Free Switch" in a 1953 pamphlet.[39] The Fleet Street newspapers initially opposed commercial television for fear of competition, but by the early 1950s were persuaded that commercialization would enlarge rather than eat into the advertising pool. Public opinion, while strongly supportive of the BBC, was divided over whether a commercial alternative should be allowed. Forty-eight percent of Britons wanted the BBC monopoly to continue, while an equal number wanted the BBC and a commercial station.[40] Finally, the Labour Party's distaste for vulgar commercialism was tempered by the growing realization that commercial television would be very popular with their core constituents in the poorer and less educated classes.[41]

The result was the 1954 Television Bill, a compromise that established a broadcasting duopoly of the BBC and Independent Television (ITV). The latter was a regional network of advertising-funded commercial stations operating under the umbrella of a public corporation, the Independent Television Authority (ITA), which was responsible for program content. Die-hard opponents of commercial television at the National Television Council denounced ITV as "Caliban in chains," but the BBC immediately and ruthlessly rose to the competitive challenge.[42] On ITV's very first day of broadcasting, the BBC caused a sensation, and stole the next day's headline, by killing off a highly popular soap opera character, Grace Archer.

The BBC's reputation for impartiality was furthered by its coverage of the Suez Crisis in 1956, when Egyptian President Gamal Abdel Nasser nationalized the Suez Canal and British and French troops were dispatched to seize it back. Despite strong pressure from the Conservative Government to support the troops, the BBC allowed Opposition leader Hugh Gaitskell to broadcast a speech criticizing the invasion. As in the General Strike, the Government threatened to invoke the Reserve Powers allowing them to take over the BBC, but the Board of Governors supported their editors so strongly that the Government backed down.[43]

The Suez affair, along with the highbrow programming policy, won the approval of the 1960 Pilkington Committee, the next Parliamentary Committee to consider broadcasting regulation. Pilkington criticized the "trivial and shoddy" output on ITV and declared that "the dissatisfaction with television can be ascribed to the independent television service."[44] Pilkington's report led to the 1963 Television Act, which explicitly brought commercial television into the public service remit rather than the other way around. The Act required the ITA to "provide the television broadcasting services as a public service for disseminating information, education and entertainment" and stressed the need to have "proper balance and wide range" in programming, and to "secure a wide showing for programmes of merit."[45] The Act also introduced a third TV channel, in line with a Conservative promise "to extend choice still further."[46] Thanks to Pilkington's stinging criticism of the commercial sector, the channel was kept public and became BBC 2.

Social Change and Editorial Upheaval: From Dignity to Impudence

Commercial competition had been the first great change in Britain's conception of public broadcasting. During the late 1950s and early 1960s, the BBC underwent an internal revolution in editorial policy and organization culture, marking a significant departure from the original policy of avoiding controversy. This was the decision, championed most strongly by Director-General Hugh Greene, that the BBC should be a force for social change, questioning and challenging prevailing social values rather than assuming them to be fixed and proper. As BBC historian Jean Seaton puts it, "somewhere in the sixties, Reithian conservatism had mutated into something like Reithian liberalism."[47]

Reith and his immediate successors had assumed national consensus on both political values and standards of taste. They had seen the BBC's proper role as to reflect the former and live up to and elevate the latter. In 1924, Reith had argued:

> Our responsibility is to carry into the greatest number of homes everything
> that is best in every department of human knowledge, endeavor and achieve-
> ment, and to avoid things which are, or may be, hurtful[48]

This view was still prevalent in 1948 when Director-General Sir William Haley
outlined his perception of the BBC's proper role. He stressed the need for impartiality and political neutrality, but then posed the rhetorical question whether the
BBC should be neutral about Christian values:

> Of course it is not. There are many demands of impartiality laid upon the Cor-
> poration but this is not one of them. We are citizens of a Christian country and
> the BBC – an institution set up by the state – bases its policy upon a positive
> attitude towards the Christian values. It seeks to safeguard those values and
> foster acceptance of them.[49]

Later Haley addressed the issue of public taste:

> The BBC's purpose is to be a source of information, education, and entertain-
> ment, as a means of raising public taste. Not reflecting it or ignoring it but of
> raising it.[50]

But by the 1950s and early 1960s, this elitist view was being challenged, partly
as a reflection of wider social changes, but also because competition from ITV
was forcing the BBC to reexamine their programming assumptions. A former
executive for Independent Television News (ITN) observed that ITN's Robin Day
"just about invented the hard-hitting, penetrating interview," including a highly
controversial one with Egyptian President Nasser at the height of the 1956 Suez
Crisis, when Britain and Egypt were effectively at war. By contrast, he recalled
a BBC journalist unctuously asking a Prime Minister, "Do you have anything
to say to the nation, sir?"[51] ITV's assertiveness prompted a reappraisal of such
interview techniques at the BBC. Director-General Ian Jacob also questioned the
notion that there was one "general public" to whom all programs could be targeted. Instead, Jacob recognized, "In broadcasting terms there is no such thing as
'the public' as some kind of solid block."[52] The reorganization of radio programming was followed, reflected, and reinforced traditional British class boundaries.
Radio 1 would play pop music for the young and less educated; soap operas and
talk shows on Radio 2 catered to the middle-brow middle classes; Radio 3 played
classical music for the cultural elites; and the news and politics on Radio 4 were
intended for the well-educated and the business community.

More significantly, Director-General Greene jettisoned Reith's belief that the
BBC should avoid the hurtful. Greene, an admirer of legendary American broadcaster Ed Murrow, argued instead that

> [t]he BBC should encourage the examination of views and opinion in an atti-
> tude of healthy scepticism. In its search for the truth – indeed, in whatever it

undertakes, a broadcasting organization must recognise an obligation towards tolerance and towards the maximum liberty of expression.[53]

The BBC should strive for impartiality, he argued, but

> [t]here are some respects in which it is not neutral, unbiased or impartial. That is, where there are clashes for and against the basic moral values – truthfulness, justice, freedom, compassion, tolerance, for example. Nor do I believe that we should be impartial about certain things like racialism or extreme forms of political belief . . . the actions and aspirations of those who proclaim these ideas are so clearly damaging to society, to peace and good order, even in their immediate effects, that to put at their disposal the enormous power of broadcasting would be to conspire with them against society.[54]

Hence, instead of taking consensus on social and political matters for granted, as Reith had done, the BBC took it upon itself, in the words of Asa Briggs, "to subject every kind of institution to fierce critical scrutiny."[55]

The BBC revolutionized programming in an intoxicating spirit of openness and innovation. Realistic dramas such as *Z Cars*, first aired in 1962, portrayed Northern working class life in stark contrast to the mostly upper-middle class 'home counties' settings of earlier decades. Searing social commentaries such as Ken Loach's *Up the Junction* (1965) about an unwanted pregnancy became regular features of both drama and documentary output, airing for the first time on British television such contentious issues as racism, extra-marital sex, homosexuality, and abortion. Loach's *Cathy Come Home* (1966), one of the notoriously controversial *Wednesday Play* series, was a particular landmark that combined elements of fly-on-the-wall drama and documentary to plot the heartbreaking descent into homelessness of a well-intentioned but unlucky young couple. It made such a powerful case against the failures of the postwar welfare state that the homeless charity Shelter was formed within a week of the broadcast.

Satire became a programming staple. Situation comedies such as *'Till Death Us Do Part* (original for the United States' *All in the Family*) tackled working-class racism. Sketch series *That Was the Week that Was* (1962–1963) drew on current events to skewer politicians, the Church of England, the Royal Family, and sundry other establishment figures, introduced by Greene specifically and successfully "to prick the pomposity of public figures."[56] It was certainly the harbinger to the anarchic, pomposity-pricking surrealism of *Monty Python's Flying Circus* (1969–1974) that ruthlessly lampooned the English establishment in sketches featuring Upper Class Twits, the Ministry for Silly Walks, and dead Anglican Bishops on the landing. In keeping with the anarchic spirit burgeoning within the Corporation, the Pythons' fattest target was the BBC itself. Ridicule was heaped mercilessly on pompous dinner-jacketed but trouser-less announcers, inane quiz show hosts, self-important arts programs, earnest nature documentaries, and gritty undercover documentaries such as the one about gangsters Doug and Dinsdale Piranha.

The swinging new look for the BBC, "Auntie in a mini-skirt" as the makeover was known, met with strong disapproval, both internal and external. Leading the external resistance was Mary Whitehouse, a self-appointed but popular and highly effective guardian of what became known as family values. According to her, Director-General Greene was personally responsible for the moral collapse of the 1960s.[57] Whitehouse was effective in restraining the more progressive forces within the BBC, because many senior managers and Governors were themselves unhappy with the controversial new content. Thus, a planned repeat of *Up the Junction*, which had included an abortion scene, was canceled by the Governors who decreed that it had caused "great offence" first time around. They came to the decision directly following a discussion on how to deal with a letter from White-house asking the BBC to make a statement about its Christian Values.[58] *That Was the Week That Was* had been canceled two years earlier. Labour Prime Minister Harold MacMillan had personally enjoyed the show, writing to the Post-Master General, still in ultimate control of BBC content, that "I hope you will not, repeat not, take any action about *That Was the Week That Was*. It is a good thing to be laughed over."[59] His sense of humor was by no means shared by other politicians. "Being anti-Establishment is one thing . . . it was hard to swallow a programme whose general bias was so extremely left wing, socialist and pacifist," wrote one Conservative.[60] In response to numerous complaints from senior politicians, the Governors canceled the satire shortly before the 1964 General Election.[61] In an illuminating side note, presenter David Frost took a version to the United States where, he says, "the programme was never allowed the freedom, whatever the limits, that it had enjoyed in Britain."[62]

The BBC itself was deeply divided internally about how far they could or should push boundaries. Many traditionalists were horrified with Greene's new direction.[63] Reith lamented in his diary that "the BBC, particularly in television, has utterly discarded everything I did."[64] Other staff were personally sympathetic to Greene's progressivism but feared the political backlash it attracted, while many of the more radical young journalists and producers thought Greene was not going far enough.[65] The struggles over the soul of the BBC came to a head with the case of *The War Game*, a controversial documentary canceled by the Gover-nors. The story is worth telling in detail not only to illustrate the Corporation's internal divisions, but also to demonstrate the ways in which political influence and self-censorship interacted, with the broadcaster's senior managers often in greater conflict with their own junior staff than their political overseers.

In 1965, Peter Watkins, a highly talented, politically radical young producer, pitched a documentary-drama about the effects of a nuclear attack on Britain.[66] Britain's possession of the H-bomb was highly controversial and since 1955, the BBC had maintained close informal consultation with the Cabinet over all pro-grams pertaining to the topic.[67] There were, naturally, deep divisions of opin-ion about Watkins' idea. Huw Wheldon, head of BBC Documentaries, supported Watkins and commissioned the film, albeit with some worries about its political acceptability. He persuaded Director-General Greene and Chairman of the Board of Governors Lord Normanbrook to agree, but they had stronger reservations.

Normanbrook, a former Cabinet Secretary with very close ties to the highest echelons of Britain's political elite, remarked that the film was "not worth attempting."[68] According to Watkins, shortly after he had contacted the Home Office in the course of his research, the Home Office contacted the BBC demanding to know why they were making such a film about such a subject.[69]

The film is a searing docudrama about the effects of a nuclear attack on Britain. Drawing on accounts of the fire and atomic bombings of Germany and Japan, it graphically depicts firestorms and the burning and blinding of victims, including young children. Other scenes dramatize food riots, the imposition of martial law, and policemen mercy-killing those too badly burned to treat. The film ridicules official optimism, for example, quoting actual Civil Defense Agency tips for surviving nuclear attack that included a post-apocalypse recipe for "Braised beefsteak, roast and mashed potatoes, and mixed vegetables." The film clearly addressed British racism, noting that thousands of Black urban Britons would have to evacuate to the homes of rural families, many of whom would be unwilling to accept them. Overall, the piece is a shocking portrayal of the consequences of nuclear war, and an indictment of what Watkins saw as the lack of public debate about the moral and practical implications of Britain's deterrence policy.[70]

After an initial in-house screening, Director-General Greene and Chairman Normanbrook were more worried than ever about the political fallout. Normanbrook promptly proposed taking "soundings" from senior civil servants about whether or not to air it.[71] He wrote to Chief Cabinet Secretary Sir Burke Trend:

> The showing of the film on television *might well have a significant effect on public attitudes towards the deterrent*. In these circumstances, I doubt whether the BBC ought alone to take the responsibility of deciding whether this film should be shown on television.[72]
>
> (Italics added)

Secret screenings were then held for officials from the Home Office, the Ministry of Defense, and the Labour Government. Afterward Trend wrote that, although the film was not generally misleading or inaccurate, it was "unbalanced." He continued:

> Lord Normanbrook and Sir Hugh Greene . . . indicated that, if it were decided on grounds of public policy that the film should not be shown, the BBC might be prepared to issue a statement to the effect that they themselves had decided on these grounds not to show it. . . . The difficulty for the BBC no less than for the Government is to think of some reason for suppressing the film which would not stir up controversy or provoke suspicion that it was motivated by political prejudice.[73]

In other words, Trend believed that the Government had the right to decide what could be shown; that the BBC's senior management accepted that right; and that the BBC were prepared to give political cover to the Government against accusations of censorship.[74] A few weeks later the BBC announced they would not air the film, arguing that "the effect of the film has been judged by the BBC to be too horrifying for the medium of television."[75] They also claimed to be worried about the effect it might have on elderly people living alone.[76] Instead, the BBC aired the film on a limited theatrical release, initially to invited audiences only, to the fury of the production staff. Nonetheless, the program won an Oscar for Best Documentary in 1966, and was finally aired on television in 1985.

But the critics of progressiveness, while they scored notable short-term victories such as *The War Game*, were fighting a rearguard action. In 1965, over 100 MPs tabled a Parliamentary motion calling for the dismissal of Greene after critic Ken Tynan used the word "fuck" on a late-night show. Prime Minister Harold Wilson defused the situation by promising to never use the "four-letter word" himself on TV, and the motion failed.[77] By the end of the decade, in the philosophical and sometimes personal confrontation between Greene and Reith, described at the time as a battle between "dignity and impudence," Greene's impudence had won.[78]

The Annan Committee and Channel 4

The 1963 Broadcasting Act had awarded the third television channel to the BBC, in part in recognition of the valuable role the broadcaster's technological know-how could play. BBC Director-General Hugh Greene had persuaded the Post-Master General that introducing color television would be a good idea because of the benefits to the electronics industry.[79] Color TV was introduced in 1967, the result of efforts by both the BBC and commercial lobbyists.

A few years later the Annan Committee was charged with allocating a fourth channel. Delayed by frequent changes of government and consequent political disruption, the Committee first met in 1974 and reported in 1977. The report reflected two significant features in the broadcasting environment. First was considerable dissatisfaction with the "comfortable duopoly" of BBC and ITV. Criticisms came from diverse sources, ranging from Mary Whitehouse's National Viewers' and Listeners' Association to economic liberals, but most agreed that the lack of accountability of both the BBC and ITV was a problem.[80] The second was a recognition that British society had changed significantly from Reith's day, and was now much more multi-racial and pluralist.[81] Annan therefore recommended that the fourth channel be awarded neither to the BBC nor ITV, but to a network devoted specifically to minority interests. Channel 4 was a commercial broadcaster with a public service remit, specifically charged with representing minority interests, but funded from subscriptions paid by ITV contractors in return for regional advertising rights. The minority interests to which programming was to be targeted included cultural niches such as opera and special interests such as fly-fishing as well as ethnic and religious groups. As such, the new channel took the onus off the BBC to become more fully representative of minority interests. On the other hand, Channel 4 was deemed a great success in expanding Britain's commitment to inclusive public broadcasting, even at the dawn of Margaret Thatcher's less progressive neoliberal era.

NHK and Postwar Democracy

NHK began television broadcasts in February 1953 with a performance of the one of Japan's most iconic cultural treasures, the Kabuki drama *Yoshitsune Zenbonzakura*, followed by a recording of President Eisenhower's inauguration and a lecture on opera.[82] The broadcaster was, like all of Japan, in a state of conflicted transition. SCAP's "Reverse Course," which had scaled back the progressive forces unleashed during the early years and begun to restore conservatives to power, continued after the Occupation ended. Events at NHK were to mirror these trends as the cosmopolitan, outspoken programs that had flourished under SCAP were swiftly replaced by more traditional fare. The fate of the CIE-inspired *Comedy Theatre* illustrates the dynamic.

In 1954, *Yumoa Gekijo* (Comedy Theatre) aired a skit about a major political scandal then gripping Japan. Satō Eisaku, Secretary-General of the ruling Liberal Party (and later Prime Minister), was on the point of being arrested in the course of criminal investigations into bribery when the Minister of Justice, also of the Liberal Party, abruptly terminated the inquiry. Sato escaped scot-free. The offending sketch, a parody radio ad, had announced "The Liberal Sugar Company can make black sugar white!" The satire was (forgive the pun) crystal clear. In Japanese the word for "sugar-manufacturer" (*seitō*) sounds the same as for "political party" (*seitō*) while the word for sugar is *satō*. The skit provoked predictable outrage from conservatives in government. Satire promptly disappeared from subsequent episodes of the show, which was permanently canceled soon after.[83]

The *Yumao Gekijo* episode proved to be a harbinger of a broader shift in NHK's programming philosophy, which evolved in the 1960s in response to the social upheavals of the time, as well as elite unease with the dramatic rise of television as a social and cultural phenomenon. A more immediate catalyst was the arrival of commercial television, with NTV beginning broadcasts just weeks after NHK. In response to these pressures, NHK adopted, or perhaps reverted to, a programming philosophy and organization culture that reflected safe, traditional values and a non-confrontational, often deferential relationship toward the state.

NHK programming would emphasize education and information at the expense of entertainment, which was left to the commercial stations. Political knowledge would be bolstered through live Diet broadcasts, news reporting, and analysis. The education channel, NHK2, was launched in 1959. On NHK's main channel, the broadcaster promised "daily broadcasts of practical lectures in the arts, cooking and etiquette."[84] The goal, as Chun puts it, was to serve as "a tool of national enlightenment that could cultivate and refine the citizenry."[85] This did not stop NHK from also broadcasting some game shows and national sports contests. It still enjoyed monopoly rights over coverage of such major national events as the 1964 Tokyo Olympics, for which the commercial broadcasters conceded full coverage.[86] But during the 1960s, entertainment came to account for less than a quarter of NHK's output.

Television viewership grew rapidly in the 1950s, despite the very high cost of sets. In the early 1950s, even the cheapest models, often imported from the United States, cost more than ten times the average monthly take-home pay.[87] Viewers often found other ways to watch, with small businesses such as coffee shops, bars, and beauty parlors owning almost half of all TV sets in the mid-1950s. Giant "Open-Air TVs" (*gaito terebi*) became hugely popular, too. NHK put sets in hospitals or official buildings in order to persuade people to buy their own, while NTV put large screens in railways and plazas to attract viewers. The fortunes of the Imperial Household and NHK had intertwined from the earliest radio days, when Emperor Hirohito's inauguration provided the impetus to create the national transmission network and greatly boosted receiver sales. The marriage of Crown Prince Akihito to Shoda Mariko in 1959 was a similar watershed, viewed by over 15 million people. Many Tokyo residents reported that they had preferred to watch the procession on the television rather than live in person.[88] Demand individual TV sets boomed after the 1959 Royal Wedding and again during the 1964 Tokyo Olympics, providing a massive boost to the nation's fledgling consumer electronics industry and a huge influx of new fees for NHK. In 1956, less than 1% of Japanese households had contracts with NHK, rising to 50% by 1960 and 90% by 1973.[89] More significantly, the audience demographics were shifting. Early ownership of televisions was concentrated overwhelmingly in Tokyo and other big cities. As transmission technologies improved and set prices fell, rural audiences grew and programming tastes changed.[90] But the spread of television prompted sharp debate about its social and political influences.

News and Impartiality

Concerns about television's malignant influence were heightened in the late 1950s against a background of social upheaval and worsening political turmoil.[91] Much of the country was still desperately poor, and the nation was bitterly divided politically. Conflict boiled over in 1960 with a wave of pro-labor strikes, often violently broken up by hired *yakuza* thugs. Meanwhile, the signing of the US-Japan Security Treaty (*Anpō*) provoked massive protests.

Television images of the demonstrations were among the factors provoking an outcry that led eventually to Prime Minister Kishi Nobusuke's resignation. Chun suggests that the particularly emotional power of television images came from their stunning newness. Demonstrations in the 1970s, while significantly larger, failed to raise the same emotions because they had become commonplace.[92] But the most shocking television image of the period, arguably in NHK's entire history, was the 1960 assassination of Socialist Party Chairman Asanuma Inejiro. Asanuma's speech to a pre-election audience was being taped when a young right-wing fanatic charged onto the stage, sword first, and stabbed Asanuma in the side.[93] The haunting footage was replayed endlessly, provoking more debate about violence and television.

Many politicians in the governing LDP were furious with NHK reporters for what they saw as exacerbating the *Anpō* crisis. They found a sympathetic ally in NHK's President Nomura Hideo, a former journalist and member of the National Public Safety Commission who had been appointed in 1957 by Minister for Posts and Telecommunications Tanaka Kakuei and Prime Minister Kishi.[94] Nomura brushed off a group of LDP Diet members demanding that NHK drop what they saw as leftist bias, but he also made sure that extreme views were downplayed and that coverage that might exacerbate the conflict was toned down.[95] Nomura declared that NHK's role was to "protect parliamentary democracy . . . and support political stability."[96] Like the BBC in the General Strike, NHK strove to appear politically neutral, with some success. A study found strong reinforcement effects in that progressives believed that coverage of the demonstrations revealed NHK's anti-government sympathies, while Conservatives believed NHK was covered the events conscientiously.[97] At the same time, both NHK and the commercial broadcasters quietly edited out "extreme" views or excessive coverage of problems.[98] The Communist Party was dropped from an NHK televised debate between the main political parties in November 1960, despite having appeared in an earlier debate.[99] In both cases, coverage reinforced a conservative framing of the protests. In 1961, newly appointed NHK President Abe Shinnosuke was invited to head an LDP-convened Council to Study Measures to Prevent Violent Crimes.[100]

The 1960s also saw NHK place much more emphasis on news coverage, stimulated in part by the unprecedented numbers of viewers who tuned in to watch the *Anpō* demonstrations. From November 1961 to March 1963, NHK aired a series of five "Talks with the Prime Minister" (*Sōri to Kataru*) in which the Prime Minister was questioned by a group of scholars and political experts. Aired between 7.30 and 9.00 p.m., and simultaneously on the radio, they proved highly popular, with the TV audience going from 4.7 million households for the first one to 15.9 million for the last.[101] Especially under Maeda Yoshinori, president from 1964 to 1973, the newsgathering operation expanded dramatically.[102] The 7 p.m. News became a daily ritual for millions of Japanese families, and NHK became the most watched and trusted source of news in Japan, the envy of foreign broadcasters.[103] However, NHK's coverage of current events, also including its documentary programming, tended to steer clear of the most controversial issues of the day, leaving the task of investigative journalism to the newspapers and even the commercial television rivals.

Media coverage of the Minamata pollution case, for example, was almost nonexistent. The case, the most notorious of a string of pollution scandals in the 1950s and 1960s, involved Chisso Chemical Corporation illegally dumping mercury into the waters of Minamata Bay. Victims of the resultant poisoning of the central nervous system were first treated in 1953, but NHK's only coverage was a radio program in 1957 and a segment on NHK General TV in late 1959. It was not until 1970 that NHK finally aired a major documentary on pollution. Even then, NHK took the sting out of any implied criticism of the LDP by discussing pollution problems in many other countries, including Britain, Sweden, and the United States.[104] Generally, the media's pursuit of "neutrality" gave the government and the chemical industry a free hand to confuse and cast doubt on the issue for years, despite clear evidence that things were going wrong.[105]

NHK also covered the Vietnam War more cautiously than the commercial stations, although the LDP tried to prevent them from covering the war at all. In 1967, TBS's Den Hideo was the first Japanese broadcaster to file reports from Hanoi, noting the high morale of the North Vietnamese and the indiscriminate nature of American bombing. LDP leaders, including Tanaka Kakuei, complained, fearful of the effect the negative reporting would have on US-Japan relations. The TBS President argued back, but within a year the reporter concerned had resigned.[106] NHK was less outspoken, but aired regular specials on Vietnam, receiving criticism from both right and left about the coverage.[107]

Krauss makes the case that NHK's leadership became thoroughly entangled in the factional infighting, which was such a central feature of LDP rule. He illustrates the close but complicated relationship between the LDP and NHK's coverage of politics with the case of the Lockheed bribery scandal of 1976. The affair centered on the arrest of Tanaka Kakuei for having accepted bribes while Prime Minister in 1972. A former Minister for Posts and Telecommunications, Tanaka had close ties with the Ministry as well as NHK, and had helped push increases in NHK viewer fees through the Diet throughout the 1960s and 1970s.[108]

NHK's president at the time the scandal broke in 1976 was Ono Kichiro, who[109] had served as administrative vice-minister for Tanaka when he was Minister for Posts and Telecommunications in 1957. Tanaka had placed Ono in an *amakudari* executive position at NHK in 1959. Tanaka had tried to get Ono appointed president in 1964 but lost out to Maeda Yoshinori, the choice of a rival faction headed by Satō Eisuke. Maeda was a graduate of Lyon University, former Rome correspondent for the Asahi Shimbun, and a long-time news broadcaster at NHK. However, Ono was appointed vice-president, a position he held throughout Maeda's tenure where he became notorious for exerting his influence over the newsroom to report favorably on the LDP.[110] When Maeda retired in 1973, Prime Minister Tanaka picked Ono to replace him.

Thanks to Maeda's expansion of the news operation, NHK had a large team of reporters covering the case.[111] Indeed, this was one of the first cases where television broadcasters deployed their own investigative reporters rather than relying on news agencies and official sources.[112] However, their own objectivity was compromised by the close ties between Ono and Tanaka.

The day after Tanaka had been released on bail following his sensational arrest, Ono paid a visit to Tanaka's home in what he later claimed was a "personal" capacity.[113] Outrage followed, with thousands of complaints from viewers and heated questions in the Upper House special committee on Lockheed. Nippōrō, the NHK union, were particularly incensed and organized a petition demanding that new president be chosen "in a democratic manner" and from within NHK, not the ranks of the bureaucracy or big business. Over 1.3 million viewers signed.[114] Ono resigned within a few weeks. In response to the public outcry, the board of governors appointed Sakamoto Tomokazu, an NHK insider with an inoffensive and non-political background in entertainment programming.[115] Ono was secretly kept on as a paid advisor, however, retiring only once the arrangement was discovered. NHK News chose not to cover this widely publicized scandal.[116]

The LDP were quick to respond to any coverage they didn't like. In May 1976, NHK News quoted a report in *Akahata*, the Communist Party newspaper, listing the names of LDP officials said to have been recipients of Lockheed bribes. LDP leaders promptly accused NHK of failing to be impartial.[117] Prime Minister Miki Takeo postponed a Diet bill raising viewer fees. This was a particularly dangerous threat because the fees had not been raised since 1968 and NHK was still suffering from huge cost increases in the wake of the 1973 Oil Shock. Miki even toyed with the ultimate threat of refusing to approve NHK's budget, with a senior LDP official quoted as saying, "The top people in NHK are all right, but there are many reds among low ranking employees."[118] The LDP did not go through with the threat, but the message was clear and helped feed NHK's culture of self-censorship.

In a postscript to the episode, in 1981, NHK planned a 15-minute segment to mark the five-year anniversary of the Lockheed scandal. Gōdo Shiro, former head of NHK's city news desk, later wrote that under pressure from management, parts of the program including a statement from Prime Minister Miki were cut and a planned opinion poll on the scandal canceled. The producers pushed back against management but to their cost. The lead editor of the documentary was promptly demoted to a research position, while other staff were variously purged from the News Bureau.[119] Tragically, Gōdo committed suicide a few years, still protesting NHK's lack of independence.[120]

Entertainment TV and National Values

Meanwhile, NHK's entertainment programming was being drawn into wider social fears that television was encouraging juvenile violence and debasing the nation's intellect and morals. In 1957, critic Ōya Soichi had noted the democratic potential of television, which could allow "one hundred million people to all become commentators."[121] Reflecting on why that wasn't happening, he excoriated NHK for being bland, unassertive, and failing to experiment despite freedom from commercial pressures.[122] However, he went on to warn that in practice television was creating *ichioku sōhakuchi*: "one hundred million idiots."[123] The precise cause of his ire was an NTV show in which an actor was hired to wave a Keio university flag in the Waseda fan section of a key baseball game.[124] Ōya blamed commercial sponsorship for what we might now call dumbing down and which he termed "idiot programming" (*hakuchi bangumi*).[125] Ōya's article hit a nerve, sparking a national debate and helping push NHK toward the inoffensive programming, which is now its hallmark. The trend is illustrated by the saga of iconic wrestler Rikidōzan.

One of America's very first exports to the infant Japanese television industry, and certainly one of the most popular, was *puroresu* (professional wrestling).[126] NHK aired the first live bout in 1954, between former sumo wrestler Yamaguchi Toshio and an American serviceman known as "Bulldog Butcher." NTV soon followed and the two broadcasters shared coverage for a number of years.[127] These faked encounters between larger-than-life characters became immensely popular, winning a 64% audience share in 1962, far outstripping the popularity of baseball, boxing, or even the popular series of the times such as *Jiken Kisha* (Police Reporter) and the US import *Rawhide*.[128] *Gaito terebi* sets in stations and parks attracted huge crowds, one estimated at 20,000.[129] An estimated 900,000 Tokyoites, or approximately one in every nine residents, watched a three-day championship match. Former sumo wrestler Rikidōzan was the undisputed star of the circuit and of television coverage.[130] A brave, scrappy fighter, Riki would grapple and beat much larger opponents, often *inchiki gaijin resura* ("cheating foreigner wrestlers").[131] His most notorious arch-nemeses were the Sharpe brothers, giant Americans who he regularly beat with a combination of bravery, perseverance, and his trademark karate-chops.[132]

Rikidōzan became a unifying national hero at a time when Japan badly needed one, perfectly embodying "*gambaru*" – the dogged perseverance of the plucky underdog.[133] Fans cheered the old wartime chant "*Nippon Banzai!*" as they watched him, but when NTV executives went to apologize to the police for having created such unruly crowds, the police thanked them for performing a valuable public service.[134] After one successful bout, Shoriki, the owner of NTV, announced "Rikidōzan, by his pro wrestling in which he sent the big white men flying, has restored pride to the Japanese and given them new courage."[135]

Schoolboys were particular fans of Riki. A Japanese friend recounted to me how his mother installed a TV in her tiny Tokyo grocery store in the mid-1950s, not minding that the dozen or so wrestling fans who always crammed into the store rarely bought anything. "Riki was our hero. He was the good guy, and the Americans were the bad guys."[136] Perhaps inevitably, a number of children were injured and at least one died, apparently from emulating Riki's stunts.[137] This prompted an equally inevitable bout of media outrage and collective national handwringing, a fire to which the deaths of an elderly couple in front of their TV, supposedly from shock after seeing pro-wrestling, added more fuel.[138] It cannot have helped wrestling's public image that Rikidōzan was knifed to death in a gang-related bar brawl in 1963, even though his funeral was organized by senior members of the LDP, including the Minister for Construction.[139]

The nation was already concerned about rising juvenile delinquency and the lax moral standards of modern youth.[140] The government had worried about the social effects of violence on TV since before broadcasting began, and had sent educational experts to the United States in 1950 to report on the problems supposedly caused by TV there.[141] There followed a series of studies on television and violence released throughout the decade. In 1958, a study by the Central Juvenile Problem Committee of the Prime Minister's Office concluded that "the recent rapid rise in juvenile crimes is mostly resultant from the bad influence of the mass communications media."[142]

President Nomura ordered a cleanup of violence on NHK in July 1960, canceling all wrestling and boxing broadcasts, then systematically removing violent scenes from other programs.[143] Hundreds of American westerns, cop shows, scenes with swords and guns, and even the enormously popular *Popeye the Sailor* were canceled or cut on the grounds of violence and immorality. Commercial stations, meanwhile, proved unwilling to clean up their acts, despite a series of attempts by the LDP and the MPT to encourage them to follow NHK's lead. These attempts at persuasion included a threat by the Minister for Posts and Telecommunications in 1961 to not renew the licenses of certain broadcasters depending on their program contents. The commercial broadcasters made more of an effort than NHK to defend their editorial independence. NHK dropped Rikidōzan, for example, but NTV carried his matches until his death. When NHK dropped *Popeye*, it offered its stock of canceled episodes to TBS. After careful consideration, the commercial broadcasters concluded, to the great benefit of their ratings, that the spinach-loving sailorman's constant brawling and womanizing would have no ill-effects on the nation's youth. They took the lot. In 1960, Fuji TV introduced daytime *yoromeki* ("infidelity") dramas for women, kicking off with *Hibi no Haishin* ("Daily Betrayal") the story of an adulterous affair, while the "Pink Mood Show" for men featured topless dancers. Not until 1972 did the commercial broadcasters announce a policy of "self-control" and banish nudity and excess to the late-night slots.[144]

NHK, meanwhile, faced big holes in its schedule because many of its most popular programs had been deemed unfit for domestic viewing. Something wholesome was needed to fill the gap, ideally something uplifting and soothing enough to heal the nation's deep, raw divisions. Unfortunately, after Rikidōzan and Popeye, the next most popular programs were American: *I Love Lucy* and *A Dog Called Lassie*.[145] NHK's response was the introduction of two new kinds of homegrown television drama.

Renzoku Terebi Shosetsu ("television novels"), more popularly known as *asa dora* ("morning dramas"), first aired in 1961. These were daytime soap operas, usually aired in 15-minute episodes, six days a week. Targeted specifically at housewives and mothers, the timing and narrative structure were designed to enable "busy housewives to keep up with the story while going about their morning tasks."[146] Usually set in the recent past (1920s–1950s), these dramas presented stories of Japanese women enduring poverty and war, but surviving and ultimately finding happiness, thanks to stoic perseverance.[147] The series began with *Musume to Watashi* ("My Daughter and I") and reached its apogee with *Oshin* (1983–1984).

Sunday-night historical dramas began in 1963 and, like the *asa dora*, are still going strong. Originally targeting men, they air for 45 minutes every Sunday evening, with each story lasting an entire year. Usually set in the 16th- and 17th-century period of unification and nation-building, they have avoided the modern era altogether: the only series set in the modern Showa period concerned Japanese-Americans during the Second World War.[148] The early heroes were Samurai, portrayed as entrepreneurs struggling to shape history in confused times.[149] The series began with *Hana no Shoga* ("Life of a Great Statesman"), set in 1860, a time of great upheaval and readjustment to Western intrusion. This was followed by *Chushingara* in 1964, the first of four versions of the story to air over the next 40 years. The earliest was based on Osaragi Jiro's novel *Akō Rōshi*, which depicted the leaderless Samurai as protestors against a corrupt and tyrannical military dictatorship, a suitable allegory for the postwar democratic impulse.[150] The climactic scene when the loyal samurai storm the treacherous leader's castle achieved the highest ratings ever for the genre. Famous nation-builders such as Toyotomi Hideyoshi, Tokugawa Ieysu, and Nobunaga Oda have all been subjects of Taiga Drama. More recent protagonists include 16th-century samurai Naoe Kanetsugu. The success of the genre prompted Fuji TV to produce its own *Sambiki no Samurai* ("Three Samurai"), about a group of warriors wandering the country hiring themselves out as bodyguards and battling evildoers.[151]

The success of the genre also sheds light onto broader concerns that new media platforms (in this case television) will invariably destroy existing, more traditional forms of entertainment. Kabuki companies had fiercely objected to the introduction of television on the grounds that it would destroy their business. Their fears were heightened with NHK's choice of *Yoshitsune Zenbonzakura* as the first show on national television, followed a few months later by the first live recording from Tokyo's Kabukiza theater. As it turned out, though, television prompted greater interest in live performance, and the Taiga dramas provided a great deal of extra employment for classically trained kabuki actors.[152]

Historian Carol Gluck argues that both Taiga and Asa dora contained clear morals for audiences in the 1960s. Men were being urged to make history. Women were being told to endure history patiently, displaying the prized Japanese quality of *gaman* (patience, endurance, or perseverance) while retaining their femininity.[153] Shunya Yoshimi notes that although the period from 1920 to 1950 proved most popular in terms of ratings for the *asa dora*, history – including the Second World War – was viewed only from the perspective of "Japanese women as victims."[154] The heroines endure shortages, privation, and American bombing. Soldiers are sent away to the front and return, if at all, often wounded. The voices of Japan's victims are never heard. More controversial historical topics were avoided. In 1964, *Fusetsu* ("Blizzard") another historical drama, planned for 100 episodes stretching from the Meiji Restoration to the end of the Second World War, was abruptly cut short before it reached the modern era.[155]

As an aside, the political violence of the era had one unintendedly positive effect: remote education. President Maeda was an enthusiastic supporter of direct educational broadcasting to benefit Japan's many rural schools and pushed the idea early in his tenure in 1964. At first the government balked at the cost, but the 1968–1969 student riots persuaded them of the attractions of a "virtual" university that could not be smashed up, occupied, or turned into a physical bastion of dissent by lefty protesters. The LDP relented and the University of the Air launched in 1971.[156]

By the mid-1970s, television was firmly entrenched as a feature of Japanese family life. In 1960, the Japanese watched on average 3 hours, 11 minutes of TV per day. This had risen to 3 hours, 26 minutes in 1975.[157] By contrast, in 1965, the average American watched 2 hours and 6 minutes.[158] A 1957 poll reported that 83% of Japanese housewives believed that their sense of family togetherness increased after buying a TV set.[159] NHK's place in Japan's television landscape was less dominant, of course, than its prewar radio monopoly. But with vast resources, serious news, and high-quality programming, the public broadcaster remained a central element of Japan's social and political consciousness.

In summary, commercial broadcasting and the explosive growth of television in the 1950s and 1960s changed the landscape entirely for public broadcasters. These changes came against a backdrop of intense social and political upheaval, with widespread, often violent, challenges to established authority and traditional values. As television became the central medium in political and social life, policymakers across the globe panicked about its supposedly damaging effects.[160] These upheavals presented the public broadcasters with similar challenges, to which each responded differently in ways that have continued to shape their organizational culture and strategic direction.

The BBC lost its broadcasting monopoly but maintained its central place in cultural and political life. This resilience was in part a result of the editorial shift from reflecting establishment values to embracing progressive change. Programming was made more inclusive and more critical of existing social and political values. NHK, by contrast, responded to widespread fears that TV was creating "a nation of 100 million idiots" by reemphasizing the traditional values of the ruling Japanese establishment. Thus, while the BBC won the loyalty from viewers of all ages, NHK secured the approval of the ruling conservative elite and older viewers. Both strategies worked in their own fashion to keep the public broadcasters safe despite the advent of commercial competition. By the 1970s, public broadcasting in both countries was in great health. But new challenges were approaching.

Notes

1 "50's Everything Was Live: Full-scale TV Broadcasting," *Fifty Years of NHK Television*, NHK, accessed March 11, 2021, www.nhk.or.jp/digitalmuseum/nhk50years_en/history/p06/index.html.

2 Jean Seaton, *Pinkoes and Traitors: The BBC and the Nation 1974–1987* (London: Profile Books, 2015), 247.

3 John Reith, "Memorandum" to *Report of the Broadcasting Committee* (Beveridge Report) Cmmd. 8117, appendix H, paper 62 (London: HMSO) 1949, 364.

4 *White Paper on Broadcasting Policy*, Cmmd. 6852 (London: HMSO), 1945–46, para 14.

5 D.A. Boyd, "Pirate Radio in Britain: A Programming Alternative," *Journal of Communication* 36, no. 2 (1986): 83–94.

6 *Pirate Radio* (2009) is an entertaining if highly fictionalized account of Caroline and other pirate stations.

7 Asa Briggs, *The History of Broadcasting in the United Kingdom: Sound and Vision*, vol. 4 (Oxford: Oxford University Press, 1979), 52.

8 "Ariel and Caliban," *The Economist*, August 15, 1953. However, the same article also noted that for technical reasons, full competition in broadcasting was currently impossible. The magazine recommended competition from a second publicly funded broadcaster, which would be "better than the present monopoly or the pure commercialism of America."

9 Briggs, *Sound and Vision*, 354.

10 F.W. Ogilvie in a letter to *The Times* on June 26, 1946, quoted in James McDonnell, *Public Service Broadcasting: A Reader* (New York, NY: Routledge, 1991), 21.
11 "BBC Memorandum: Monopoly and Competition in Broadcasting," paper 22, in *Report of the Broadcasting Committee* (Beveridge Report) Cmmd. 8117, appendix H, paper 62 (London: HMSO) 1949, para. 10–12.
12 "BBC Memorandum: Monopoly and Competition in Broadcasting."
13 Briggs, *Sound and Vision*, 355.
14 Briggs, *Sound and Vision*, 911.
15 Reith, "Memorandum."
16 Paul Litt, "The Massey Report Fifty Years Later," *Beaver* 51, no. 3 (June/July 2001).
17 Valeria Camporesi, "The BBC and American Broadcasting 1922–1955," *Media, Culture and Society* 16 (1994): 625–639.
18 Andrew Crisell, *An Introductory History of British Broadcasting* (Abingdon: Routledge, 2nd edition, 1997), 85–86.
19 "Ariel and Caliban," *The Economist*.
20 Derek Johnson, "The BBC versus 'Science Fiction': The Collision of Transnational Genre and National Identity in Television in the Early 1950s," in *British Science Fiction Film and Television*, eds. Tobias Hochscherf and James Leggot (Jefferson, NC and London: McFarland and Company, 2011).
21 Su Holmes, *Entertaining Television: The BBC and Popular Television Culture in the 1950s* (Manchester: Manchester University Press, 2008).
22 Holmes, *Entertaining Television*, 205.
23 Labour Party, "Memorandum of Evidence," *Report of the Broadcasting Committee*, Cmmd. 8117, appendix H, paper 59 (London: HMSO, 1949), 345.
24 Labour Party, "Memorandum of Evidence," 345.
25 Labour Party, "Memorandum of Evidence," 347.
26 Labour Party, "Memorandum of Evidence," 345.
27 Briggs, *Sound and Vision*, 914.
28 *Report of the Broadcasting Committee*, Cmmd. 8116 (London: HMSO, 1949), para. 376.
29 *Report of the Broadcasting Committee*, Cmmd. 8116, para. 376.
30 *Report of the Broadcasting Committee*, Cmmd. 8116, para. 378.
31 Speech to Parliament on July 19, 1949, quoted in McDonnell, *Public Service Broadcasting*, 30.
32 Des Freedman, "Modernising the BBC: Wilson's Government and Television 1964–1966," *Contemporary British History* 15, no. 1 (Spring 2001): 21.
33 Briggs, *Sound and Vision*, 110.
34 Cain, *The BBC: Seventy Years*, 72.
35 Crisell, *An Introductory History of British Broadcasting*, 84.
36 Crisell, *An Introductory History of British Broadcasting*, 86.
37 "Ariel and Caliban," *The Economist*.
38 Briggs, *Sound and Vision*, 923.
39 Briggs, *Sound and Vision*, 914.
40 Briggs, *Sound and Vision*, 923.
41 Cain, *The BBC: Seventy Years*, 72.
42 Briggs, *Sound and Vision*, 101.
43 Cain, *The BBC: Seventy Years*, 82.
44 Cain, *The BBC: Seventy Years*, 85.
45 Television Act, c. 50, 1963.
46 Alec Douglas-Home, "1964 Conservative Party General Election Manifesto," accessed 2001, www.conservative-party.net/manifestos/1964/1964-conservative-manifesto.shtml.
47 Seaton, *Pinkoes and Traitors*, 247.
48 John Reith, *Broadcast Over Britain* (London: Hodder and Staunton, 1924), 34.

49 William Haley, "Moral Values in Broadcasting: Address to the British Council of Churches" in 1948, quoted in McDonnell, *Public Service Broadcasting*, 23.

50 McDonnell, *Public Service Broadcasting*, 23.

51 David Nichols, "Television News," *The Independent on Sunday*, July 10, 2011.

52 Ian Jacob, "The Tasks Before the BBC Today," *The BBC Quarterly* 9, no. 3 (Autumn 1954): 132–133.

53 Hughe Greene, *The Third Floor Front: A View of Broadcasting in the Sixties* (London: Bodley Head, 1969), 102, quoted in McDonnell, *Public Service Broadcasting*, 51.

54 McDonnell, *Public Service Broadcasting*, 107.

55 Asa Briggs, *The History of Broadcasting in the United Kingdom: Competition*, vol. V (Oxford: Oxford University Press, 1995), 326.

56 Crisell, *An Introductory History of British Broadcasting*, 124.

57 Briggs, *Sound and Vision*, 309.

58 Briggs, *Sound and Vision*, 525.

59 Briggs, *Sound and Vision*, 360.

60 G.W. Goldie, "Facing the Nation: Television and Politics 1936–1976," quoted in Briggs, *Sound and Vision*, 363.

61 Mike Wayne, "Failing the Public: The BBC, The War Game and Revisionist History: A Reply to James Chapman," *Journal of Contemporary History* 42, no. 4 (2007): 629.

62 Briggs, *Sound and Vision*, 375.

63 Author's own interviews with BBC staff, March 2008.

64 Reith diary entry, September 7, 1963, quoted in Briggs, *Sound and Vision*, 317.

65 BBC staff interviews, March 2008.

66 James Chapman, "The BBC and the Censorship of The War Game (1965)," *Journal of Contemporary History* 41, no. 1 (2006): 75–94.

67 Wayne, "Failing the Public," 631.

68 Chapman, "The BBC and Censorship," 81.

69 Peter Watkins, "The War Game," accessed June 1, 2015, http://pwatkins.mnsi.net/warGame.htm#update.

70 Watkins, "The War Game."

71 Minutes of BBC Controller's meeting on September 6, 1965, quoted in Chapman, "The BBC and Censorship," 84.

72 Chapman, "The BBC and Censorship," 85.

73 Sir Burke Trend quoted in Chapman, "The BBC and Censorship," 87.

74 Wayne, "Failing the Public," 634–635.

75 Quoted in Briggs, *Competition*, 534.

76 Chapman, "The BBC and Censorship," 88.

77 Briggs, *Sound and Vision*, 530.

78 Briggs, *Sound and Vision*, 318.

79 Des Freedman, "Modernising the BBC: Wilson's Government and Television 1964–1966," *Contemporary British History* 15, no. 1 (Spring 2001): 25.

80 Crisell, *British Broadcasting*, 202.

81 Crisell, *British Broadcasting*, 203.

82 "Television Broadcasting Officially Opens in Japan," *Japan Times*, February 2, 1953.

83 NHK, *Broadcasting in Japan: The Twentieth Century Journey from Radio to Multimedia* (Tokyo: NHK Publications, 2002), 92–93.

84 Jayson Makoto Chun, *A Nation of a Hundred Million Idiots: A Social History of Japanese Television 1953–1973* (New York: Routledge, 2007), 54–55.

85 Chun, *Hundred Million Idiots*, 55.

86 "NHK to Televise All of Olympics," *Japan Times*, February 6, 1964.

87 NHK, *Broadcasting in Japan*, 127.

88 Akira Takahashi, "CBC Report," June 1959, quoted in Hidetoshi Sato, ed., *Japanese Research in Communications (Selected Abstracts)* (Honolulu: University Press of Hawaii, 1974), 14.

89 Motohama Ryōichiro and Kōsaka Kenji, 'The Effects of Television on People's Consciousness," in *A Social History of Science and Technology in Japan Volume 3 High Economic Growth Period 1960–1969*, eds. Shigeru Nakayama and Kunio Gotō (Tokyo: Transpacific Press, 2006), 516–527.

90 "40 Turbulent Years Recalled," *Japan Times*, March 22, 1965.

91 Ellis Krauss, *Broadcasting Politics in Japan: NHK and Television News* (Ithaca: Cornell University Press, 2000), 245.

92 Chun, *Hundred Million Idiots*, 228.

93 This footage, along with newsreels of the Anpō Demonstrations and the Miike Coalmine strike, can be seen in the video documentary "Inside Japan, Inc."

94 "Nomura May be Selected Head of NHK," *Japan Times*, November 10, 1957.

95 Krauss, *Broadcasting Politics*, 126–127; NHK, *Broadcasting in Japan*, 144–145.

96 "Diet Sessions and Debate," *Fifty Years of NHK Television*, NHK, accessed March 11, 2021, www.nhk.or.jp/digitalmuseum/nhk50years_en/history/p13/index.html.

97 Masaki Takizawa and Sakuichi Nakagawa, *Terebi to Seiji Mondai* [TV and the Political Crisis], August 1960, quoted in Hidetoshi Kato, *Communications Policies in Japan* (Belgium: UNESCO, 1978), 37.

98 Krauss, *Broadcasting Politics*, 127.

99 "Second TV Three-party Debate set for Tonight," *Japan Times*, November 16, 1960.

100 "25 Named to Anticrime Council," *Japan Times*, March 21, 1961.

101 NHK, *History of Broadcasting*, 180.

102 Krauss, *Broadcasting Politics*, 128–129.

103 Judith Geller, *Japanese Broadcasting: A Promise Fulfilled* (Queenstown, MD: The Aspen Institute, 1979).

104 NHK, *History of Broadcasting*, 207.

105 Timothy S. George, *Minamata: Pollution and the Struggle for Democracy in Postwar Japan* (Cambridge, MA: Harvard University Asia Center, 2002), 118.

106 NHK, *History of Broadcasting*, 188.

107 NHK, *History of Broadcasting*, 185.

108 Greg Noble, "Let a Hundred Channels Contend: Technological Change, Political Opening and Bureaucratic Politics in Japanese Television Broadcasting," *Journal of Japanese Studies* 26, no. 1 (Winter 2000): 87.

109 This paragraph draws largely on Krauss, *Broadcasting Politics*, 130–133.

110 "JSP Demand Ono Step Down," *Japan Times*, September 3, 1976.

111 Between 40 and 50 reporters, according to Krauss, *Broadcasting Politics*, 133.

112 NHK, *History of Broadcasting*, 221.

113 "NHK's Ono Apologizes for Visiting Tanaka," *Japan Times*, September 2, 1976.

114 "Group Calls for Care in Choosing NHK Head," *Japan Times*, September 8, 1976.

115 "Sakamoto Nominated NHK President," *Japan Times*, September 22, 1976.

116 "NHK President Ono Resigns," *Japan Times*, September 4, 1976; Krauss, *Broadcasting Politics*, 133–135; Makoto Odagiri, *NHK wa Naze Okanemochi na no ka?* [Why is NHK so Rich?] (Tokyo: Futabashi Press, 2014), 247.

117 "NHK Troubled by Diet Delay," *Japan Times*, May 9, 1976.

118 "NHK Troubled by Diet Delay."

119 Krauss, *Broadcasting Politics*, 135. See also Akemi Nakamura, "Fourth Estate Takes NHK to Task for Abusing Trust," *Japan Times*, February 11, 2005.

120 "Ex-NHK City News Chief Takes His Own Life," *Japan Times*, May 3, 1987; Krauss, *Broadcasting Politics*, 139.

121 Quoted in Kenji Kosaka and Ryoichi Motohama, "The Effects of Television on People's Consciousness," in *A Social History of Science and Technology in Contemporary Japan Volume 3 The High Growth Period 1960–1969*, eds. Shigeru Nakayama and Kunio Goto (Tokyo: Transpacific Press, 2006), 521.

122 Soichi Ōya, "Hōshasen," *Tokyo Shimbun*, January 21, 1957, quoted in Chun, *Hundred Million Idiots*, 163.

123 Quoted in Hidetoshi Kato, "Japan," in *Television: An International History*, ed. Antony Smith (Oxford: Oxford University Press, 1998), 174.
124 Chun, *Hundred Million Idiots*, 162.
125 Chun, *Hundred Million Idiots*, 165.
126 Lee Austin Thompson, "Professional Wrestling in Japan – Medium and Message," *International Communication Review of the Sociology of Sport* 21, no. 1 (March 1986): 65–81; Shunya Yoshimi, "Japanese Television: Early Development and Research," in *A Companion to Television*, ed. Janet Wasko (Oxford: Blackwell's, 2005).
127 Thomas, "Professional Wrestling in Japan," 69.
128 "Grunt and Groan Marches On, Right at the Head of the Hit Parade," *Japan Times*, July 1, 1962.
129 Chun, *Hundred Million Idiots*, 63.
130 "The Rags to Riches Story of Rikidōzan," *Japan Times*, August 19, 1963. The full bizarre story of Rikidōzan's rise from Sumo wrestler to national icon and eventual yakuza murder victim is vividly told in: Robert Whiting, *Tokyo Underworld: The Fast Times and Hard Life of an American Gangster in Tokyo* (New York: Random House, 1999).
131 Whiting, *Tokyo Underworld*, 54.
132 In a nice parallel, the 1993 World Wrestling Federation featured matches between Yokozuna, an enormous Japanese sumo wrestler – who was booed by the American crowds – and Jim Duggan, a brave, scrappy American delivering redneck whoops to background chants of "U-S-A! U-S-A!" See Michael Billig, *Banal Nationalism* (Thousand Oaks, CA: Sage Publications Ltd, 1995), 152.
133 Thompson documents how Rikidōzan's status as Japan's "Ethnic Hero" was fueled by both wounded national pride and considerable racism directed at his foreign opponents. Thompson, "Professional Wrestling in Japan," 71–76. Ironically, Riki was of Korean origin, and had turned to wrestling only after he had failed to progress in the closed world of Sumo because of his ethnicity. The irony was compounded by the fact that the supposedly bad-guy Yankees, the Sharpe brothers, were actually Canadian. Chun, *Hundred Million Idiots*, 63.
134 Chun, *Hundred Million Idiots*, 63–64.
135 Whiting, *Tokyo Underworld*, 51.
136 Author's personal conversation, Tokyo August 2000. See also Chun, *One Hundred Million Idiots*, 60–61, who notes that early demand for TV came from small shopkeepers as much as individual homes.
137 "Pro Wrestling Alarms TV," *Japan Times*, November 26, 1955.
138 Kosaka and Motohama, "The Effects of Television," 521.
139 "Ohno, Kono to Direct Rites for Riki," *Japan Times*, December 17, 1963.
140 Chun, *Hundred Million Idiots*, 175.
141 Ishiyama Shuhei, *TV and the Contents of Education* (Tokyo: Hoso Bunka, 1952).
142 Quoted in Nishimoto Mitoji, *The Development of Educational Broadcasting in Japan* (Tokyo: Sophia University Press, 1969), 32.
143 NHK's ban on boxing was finally lifted in 1989, when the *Sugar Ray Leonard vs. Tom Hearns* bout was aired live.
144 NHK, *History of Broadcasting*, 176.
145 Yoshimi, "Japanese Television: Early Development," 543.
146 NHK, *History of Broadcasting*, 158–159.
147 Yoshimi, "Japanese Television: Early Development," 554.
148 Carol Gluck, "The Past in the Present," in *Postwar Japan as History*, ed. Andrew Gordon (Berkeley, CA: University of California Press, 1993), 74.
149 Anne Cooper-Chen, *Mass Communication in Japan* (Hoboken, NJ: Wiley-Blackwell, 1991), 119.
150 Henry D. Smith II, "The Capacity of Chushingura," *Monumenta Nipponica* 58, no. 1 (Spring 2003): 32.

151 NHK, *History of Broadcasting*, 162.
152 Samuel L. Leiter, *Kabuki at the Crossroads: Years of Crisis 1952–1965* (Leiden: Brill, 2014), 235.
153 Gluck, "The Past in the Present."
154 Shunya Yoshimi, "Television and Nationalism: Historical Change in the National Domestic TV Formation of Postwar Japan," *European Journal of Cultural Studies* 6, no. 4 (2003): 479. Brian Moeran puts different emphasis on the genre, noting that television samurai dramas tended to mix historical myth and contemporary commentary to generate "Confucian confusion" rather than clear moral messages. Brian Moeran, "Confucian Confusion: The Good, The Bad and the Noodle Western," in *The Anthropology of Evil*, ed. David Parkin (Oxford: Blackwell, 1985).
155 NHK, *History of Broadcasting*, 178.
156 "University of the Air," *Japan Times*, February 28, 1970.
157 Smith, *Television: An International History*, 174.
158 Chun, *Hundred Million Idiots*, 75.
159 Jiro Hino, "Shufu to kodomo ni taisuru terebi no eikyo [Impact of TV on Households and Children]," in Sato, ed., *Japanese Research in Communications*, 18.
160 In the United States, elite fears, not widely shared by the public, that the low quality of commercial TV was dangerous for America's educational, political, and cultural health prompted the passage of the Public Broadcasting Act, which established PBS and NPR.

References

"25 Named to Anticrime Council," *Japan Times*, March 21, 1961.
"40 Turbulent Years Recalled," *Japan Times*, March 22, 1965.
"50's Everything Was Live: Full-scale TV Broadcasting," *Fifty Years of NHK Television*, NHK, accessed March 11, 2021, www.nhk.or.jp/digitalmuseum/nhk50years_en/history/p06/index.html.
"Ariel and Caliban," *The Economist*, August 15, 1953.
"BBC Memorandum: Monopoly and Competition in Broadcasting," paper 22, in *Report of the Broadcasting Committee* (Beveridge Report) Cmmd. 8117, appendix H, paper 62, (London: HMSO, 1949), para. 10–12.
Billig, Michael, *Banal Nationalism* (Thousand Oaks, CA: Sage Publications Ltd, 1995), 152.
Boyd, D. A., "Pirate Radio in Britain: A Programming Alternative," *Journal of Communication* 36, no. 2 (1986): 83–94.
Briggs, Asa, *The History of Broadcasting in the United Kingdom: Sound and Vision*, vol. 4 (Oxford: Oxford University Press, 1979).
Briggs, Asa, *The History of Broadcasting in the United Kingdom: Competition*, vol. V (Oxford: Oxford University Press, 1995).
Camporesi, Valeria, "The BBC and American Broadcasting 1922–1955," *Media, Culture and Society* 16 (1994): 625–639.
Chapman, James, "The BBC and the Censorship of The War Game (1965)," *Journal of Contemporary History* 41, no. 1 (2006): 75–94.
Chun, Jayson Makoto, *A Nation of a Hundred Million Idiots: A Social History of Japanese Television 1953–1973* (New York: Routledge, 2007).
Cooper-Chen, Anne, *Mass Communication in Japan* (Hoboken, NJ: Wiley-Blackwell, 1991), 119.
"Diet Sessions and Debate," *Fifty Years of NHK Television*, NHK, accessed March 11, 2021, www.nhk.or.jp/digitalmuseum/nhk50years_en/history/p13/index.html.

Douglas-Home, Alec, "1964 Conservative Party General Election Manifesto," accessed 2001, www.conservative-party.net/manifestos/1964/1964-conservative-manifesto.shtml.

Geller, Judith, *Japanese Broadcasting: A Promise Fulfilled* (Queenstown, MD: The Aspen Institute, 1979).

George, Timothy S., *Minamata: Pollution and the Struggle for Democracy in Postwar Japan* (Cambridge, MA: Harvard University Asia Center, 2002).

Gluck, Carol, "The Past in the Present," in *Postwar Japan as History*, ed. Andrew Gordon (Berkeley, CA: University of California Press, 1993).

"Group Calls for Care in Chosing NHK Head," *Japan Times*, September 8, 1976.

"Grunt and Groan Marches on, Right at the Head of the Hit Parade," *Japan Times*, July 1, 1962.

Hino, Jiro, "Shufu to kodomo ni taisuru terebi no eikyo [Impact of TV on Households and Children]," in *Japanese Research in Communications (Selected Abstracts)*, ed. Hidetoshi Sato (Honolulu: University Press of Hawaii, 1974).

Jacob, Ian, "The Tasks Before the BBC Today," *The BBC Quarterly* 9, no. 3 (Autumn 1954): 132–133.

"JSP Demand Ono Step Down," *Japan Times*, September 3, 1976.

Kato, Hidetoshi, *Communications Policies in Japan* (Belgium: UNESCO, 1978).

Labour Party, "Memorandum of Evidence," *Report of the Broadcasting Committee*, Cmmd. 8117, appendix H, paper 59 (London: HMSO, 1949).

Leiter, Samuel L., *Kabuki at the Crossroads: Years of Crisis 1952–1965* (Leiden: Brill, 2014).

Litt, Paul, "The Massey Report Fifty Years Later," *Beaver* 51, no. 3 (June/July 2001).

McDonnell, James, *Public Service Broadcasting: A Reader* (New York, NY: Routledge, 1991).

Mitoji, Nishimoto, *The Development of Educational Broadcasting in Japan* (Tokyo: Sophia University Press, 1969).

Moeran, Brian, "Confucian Confusion: The Good, The Bad and the Noodle Western," in *The Anthropology of Evil*, ed. David Parkin (Oxford: Blackwell, 1985).

"NHK President Ono Resigns," *Japan Times*, September 4, 1976.

"NHK's Ono Apologizes for Visiting Tanaka," *Japan Times*, September 2, 1976.

"NHK to Televise All of Olympics," *Japan Times*, February 6, 1964.

Nichols, David, "Television News," *The Independent on Sunday*, July 10, 2011.

Noble, Greg, "Let a Hundred Channels Contend: Technological Change, Political Opening and Bureaucratic Politics in Japanese Television Broadcasting," *Journal of Japanese Studies* 26, no. 1 (Winter 2000).

"Nomura May be Selected Head of NHK," *Japan Times*, November 10, 1957.

Odagiri, Makoto, *NHK wa Naze Okanemochi na no ka?* [Why is NHK so Rich?] (Tokyo: Futabashi Press, 2014).

"Ohno, Kono to Direct Rites for Riki," *Japan Times*, December 17, 1963.

"Pro Wrestling Alarms TV," *Japan Times*, November 26, 1955.

"The Rags to Riches Story of Rikidōzan," *Japan Times*, August 19, 1963.

Reith, John, *Broadcast Over Britain* (London: Hodder and Staunton, 1924).

Reith, John, "Memorandum" to *Report of the Broadcasting Committee* (Beveridge Report) Cmmd. 8117, appendix H, paper 62, (London: HMSO) 1949.

"Sakamoto Nominated NHK President," *Japan Times*, September 22, 1976.

Sato, Hidetoshi, ed., *Japanese Research in Communications (Selected Abstracts)* (Honolulu: University Press of Hawaii, 1974).

Seaton, Jean, *Pinkoes and Traitors: The BBC and the Nation 1974–1987* (London: Profile Books, 2015).

"Second TV three-Party Debate Set for Tonight," *Japan Times*, November 16, 1960.

Shuhei, Ishiyama, *TV and the Contents of Education* (Tokyo: Hoso Bunka, 1952).

Smith II, Henry D., "The Capacity of Chushingura," *Monumenta Nipponica* 58, no. 1 (Spring 2003).

Television Act, c. 50, 1963.

"Television Broadcasting Officially Opens in Japan," *Japan Times*, February 2, 1953.

Thompson, Lee Austin, "Professional Wrestling in Japan: Medium and Message," *International Communication Review of the Sociology of Sport* 21, no. 1 (March 1986): 65–81.

Watkins, Peter, "The War Game," accessed June 1, 2015, http://pwatkins.mnsi.net/warGame.htm#update.

Wayne, Mike, "Failing the Public: The BBC, The War Game and Revisionist History: A Reply to James Chapman," *Journal of Contemporary History* 42, no. 4 (2007): 629.

White Paper on Broadcasting Policy, Cmmd. 6852 (London: HMSO), 1945–46.

Whiting, Robert, *Tokyo Underworld: The Fast Times and Hard Life of an American Gangster in Tokyo* (New York: Random House, 1999).

Yoshimi, Shunya, "Japanese Television: Early Development and Research," in *A Companion to Television*, ed. Janet Wasko (Oxford: Blackwell's, 2005).

Yoshimi, Shunya, "Television and Nationalism: Historical Change in the National Domestic TV Formation of Postwar Japan," *European Journal of Cultural Studies* 6, no. 4 (2003).

7 Video Didn't Kill the Radio Star (Satellite TV 1980s–1990s)

Cable and satellite television exploded in the 1980s, offering vastly more viewing choices and destroying one of the main rationale for public broadcasting. The election of Margaret Thatcher in 1979 ushered in neoliberal reforms, including aggressive deregulation of telecommunications and media markets. Privatization seemed inevitable, yet the BBC escaped the axe, saved in large part, by the popularity and quality of its programming. In Japan, by contrast, neoliberalism never really took off and NHK never faced any sustained similar ideological threats to its survival. Indeed, the 1980s were something of a golden era for NHK, which launched ambitious projects to develop satellite and high-definition television technology and to expand globally. Programming continued to entertain, educate, and edify in ways that tended to reflect the concerns and values of the conservative patricians of the ruling LDP. By the end of the 1990s, however, with the failure of the HDTV and expansion plans and with growing audience dissatisfaction, NHK faced its own crisis of trust.

Thatcher and Neoliberalism

By the late 1970s, economic and political storm clouds were looming over the BBC. The economy was stagnant and television production and broadcasting costs were rising much faster than license fee revenues. *Variety*, the UK trade magazine, wondered "how far into the 1980s can the BBC be sustained as a public service financed by licence fees?" given the rise in inflation, as well as competition from satellite, cable, and subscription services.[1]

The election of Thatcher's Conservative Party in 1979 marked a decisive shift toward the neoliberal philosophy of free markets and away from the corporatism embodied by the BBC. Thatcher's government aggressively privatized or partially privatized a swathe of national enterprises, including the coal, steel, and car industries, as well as public housing, gas, electricity, and the water supply. Amidst such politically sensitive targets, it was no surprise to public broadcasting under ideological attack. The broadcasting duopoly, declared the Prime Minister, "encouraged restrictive practices, increased costs, and kept out talent."[2] Thatcher wanted to end the BBC license fee, fully privatize Channel 4, liberalize the ITV auctions, develop the cable and satellite markets, and ultimately break the existing

DOI: 10.4324/b23015-7

duopoly. "I wanted to give viewers a far wider choice," she wrote, adding "I would have liked to find an alternative to the BBC licence fee."[3]

Thatcher had political as well as economic reasons to dislike the BBC, agreeing with one of her backbenchers that the Corporation demonstrated "an utter lack of patriotism and continuing left-wing bias."[4] It was true that over the decade, programming became more daring and controversial than hitherto. The *Panorama* investigation "Maggie's Militant Tendency" (1984) explored right-wing extremists within the Conservative Party. Dramas such as *Boys from Black Stuff* (1982), about the social impact of mass unemployment in Liverpool, were seen as critical of Thatcherite economic policy, while *The Monocled Mutineer* (1987) and *Tumbledown* (1988) questioned traditional narratives of patriotism and military glory. Social conventions were also challenged. *Eastenders*, a soap opera so popular that some episodes were watched by up to 70% of the country, began featuring mainstream gay characters in 1985. When a kiss between two gay men aired in 1989, traditionalists were outraged. The *Sun*'s Piers Morgan joined Mary Whitehouse and several conservative MPs in demanding, unsuccessfully, that the program be axed.[5] Meanwhile, on Radio 1, John Peel was popularizing the protest punk of the *Clash, Joy Division, UB40*, the *Tom Robinson Band, Stiff Little Fingers* and others, bringing their angry, highly progressive messages about race, class, inequality, gay rights, and Northern Ireland to national audiences.[6]

The BBC's coverage of two highly controversial issues contributed particularly to Conservative antagonism. The first was Northern Ireland, where relations between the majority Protestant and minority Catholic communities had deteriorated violently as the latter protested ongoing discrimination in the late 1960s. By the 1970s, thousands of British troops had been sent in, ostensibly to keep the peace but in practice also stoking more hostility with sometimes violent tactics. Meanwhile, paramilitaries from both communities were waging guerilla terror campaigns, which were to kill several thousand people over the decade. As Seaton argues, giving fair and appropriate coverage to all sides of this violently polarized situation was almost impossible.[7] The BBC had particular problems securing the trust of the Catholic community because they were so closely associated with the hated British state. Indeed, the BBC was legally required to uphold the integrity of the state, even though that was precisely what was being challenged. On the other hand, attempts at balance were denounced as treason by the pro-British protestants and Conservatives in London. Giving voice to paramilitaries was condemned as condoning violence, while ignoring them could be seen as taking sides, and was in any case antithetical to the journalistic mission of getting at the truth. Over the decades, Seaton argues, the life-or-death difficulties of the challenge caused a dramatic improvement in the BBC's understanding and practice of genuine impartiality in news reporting.[8] The cost was that Thatcher absolutely detested BBC coverage of Northern Ireland, which she considered too sympathetic to the Republican cause and which "played into the hands of terrorists and criminals."[9]

Thatcher had also been enraged by BBC coverage of the Falklands War in 1982, describing as "chilling" the practice of reporters referring to "British" and "Argentinean" forces rather than "ours" and "theirs."[10] As Seaton points out, the BBC had adopted this practice in the Second World War, and was generally regarded as having done a remarkably good job of covering the conflict with fairness to both sides.[11] Once again, though, the BBC's commitment to impartial reporting could never satisfy those who insisted that the Corporation put loyalty to the nation over loyalty to the truth whenever British lives were at stake.

Paradoxically for a self-described believer in individual freedom, Thatcher also wanted greater regulation of obscene or blasphemous content. She admired public morals crusader Mary Whitehouse and wrote that the permissive programming of the post-1960s BBC often "outraged the sense of public decency."[12] Thatcher sought an expansion of the powers of the Broadcasting Complaints Commission (BCC) and the Broadcasting Standards Council (BSC) she had introduced in 1981 and 1988, respectively. Yet despite a decade of debate culminating in the 1990 Broadcasting Act, and despite having all the powers available to a British Prime Minister commanding a comfortable Parliamentary majority, Thatcher proved unable to overhaul the BBC.

The crucial intellectual battle over the future of public broadcasting took place within the Peacock Committee, which Thatcher convened in 1985 to consider alternative funding sources to the license fee, including advertising. Committee Chair Professor Alan Peacock, a leading neoclassical economist and an outspoken supporter of free markets, had been handpicked by Thatcher on the basis of his sympathy with her cause. As such, Peacock posed an existential threat to the BBC greater than any of the previous Committees on public broadcasting convened since 1922. Yet, although Peacock made a powerful intellectual case for a free market in broadcasting, his Committee ultimately recommended against advertising on the BBC and in favor of its continuation as a publicly funded non-profit broadcaster.

The Peacock Report began by listing the problems with the license fee: that it was regressive; unfair to viewers who preferred ITV; expensive to administer; easy to evade, and facilitated political control over broadcasting.[13] Peacock went on to articulate a radically different ideal for broadcasting policy based, for the first time in British broadcasting debate, on the principle of consumer sovereignty. The fundamental aim of broadcasting policy should be "enlarging the freedom of choice of the consumer and the opportunities to programme makers to offer alternative wares."[14]

Peacock's neoliberalism was accompanied by a strong commitment to the principle of free speech. The Report recounted the intellectual history of free speech and censorship in British history, and approvingly quoted the First Amendment to the US Constitution.[15] This provision, remarked one committee member, "is in flat contradiction to the British system."[16] Peacock argued that Britain's broadcasting duopoly represented a form of censorship, and cited Ronald Coase's observation that "no balanced appraisal of the strengths and weaknesses of public service broadcasting should overlook the role of the BBC in keeping Winston Churchill off the air before WW2."[17] Finally, the Committee noted that the rapid adoption of new media technologies, including cable and satellite television, were rendering the old broadcasting structure obsolete. Not to adapt would be to act like King Canute, the ancient British monarch who famously and futilely commanded the sea to recede.

Peacock recommended against reform of the license fee. In fact, the report made a powerful case for continued support for public broadcasting.[18] Peacock justified this conclusion in two ways, both compatible with his neoliberal principles. First was the public goods argument that programs promoting knowledge and culture, or were innovative and experimental, were socially valuable but would be underprovided by the market. "Programmes which viewers and listeners are willing to support in their capacity as taxpayers and voters, but not directly as consumers."[19] Public support for such content could be reconciled with the principle of consumer sovereignty in three ways. First, viewers may appreciate or enjoy programming they would not necessarily have chosen for themselves. Second, many people accept guidance from others on matters where they believe their knowledge is limited. Finally, many people want high-quality programming to be available even if they would not willingly watch or listen to it in large enough numbers to pay for it directly.[20]

Peacock was careful to distinguish between *patronage*, which could be justified on market failure grounds, and *paternalism*, which could not. This was the first official rejection of Reith's elitist contention that someone other than the viewers should decide what should be aired:

> If one believes that people should be allowed to make their own decisions, and they appear content with a diet of junk food, then we can support all kinds of activities designed to enlarge their tastes and inform them of the merits of other foods. But if after all these efforts they still make for junk food, that is their privilege in a free society.[21]

The economic rationale for the BBC was that the broadcasting market was currently imperfect. Limited spectrum meant limited competition, so full consumer choice was impossible.

> In the highly imperfect broadcasting market we have known and which continues to exist, the role of public service is much wider. So long as the number of television channels is severely limited by spectrum shortage, and there is no direct payment by viewers and listeners [*i.e.* no commercially viable technology to facilitate direct payment], an unregulated advertiser-financed broadcasting system, so far from satisfying consumer demand, can actually distort it [by undersupplying minority programs.][22]

Peacock believed that the BBC and ITV had done an excellent job of mimicking the market under conditions of imperfect competition, and warmly praised their output.[23] However, while the public goods rationale for the BBC would continue to hold up, the spectrum scarcity rationale would become less and less persuasive as technologies improved.

The Report therefore recommended that the Government pave the way for greater competition by encouraging the development of more channels and requiring all new TV sets to have technology compatible with subscription television.

In the medium term, Peacock saw the license fee being replaced by a subscription for willing viewers. Longer term, he seems to have agreed with his advisor and fellow committee member Peter Jay that the BBC was ultimately doomed by the advent of a fiber-optic society in which all viewers would be individually wired up.[24] These widely held expectations proved wrong. The digital revolution and the explosion of media competition demolished the spectrum scarcity rationale for public broadcasting but made the public goods argument stronger.

Despite his ideological sympathy with Thatcher and Reagan, Peacock flatly rejected the American free-market fundamentalism of the then FCC Chairman: "The [Mark] Fowler model should not form the eventual aim for the UK."[25] The Report noted drily that over the course of the hearings, "the U.S. model has been cited countless times by organizations and individuals as an example of how broadcasting should *not* be run."[26] Peacock concluded that for the time being, advertising on the BBC would not reap the benefits of market competition and would lose the considerable benefits of the license fee system. Indeed, one of the Report's final conclusions is that "there will be a distinct and important role for the BBC for as long ahead as anyone cares to look."[27]

Labour supporters of the BBC were jubilant. "A collection of trustees hand-picked to give the right answer have failed to oblige," crowed Labour shadow cabinet minister Gerald Kaufman, who went on to celebrate the BBC's escape from twin perils of either being turned into "the TV equivalent of junk food" or being driven "into a cultural ghetto."[28]

Margaret Thatcher was predictably disappointed by the Report, not least because it came in the wake of a vicious fight with the BBC over *Real Lives: At the Edge of the Union*, a documentary that interviewed political extremists on both sides of the Northern Irish conflict, and that had become the ugliest battle between government and BBC since the General Strike.[29] The case showed both willingness of certain UK politicians to interfere with the BBC's editorial auton-omy, and the internal turmoil as the BBC responded.[30] In 1985, responding to an Irish Republican Army (IRA) terror campaign that had included the bombing of the Brighton Hotel where she was staying, killing five people, Thatcher declared the terrorists should be denied "the oxygen of publicity." She would later pass legislation prohibiting representatives from designated terrorist organizations from speaking directly on public media. When she discovered that the *Real Lives* team had interviewed a senior Republican paramilitary, Home Secretary Leon Brittan demanded the episode be canceled. The BBC Governors took the almost unprecedented step of previewing the episode and agreed not to air it. Many BBC staff promptly went on strike, alleging censorship, and public outrage against the government followed. In the face of deep distrust between Governors and senior management, and in turn between senior management and staff, Director-General Alisdair Milne reversed the decision and the program aired. He was sacked 18 months later. Ironically, his defenestration was probably delayed because the Gov-ernors did not want to appear vindictive.[31] Even more ironically, the interviewee at the center of the storm, Martin McGuinness, was later to become Deputy First Minister of Northern Ireland.

Thatcher's failure to reform the BBC was in part a result of divisions within the Conservative Party, which had always been ambivalent about public broadcasting. The so-called drys, neoliberals such as Chancellor Nigel Lawson and Home Secretary Leon Brittan, agreed with the Prime Minister on the need for competition. In contrast, the "wets," traditional patricians such as Douglas Hurd and William Whitelaw, supported the BBC as it was, the latter threatening to resign from the Cabinet if advertising were introduced.[32] Moreover, many neoliberals, including both Peacock and Thatcher herself, privately admired much of the BBC's programming. Thatcher did not simply have had ITV in mind when she wrote that British television is "internationally in a class of its own."[33] Her proposals to enact far stricter controls on sex and violence weakened the philosophical thrust of her calls for reform, and struck old-school Tories such as Hurd as censorship.[34]

The BBC had the support of what Thatcher describes as a "powerful lobby,"[35] which included the Labour Party, a majority of public opinion, and even its rivals in commercial broadcasting. The Deputy Chairman of Granada TV likened privatization of the BBC to Disneyland taking over the British Museum.[36] The British public remained solidly, although by no means universally, fond of the BBC: 71% of TV viewers thought the license fee represented fairly or very good value at a little over one pound per week.[37] Nor did the public share Thatcher's perception of left-wing bias at the Corporation. A 1985 survey found 22% of viewers believed BBC 1 favored the Conservatives, while only 4% thought the channel favored the Labour Party. By contrast, 6% believed ITV favored Conservatives and 8% thought it favored Labor.[38]

Meanwhile, Peacock's conclusions overshadowed deliberations for the 1988 Broadcasting White Paper and then the neoliberal 1990 Broadcasting Act, which introduced greater competition to the wider broadcasting market. The Act liberalized the ITV auctions, and facilitated expansion of multichannel satellite TV. Rules were introduced to restrict media cross-ownership but a specific exemption, the "Murdoch Loophole," permitted News International to expand its newspaper holdings (notably *The Times* and the *Sun*) and its satellite TV ventures.[39] The Act broke the IBA into two separate bodies, the Independent Television Commission (ITC) and the Radio Authority, both of which were to be "light touch" regulators. The roles of the BCC and BSC were formalized.

The BBC was left largely untouched by the Act, save for a requirement inspired by the success of Channel 4 that at least 25% of its total programming be obtained from independent production companies.[40] This was to prove a momentous decision, leading to a major shift in the Corporation's internal dynamics as program production shifted from being largely in-house to being predominantly outsourced over the next two decades.[41] This shift contributed to the vitality of Britain's broader creative economy, giving a boost to independent production companies and producing global successes such as *Wallace and Grommit* and *Downton Abbey*.[42] This dynamic, in turn, has given policymakers economic incentives to keep the BBC itself healthy.

Meanwhile, many Conservative politicians remained sympathetic to the BBC because of the perceived excellence of its programming. In a 1995 Parliamentary debate on renewal of the Royal Charter, Conservative Secretary of State for National Heritage Stephen Dorrell declared:

> Although we are all occasionally annoyed by material produced by the BBC . . . the unavoidable and welcome truth is that throughout its history the BBC has made a serious effort to maintain independence and has established a public reputation in doing so.[43]

David Mellor, his fellow Conservative and predecessor as Minister for National Heritage, agreed:

> One can go to New York, as I did not so long ago, push one's way through thirty channels on television and find nothing that remotely engages one's attention. That is not choice, that is the absence of choice. . . . It is trash and rubbish from the archives, badly presented, thrown into a pot. It is not quality broadcasting of the type that we want to watch.[44]

The Charter was renewed until 1996, and then again until 2006. The BBC had weathered Thatcherism.

NHK, Industrial Policy, and Expansion

In the early 1980s, Japanese broadcasting remained a cozy oligopoly of NHK and five commercial broadcasters. NHK maintained a secure position, with about 25% of audience share and 30% of the total broadcasting staff.[45] NHK's annual revenues of ¥600 billion were approximately twice those of any other broadcaster. The broadcaster thus faced the challenges of the era – neoliberalism, globalization, and technological change – in a stronger position than its British counterpart. Nonetheless, these challenges required response. NHK's strategic decisions, including aggressive technological development, global expansion, and commercialization, were to create further problems, but NHK entered the period enjoying the support of three key constituencies: the government, the bureaucracy, and even the commercial networks.

Politically, NHK retained the favor of the LDP and the political establishment. Neoliberalism never took hold in Japan to the degree it did in the United States or Britain, and NHK stayed safe from ideological attack. The LDP's firm grip on power, loosened only somewhat by the Lockheed Scandal, was resumed during the economic boom. Nakasone Yasuhiro, Prime Minister from 1982 to 1987, was a close friend of Ronald Reagan and shared his faith in free markets to a greater degree than most LDP leaders. Nakasone privatized telecommunications monopoly NTT and began deregulating some sectors, usually those most exposed to global competition such as financial services. In these cases, though, liberalization was undertaken as a response to demands from Japanese business interests rather than for ideological reasons.[46] Few powerful voices, and none in the LDP, called for such radical reform at NHK. This was in large part due to the close ties between the ruling LDP and NHK, and to the fact that NHK's non-confrontational news and uncontroversial, wholesome content served status quo interests. McCargo, among others, notes that the LDP, unusually for a conservative party, generally preferred NHK to the commercial networks.[47]

However, the commercial broadcasters, represented by *Minpōren*, were generally tolerant, even supportive of NHK. They complained almost ritualistically about NHK's power but fell far short of demanding its privatization. Japan's commercial TV stations were reluctant to propose radical reform of NHK in large part because they were very comfortable with their own protected positions.[48] As a commercial enterprise, NHK's wealth of assets and high reputation would have made it an extraordinarily powerful competitor. In the ever-more-important area of sports coverage, moreover, NHK was able to use its political clout and bargaining power to hold down costs to broadcast rights, for which all broadcasters benefitted.[49] NHK management were also said to be adept at placating their commercial rivals by striking behind-the-scenes deals to split coverage of certain expensive events.[50] Finally, NHK's presence relieved pressure on commercial broadcasters to produce expensive or less popular programming such as news and education.

NHK also enjoyed the support of the bureaucracy, and two key policymaking ministries in particular. *Yuseishō*, the Ministry of Posts and Telecommunications (MPT), had the job of regulating the entire broadcasting sector, and saw its primary role as being to protect the interests of the industry itself rather than those of the viewing public.[51] NHK was seen as the jewel in the crown of this industry, with the international reputation of its documentaries and costume dramas being sources of great pride in the Japanese establishment. In addition, NHK, through its research and development laboratories, enjoyed a close and productive relationship with MITI (the Ministry of Economy, Trade and Industry), chief architect of Japan's fabled industrial policy.[52]

Of greater concern to NHK than political assault, then, were financial problems that grew during the 1980s. The growth in viewer fees stagnated as the uptake of color television sets leveled out. The quality of commercial television had also vastly improved as advertising revenues had risen strongly over the past decade or so, putting upward pressure on program budgets. Finally, of course, the new satellite and cable technologies required some strategic response. In response, NHK developed three broad new strategies to maintain its position in this changing environment.

First, NHK would aggressively develop new technologies, most notably in satellite broadcasting and High Definition Television (HDTV) in order to dominate the new media landscape against commercial rivals both domestic and foreign.[53] Second, NHK joined the *kokusaika* (globalization) trend sweeping Japan in the 1980s with plans for the Global News Network (GNN) to rival CNN and the BBC. Finally, NHK sought permission to expand into commercial businesses via subsidiary companies.

NHK began developing satellite broadcasting in the mid-1960s as a way to provide television coverage to every household in Japan, as required by the

Broadcast Law.[54] At that time, the country's mountainous geography meant that over 100,000 households could not receive a proper signal.[55] Both Krauss and Noble, however, argue that NHK also developed satellite technology with an eye to using it to broadcast HDTV.[56] Development in direct broadcast satellite television (DBS) continued in conjunction with the National Space Development Agency and the MPT. NHK launched trial DBS broadcasting on the NHK BS-1 Channel in 1984. Boosted in part by the popularity of the 1988 Seoul Olympics, regular full-scale broadcasts began in 1989. The service required an additional monthly fee, and proved popular, achieving ten million subscribers, roughly one in four households, by 2000. Commercial broadcasters clamored to be allowed to follow suit. The MPT merged them all into a single private DBS operator using NHK's satellite platform and a rented decoder.[57] The new service, Wowow, commenced broadcasts in 1991 but never achieved the popularity of NHK's satellite service. DBS may thus be claimed a technological success for the public broadcaster. NHK, or more accurately, the fee-paying public, was bearing most of the costs of what had become, in effect, national industrial policy.[58]

HDTV, however, was to prove a spectacular financial failure for NHK.[59] Like DBS, HDTV was a product of NHK research and funding stretching back to the 1960s. In 1978, NHK made a fateful decision to adopt a transmission standard that could broadcast on the bandwidth of existing BS satellite channels.[60] This standard, Hi-vision MUSE, was a hybrid system in which images were compressed digitally and then transmitted through analog signals. It produced far superior image quality to alternatives, but was not compatible with any of the world's existing TV formats. In addition, all related equipment such as the cameras and, most importantly, compatible TV sets, had to be designed and produced from scratch.[61] MPT and the electronics manufacturers preferred a broadcast system that used existing television systems, but NHK persevered with their system. As MUSE improved, the MPT, the economic planning ministry MITI, and the electronics industry finally came on board.

By 1987, Hi-vision Muse, backed now by the key government agencies as well as NHK, was accepted as the only HDTV transmission standard in Japan.[62] President Shima Keiji was so confident of NHK's technological capabilities that he accused US commercial broadcasters of being too optimistic about their survival in the new multichannel world, taunting them for "not moving aggressively into the future" of analog HDTV.[63] Japanese electronics firms had concluded that if they could dominate this technology, and if it became the global standard, they would dominate a whole series of related technologies such as recording devices, and filming equipment. Sony and Matsushita joined forces to refine the technology and push down the prohibitively expensive prices of HDTV sets. The electronics giants also rushed to secure the killer content needed to sell their hardware, paying handsomely for big-name producers such as Columbia Pictures, whose acquisition by Sony in 1989 raised a storm of controversy in the United States.[64] Meanwhile, the Japanese government aggressively tried to get Hi-Vision MUSE adopted as the international broadcast standard.[65] NHK poured resources into

HDTV coverage of the 1988 Seoul Olympics. The technology had become a key gamble in Japan's new industrial policy.[66]

But the bet never paid off. Full-time HDTV broadcasting began in Japan in 1991, but the system found no international support. Neither the United States nor the EU were interested in adopting the Japanese standards. This refusal was partly to protect their own electronics manufacturers and partly because of the well-founded belief that Japan's system, as impressive as it was, would rapidly become obsolete. The FCC, for example, had decided by the very early 1990s that next-generation TV formats would have to be in full digital format.[67] Moreover, with compatible receivers costing in excess of $8,000, the service attracted very few domestic subscribers. By 1994, the MPT had reluctantly concluded that their system was dead and began to focus on digital broadcasting. Estimates of NHK's direct costs for developing the stillborn analog transmission system were as high as $200 million.[68] Meanwhile, the saga became a byword for the "Galapagos Effect," referring to the exotic animals discovered by Charles Darwin that were exquisitely evolved for a specific closed environment but utterly helpless in the outside world.[69]

The second part of NHK's three-pronged strategic response to the multichannel environment was globalization. The plan was to achieve a greater international presence with a new venture, the Global News Network (GNN). GNN was the brainchild of NHK President Shima Keiji, who had ambitions to rival the BBC in international reputation, and who believed that CNN was "trying to force U.S. news on the rest of us."[70] The service would have been based in New York, broadcast in English, and cost around $800 million a year to produce. However, the initiative never enjoyed much internal support, and did not last long.[71] First proposed in 1990, GNN was dropped a year later after Shima, a highly controversial President, resigned in disgrace.[72] He had lied to the Diet, claiming to have been at the failed launch of a US rocket carrying an NHK satellite when he had in fact been in a Los Angeles hotel with his mistress.[73]

As at the BBC, globalization pushed NHK toward greater entrepreneurialism. For both broadcasters, the arrival of very well-funded commercial competition had pushed up costs for technology and content, management feared that reliance on viewer fees was unsustainable. Cost-cutting measures such as subcontracting drama production could only go so far, especially because such measures provoked loud opposition from *Nipōren*.[74] Management accordingly sought permission to generate alternative sources of revenue. In 1982, the MPT and LDP agreed to revise the Broadcast Law to allow NHK to invest in affiliated companies. Further revisions in 1988 allowed even greater leeway. Some affiliates, such as the NHK Symphony orchestra and NHK Publishing, had been around for decades. Other affiliated companies, of which NHK Enterprises became the best known, grew rapidly in number and size. NHK Enterprises in turn established related ventures such as Media International Corp, a video software distribution company. Each new enterprise in turn was resisted by commercial broadcasters.[75] By 1992, NHK had 30 affiliates, with total sales equivalent to those of an average Tokyo commercial TV station.[76]

But the more successful the commercialization strategy became, the more opposition it generated.[77] *Minpō* argued that NHK's pursuit of profit was a violation of the Broadcasting Law, and that "NHK is taking unfair advantage of the number of media it controls."[78] The authorities responded by restricting NHK's commercial activities and easing restrictions on the commercial channels. For example, when *Minpō* argued in 2001 that it was "unfair that only NHK can operate multiple channels," the newly formed Ministry of Public Management, Home Affairs, Posts and Telecommunications Ministry (*Sōmushō*) agreed to allow the commercial broadcaster to merge local stations and operate multiple channels.[79]

Programming, meanwhile, remained the sort of safe, high-quality but staid fare developed in the 1960s and 1970s. News and information, in particular, remained trusted but uncontroversial and non-confrontational, as Krauss documents.[80] However, Krauss also confirms what the Trilateral commission reported in 1975: "NHK clings more strictly to the principle of nonpartisanship and to a less critical spirit than the newspapers."[81] For example, according to Elizabeth MacLachen's careful account, during the 1995 Kobe earthquake, NHK was able to provide coverage that was "detailed, compassionate, authoritative, and journalistically responsible."[82] Yet NHK refused to broadcast criticisms of the government for the first several days of the earthquake, unlike the commercial broadcasters who aired their own observations if the Government line was late or clearly inaccurate.[83] The public broadcaster was regarded as the station that most downplayed the extent of the damage. This was in part a reflection of the broadcaster's laudable editorial insistence on confirmed numbers rather than speculation or sensationalism. According to NHK news staff, "It was not our duty to dramatize the events . . . we were told to encourage people."[84] On the other hand, reliance on official numbers meant dependency on the state. Only when smaller broadcasters aired foreign criticisms of government action did NHK reports begin to air such criticism.[85]

Documentaries and documentary-style dramas became a hallmark of NHK programming. Science programming continued to be both popular and accessible to wide audiences, with the Monday evening Science Specials getting an approximate 24% market share.[86] On the other hand, Japanese scientists were critical of NHK's reluctance to tackle controversial scientific issues.[87] The era's standout piece of educational filmmaking was *The Silk Road* (1980–1984), an epic documentary series co-produced with Chinese state television and winner of numerous global awards.

Japanese high culture was an important source of content. NHK was the only broadcaster consistently to air classical music and dance. Traditional theater performances of Noh, Kyogen, Bunraku, and Kabuki made up almost one-eighth of all television drama in the late 1960s.[88] NHK was also an important curator of national folk culture, taking an active role in recording traditional folk songs as soon as the technologies became available.[89] In the early 1980s, NHK took up the cause of *taishu engeki*, small-scale street theater, reviving it from near extinction.[90] *Butoh* also found a home at NHK. Performances of this disturbing, avant-garde dance form were rare on television, but produced and aired by NHK, albeit under the heading of "culture" rather than "dance."[91] But there were also signs that NHK were more concerned with presenting a stereotyped image of national tradition than reflecting messy reality, as is illustrated in D.P. Martinez's discussion of the making of a documentary about the village of Kuzaki, home of a traditional ritual of diving for and making *noshi awabi* (dried abalone used ceremonially at Ise shrine). The documentary-makers insisted the old men wear traditional clothes, usually worn only for the initial ceremony, throughout the process. The producer also instructed participants to remove wristwatches and other modern accessories that would jar with the "traditional" look.[92]

The era's standout work of entertainment was the Morning drama *Oshin* (1983–1984), which won an astonishing 65% audience share in Japan and aired in 57 different countries.[93] It may not be coincidental that this most successful of the *asa dora* was also the first to be directed by a woman, Hashida Sugako. The eponymous heroine was born into poverty and sent away to work as a maid at age 7. Patiently and heroically, she endures cruel employers, mothers-in-law, earthquakes, and wars. She suffers a miscarriage, her son is killed in the war, and her husband commits suicide. Finally, she achieves success as the owner of a small supermarket. The message of approval for working women was underscored by the writer's guide for the series, which included a chart of women's contributions to recent Japanese history. Hashida denied that this had any connection to the then government policy of encouraging women to work.[94] But a viewer survey conducted by NHK six months into the series revealed another subtext. Viewers were asked such leading questions as whether Oshin made them "realize the importance of perseverance and patience, things that tend to be forgotten in our affluent society." Over 40% agreed that it did, and even more admitted to crying.[95] Critics, including Paul Harvey, saw in Oshin's rise an allegory for Japan's own postwar rebirth, and an essentially conservative indictment of the decadent affluence of the 1980s.[96]

NHK tended to follow rather than lead in tackling issues of gender and sexuality. Although NHK made documentaries about gay issues, and indeed were the first major TV network to publicize the problems of AIDS sufferers, it was the commercial stations rather than NHK that made gayness visible in mainstream entertainment.[97] NTV aired the first major drama series to tackle gay themes. The 1993 melodrama *Dōsōkai* ("Reunion"), concerning a young married Tokyoite coming to terms with being gay, was a big success, with a 20% audience share.[98] *Dōsōkai* was followed by TBS's *Inochi Sasete Mama, Papa wa AIDS Nan* ("Does Dad Have AIDs? Support Him Mama!") aired in the same year, and Fuji TV's *Kami-sama, Mo Sukoshi Dake* ("Please God, Just a Little More Time") aired in prime time in 1998.[99]

NHK treatment of women, both in front of and behind the camera, continued to reflect rather than challenge traditional gender norms, although the period saw some progress: the first female co-anchor of an evening news program only appeared in 1979.[100] News programs, though, followed the pattern of older, more serious-sounding male newscasters partnered with younger, more deferential women, with the men doing the overwhelming majority of the talking.[101] Krauss describes the appointment of NHK journalists as a "highly selective recruitment through merit through examination."[102] But he also notes that of the 140 successful applicants for reporter positions in 1984, there were 131 men and only 9 women. Such gender imbalance is seen in many countries, although Japan was outlier even so. In 1993, women represented 0.4% of senior positions in Japanese broadcasting, versus 14.1% in France and 13.9% in the United Kingdom.[103] Sakurai Yoshiko, the main newscaster for a commercial station in the 1990s, reported a co-worker telling her: "A woman has to be cute."[104] And even in an already male-dominated sector, NHK's hiring practices seem less progressive than at commercial stations, although both are improving. In 1990, women represented 5.9% of all NHK employees, and 0.2% of reporters. At the private broadcasters, women represented 18.5% of all employees and 0.4% of reporters.[105] By 2007, women represented 26.6% of newly hired employees at NHK and 31.8% at the commercial stations. By contrast, women comprised 39% of new graduate hires at the Mainichi Shimbun.[106]

Staid, conservative, and uncontroversial programming undoubtedly helped ensure the support of political elites, but at an increasing cost in viewer loyalty, especially among the young. As the economic recession of the 1990s dragged on, and as alternative sources of entertainment grew, more and more viewers and commentators began to question the legitimacy of the viewer fee.[107] By the end of the 1990s, NHK was facing a dramatic loss of viewers. One wrote:

> I have lived alone for about a year since I started going to college. Throughout that period, I have been very much annoyed by one thing: the fee for NHK. Although it is our legal duty to pay for the broadcasting, I just can't understand why I should pay it since I am not a viewer of NHK programs. As a college student living alone, I can't afford to pay it. People around me, who also live alone, say the same thing. It is too much of a burden for us to pay.[108]

Declining viewer rates presented a new challenge for NHK management. Tellingly, they looked for the solution not at changing the tenor of their content, but at developing a new technology, digital television.[109]

The technological, economic, and ideological developments of the 1980s strained almost to breaking point the relationship between conservative politicians and the BBC, multichannel television eroded the scarcity rationale for public broadcasting, while neoliberalism attacked its core philosophy. The BBC's outspoken programming and choice to champion social change on issues such as gay rights heightened the conflict with the state. However, Margaret Thatcher's attempt to privatize the BBC failed, lacking support from either the public or paternalistic elements of her own Conservative Party. NHK avoided political attack, in part because the LDP, bureaucrats, and powerful electronics manufacturers all valued NHK's technology research capacities. The HDTV debacle demonstrated the dangers of such close state–broadcaster relationships, but did not prompt widespread calls for reform. Political support for NHK was also encouraged by its non-confrontational news reporting and traditional, inoffensive entertainment. The downside of this traditional programming philosophy was declining loyalty among young viewers and rising criticism of the viewing fee.

Notes

1 Bert Baker, "The BBC has to Struggle," *Variety*, January 9, 1980.
2 Margaret Thatcher, *The Downing Street Years* (New York: Harpercollins, 1993), 635.
3 Thatcher, *The Downing Street Years*, 635–636.
4 John Stokes MP (Halesowen and Stourbridge) 'Debate on BBC Financing House of Commons' 3 July 1986, *Hansard*, vol. 100, 1191, accessed October 28, 2021, https://hansard.parliament.uk/Commons/1986-07-03/debates/7efc8223-2a4c-46a7-8620-ecf21d0ba4c6/BbcFinancing(PeacockReport).
5 Chris Godfrey, "How Michael Cashman Changed the World," *The Guardian*, January 29, 2020.
6 "John Peel," *The Economist*, November 6, 2004. The lack of interest in gender equality by otherwise progressive British punk bands should be noted.
7 Jean Seaton, *Pinkoes and Traitors: The BBC and the Nation 1974–1987* (London: Profile Books, 2015), 58–84.
8 Seaton, *Pinkoes and Traitors*, 63.
9 Thatcher, *The Downing Street Years*, 634.
10 Thatcher, *The Downing Street Years*, 81.
11 Seaton, *Pinkoes and Traitors*, 161–185.
12 Thatcher, *The Downing Street Years*, 634.
13 *Report of the Committee on Financing the BBC (Peacock Report)*, Cmmd. 9824 (London: HSMO, 1986), para. 209.
14 Peacock Report, para. 592.
15 Peacock Report, paras 16–27 and 548–549.
16 Samuel Brittan, "The Fight for Freedom in Broadcasting," *The Political Quarterly* 58, no. 1 (January–March 1987): 9.
17 Coase, cited in *Peacock Report*, para 596.
18 *Peacock Report*, para 580.
19 *Peacock Report*, para 580.
20 *Peacock Report*, para 564.
21 *Peacock Report*, para. 566.
22 *Peacock Report*, para. 581.
23 *Peacock Report*, para. 582.
24 Alistair Milne, *D.G.: Memoirs of a British Broadcaster* (London: Hodder and Stoughton, 1988), 170.
25 *Peacock Report*, para. 573.
26 *Peacock Report*, para. 140 (emphasis added).
27 Alan Budd, "The Peacock Committee and the BBC: Liberal Values versus Regulation," *Public Money & Management* 6, no. 3 (December 1986): 29–33.
28 "Debate on BBC Financing," House of Commons 3rd July 1986 *Hansard*, vol. 100. 1180–1193, accessed October 28, 2021, https://hansard.parliament.uk/Commons/1986-07-03/debates/7efc8223-2a4c-46a7-8620-ecf21d0ba4c6/BbcFinancing(PeacockReport).
29 BBC, "History of the BBC: Real Lives," accessed October 28, 2021, www.bbc.com/historyofthebbc/anniversaries/june/real-lives/.
30 Discussed in detail in Seaton, *Pinkoes and Traitors*, 313–317.
31 Roy Greenslade, "After 30 Years, More Light Is Cast on BBC's Real Lives Drama," *The Guardian*, August 3, 2015.
32 Mark Stuart, *Douglas Hurd: An Authorized Biography* (Edinburgh: Mainstream Publishing, 1998), 157.

33 Thatcher, *The Downing Street Years*, 634.
34 Stuart, *Douglas Hurd*, 159.
35 Thatcher, *The Downing Street Years*, 637.
36 McDonnell, *Public Service Broadcasting*, 106.
37 "Financing the BBC: A Survey of Public Opinion," *NOP Market Research* (London: HMSO, 1985), 11.
38 Robert Mullan, *Consuming Television* (Oxford: Blackwell's, 1997), 118.
39 John Dugdale, "1990 Broadcasting Act," *The Guardian*, November 19, 2000, www.guardian.co.uk/media/2000/nov/20/broadcasting.mondaymediasection2.
40 BBC, accessed May 16, 2018, www.bbc.co.uk/commissioning/tv/how-we-work/how-we-commission.shtml.
41 Author's interview with a BBC producer on May 5, 2016.
42 L. Lazzeretti, ed., *Creative Industries and Innovation in Europe: Concepts, Measures and Comparative Case Studies* (London: Routledge, 2012).
43 Stephen Dorrell, House of Commons Debate "The Future of the BBC" 9th February 1995, *Hansard*, vol. 254, 473, accessed October 28, 2021, https://hansard.parliament.uk/Commons/1995-02-09/debates/4f7f2e37-8c9c-4385-ab39-76509410512e/Bbc.
44 David Mellor, House of Commons Debate "The Future of the BBC" 9th February 1995, *Hansard*, vol. 254, 491, accessed October 28, 2021, https://hansard.parliament.uk/Commons/1995-02-09/debates/4f7f2e37-8c9c-4385-ab39-76509410512e/Bbc.
45 Greg Noble, "Let a Hundred Channels Contend: Technological Change, Political Opening and Bureaucratic Politics in Japanese Television Broadcasting," *Journal of Japanese Studies* 26, no. 1 (Winter 2000): 83.
46 As I have argued elsewhere. Henry Laurence, *Money Rules: The New Politics of Finance in Britain and Japan* (Ithaca, NY: Cornell University Press, 2001).
47 Duncan McCargo, *Media and Politics in Pacific Asia* (London: RoutledgeCurzon, 2003), 67.
48 Author's interview with commercial broadcasting staff in Tokyo in September 2000.
49 Author's own interview with a media analyst in Tokyo in September 2000.
50 Author's own interview with a media analyst in Tokyo in September 2000.
51 Koichi Nakano, "Becoming a Policy Ministry: The Organization and Amakudari of the Ministry of Posts and Telecommunications," *Journal of Japanese Studies* 24, no. 1 (Winter 1980).
52 Chalmers Johnson, *MITI and the Japanese Miracle: The Growth of Industrial Policy 1925–1975* (Stanford: Stanford University Press, 1982).
53 Noble, "Let a Hundred Channels Contend," 90.
54 NHK staff member. Author interview, Tokyo, October 10, 2000.
55 NHK, *Broadcasting in Japan*, 249.
56 Noble, "Let a Hundred Channels Contend," 90; Krauss, *Broadcasting Politics*, 185.
57 Noble, "Let a Hundred Channels Contend," 91.
58 Roya Akhavan-Majid, "Public Service Broadcasting and the Challenge of New Technology: A Case Study of Japan's NHK," *International Communication Gazette* 50, no. 21 (1992): 29.
59 The full story is told in Jeffrey Hart, *Technology, Television and Competition* (Cambridge: Cambridge University Press, 2004).
60 NHK, *Broadcasting in Japan*, 253.
61 Krauss, *Broadcasting Politics*, 186.
62 Sheridan Tatsuno, *Created in Japan: From Imitators to World-Class Innovators* (New York: Harper and Row, 1990), 129–149.
63 "NHK Executive Sees Future in HDTV, DBS," *Broadcasting* 114, no. 11 (March 14, 1988).
64 Garth Alexander and Andrew Davidson, "Japan Takes a Wide View of TV," *Sunday Times*, August 4, 1991.
65 Krauss, *Broadcasting Politics*, 187–190.

66 Tatsuno, *Created in Japan*, 130.
67 Takashi Masuko, "Time to Rethink Hi-Vision," *Nikkei Weekly*, September 19, 1992.
68 Henny Sender, "Image Problems," *Far Eastern Economic Review*, October 6, 1994, 81.
69 Author's own interview with a media analyst in Tokyo in September 2000.
70 Howard French, "NHK of Japan Ends Plan for Global News Service," *New York Times*, November 8, 1991.
71 The full story is told in Krauss, *Broadcasting Politics*, 198–204.
72 "NHK Shelves Plan," *Japan Times*, December 12, 1991.
73 "NHK Chief Announces Resignation over False Statements Made to Diet," *Japan Times*, July 16, 1991.
74 "Union Raps NHK Sub-contracting," *Daily Yomiuri*, March 15, 1991.
75 "NHK Venture's Commercialism Criticized," *Japan Times*, July 21, 1990.
76 Suzuki, "NHK Under Fire," 11.
77 Yoshikazu Suzuki, "NHK Under Fire for Commercial Tilt," *Daily Yomiuri*, January 22, 1992.
78 Ai Nakajima, "NHK Software Ties Worry Commercial Rivals," *Japan Economic Journal*, September 1, 1990.
79 "Broadcasting Regulations under Ministry Scrutiny," *Japan Times*, March 3, 2001. The new ministry was the result of a 2001 merger of the Ministry of Posts and Telecommunications, the Ministry of Home Affairs and the Management and Coordination Agency. In 2004, its English name became the Ministry of Internal Affairs and Communication. *Sōmushō*, its short Japanese name, refers to the "General Affairs Ministry."
80 Krauss, *Broadcasting Politics in Japan*.
81 Michel Crozier, Samuel Huntington, and Joji Watanuki, *The Crisis of Democracy* (New York: New York University Press, 1975), 134.
82 Elizabeth MacLachlan, "Turning Seeing into Believing," in *Asian Media Productions*, ed. Bruce Moeran (Richmond: Curzon Press, 2001), 118.
83 MacLachlan, "Turning Seeing into Believing," 122.
84 MacLachlan, "Turning Seeing into Believing," 121.
85 MacLachlan, "Turning Seeing into Believing," 121.
86 Marcel Chotkowski La Follette, "Science on Japanese Public Television: An Adaptable Model for the U.S.?" *Science, Technology and Human Values* 4, no. 27 (Spring 1979): 61.
87 La Follette, "Science on Japanese Public Television," 63.
88 Martin Cobin, "Traditional Theatre and Modern Television in Japan," *Educational Theatre Journal* 21, no. 2 (May 1969): 162.
89 Takashi Ogawa, "The Collection and Preservation of Japanese Folk Songs by the Japan Broadcasting Corporation (NHK)," *Journal of the International Folk Music Council* 13 (1961): 83–84.
90 Marylin Ivy, "Formation of Mass Culture," in *Postwar Japan as History*, ed. Andrew Gordon (Berkeley, CA: University of California Press, 1993), 257.
91 Author's own interview with Butoh performer in Tokyo in November 2000.
92 D.P. Martinez, "NHK Comes to Kuzaki," in *Ideology and Practice in Modern Japan*, eds. Roger Goodman and Kirsten Refsing (London: Routledge, 1992), 153–170.
93 Anne Cooper-Chen, *Mass Communication in Japan* (Hoboken, NJ: Wiley-Blackwell, 1991), 118.
94 Paul Harvey, "Nonchan's Drama: NHK Morning Serialized Television Novels," in *The Worlds of Japanese Pop Culture*, ed. D.P. Martinez (Cambridge: Cambridge University Press, 1998), 138.
95 NHK, *History of Broadcasting*, 236.
96 Harvey, "Nonchan's Drama." See also Wilhelmina Penn, *The Couch Potato's Guide to Japan: Inside the World of Japanese TV* (Japan: Forest River Press, 2003), 43.
97 Ann Saphir, "A Policy of Silence," *Look Japan*, August 1994.
98 Steven D. Miller, "The (Temporary?) Queering of Japanese TV," *Journal of Homosexuality* 39, no. 3 (April 2000): 83–109.

99 Penn, *Couch Potato's Guide*, 115.
100 Miiko Kodama, "Nyūsu no okurite toshite no josei [Women as Newscasters]," in *Hyogen to Mejia*, eds. Teruko Inoue, Chizuko Ueno, and Yumiko Ehara (Tokyo: Iwanami Shoten, 1995), 203. At the BBC, Nan Winton read the evening news in 1960 and Angela Rippon became the first woman to act as regular sole presenter of prime-time news in 1974.
101 Kodama, *Nyūsu*, 204.
102 Krauss, *Broadcasting Politics*, 151.
103 Barbara Gatzen, "Japanese Media: The Stone Unturned," *Japan Media Review* (2003), quoted in MacLachlan, "Turning Seeing into Believing," 149.
104 Eiji Oshita, *Hōdō Sensō: Nyūsukyasutatachi no tataki* [Broadcast Wars: Newscasters Fights] (Tokyo: Kondansha, 1995), 145.
105 Midori Fukunishi Suzuki, "Women and Television: Portrayal of Women in Mass Media," in *Japanese Women*, eds. Kumiko Fujimura-Faneslow and Atsuko Kaneda (New York: The Feminist Press, 1995), 84.
106 Japan Newspaper Publishers and Editors Survey, quoted in "Media Women in Japan Have Achieved Slow but Steady Progress," *Media Report to Women* (Fall 2007).
107 Katsuichi Honda, *NHK jushinryō kyohi no ronri* [The Logic of Refusing NHK's Viewer Fee] (Tokyo: Asahi Shimbun Press, 1991). Akifumi Inaba, *NHK Jushinryo o Kangaeru* [Considering NHK's Viewer Fee] (Tokyo: Aoki Shōten, 1985).
108 Nobue Sungawa, "Go Away NHK," Letter to the Editor, *Asahi Evening News*, February 3, 1997.
109 Author's own interview with an NHK staff member, Tokyo, November 2000.

References

Akhavan-Majid, Roya, "Public Service Broadcasting and the Challenge of New Technology: A Case Study of Japan's NHK," *International Communication Gazette* 50, no. 21 (1992).

Alexander, Garth, and Andrew Davidson, "Japan Takes a Wide View of TV," *Sunday Times*, August 4, 1991.

Baker, Bert, "The BBC Has to Struggle," *Variety*, January 9, 1980.

Brittan, Samuel, "The Fight for Freedom in Broadcasting," *The Political Quarterly* 58, no. 1 (January–March 1987).

"Broadcasting Regulations Under Ministry Scrutiny," *Japan Times*, March 3, 2001.

Cobin, Martin, "Traditional Theatre and Modern Television in Japan," *Educational Theatre Journal* 21, no. 2 (May 1969).

Cooper-Chen, Anne, *Mass Communication in Japan* (Hoboken, NJ: Wiley-Blackwell, 1991).

Crozier, Michel, Samuel Huntington, and Joji Watanuki, *The Crisis of Democracy* (New York: New York University Press, 1975).

Dugdale, John, "1990 Broadcasting Act," *The Guardian*, November 19, 2000, www.guardian.co.uk/media/2000/nov/20/broadcasting.mondaymediasection2.

French, Howard, "NHK of Japan Ends Plan for Global News Service," *New York Times*, November 8, 1991.

"Financing the BBC: A Survey of Public Opinion," *NOP Market Research* (London: HMSO, 1985).

Godfrey, Chris, "How Michael Cashman Changed the World," *The Guardian*, January 29, 2020.

Greenslade, Roy, "After 30 Years, More Light is Cast on BBC's Real Lives Drama," *The Guardian*, August 3, 2015.

Hart, Jeffrey, *Technology, Television and Competition* (Cambridge: Cambridge University Press, 2004).

Harvey, Paul, "Nonchan's Drama: NHK Morning Serialized Television Novels," in *The Worlds of Japanese Pop Culture*, ed. D.P. Martinez (Cambridge: Cambridge University Press, 1998).

Honda, Katsuichi, *NHK jushinryō kyohi no ronri* [The Logic of Refusing NHK's Viewer Fee] (Tokyo: Asahi Shimbun Press, 1991).

Inaba, Akifumi, *NHK Jushinryo o Kangaeru* [Considering NHK's Viewer Fee] (Tokyo: Aoki Shōten, 1985).

Ivy, Marylin, "Formation of Mass Culture," in *Postwar Japan as History*, ed. Andrew Gordon (Berkeley, CA: University of California Press, 1993).

"John Peel," *The Economist*, November 6, 2004.

Johnson, Chalmers, *MITI and the Japanese Miracle: The Growth of Industrial Policy 1925–1975* (Stanford: Stanford University Press, 1982).

Kodama, Miiko, "Nyūsu no okurite toshite no josei [Women as Newscasters]," in *Hyogen to Mejia*, eds. Teruko Inoue, Chizuko Ueno, and Yumiko Ehara (Tokyo: Iwanami Shoten, 1995).

La Follette, Marcel Chotkowski, "Science on Japanese Public Television: An Adaptable Model for the U.S.?" *Science, Technology and Human Values* 4, no. 27 (Spring 1979).

Laurence, Henry, *Money Rules: The New Politics of Finance in Britain and Japan* (Ithaca, NY: Cornell University Press, 2001).

Lazzeretti, L., ed., *Creative Industries and Innovation in Europe: Concepts, Measures and Comparative Case Studies* (London: Routledge, 2012).

Machlachlan, Elizabeth, "Turning Seeing into Believing," in *Asian Media Productions*, ed. Bruce Moeran (Richmond: Curzon Press, 2001).

Martinez, D.P., "NHK Comes to Kuzaki," in *Ideology and Practice in Modern Japan*, eds. Roger Goodman and Kirsten Refsing (London: Routledge, 1992).

Masuko, Takashi, "Time to Rethink Hi-Vision," *Nikkei Weekly*, September 19, 1992.

McCargo, Duncan, *Media and Politics in Pacific Asia* (London: RoutledgeCurzon, 2003).

"Media Women in Japan Have Achieved Slow But Steady Progress," *Media Report to Women* (Fall 2007).

Miller, Steven D., "The (Temporary?) Queering of Japanese TV," *Journal of Homosexuality* 39, no. 3 (April 2000): 83–109.

Milne, Alistair, *D.G.: Memoirs of a British Broadcaster* (London: Hodder and Stoughton, 1988).

Mullan, Robert, *Consuming Television* (Oxford: Blackwell's, 1997).

Nakajima, Ai, "NHK Software Ties Worry Commercial Rivals," *Japan Economic Journal*, September 1, 1990.

Nakano, Koichi, "Becoming a Policy Ministry: The Organization and Amakudari of the Ministry of Posts and Telecommunications," *Journal of Japanese Studies* 24, no. 1 (Winter 1980).

"NHK Chief Announces Resignation over False Statements Made to Diet," *Japan Times*, July 16, 1991.

"NHK Executive Sees Future in HDTV, DBS," *Broadcasting* 114, no. 11 (March 14, 1988).

"NHK Shelves Plan," *Japan Times*, December 12, 1991.

"NHK Venture's Commercialism Criticized," *Japan Times*, July 21, 1990.

Noble, Greg, "Let a Hundred Channels Contend: Technological Change, Political Opening and Bureaucratic Politics in Japanese Television Broadcasting," *Journal of Japanese Studies* 26, no. 1 (Winter 2000).

Ogawa, Takashi, "The Collection and Preservation of Japanese Folk Songs by the Japan Broadcasting Corporation (NHK)," *Journal of the International Folk Music Council* 13 (1961).

Oshita, Eiji, *Hōdō Sensō: Nyūsukyasutatachi no tataki* [Broadcast Wars: Newscasters Fights] (Tokyo: Kondansha, 1995).

Penn, Wilhelmina, *The Couch Potato's Guide to Japan: Inside the World of Japanese TV* (Japan: Forest River Press, 2003).

Report of the Committee on Financing the BBC (Peacock Report), Cmmd. 9824 (London: HSMO, 1986), para. 209.

Saphir, Ann, "A Policy of Silence," *Look Japan*, August 1994.

Seaton, Jean, *Pinkoes and Traitors: The BBC and the Nation 1974–1987* (London: Profile Books, 2015).

Sender, Henny, "Image Problems," *Far Eastern Economic Review*, October 6, 1994, 81.

Stuart, Mark, *Douglas Hurd: An Authorized Biography* (Edinburgh: Mainstream Publishing, 1998).

Sungawa, Nobue, "Go Away NHK," Letter to the Editor, *Asahi Evening News*, February 3, 1997.

Suzuki, Midori Fukunishi, "Women and Television: Portrayal of Women in Mass Media," in *Japanese Women*, eds. Kumiko Fujimura-Faneslow and Atsuko Kaneda (New York: The Feminist Press, 1995).

Suzuki, Yoshikazu, "NHK Under Fire for Commercial Tilt," *Daily Yomiuri*, January 22, 1992.

Tatsuno, Sheridan, *Created in Japan: From Imitators to World-Class Innovators* (New York, NY: Harper and Row, 1990).

Thatcher, Margaret, *The Downing Street Years* (New York: Harpercollins, 1993).

"Union Raps NHK Sub-contracting," *Daily Yomiuri*, March 15, 1991.

8 Moving Online (Internet 2000s)

The internet posed an existential threat to public broadcasters. New forms of what used to be called broadcasting, including social media, podcasts, or blogs, create the exact opposite of the conditions that shaped the formation of the BBC and NHK. In Lord Reith's day, spectrum was so cramped that tight regulation of content was deemed essential but now, anyone can broadcast whatever they like, whenever they want to. In the old world, a handful of paternalistic gatekeepers decided how their audiences would be educated, informed, and maybe entertained. Now, individuals create their own content, TikTok videos being infinitely more entertaining than lavishly costumed period dramas for increasing numbers of people. Smartphone footage of a violent arrest can prove more educational than *Panorama* or an NHK Special, and millions of citizens are turning from the evening news to Facebook.[1]

Paradoxically, however, the internet also presents a golden opportunity to public broadcasters to reinvent themselves, develop new content, and reach wider, often younger, audiences. On-demand services allow them to recycle their vast archives of beloved old content onto new platforms. Interactivity allows them to put the public actively at the heart of public broadcasting, rather than passively at the receiving end. Most importantly, the internet hastened the collapse of old models of journalism and the rise of sensationalist, rabidly partisan, and often fake news, generating an even greater need for reliable, impartial reporting.

The questions new media posed for public broadcasters are simultaneously legal, economic, political, and philosophical. First were the legal constraints on how much publicly funded media could expand onto new platforms. What was possible given the specific terms of their charters or founding legislation? Second, online expansion was expensive, requiring heavy investment in completely untested new technologies and platforms. Where would the money come from? Could new media somehow be used to raise money without eroding the nonprofit ethos? Closely related was the political challenge: private media corporations large and small resisted the intrusion of publicly funded rivals into what was already an unknown and viciously competitive new environment. How could public broadcasters answer criticism that their online expansion was crowding out desirable commercial competition? Finally, the broadcasters were internally divided over the most appropriate strategic responses to the internet. At the

DOI: 10.4324/b23015-8

broadest level, online expansion meant reassessing the fundamental question of what programming public broadcasters should provide: universal content, popular for all audiences, or niche offerings for specific, underserved constituencies? The internet's global reach also introduced new questions about national versus global broadcasting. Should national public broadcasters continue to serve only domestic interests, or should they attempt to reach international audiences? If so, to what purpose, and with what mandate? As we will see, the BBC was an enthusiastic early adopter of new media, with NHK both more cautious and more constrained in its embrace of the new world.

The transition from analog to digital television broadcasting in the early 2000s is worth noting because it offered a preview of the differences between the BBC and NHK's digital strategies.[2] Digital television might have been a death blow for public broadcasters by ending spectrum scarcity and destroying a key rationale for their existence. However, both the BBC and eventually NHK made themselves central to their governments' transition strategies and in doing so reinforced their positions as vital elements of their respective national media systems. Their approaches to the issue, though, were quite different. Under Director-General Greg Dykes entrepreneurial leadership, the BBC made itself central to the Labour government's transition policy; indeed, the BBC showed its customary adaptability in thrusting itself onto center stage when successive governments had tried to pursue more free-market approaches to the policy challenge. NHK was also at the heart of events. However, under Chairman Ebisawa Katsuji, NHK's commitment to the analog high-definition television their laboratories had developed helped delay Japan's initial adoption of the digital format. Only after their analog venture had proved an expensive failure did NHK throw itself into solving the collective action problem of persuading the population to make the switch to digital.[3]

New Media Strategies at the BBC

John Birt was Director-General of the BBC when internet use took off in the late 1980s. Birt saw the internet as both a source of renewed legitimacy for public broadcasting and as an opportunity for commercial development that would not undermine the license fee/free-to-air model. First, he articulated the new threats to civic culture and hence the continued need for the BBC.

> The digital age brings with it risks as well as opportunities- the risk that globalization of culture will threaten national identities; that the powerful gateway controllers will restrain rather than promote diversity; the risk of a two-class society, the information rich, ready and able to pay for their increasingly expensive media, and the information poor who cannot.[4]

Therefore, he promised that "in the digital age the BBC will safeguard national culture, encourage diversity and extend choice, and strive to bring the benefits of the new technologies universally to every home in the land."[5] However, Birt was also aware of the enormous new commercial possibilities, and was anxious to avoid the mistake he believed the BBC had made in earlier dealings with the American Discovery and A&E Channels. The BBC had provided much of the programming but had failed to secure an equity stake in the channels and so missed out on their enormous growth. In future, Birt wanted a better return on the BBC's considerable assets.[6]

Birt's ideas about commercial enterprises raised considerable legal confusion within the organization about what sorts of activities the BBC was permitted to do under the terms of the Charter.[7] In addition, new media exacerbated existing philosophical differences about the appropriate direction for public broadcasting in a multichannel world. Some saw the success of the BBC websites as potential salvation for the corporation. Others saw the use of advertising as the thin end of the wedge of commercialization that would ultimately destroy the soul of public broadcasting.[8] Producers of traditional programs feared that they would be forgotten as scarce resources were diverted to "shiny new toys" (i.e., new technologies) and the latest programming fads.[9] Birt and the advocates for embracing new platforms eventually won the day but not without considerable argument and bruised feelings.

The BBC's first forays online began in 1994 with the Multimedia Centre and, later, the BBC Networking Club, which was a bulletin board run by the Education division. *Beeb.com* was established by BBC Worldwide, the commercial arm of the BBC, to sell merchandise. BBC News Online (later *bbc.co.uk*) was launched in 1997 in an attempt to win back the younger generation who were far less likely to watch traditional TV news than their parents and grandparents. The corporation-wide *BBC Online*, as well as websites for BBC Education and the World Service soon followed.

The expanded role of new media within the Corporation was institutionalized in 2006 with the creation of the Future Media and Technology division (FMT), a cross-departmental organization that broke important new ground organizationally because it included the news division rather than, as before, treating news as a distinct entity.[10] The first priority was to streamline services so that all programming could be made available on demand across different media. The division also spearheaded the use of new media across the organization, rather than within one or two "techie" divisions. "Get web-savvy or we die," proclaimed FMT Director Ashley Highfield in 2007.[11]

The new media environment also stimulated a long-overdue streamlining of the BBC's sprawling, frequently overlapping newsgathering services.[12] In 2008, BBC News 24, World News, *bbc.co.uk*, and all the myriad other radio and regional BBC news bulletin teams were merged into a single unit, BBC Multimedia newsroom.[13] Previously, there had been considerable duplication of effort among the multiple BBC news departments. One celebrity told me she had once been contacted by four different BBC journalists over one evening, all covering the same story.[14]

The BBC was quick to embrace user-generated content (UGC). The ubiquity of email and digital cameras combined with the overwhelming willingness of people across the globe to upload and share content seemed, at first, like a godsend for cash-strapped news media who were in the process of cutting full-time report-ers, especially foreign correspondents. UGC promised a costless way to farm out newsgathering to unpaid volunteers, as well as to expand news coverage to regions and entire countries hitherto unserved by conventional reporters usually based in urban centers. However, news organizations soon ran into two problems. First was veracity. News sites that allowed anyone to publish content unfiltered were frequently embarrassed by glaring inaccuracies such as when photos of a natural disaster turned out to be of a totally different event.[15] The solution was to moderate what was published, but the sheer volume of contributions made this difficult or impossible for most hard-pressed news organizations.[16] Unlike most rivals, the BBC had the resources and personnel to devote full-time to cultivating and curating UGC, and it did so enthusiastically. In 2006, the BBC established a UGC hub with 23 full-time staff. The 2005 terrorist bombings in London and the 2006 Asian Tsunami had demonstrated to management the enormous potential of eyewitness videos, photos, and stories to improve coverage of breaking news events.[17] The corporate embrace of social media, though, caused considerable cul-ture shock as broadcasters had to adjust to listening to their audiences instead of merely talking down to them.[18]

The ease of acquiring and publishing user content presented a new version of the old editorial challenge of balancing the journalistic values of objectivity and fact-checking with the democratic values of allowing everyone to have their say regardless of how banal, prejudiced, or ill-informed they were.[19] As with inter-net expansion, there was considerable internal opposition to both blogging and UGC, with many journalists worried about the dangers of publishing comments or input without proper fact-checking. Peter Horrocks, head of BBC News, sug-gested in 2007, "I don't expect to see a huge amount of UGC on Newsnight in the future."[20] But the two-way interaction with audiences proved helpful in enabling journalists to know their audiences. In addition, surveys found that although audiences approved of the use of social media, they were also happy to allow the BBC and other news sources to filter and check input.[21] By 2010, Horrocks was not merely encouraging but ordering BBC journalists to embrace social media, telling staff, "This isn't just a kind of fad. . . . You aren't doing your job if you can't do these things. It's not discretionary."[22] Leading present-ers and journalists were encouraged to blog, and Business Editor Robert Preston became the United Kingdom's most read blogger in 2009, with up to six million weekly visitors.[23]

The BBC's entrepreneurial embrace of the digital age revived its role in devel-oping media technology. Secure funding, guaranteed audiences, and longer time horizons allowed the Corporation to take more risks and make bigger and longer-term investments than most private companies. In the words of one observer, "the BBC is playing a far more aggressive role than other broadcasting companies in new technology development."[24] FMT identified the internet as the key platform, with mobile phones as the so-called fourth screen after cinema, TV, and com-puters. The Corporation launched content channels on YouTube and distribution deals with Facebook and other social media platforms.[25]

In 2007, the BBC developed and launched iPlayer, an online radio and TV streaming service providing full-length BBC shows on demand for seven days after first transmission. iPlayer became hugely popular, especially and perhaps surprisingly among older viewers. One analyst described iPlayer's success as providing a model, and a vital kick-start, for commercial networks in the United Kingdom, the United States, and Europe to commit more fully to online TV.[26] The iPlayer also prompted development of a system of broadband delivery to home TVs in alliance with British Telecom.

To support these online initiatives, the BBC's research division developed Dirac, a code useful for both studio video-coding and for simple internet streaming. Dirac opened natively in internet browsers, without the need for plug-ins or royalty payments, and so helped the BBC sell streaming video content in global markets. Also in 2008, the BBC joined a consortium of European broadcasters to develop an open-source platform for the delivery of high-definition video content to home televisions via set-top boxes.[27] The BBC began to distribute online through BBC Motion Gallery, which manages clip sales worldwide. In 2010, it went into strategic partnership with Thought Equity Motion, a leader in digitizing, delivering, and monetizing video content.[28] Ultimately, though, as Mark Thompson argued, "The point about the future of the BBC is about the willingness of the public to pay for high-content broadcasting, not about technology."[29]

The rapid expansion of the new websites attracted loud complaints of unfair competition from the commercial broadcasters and the British Internet Publishers Association (BIPA).[30] The BIPA argued that "there is manifestly no spectrum scarcity on the internet, and no need for a publicly subsidized remedy for market failure."[31] They accused the BBC of using "unfair cross-promotional activities" to crowd out private companies in "markets which are entirely inappropriate to its purposes."[32] BSkyB's strategy director argued, "If they don't already, new media companies will come to understand the severe problems that arise when a well-funded BBC decides that its remit now needs to extend to include their fledgling line of business."[33] The notion of advertising on websites, even those only accessed by foreign readers, had also divided BBC management and politicians. However, early reports from Ofcom and others found little direct evidence of crowding out, and while politicians demanded transparency, there was little effort within Parliament to prevent the BBC from expanding.[34]

One new broadcasting platform where the BBC does seem to have stifled independent creators is podcasting. Podcasting began in the United States in 2004, and within a few months the BBC was putting some of its voluminous daily radio output into podcast form.[35] With ready-made audiences and high brand recognition, BBC radio shows-cum-podcasts such as Melvyn Bragg's *In Our Time* came to dominate the UK podcasting scene, with little space for the commercial start-ups such as Gimlet Media that flourished in the United States.[36] In 2018, the BBC replaced iPlayer Radio with BBC Sounds to serve as the "Netflix for podcasts" and consolidate its position as the United Kingdom's leading producer in the medium.[37]

Table 8.1 Internet Presence of Selected Media Websites 2011

	bbc.co.uk	*nhk.co.jp*	*sky.com* *(United Kingdom)*	*asahi.com* *(Japan)*
% global traffic(i)	2.18	0.16	0.16	0.19
Global Traffic ranking (ii)	44th	815th	856th	661st
Home country ranking (iii)	5th	54th	33rd	34th
Avg. time per visit (min) (iv)	6.6	3.3	4.9	3.9

Source: Alexa Web Information.
www.alexa.com/ (accessed August 2, 2011).

(i) Estimated percentage of total global internet users who visited website.
(ii) Rank by traffic, all websites.
(iii) Rank by traffic, all websites in home country.
(iv) Estimated average time per visit in minutes.

(Three-month average from May to June 2011).

The first decade of the new millennium, in other words, found the BBC in excellent shape online. In 2010, 98% of adults were using at least one BBC service each week, and *bbc.co.uk* was receiving 20 million British visitors a month.[38] The news website quickly became by far the most successful online news source in the United Kingdom, with 13 million unique visitors per week in 2007, compared with 10 million per month for the *guardian.co.uk*, the most popular newspaper site, or 4.6 million per month for Sky News online.[39] The BBC's success online was understandable in hindsight. It had the financial freedom to research and to experiment with new technologies, a huge library of proprietary content, tremendous brand recognition, and the capacity, exploited shamelessly, for cross-platform promotion.[40] As we will see in the next chapter, online expansion brought vocal opposition from a growing number of aggrieved commercial rivals. But the BBC's ambitiously proactive new media strategy stands in marked contrast to their more restrained Japanese counterparts.

NHK and the Internet

NHK's early engagement with the internet and new media was both slower and less aggressive than the BBC's. According to the 2020 Reuters Institute Digital News Report, NHK online news is the top brand for just 11% of consumers of online news, far behind Yahoo News, the top brand for 58%. NHK is, however, still the most popular source of offline news in Japan, the top source for 48% of respondents, just above Nippon TV News at 45%. By contrast, *BBC.co.uk* is by far the most popular news website in the United Kingdom, the top news brand for 45% of the population compared with 18% for the next best, Guardian Online. Like NHK, the BBC is also overwhelmingly the most popular source for traditional news, the top source for 56%, compared with 27% for ITV news.[41]

NHK's comparatively lukewarm approach to the internet had several causes. Interviewees often noted legal constraints.[42] The Broadcast Law forbade the broadcaster from spending viewer fees for anything other than prespecified types of broadcasting, which included radio and terrestrial and satellite broadcasting.[43] The law further stipulated that any broadcasting undertaken by NHK must be received all over the country, and available to all fee-payers.[44] Money taken from the whole population could not be used for programs targeting only a specific, restricted group. This provision, for example, meant that revenue from satellite viewer fees could only be spent on satellite broadcast services. In the late 1990s and early 2000s, any internet services would assuredly not be accessible in most households. Thus, a strict interpretation of the Broadcast Law would suggest that internet services that went beyond support for television broadcasts would be legally problematic. However, this explanation, while valid as far as it goes, does not explain why the BBC, faced with similar legal obstacles, was able to get around them so much more quickly and thoroughly, chiefly through the use of independent affiliated companies such as BBC Worldwide.

Similarly, NHK staff note that commercial networks and internet services resisted their online expansion.[45] However, the same is also true of the BBC. In addition to these factors, I argue that the differences in BBC and NHK strategy are more fully explained by reference to (1) the broader digital environment in both countries; (2) the more proactive role played by Japanese regulators in balancing NHK's interests online with those of commercial rivals; (3) prior strategic choices by both broadcasters, most notably that NHK was deeply invested in managing a series of expensive earlier technological innovations, including HDTV and Direct Broadcast Satellite (DBS) broadcasting; (4) differences in managerial philosophy and organizational culture, themselves both a cause and a reflection of the earlier constraining choices. NHK took online its narrower, more information-oriented conception of public broadcasting compared to the BBC's expansive programming vision. Moreover, while traditionalists at both organizations were initially reluctant to embrace new media, NHK's leadership and organizational culture were far more cautious and less entrepreneurial than at the BBC.

NHK's relatively slow online expansion reflected an initially slow adoption of the internet in Japan more generally. In 1999, the ratio of internet users to total population was 13.5%, compared to approximately 25% in the United Kingdom and 30% in the United States.[46] Even South Korea, long a follower of Japan's technological lead, had vaulted ahead in IT, thanks to a nationally integrated "cyber-Korea" strategy launched in 1995. By 2000, 53% of the South Korean population used the internet regularly, with one official even boasting that Korea had "very little to learn from Japan" about IT.[47] The situation in Japan was so bad, by contrast, that foreign investors were reporting shortages of technically qualified IT workers.[48] In response, and seeking new ways out of the economic slump, Prime Minister Mori Yoshiro's LDP passed with wide support the Information Technology Basic Bill in 2000.[49] The Bill called for an e-government initiative, expansion of the broadband network, more e-commerce, and more training of IT experts.[50]

NHK, however, were deeply invested in earlier initiatives in broadcast television, including HDTV and digital satellite broadcasting (DSB), which had begun with great fanfare in 2000.[51] The enormous investments looked vulnerable given lukewarm audience response. At the time, only around 100,000 people had the extremely expensive equipment necessary to receive DBS.[52] Even the most enthusiastic supporter of NHK's DBS ambitions, the Japan Electronics and Information Technology Industries Association (*Denshi Jōhō Gijutsu Sangyo Kyōkai*), predicted that it would take until 2010 until all 70 million households in Japan were digitally equipped.[53] Meanwhile, according to some staff, managerial attention became preoccupied with these ventures to the exclusion of an internet strategy.[54] Indeed, online services and the internet barely rated a mention in NHK's 2000 Annual Report.[55]

NHK's organizational culture worked against the leap of faith needed to jump online. The seniority system of promotion common to Japan's bureaucracies did not encourage fresh or innovative managerial thinking. Senior managers were steeped in the traditional broadcasting culture, more comfortable with the technicalities of hardware development than in generating creative new media strategies. Most managers simply did not see the internet as a priority.[56] At the BBC, affiliated companies had been the vehicles for younger managers to experiment with online activities. At NHK's affiliates, the organizational culture was often, although not always, even more resistant to innovation. Affiliate companies had long been an abundant source of well-paid but undemanding *amakudari* positions for MPT officials or passed-over NHK managers. According to one NHK insider, "About one third of the management [at the affiliates] are old guys enjoying an easy life who do no work. About one third don't want to work, but will if you make them. Only about one third are really enthusiastic and active."[57]

NHK's institutional conservatism was reinforced by the leadership of Ebisawa Katsuji as Chairman from 1997 until his forced resignation in 2005. Ebisawa had risen through NHK's ranks as a political journalist with close connections with the conservative Takeshita faction of the LDP.[58] A self-confessed missionary for HDTV, Ebisawa showed less interest in the internet.[59] He also demonstrated far less of the commercial entrepreneurialism, which drove John Birt and Greg Dyke to embrace new media. Opposing liberalization of international trade in television programs, for example, Ebisawa announced, "Broadcasting is a part of culture and in that context we could not support treating the audiovisual sector like any other."[60]

NHK's first forays online came in the late 1990s, with the posting of program information to the corporate website *www.nhk.or.jp*. The first use of multimedia came with an experimental educational program for schools produced by an affiliated company, NHK Enterprise 21 (NEP 21) in 1999.[61] Even these limited initiatives raised legal difficulties, and in April 2000, Ebisawa called for a cautious revision of the Broadcasting Law to allow NHK to provide internet services. The services he proposed were defined narrowly, confined mostly to electronic program guides and national weather and emergency reports.[62] Granted permission to proceed, NHK expanded its website, but devoted it exclusively to its own programming and organization. Online news was introduced on an experimental basis in December 2000, restricted to audio reports without images. Even this small step was taken a full three years after the BBC.[63]

As in Britain, these moves set off waves of protest from commercial broadcasters and major newspapers, who opposed any NHK presence online.[64] According to the *Minpōren* Chairman Ujie Seiichiro:

> NHK's licence fee . . . is in effect a semi-tax. A public corporation should not be allowed to use those funds to expand its activities indiscriminately. Properly speaking, all of NHK's content, which has been produced using licence fees, belongs to the public.[65]

The Newspaper Publishers and Editors Association (*Nihon Shimbun Kōkai*, NSK) noted the unfair competitive advantage that NHK enjoyed from its guaranteed viewer fees. They also pointed out the unfairness of viewers paying for internet services available to non-subscribers; as an editorial in the Mainichi Shimbun expressed it:

> It would not make sense if people who paid the fee were prohibited from receiving broadcast services from NHK. On the other hand, it is equally illogical for NHK to use the fees to underwrite services extended to non-subscribers.[66]

Newspaper owners also felt threatened by NHK's expansion into online services via mobile phones, and urged the authorities to prevent NHK from entering the internet via subsidiaries.[67]

The MPT's policy of balancing competing demands slowed NHK's online expansion. Restructuring of the regulatory framework was slow and piecemeal as the bureaucrats balanced limited relaxation of restrictions on what NHK could do with concessions to private interests. In 2001, the Ministry's Study Group on Broadcasting Policies recommended that NHK be restricted in what information it could put online for three years, so as to protect commercial rivals, including both TV and newspaper companies. The regulator further recommended NHK only post online segments of previously aired programs and information, and that this content should be restricted to programming related to education, welfare, and medical services. The Ministry argued it would be inappropriate for NHK to produce content specifically for the web, or to sell content directly to viewers. In other words, online services should be secondary and supplementary to TV broadcasting, and cast within a tight public service remit.[68]

The Broadcast Law was revised in 2002 to permit NHK to engage in internet activities as long as they were related to broadcasting. The MPHPT issued separate guidelines for NHK subsidiaries, warning them specifically against expansion into internet activity. In addition, MPHPT limited NHK's internet budget to ¥1 billion annually. The revisions were undertaken, as usual, in the face of outrage from the usual opponents, with NSK warning that "NHK will enlarge itself and expand its operations, which may cause a grave situation surrounding the nation's mass media."[69]

NHK, like the BBC, stood to benefit from using the internet for on-demand services for its back catalog. In the late 2000s, NHK managers raised the possibility of a video-on-demand service along the lines of BBC iPlayer. NHK's proposed service would, as at the BBC, be free to NHK subscribers with fees for non-subscribers. Programs would be available for one week after airing, and be copyright protected.[70] NHK had a vast archive of programs that had been digitized in a project begun in 1997 in preparation for the advent of digital television, and completed with the opening of a 37-acre storage site in Kawaguchi. However, copyright and image right laws were so strict that NHK officials had to visit all living individuals featured in these programs to get their permission for rebroadcasting on other media, a laborious and expensive process that continued for a decade until the on-demand video service was launched.[71] Even without the copyright problems, NHK could not use most of this material online, thanks to MIAC's existing restrictions on online content. In 2006, of some 58,000 stored programs, only 5,700 were available online: the rest could only be viewed in person at the Kawaguchi site.[72]

MIAC Minister Takanaka Heizō agreed that the entire archive should be available online, and enabling revisions to the Broadcast Law went into effect in April 2008. These revisions raised the limit on NHK internet revenues from ¥1 billion to ¥4 billion, and allowed NHK to distribute selected current and archived programs online. However, MIAC insisted that the service be fee-based (originally ¥315), and that the revenues were to be kept separate from the regular viewer fees. These strictures came in response to complaints of unfair competition from commercial broadcasters, including Fuji TV and NTV, who had begun on-demand services in 2005.[73] NHK's selections could include up to 90 recently aired "missed programs" such as *NHK Special*, or choices from around 130 titles in the special selection library, including old episodes of the *Project X* documentary series. NHK, like the BBC, was to use its highly regarded documentaries as a central element in developing online presence.[74] In December 2008, NHK selected Omniture, a US-based provider of online business software, to provide the platform for the new service, *NHK On Demand*.[75] Foreign rights for NHK Archives were handled by a specially established affiliate, NHK International Inc., which in 2006 appointed BBC Motion Gallery to distribute the archives outside Japan.[76] NHK's service did not match the popularity of the iPlayer, however. In 2009, one year after launch, 60% of Japanese didn't know about the service and only 1% used it "often or sometimes." This compared with 44% of Britons who used the BBC's on-demand service often or sometimes, and 7% who were unaware of the service.[77]

Meanwhile, NHK's research laboratories continued to contribute to national policy goals of technology development. This time NHK was a central play in Japan's ambitious policy of platform convergence. Policymakers at MPT were trying to coordinate transmission and broadcast standards across platforms so that any digital content could be carried on any platform: computer, television, or mobile phone. Such a policy would require the purchase of highly sophisticated new equipment and hence be a boon to the consumer electronics industry. Equally important, the MPT believed that platform convergence would stimulate growth in the so-called creative industries, especially *anime* and *manga*, which were seen as key future players in the post-industrial economic revitalization of "Cool Japan."[78] Platform convergence was clearly essential to serve the MPT's goal for households to require only one receiving device.[79] Thus, in 2005 MIAC (*Sōmushō*) announced plans and funding to allow DTT broadcasts to be simultaneously streamed to internet users via fiber-optic networks, hoping this would ease problems of poor TV reception, and also further break down the barrier between broadcasting and communication.[80] The Ministry also permitted the transmission of DTT directly to cell phones.[81] Broadcast of NHK's regular terrestrial offerings onto cell phones was a legal and managerially uncontroversial way to help boost the uptake of DTT-enabled phones, aiding both Japan's electronics manufacturers, NHK, and the commercial broadcasters. By 2007, 82% of the Japanese population (104 million) owned cell phones, of which 80% were capable of receiving digital terrestrial signals.[82] "One-Seg" broadcasting of high-definition digital TV direct to mobile phones and cars began in 2008, with NHK labs developing the necessary transmission standards.[83]

Thus, by the close of the decade, NHK had established a solid if unspectacular presence online, with a lower profile than either the BBC or Japan's commercial broadcasters. In February 2009, *NHK.or.jp* received 3.8 million unique visitors, representing just 7% of the total internet audience for that month of 62 million visitors, making it the 14th most visited site in Japan, well behind Sony online, and the online sites of Fuji and Nippon TV.[84] A 2009 survey found that only 3% of Japanese visited an NHK website more than twice per week, compared to 44% of Britons who reported visiting a BBC website that frequently. Three-quarters of Japanese people rarely or never accessed NHK online, compared with fewer than one quarter in Britain.[85]

The internet threatened public broadcasters in at least two ways. First, the spectrum scarcity rationale for public broadcasting, already eroded by multichannel television, was entirely demolished by the multiplication of new sources of news, information, and entertainment content. Second, the new platforms did not fit the existing regulatory structure for public broadcasting. The BBC and NHK's early attempts to adopt the new technologies faced fierce opposition from new players such as internet service providers as well as existing commercial rivals. The BBC was more aggressive and more successful in overcoming regulatory challenges and adopting innovative platform and programming strategies to keep existing audiences and generate new ones. NHK's conservative organizational culture, as well as somewhat more stringent legal obstacles to cross-platform broadcasting, made it a less active player online.

Notes

1 See, for example, Michael Tracy, *The Decline and Fall of Public Service Broadcasting* (Oxford: Oxford University Press, 1998) or Bruce M. Owen, *The Internet Challenge to Television* (Cambridge, MA: Harvard University Press, 1999).
2 Three books stand out in telling the full story: Jeffrey Hart, *Technology Television and Competition* (Cambridge: Cambridge University Press, 2004); Hernan Galperin, *New*

Television, Old Politics: The Transition to Digital TV in the United States and Britain (New York: Cambridge University Press, 2004); Michael Starks, *Switching to Digital Television: UK Public Policy and the Market* (Bristol: Intellect, 2007).

3 For a more detailed account, see Henry Laurence, "The Political Economy of Digital Switchover in Japan and the US," in *The East Asian Development Model: 21st Century Perspectives*, ed. Shiping Hua (London: Routledge, 2015).

4 "Public Service Will Remain at Heart of the BBC in the Digital Ages Pledges Director-General," *M2 Communications Presswire*, January 22, 1998.

5 "Public Service Will Remain at Heart of the BBC in the Digital Ages Pledges Director-General," *M2 Communications Presswire*.

6 Mathew Horsman, "The Reith Thing," *The Guardian*, January 26, 1998.

7 Hallvard Moe, "Public Service Media Online? Regulating Public Broadcasters' Internet Services – A Comparative Analysis," *Television and New Media* 9, no. 3 (May 2008): 226.

8 Jamie Doward, "Showdown at White City," *The Observer*, January 28, 2001.

9 Author's own interviews with BBC staff in London, July 2009.

10 "BBC Restructures for Digital Age," *BBC*, July 19, 2006, http://news.bbc.co.uk/2/hi/entertainment/5194046.stm; Peter Lee-Wright, "Culture Shock: New Media and Organizational Change at the BBC," in *New Media, Old News: Journalism and Democracy in the Digital Age*, ed. Natalie Fenton (London: Sage Publication, 2010), 72.

11 Lee-Wright, "Culture Shock," 77.

12 Author's own interviews with BBC staff in London, July 2009.

13 Cathy Loughran, "Big Bang for TV News," *Ariel* (BBC: London, April 22, 2008).

14 Author's own interview in Oxford, UK, October 2007.

15 "Struggling to Stay on Top of Fake Social Media Posts," *Japan Times*, June 23, 2018.

16 Author's own interview in Oxford, UK, 2007.

17 Nic Newman, "The Rise of Social Media and Its Impact on Mainstream Journalism," *Working Paper, Reuters Institute for the Study of Journalism at Oxford University*, Working Paper, 2009, http://reutersinstitute.politics.ox.ac.uk/publications/risj-working-papers.html.

18 Newman, "The Rise of Social Media," 9.

19 John Kelly, "Red Kayaks and Hidden Gold: The Rise, Challenges and Value of Citizen Journalism," Reuters Institute for the Study of Journalism at Oxford University, 2009. For a different take, comedy duo Mitchell and Webb satirized the BBC's obsession with audience participation in a sketch in which a presenter asks: "Yes, why not email us? Certainly ignorance shouldn't be a bar . . ."

20 Lee-Wright, "Culture Shock," 86.

21 Newman, "The Rise of Social Media," 2, 8–9.

22 Mercedes Bunz, "BBC Tells News Staff to Embrace Social Media," *The Guardian*, February 10, 2010.

23 Newman, "The Rise of Social Media," 35.

24 Junko Yoshida, "Broadcasters Look for New Hits among Golden Oldies," *Electronic Engineering Times*, September 22, 2008.

25 Lee-Wright, "Culture Shock," 6.

26 Mark Scott, "BBC Leads the Way on the Web," *BusinessWeek Online*, July 3, 2008.

27 Yoshida, "Broadcasters Look for New Hits."

28 "BBC Motion Gallery and Thought Equity Motion Launch Strategic Partnership," *Marketwire*, March 18, 2010.

29 Rosa Price, "Licence Fee on Death Row," *Daily Telegraph*, July 9, 2008.

30 Stewart Purvis, "Why ITN Is Taking the BBC to Court," *The Guardian*, July 17, 2000. Owen Gibson, "BBC Web Chief Defends Spending Spree," *The Guardian*, July 22, 2002.

31 British Internet Providers Association, "Memorandum," *The Funding of the BBC*, vol. II (London: HMSO, December 15, 1999), 36–37.

32 British Internet Providers Association, "Memorandum."
33 Emiko Terazono, "BBC Chief Denies Crowding Out Commercial Rivals," *Financial Times*, May 4, 2006.
34 Terazono, "BBC Chief."
35 "Podcasts Go Mainstream," *PC World*, May 1, 2005, 28.
36 Nicholas Quah, "Hot Pod: Is the BBC's Power to Blame for the U.K. Podcasting Scene's Underdevelopment?" *Nieman Lab*, June 28, 2016, www.niemanlab.org/2016/06/hot-pod-is-the-bbcs-power-to-blame-for-the-u-k-podcasting-scenes-underdevelopment/.
37 Richard Berry, "Radio, Music, Podcasts – BBC Sounds: Public Service Radio and Podcasts in a Platform World," *Radio Journal: International Studies in Broadcast & Audio Media* 18, no. 1 (2020): 63.
38 "No Surrender," *The Economist*, March 6, 2010.
39 Des Freedman, "The Political Economy of the New News Environment," *New Media, Old News*, ed. Natalie Fenton (Thousand Oaks, CA: SAGE Publications Ltd, 2009), 43.
40 Scott, "BBC Leads the Way onto the Web."
41 "Digital News Report 2020," Reuters Institute for the Study of Journalism at Oxford University, 2020, www.digitalnewsreport.org/interactive/.
42 Author's own interviews with NHK staff, Tokyo, August 2006.
43 Broadcast Law of Japan, law no. 132, Article 39 (1).
44 Broadcast Law of Japan, law no. 132, Article 9 (5).
45 Author's own interviews with NHK staff in August 2006.
46 MPT, "Tsushin Hakushō [White Paper on Telecommunications]" (Tokyo: MPT, 1999).
47 "Japan No Tutor for IT-Savvy South Korea," *Japan Times*, December 5, 2000.
48 "Foreign Firms Here Find Dearth of IT Experts," *Japan Times*, November 29, 2000.
49 "5-Year Goal Set to Make Japan the World's Leading IT Nation," *Daily Yomiuri*, November 28, 2000.
50 "Diet Passes Bill to Promote IT," *Japan Times*, November 30, 2000.
51 Yūseishō, *Maruchimedia Hakusho 200: kontentsu-komasu ni mukete [Multimedia White Paper 2000: Towards Contents-Commerce]* (Tokyo: Yūseishō, 2000).
52 "BS dejitaru: asu hōsō o kaishi [BS Digital Broadcasting Starts Tomorrow]," *Asahi Shimbun*, November 30, 2000.
53 "Terebi Mekaa teikai ni hashiru [TV Makers Cooperate]," *Asahi Shimbun*, November 30, 2000.
54 Author's own interviews with NHK staff, Tokyo, November 2000.
55 NHK, *Annual Report* (Tokyo: NHK, 2000).
56 Author's own interviews with NHK staff, Tokyo, November 2000.
57 Author's own interviews with NHK staff, Tokyo, October 2000.
58 Shūkan Kinyōbi, *Abe Seiji to Genron Tōsei [Abe's Politics and Speech Control]* (Tokyo: Kinyōbi Press, 2016), 35; Tad Osaki, "A Man of Vision," *Television Asia*, June 1, 2000.
59 "Dijitaru kōkyō hōsōron: NHK Kaicho Ebisawa Katsuji ga Kataru [Digital Public Broadcasting Debate: NHK Chairman Ebisawa Katsuji speaks]," *Gekkan Nyūmedia Henshūbu* [New Media Monthly, Editors] (Tokyo: New Media Company, 2000).
60 Mark Woods, "Pubcasters Nix Free Product," *Daily Variety*, November 15, 1999.
61 "NHK Begins Net Programs for Schools," *Daily Yomiuri*, November 9, 1999.
62 "NHK May Seek Law Revision to Let NHK Use Net," *Kyodo Newswire*, April 6, 2000.
63 NHK, *Annual Report*, 2000.
64 "TV Industry Stands against NHK Internet Business," *Jiji Press Ticker Service*, December 26, 2000.
65 Yamada Shinichi and Miyashita Hiroshi, "Broadcasters at Odds over Updating of Law," *Daily Yomiuri*, June 22, 2000.
66 "NHK Internet Plans to Cause Licensing Problems," *Mainichi Daily News*, February 28, 2001.

67 "Newspaper Industry Concerned about NHK's Internet Business," *Jiji Press Ticker Service*, December 5, 2000.
68 "Ministry Panel Proposes Limits on NHK's Internet Services," *Japan Economic Newswire*, December 21, 2001.
69 "Limit Set on NHK's Internet Activities," *Kyodo News Service*, March 8, 2002.
70 "NHK is First Broadcaster to Offer Aired TV Programs on Internet," *Kyodo News Service*, July 18, 2007.
71 "Digitization Budgets Cut Profits," *Nikkei Weekly*, June 6, 2005.
72 *Daily Yomiuri*, May 7, 2006.
73 Suzuki Yoshikazu, "Will NHK's On-Demand Service Be a Hit?," *Daily Yomiuri*, November 28, 2006.
74 Audrey Stuart, "TV Documentaries Take Leap into Digital World," *Agence France Presse*, March 30, 2009.
75 "Japan's Only Public Broadcaster Selects Omniture for Advanced Video Measurement of New Internet TV Service," *Market News Publishing*, December 11, 2008.
76 "BBC Distribution Deal with NHK Japan," *BBC Worldwide*, April 5, 2006.
77 Yoshihiko Nakamura and Ritsu Yonekura, "How Public Service Broadcasting Is Talked About: A Comparative Web Survey of Japan, the ROK and the United Kingdom," *NHK Broadcasting Studies*, no. 8 (Tokyo: NHK Broadcasting Culture Research Institute, 2010), 123.
78 Yūseishō, *Maruchimedia hakusho 200: Kontentsu-Komasu ni Mukete* [Multimedia White Paper 2000: Towards Contents-Commerce] (Tokyo: Yūseishō, 2000).
79 Author's own interviews with NHK staff, Tokyo, February 2001.
80 "DTV Broadcasts to be Simulcast on Internet," *Nikkei Weekly*, July 16, 2005.
81 "DTV Broadcasters to Reach Cell Phone Users," *Nikkei Weekly*, October 3, 2005.
82 Ministry of Internal Affairs and Communications *Telecommunications Usage Trend Survey 2007*. MIAC, April 18, 2008, accessed October 31, 2021, www.soumu.go.jp/johotsusintokei/tsusin_riyou/data/eng_tsusin_riyou02_2007.pdf.
83 Japan's standard for digital terrestrial broadcasting was ISDB-T. A single band of 6 MHz radio spectrum is composed of 13 segments, 12 of which are devoted to home transmission, with one segment (hence "one-seg") reserved for transmission to mobile devices, including cell phones or cars. NHK, "NHK Digital," accessed June 28, 2021, www.nhk.or.jp/digital/en/digitalbroad/02_spec.html.
84 "Japanese Internet Users Glued to Entertainment Sites," *PR Newswire*, April 9, 2009.
85 Nakamura and Yonekura, "How Public Service Broadcasting Is Talked About."

References

"5-Year Goal set to Make Japan the World's Leading IT Nation," *Daily Yomiuri*, November 28, 2000.
"BBC Distribution Deal with NHK Japan," *BBC Worldwide*, April 5, 2006.
"BBC Motion Gallery and Thought Equity Motion Launch Strategic Partnership," *Marketwire*, March 18, 2010.
"BBC Restructures for Digital Age," *BBC*, July 19, 2006, http://news.bbc.co.uk/2/hi/entertainment/5194046.stm.
Berry, Richard, "Radio, Music, Podcasts – BBC Sounds: Public Service Radio and Podcasts in a Platform World," *Radio Journal: International Studies in Broadcast & Audio Media* 18, no. 1 (2020): 63.
British Internet Providers Association, "Memorandum," *The Funding of the BBC*, Vol. II (London: HMSO, December 15, 1999), 36–37.
"BS dejitaru: asu hōsō o kaishi [BS Digital Broadcasting Starts Tomorrow]," *Asahi Shimbun*, November 30, 2000.

Bunz, Mercedes, "BBC Tells News Staff to Embrace Social Media," *The Guardian*, February 10, 2010.
"Diet Passes Bill to Promote IT," *Japan Times*, November 30, 2000.
"Digital News Report 2020," Reuters Institute for the Study of Journalism at Oxford University, 2020, www.digitalnewsreport.org/interactive/.
"Digitization Budgets Cut Profits," *Nikkei Weekly*, June 6, 2005.
Doward, Jamie, "Showdown at White City," *The Observer*, January 28, 2001.
"DTV Broadcasters to Reach Cell Phone Users," *Nikkei Weekly*, October 3, 2005.
"DTV Broadcasts to be Simulcast on Internet," *Nikkei Weekly*, July 16, 2005.
"Foreign Firms Here find Dearth of IT Experts," *Japan Times*, November 29, 2000.
Freedman, Des, "The Political Economy of the New News Environment," in *New Media, Old News*, ed. Natalie Fenton (Thousand Oaks, CA: SAGE Publications Ltd, 2009).
Galperin, Hernan, *New Television, Old Politics: The Transition to Digital TV in the United States and Britain* (New York: Cambridge University Press, 2004).
Gibson, Owen, "BBC Web Chief Defends Spending Spree," *The Guardian*, July 22, 2002.
Hart, Jeffrey, *Technology Television and Competition* (Cambridge: Cambridge University Press, 2004).
Horsman, Mathew, "The Reith Thing," *The Guardian*, January 26, 1998.
"Japanese Internet Users Glued to Entertainment Sites," *PR Newswire*, April 9, 2009.
"Japan No Tutor for IT-Savvy South Korea," *Japan Times*, December 5, 2000.
"Japan's Only Public Broadcaster Selects Omniture for Advanced Video Measurement of New Internet TV Service," *Market News Publishing*, December 11, 2008.
Kelly, John, "Red Kayaks and Hidden Gold: The Rise, Challenges and Value of Citizen Journalism," Reuters Institute for the Study of Journalism at Oxford University, 2009.
Kinyōbi, Shūkan, *Abe Seiji to Genron Tōsei* [Abe's Politics and Speech Control] (Tokyo: Kinyōbi Press, 2016).
Laurence, Henry, "The Political Economy of Digital Switchover in Japan and the US," in *The East Asian Development Model: 21st Century Perspectives*, ed. Shiping Hua (London: Routledge, 2015).
Lee-Wright, Peter, "Culture Shock: New Media and Organizational Change at the BBC," in *New Media, Old News: Journalism and Democracy in the Digital Age*, ed. Natalie Fenton (London: Sage Publication, 2010).
"Limit Set on NHK's Internet Activities," *Kyodo News Service*, March 8, 2002.
Loughran, Cathy, "Big Bang for TV News," *Ariel* (BBC: London, April 22, 2008), 1.
"Ministry Panel Proposes Limits on NHK's Internet Services," *Japan Economic Newswire*, December 21, 2001.
Moe, Hallvard, "Public Service Media Online? Regulating Public Broadcasters' Internet Services, A Comparative Analysis," *Television and New Media* 9, no. 3 (May 2008).
MPT, "Tsushin Hakushō [White Paper on Telecommunications]" (Tokyo: MPT, 1999).
Nakamura, Yoshihiko, and Ritsu Yonekura, "How Public Service Broadcasting is Talked About: A Comparative Web Survey of Japan, the ROK and the United Kingdom," *NHK Broadcasting Studies*, no. 8 (Tokyo: NHK Broadcasting Culture Research Institute, 2010).
Newman, Nic, "The Rise of Social Media and its Impact on Mainstream Journalism," *Working Paper, Reuters Institute for the Study of Journalism at Oxford University*, Working Paper, 2009, http://reutersinstitute.politics.ox.ac.uk/publications/risj-working-papers.html.
"Newspaper Industry Concerned about NHK's Internet Business," *Jiji Press Ticker Service*, December 5, 2000.

NHK, *Annual Report* (Tokyo: NHK, 2000).

"NHK Begins Net Programs for Schools," *Daily Yomiuri*, November 9, 1999.

"NHK Internet Plans to Cause Licensing Problems," *Mainichi Daily News*, February 28, 2001.

"NHK is First Broadcaster to Offer Aired TV Programs on Internet," *Kyodo News Service*, July 18, 2007.

"NHK May Seek Law Revision to Let NHK Use Net," *Kyodo Newswire*, April 6, 2000.

NHK, "NHK Digital," accessed June 28, 2021, www.nhk.or.jp/digital/en/digitalbroad/02_spec.html.

"No Surrender," *The Economist*, March 6, 2010.

Osaki, Tad, "A Man of Vision," *Television Asia*, June 1, 2000.

Owen, Bruce M., *The Internet Challenge to Television* (Cambridge, MA: Harvard University Press, 1999).

Price, Rosa, "Licence Fee on Death Row," *Daily Telegraph*, July 9, 2008.

"Public Service Will Remain at Heart of the BBC in the Digital Ages Pledges Director-General," *M2 Communications Presswire*, January 22, 1998.

Purvis, Stewart, "Why ITN is Taking the BBC to Court," *The Guardian*, July 17, 2000.

Quah, Nicholas, "Hot Pod: Is the BBC's Power to Blame for the U.K. Podcasting Scene's Underdevelopment?" *Nieman Lab*, June 28, 2016, www.niemanlab.org/2016/06/hot-pod-is-the-bbcs-power-to-blame-for-the-u-k-podcasting-scenes-underdevelopment/.

Scott, Mark, "BBC Leads the Way on the Web," *BusinessWeek Online*, July 3, 2008.

Shinichi, Yamada, and Miyashita Hiroshi, "Broadcasters at Odds Over Updating of Law," *Daily Yomiuri*, June 22, 2000.

Starks, Michael, *Switching to Digital Television: UK Public Policy and the Market* (Bristol, UK: Intellect, 2007).

"Struggling to Stay on Top of Fake Social Media Posts," *Japan Times*, June 23, 2018.

Stuart, Audrey, "TV Documentaries Take Leap into Digital World," *Agence France Presse*, March 30, 2009.

Terazono, Emiko, "BBC Chief Denies Crowding Out Commercial Rivals," *Financial Times*, May 4, 2006.

"Terebi Mekaa teikai ni hashiru [TV Makers Cooperate]," *Asahi Shimbun*, November 30, 2000.

Tracy, Michael, *The Decline and Fall of Public Service Broadcasting* (Oxford: Oxford University Press, 1998).

"TV Industry Stands Against NHK Internet Business," *Jiji Press Ticker Service*, December 26, 2000.

Woods, Mark, "Pubcasters Nix Free Product," *Daily Variety*, November 15, 1999.

Yoshida, Junko, "Broadcasters Look for New Hits among Golden Oldies," *Electronic Engineering Times*, September 22, 2008.

Yoshikazu, Suzuki, "Will NHK's On-Demand Service Be a Hit?" *Daily Yomiuri*, November 28, 2006.

Yūseishō, *Maruchimedia hakusho 200: kontentsu-komasu ni mukete* [Multimedia White Paper 2000: Towards Contents-Commerce] (Tokyo: Yūseishō, 2000).

9 Battles for the BBC (2000–2021)

The first two decades of the 21st century were tumultuous for all traditional media organizations, and especially difficult for public broadcasters. New media exacerbated the common challenges of greater competition, declining audiences and escalating costs. Other wounds were self-inflicted, with top officials forced to resign in disgrace. The BBC's editorial autonomy was challenged as it became embroiled in a bitter fight with Tony Blair's Labour Government over allegations of deception in the run-up to the Iraq War. The Corporation was rebuked by the subsequent Hutton Inquiry but fighting back against political interference burnished the BBC's reputation for independence. Next, the Corporation was engulfed in a wave of scandals, including misleading footage of the Queen, manipulated phone-in shows, and the overpayment of star performers, all culminating in the awful revelations concerning presenter Jimmy Savile's sexual abuse and pedophilia. After the Conservatives returned to power in 2010, the BBC also faced austerity and renewed ideological hostility. The extreme polarization of the Brexit debate posed enormous challenges for the BBC's impartiality, while attempts to improve diversity and inclusion on-screen and within the Corporation fueled a cultural backlash. However, populist attacks launched by Prime Minister Boris Johnson and others were blunted by the vital role the BBC played during the COVID-19 pandemic.

NHK too was mired in scandals involving political interference and nationalistic historical revisionism, managerial embezzlement, and insider trading. The consequent fee-boycott by millions of viewers only exacerbated the problem of declining audiences and collapsing trust. Prime Minister Koizumi Jun'ichro's promise to reform Japan's economy "with no sacred cows" briefly threatened NHK's privileged status, but the expected economic assault never materialized. However, Prime Minister Abe Shinzō's attacks on press freedom undermined NHK's editorial autonomy throughout his long reign from 2012 to 2020. Nevertheless, while the existence of public broadcasting became once again the subject of intense political debate, the public broadcasters themselves managed to defend themselves against forces that seemed likely to result in their imminent demise. Their survival strategies followed earlier patterns. The BBC fought back against political interference and won public support in its defense. NHK avoided political conflict where possible, and backed down when confronted.

DOI: 10.4324/b23015-9

The following two chapters explore four interrelated themes. The first is the ongoing ideological threats from neoliberalism. Tony Blair's New Labour and Koizumi Junichiro's revitalized LDP deregulated media markets, but the public broadcasters survived, each following their own well-worked strategies for enlisting political support. Second, internal scandals created by poor managerial decisions generated crises of legitimacy at both organizations. Again, while their self-inflicted problems were superficially similar, responses differed as the BBC proved more transparent in its self-reflection and self-criticism. Third, the chapters explore cases of political interference and the defense of editorial independence. Both broadcasters were attacked by their governments in the 2000s. One case saw the BBC engage in a "fight to the death" with the government over coverage of the 2003 Iraq War. The other case saw NHK submit meekly to the government over its coverage of Japan's Second World War era war record. The cases will be explored in depth to illustrate the distinctive patterns of government–media interaction. Finally, we examine some of the complicated ways in which entertainment programming and organizational culture either challenge or reaffirm prevailing social norms and values, with NHK more often an agent of social stability and the BBC more likely an agent of change.

New Labour and the BBC

The election of Prime Minister Tony Blair in 1997 presented both dangers and opportunities for the BBC. The modernizing doctrine of "New Labour" embraced market forces and stressed the benefits of private enterprise over public provision, especially in sectors such as media and telecommunications.[1] The new government had specifically identified creative industries such as television as a vital engine for future economic growth in the post-industrial "knowledge economy" and was actively seeking to deregulate and promote entrepreneurialism in the relevant sectors.[2] In addition, Blair's close political alliance with Rupert Murdoch and the backing of News International media, including the *Sun* and the *Times*, were seen as pivotal elements in Blair's electoral success. Murdoch was widely expected to be rewarded for his support with favorable media policies and a more constrained BBC was high on his wish-list. Set against these threats, though, Labour were still publicly committed to public services, and there was considerable sympathy for the BBC within the party, especially in light of its resistance to what many had seen as Thatcherite bullying.

Greg Dyke replaced John Birt as Director-General of the BBC in 2000, in what was to prove a pivotal year for the Corporation. Dyke had earned fame and considerable fortune in commercial television, and became the first outsider Director-General in 60 years. His background prompted fears that he would push the BBC down-market in an effort to replicate his commercial ratings successes. His close friendship with Sir Christopher Bland, Chairman of the Governors, and his large donations to the Labour Party only made his appointment more controversial. William Hague, leader of the Conservative Party, formally opposed Dyke's selection on the grounds of his open political partisanship.[3]

Dyke's appointment went ahead despite the protests, but the issues raised fore-shadowed two of the key debates over the next decade. The first set of questions arose from thorough reexamination of the meaning of "public service broadcasting" in an era where the original rationale, spectrum scarcity, was no longer an issue and where "broadcasting" itself was an increasingly ambiguous concept. What public services should the BBC provide, and which could they do better than commercial media? Who would pay for these increasingly expensive services, and why should they? Would the BBC become too commercial under the entrepreneurial Dyke, and if so, how would that hurt the private sector? What was the appropriate relationship between the BBC and an increasingly broad and eclectic set of commercial rivals that now included internet service providers and global media conglomerates, as well as the usual newspaper owners and independent broadcasters?

The second, far uglier set of issues, concerned the BBC's alleged partisanship and editorial autonomy. Dyke was a close associate and financial backer of Blair, quintessentially one of "Tony's Cronies." Did Dyke's appointment give the Prime Minister too much power over the broadcaster? How could such a nakedly politi-cal appointment maintain editorial impartiality? Indeed, was neutrality possible, or even desirable, in an increasingly polarized political landscape? In the event, ironically, Dyke was to lead the BBC into the most dangerous political battle in its existence, as the corporation fought viciously with the Labour Government over issues of journalistic integrity and editorial independence.

Dyke arrived against a backdrop of audience fragmentation and declining inter-est in news, especially by younger and poorer audiences. Seven in ten viewers were satisfied with the BBC, but only 45% thought the license fee was good value for money. Nearly 60% favored replacing the license fee with adverts.[4] Morale among staff was very low, in part as a result of John Birt's bureaucratic manage-ment style.[5] Meanwhile, the internet was raising new and difficult challenges, with staff deeply divided about the appropriate responses. "At the end of my first week at the BBC," Dyke recalled, "I was deeply depressed."[6]

Questions of sustainable funding in the digital age were addressed by a 1999 report to the Department of Culture, Media and Sport (DCMS) by an indepen-dent review panel led by Gavin Davies, an economist and managing director at Goldman Sachs. *The Future Funding of the BBC* proposed increased funds for the BBC to engage in digital and new media.[7] The DCMS obliged awarding a greater-than-inflation increase in the license fee, which yielded increased reve-nues that were less than requested but more than enough to enrage commercial rivals, especially those investing in the soon-to-be-doomed Ondigital DTV ven-ture.[8] The DCMS also approved the BBC's request to place advertising on BBC Worldwide's foreign services, illustrating both the increasingly entrepreneurial organization culture and state approval for the trend. Parliamentary opposition to the plan had come from both traditionalists who feared that commercialization would erode the BBC's public service ethos and free-marketeers who feared that adverts would unfairly crowd out commercial media.[9] Davies was rewarded for his passionate and articulate defense of public broadcasting by being appointed Chairman of the Board of Governors in 2001.

Labour's 2003 Communications Act further liberalized media markets, selectively easing ownership rules in ways generally assumed to have been for Rupert Murdoch's benefit.[10] The Act also streamlined oversight of the rapidly converging communications sector with the creation of a single regulatory body, the Office of Communications (Ofcom). The BBC's special place within the media ecology was underlined by the decision to leave the Corporation outside Ofcom's jurisdiction. This decision was made despite lingering dissatisfaction with the role of the Board of Governors and calls for an independent regulator for the BBC.

The BBC thus emerged from the 2003 Act intact, but the competitive pressures generated by liberalization fueled the entrepreneurialism already growing in the organizational culture since Birt's reforms. Indeed, sociologist and BBC critic Tom Mills notes that Birtism was itself a continuation of the pattern of commercialization begun by Michael Checkland in the Thatcher era, with reforms including producer choice and the 25% independent production quota. Mills argues that, as with neoliberalism more generally, the outcome of the reforms had not been the promised efficiencies but even greater layers of financial bureaucracy and an erosion of the public service ethos.[11] While the latter point is debatable, BBC staff were certainly becoming conversant with the language and practices of the market. As the dust from the Communications Act was settling, however, the BBC was hit by its greatest political battle since the General Strike. At issue was a case that struck at the core of the BBC's journalistic responsibilities, editorial autonomy, and relationship to government.

The Iraq War and the Hutton Inquiry

The issue was the BBC's coverage of government statements in the run-up to the 2003 Iraq War. A vital part of the rationale Blair had presented for invasion was that Iraq possessed weapons of mass destruction (WMD), which posed an imminent threat to UK interests. But early one morning in May 2003, reporter Andrew Gilligan made an off-the-cuff remark on Radio 4's *Today* show that he had a source claiming that the Government "probably knew" that information it had presented to Parliament in 2002 on Iraq's possession of WMD was false. Gilligan further stated that his source, whom he kept anonymous, had claimed Number Ten had "sexed-up" the case for war by deliberately exaggerating the reliability of the evidence supporting the government case. Blair and Alistair Campbell, his notoriously short-tempered Communications Director, furiously denied the charges of dishonesty and demanded a full retraction and apology from the BBC.

Director-General Dyke and Chairman Gavyn Davies instinctively defended the BBC's independence. They refused to apologize, backing their journalist even before they had properly checked his story. They continued to support Gilligan even after they discovered that he could not produce satisfactory evidence to substantiate his allegations and had clearly been sloppy in his journalistic practices and on-air statements. In the subsequent political uproar, Campbell engineered the exposure of Gilligan's source, a respected scientist and former weapons inspector named David Kelly. Soon after, under intense public scrutiny and hounded by the press, Kelly committed suicide. Blair then appointed Lord Hutton to head a public inquiry into Kelly's death, and this inquiry became the battleground for an epic fight between the BBC and the government.[12]

Blair and Campbell's charge in the court of public opinion was that the BBC had failed to produce any evidence in support of Gilligan's accusations of dishonesty. The BBC's defense was that the gist of what Gilligan had said had been true, although they admitted he had been too loose in his on-air language.[13] Much of the evidence for the Government's claims about Iraq's WMD program had indeed been of dubious value, yet the government had presented an uncertain case with unwarranted certainty, as Gilligan had so colorfully charged. Gilligan and the BBC's version of events was eventually corroborated by a 2016 public inquiry into the origins of the Iraq War headed by Sir John Chilcot. The Chilcot Report noted that Prime Minister Blair had publicly stated that "the assessed intelligence has established beyond doubt" that Saddam Hussein was producing chemical and biological weapons when, in fact the evidence was very far from conclusive, largely because Iraq was not producing any such weapons. In Chilcot's words: "Intelligence and assessments [about Iraq's possession of WMD] were used to prepare material to be used to support Government statements in a way which conveyed certainty without acknowledging the limitations of the intelligence."[14]

Back in 2003, though, the Hutton Inquiry had chosen to focus narrowly on the BBC's editorial policies and ignored completely the wider issue of the veracity of the government's case for war. Hutton found the BBC guilty of editorial misconduct.[15] Dyke promptly resigned, replaced by Mark Thompson, a long-time BBC producer (and later CEO of the *New York Times*) who was then Chief Executive at Channel 4. BBC journalists were generally aghast at the verdict and dismayed at the popular Dyke's departure, although some were annoyed at Dyke's short-sighted decision to stake the BBC's reputation on shaky ground, having not properly vetted Gilligan's journalism before "betting the farm" on it.[16] Nonetheless, BBC reporting of the entire affair was generally acclaimed as both thorough and fair, with the Panorama documentary *A Fight to the Death* an example of an organizational culture that did not flinch from institutional self-criticism.[17]

The British public largely rejected Hutton's critical conclusions about the BBC. A poll taken immediately after the findings asked: "Was it fair or unfair for the BBC to receive most of the blame for the Kelly affair in the Hutton Report?" While 56% of the public found it unfair, only 35% found it fair.[18] Later polls revealed similar findings: By margins approaching two to one, Britons thought Hutton guilty of one-sidedness at best and "a whitewash" at worst.[19] And while Hutton's conclusions dented the BBC's reputation for reliability, they ultimately did greater damage to the reputations of Blair and Campbell. A survey for the *Daily Telegraph* found that 67% of respondents still trusted BBC journalists to tell the truth, compared with 31% who trusted the government.[20] Criticisms of Hutton were also widespread within the ruling establishment. Former Chairman of the BBC Governors Sir Christopher Bland called the report "a whitewash" that had "tarred and feathered" the BBC, while former Cabinet Minister Clare Short accused Hutton of being "completely one-sided."[21] Even the conservative press, usually quick to criticize the BBC, came out in its support. Max Hastings, a high-profile conservative columnist at the *Daily Mail* lamented:

> Just as the Hutton Report washes Mr. Blair and his little Downing Street cabal whiter than they deserve, so it blackens the BBC beyond any possible desert. For all its limitations, failings, weaknesses and follies the Beeb remains one of the world's great beacons of public service and global information. . . . This is a travesty of justice.[22]

The *Daily Telegraph* also worried about the degree of political interference the case had revealed. "The BBC does not belong to the politicians. It is a national institution. If it is simply left to this government to fiddle with it we shall go from bad to worse. The BBC will become more not less politicised."[23] Indeed, of the major newspapers, only the Murdoch-owned titles were enthusiastic about the Hutton findings, with *The Times* calling Dyke's behavior "little short of disgraceful" and calling for multiple resignations.[24]

Charter Renewal and the Future of the BBC

The Hutton Report roiled discussions over the BBC's 2006 Charter Renewal and revealed deep divisions within the Labour Government.[25] Most Labour MPs and Ofcom regulators were broadly sympathetic to the BBC and held few ideological objections to publicly funded media. On the other hand, a central tenet of Blair's highly successful rebranding of "New Labour" was a loudly professed faith in the market. As the digital switchover story illustrated, Labour were anxious to be seen as business-friendly. Complicating matters further, Blair's electoral strategy involved cultivating good relationships with the media, especially the vitally important and popular newspapers *The Times* and *The Sun*. Labour therefore took Rupert Murdoch's objections to the BBC very seriously. The 2003 Communications Act reforms had largely spared the BBC, but Hutton had reignited doubts about the privileged status and lack of accountability of the publicly funded behemoth. Complicating matters still further, the widespread repudiation of Hutton's findings made the Government anxious to avoid the appearance of acting out of revenge. So intense was public feeling on this matter that DCMS Minister Tessa Jowell felt compelled to promise: "There is no question whatsoever of the [Gilligan] dispute affecting in any shape or form the BBC's licence fee or its charter."[26] The discussions, therefore, went in several different directions before arriving at a vision of the BBC that was not so different in principle from that of 1996, or, for that matter, 1926.

Debate began in 2004 with Ofcom's Public Service Television Review, notable for being the first time in BBC history that the government had actually tried to define public service broadcasting.[27] Gareth Davies's report for the DCMS, for example, had ducked the question, stating, "We may not be able to offer a tight new definition of public service broadcasting but we nevertheless each felt that we knew it when we saw it."[28] But while a great deal of time and effort was spent on coming up with a more precise definition of public service media's mission than "to educate, inform and entertain," a better summary was not forthcoming. The Charter came up with a list of priorities, discussed subsequently, but this was hardly the same thing. Ofcom also attempted to quantify the economic value to society of public service broadcasting, also for the first time. "Public value" was measured by surveying viewers on what they would be willing to pay for BBC services, or by calculating what profits those services would make in private markets. This approach drew considerable criticism from observers for whom the most valuable aspects of the BBC, such as its contributions to informed democratic debate and national culture, were unquantifiable. As one academic was reported to have told Ofcom, one cannot measure quality, because if you do, it becomes quantity.[29]

Ofcom's review reflected New Labour thinking in stating that "a competitive marketplace is a good starting place" in the quest for high-quality programming.[30] The debate on value thus became subsumed in broader concerns about "crowding out" and the BBC's impact on commercial markets.[31] Media companies and internet providers argued that the BBC was engaged in too many activities that were not public service at all, or were so only in the tautological sense that the BBC provided them. Ofcom acknowledged the complaints, but found no hard evidence that the BBC was harming commercial rivals. Indeed, later studies have also failed to show evidence of crowding out: a 2017 survey found that people who get their news from the BBC or NHK were no less likely to be willing to pay for online news.[32] This did not stop considerable debate over how to make the BBC more accountable for how it spent the license fee in the absence of genuine competition. A popular suggestion was "top-slicing," that is, forcing the BBC to share the license fee with other independent producers of public service content. The idea was dropped for the 2006 Renewal, but was revived and subsequently dropped again in 2008.

Ofcom concluded that the BBC was "at the heart of the UK public service broadcasting system":

> [A]s a society, we clearly demand a wider range of high quality UK content than would be provided by the market. . . . We value trustworthy and independent news, programmes which increase our knowledge of the world, and content which reflects the different parts of the UK, and informs our cultural identity. Although commercial broadcasters will provide some of this content, intervention is needed to ensure that there is sufficient range, volume and quality of programming made in the UK and for UK audiences.[33]

The 2006 Charter largely reaffirmed the existing institutional structure and traditional rationale for public broadcasting, declaring: "The BBC exists to serve the public interest." Six "public purposes" had emerged from the debates: (1) sustaining citizenship and civil society; (2) promoting education and learning; (3) stimulating creativity and cultural excellence; (4) representing the United Kingdom, its nations, regions, and communities; (5) bringing the United Kingdom to the world and the world to the United Kingdom; and (6) in promoting its other purposes, helping to deliver to the public the benefit of emerging communications technologies and services and, in addition, taking a leading role in the switchover to digital television.³⁴ The Corporation was charged to promote these public purposes "through the provision of output which consists of information, education and entertainment."³⁵ Striking about this articulation of the BBC's public purposes is that with the exception of item six, the commitment to help deliver new technologies and the specific instruction to promote digital switchover, these priorities were at heart virtually unchanged from Lord Reith's day.

The 2006 Charter's most significant reform was to the governance structure, seen as a necessary response to Hutton's criticisms. The Board of Governors was replaced with the BBC Trust. The conflict of interest inherent in the Board's role as both defender and overseer of the BBC had long been clear, and abolition had seemed imminent in 2000, when DCMS Minister Smith expressed fears that the Board would simply rubber-stamp Greg Dyke's more commercially minded plans. Dyke's close friendship with Chairman Christopher Bland had exacerbated Smith's fears, but when Dyke withdrew the offending proposals, the proposed governance reform was dropped.³⁶ But the Board's perceived failings during the Gilligan affair were the last straw. A 14-person Trust would be appointed by Parliament and charged with acting as "guardians of the licence fee and the public interest."³⁷

With the Charter approved, Parliament passed the license fee renewal. The settlement amount was below inflation, but was guaranteed to last until 2016. However, for the first time in BBC history, a sum had been earmarked for a specific use: £600 million to help pay for digital switchover. While this was what the BBC needed, some warned that this represented an unwelcome increase in political control over the broadcaster's funds, with the implication, later born out, that future governments might do the same thing.

Meanwhile, the BBC continued to expand aggressively onto the proliferation of new media platforms, provoking further criticism. So successful had the Corporation become, in fact, that the concern was less that the BBC was too weak to survive than that it had become too powerful. For example, in 2008, the BBC launched the reality show *Any Dream Will Do* to select some of the cast for a commercial West End production of *Joseph and the Amazing Technicolor Dreamcoat*. High-profile theater luminaries argued that the BBC was abusing the license fee, echoing complaints made by music-hall owners 90 years earlier. BBC imperialism was also the problem in 2007 when BBC Worldwide bought up the *Lonely Planet* travel guide to enhance its global information services across media platforms. The move provoked outrage from commercial publishers and MPs, one of whom condemned it as "the most egregious example" of unjustified commercial expansion by the BBC.³⁸ Ofcom were unmoved. The 2009 Public Service Broadcasting Review had as its first priority: "to maintain the BBC's role and funding for its programmes and services at the heart of the overall system."³⁹

In March 2010, the BBC unveiled *Putting Quality First*, the strategy review for the second half of the 2006–2016 Charter period, against the backdrop of the economic recession brought on by the 2008 stock market crash.⁴⁰ The first order of business was cutbacks, including cancelation of two radio stations (BBC 6 and the Asian Network), and cuts of 25% to website spending and 20% to foreign content acquisition. Director-General Thompson described the internet cutbacks as "rationalisation after a period of very broad activity," but they were generally believed to be a preemptive response to the expected Conservative Party election victory.[41] The BBC Trust subsequently saved BBC 6, the music station, in response to an outpouring of support for it on Twitter and Facebook.[42]

Next, the review stressed future priorities: quality programming, tighter focus, greater efficiency, and more awareness of market impact. Mark Thompson elaborated on his blog:

> Quality is our raison d'être. The BBC exists to deliver to audiences in the UK and around the world, programmes and content of real quality and value – content which audiences would never enjoy if the BBC did not exist.
>
> We will refocus licence fee investment around five clear priorities: the best journalism; inspiring knowledge, music and culture; ambitious UK drama and comedy; outstanding children's content; and events that bring communities and the nation together. We will focus on the areas which most clearly build public value and which are most at risk of being ignored or under-invested in by commercial players.
>
> The BBC will live or die by the quality of its programmes and content. We will retain an unswerving, unwavering, unflagging focus on quality. To ensure we do, we are committing to unprecedented investment in high-quality, original UK content.
>
> We will also deliver a more focused BBC doing fewer things better and leaving space for others by setting clearer boundaries.[43]

The concerns about market impact, so important in 2006, were still apparent. But in interviews Thompson articulated a far grander vision for the BBC than simply filling in where markets failed, instead invoking quality, public space, and the creation of a common culture.[44] His language marked a shift away from the economic terminology of "value" and market failure used for much of the 1990s and in the 2006 Review.

The 2010 electoral victory of the Conservative Party, senior partners in a coalition with the Liberal-Democrat party, revived both ideological and economic threats to the BBC. The 2008 crash and recession had fueled rising budget deficits, prompting massive cuts in public sector spending. The BBC was a prime target for austerity measures, described by one conservative MP as "the bloated, nationalised state broadcasting service."[45] In opposition, the Conservatives had revived the idea of "top-slicing" the license fee to promote competition and "to keep the BBC on its toes."[46] Sir Michael Lyons, Chairman of the BBC Trust, had fought back. "The licence fee belongs to the licence payers. [It] is not a back pocket for the government. . . . It is not a spare pot of cash to be raided."[47] The Labour government had supported the BBC, with Culture Secretary Ben Bradshaw describing it as "a great British asset" and urging it to demonstrate greater confidence in the face of Conservative threats.[48] Incoming Conservative Culture Secretary Jeremy Hunt had pointedly asked while in opposition: "Will the BBC be less expansionist? Will it think carefully about its impact on the independent sector? Above all, will it spend licence fee payers' money on quality public service content that they want to see?"[49]

Once again, the BBC's carefully nurtured reputation for great programming limited how far its critics were prepared to reform it. Hunt described the BBC as the "quality benchmark" in TV and radio, adding "I understand that it is difficult for newspapers to charge because of the quality of BBC News Online, but we are not going to turn the clock back."[50] Conservative Prime Minister David Cameron even took space in *The Sun* to claim he was a fan of the BBC.

> You can come up with all the arguments in the world for how – theoretically – a different, more market-driven structure would work better. But frankly, I would rather stick with a structure that has produced good television and radio programmes, led by an institution – the BBC – that is still respected at home and abroad.[51]

Cameron did, however, criticize the BBC for being "oversized and overreaching." He called it out of touch with viewers, invoking presenter Jonathan Ross's astronomic £6 million salary and "sick" phone-calls.[52] Cameron didn't like "the squeezing and crushing of commercial competitors online or in publishing," citing the Lonely Planet purchase. He preferred the Trust to the Board of Governors, but still wanted a fully independent regulator. Nonetheless, he claimed "I am a fan of the BBC . . . and I even approve of the way it is funded."[53]

Scandals

Political discussions were conducted and often inflected by periodic scandals, usually program related, and the 2006–2016 period was rife with scandal for the BBC. Some were relatively minor affairs, such as the "Crowngate" saga when the documentary *A Year in the Life of the Queen* (2007) was misleadingly edited so that Her Majesty was made to look as if she were storming grumpily out of a photo shoot.[54] In the "Socksgate affair," the much-loved children's show *Blue Peter* was caught faking the results of a viewer poll to name the show's new cat.[55] The revelation that presenter Jonathan Ross was being paid a salary of approximately £6 million prompted outcry about misspent license fee money, with Ross compounding the public relations problem by making offensive on-air calls.[56]

Next, Director-General Thompson was roundly criticized from the political left for his refusal to air an appeal for humanitarian aid to Gaza. Early in 2009, a group of UK charities, including the Red Cross, Save the Children and Oxfam, formed the Disasters Emergency Committee (DEC) to raise money for aid relief and reconstruction in the Gaza Strip. DEC ran a TV appeal that was carried on the commercial stations, ITV and Channel 4. Thompson refused to air it on the grounds that to do so "could be interpreted as taking a political stance on an ongoing story" and would thus breach the BBC's impartiality obligations.[57] The decision provoked criticism from the Government's Minister for International Development and thousands of protesters outside Broadcasting House.

The episode vividly illustrated the difficulties of maintaining editorial neutrality while attempting to serve the public interest on the increasingly frequent occasions when there are partisan disagreements about what precisely is in the public interest. But among all these controversies, none prompted more serious demands for fundamental reform than the shocking revelations of the Jimmy Savile scandal and the shame they brought on the BBC.

Savile

Jimmy Savile was a flamboyant, long-serving BBC presenter, working chiefly with youth-oriented shows such as *Top of the Pops* and *Jim'll Fix It* from the 1960s until the mid-2000s.[58] A prolific fundraiser for hospitals and children's charities, he was hugely popular at the time of his death in 2011. Posthumously, however, it soon emerged that he had engaged for decades in serial pedophilia and other forms of sexual abuse.[59] Investigations brought to light thousands of alleged incidents involving, among others, children at the hospitals for which he raised money or teenagers on the sets of his BBC shows. Other popular presenters were also found to have engaged in sexual abuse. The revelations wrought huge damage on the BBC's reputation in two areas, the corporate culture and the disastrous handling of the revelations themselves. First, harsh questions were raised about how much, and for how long, BBC management had enabled the abuses. An internal inquiry led by Dame Janet Smith confirmed subsequently that for decades awareness of Savile's abuse had been widespread within the Corporation.[60] She described the organizational culture that had allowed Savile and others to continue their practices as macho, hierarchical, deeply deferential to management, and fearful of the power of celebrities.[61] Clearly, reform was needed.

A more immediate problem was the unsatisfactory way in which BBC management responded to the revelations of abuse. As soon as Savile died, a *Newsnight* team led by reporters Meiron Jones and Liz McKean began investigating the abuse allegations, which had already been under police inquiry.[62] Their findings were due to air in December 2011 but at the last minute *Newsnight's* editor Peter Rippon canceled the program.[63] Shortly thereafter, a gushing posthumous tribute to Savile was broadcast over the Christmas holidays. Jones and McKean were furious with Rippon's decision, seeing it as a betrayal of the abuse survivors who had had the courage to speak to out. They took their findings to ITV who broke the Savile story a few months later on the current affairs show *Exposure*.[64] Naturally, the decision to drop the *Newsnight* broadcast looked suspiciously like a management-ordered whitewash, and outrage against the BBC intensified after the cancelation became known. An internal inquiry led by Nick Pollard, a well-respected independent broadcaster, found no evidence of a cover-up. Pollard accepted that Rippon had in good faith canceled the program for editorial reasons, principally that the original allegations were not properly substantiated.[65] Such caution, I was told, seems to have been in large part a reaction to the trauma of the Gilligan affair.[66] However, Pollard found much fault with the BBCs internal editorial and management structures, describing "a critical lack of leadership and of organization" in dealing with the aftermath of the revelations.[67] Many BBC staff expressed frustration and anger at the way management had handled the affair, especially the subsequent marginalization of Jones and McKean.[68] However, evidence of institutional transparency can be found in the fact that within a few months *Panorama* aired their own investigation into the canceled *Newsnight* episode, including an interview with McKean who accused the BBC of misleading the public.[69]

The BBC's image problems were compounded by another *Newsnight* episode, aired in November 2012, that investigated alleged child abuse in the 1970s. The program falsely implied that the abuser was Lord Alistair MacAlpine, a senior Conservative politician. It was a case of mistaken identity, caused in large part by the reporters, who had failed to contact MacAlpine or verify his photograph with the accuser.[70] In the subsequent outrage, the BBC was forced again to apologize, and newly appointed Director-General George Entwhistle resigned. Entwhistle had replaced Mark Thompson, who had announced his resignation just before the Savile scandal blew up.[71]

The damage to the BBC's reputation, while grave, was less than many expected. An extensive survey found that just under half of the public trusted the Corporation less after the scandals. However, the BBC remained the most trusted news source for a plurality (39% of respondents, compared with 13% for ITV and 10% for Sky News). Helping protect the broadcaster were the very high levels of goodwill, with many describing it as a "national treasure" and almost 40% regarding it with great respect, compared with 7% for Parliament or News International. In addition, there was a widely held sense that the Savile scandal was about an evil individual rather than the institution, although many believed that management was deeply complicit in enabling his behavior. Only one-third of respondents blamed the BBC for what Savile did.[72] The departure of the Director-General seemed to allow the Corporation to move forward again, but the respite was short-lived with the 2016 Charter Renewal discussions looming, and now under a cloud.

After 2015: Brexit, COVID, and Conservative Attacks

The Conservatives' outright victory in the 2015 election came during discussions over the 2016 Charter Renewal, raising fears within the BBC and hope among many Conservatives that reform might once again be imminent. Since the 2006 Charter Renewal, the BBC's editorial reputation had been badly tainted by the scandals, allegations of profligacy, and the continued criticism leveled by the right-wing press. Many Conservatives were further aggrieved at what they saw as unfair coverage during the 2015 election campaign. Expectations of a sustained ideological assault were compounded by the appointment of John Whittingdale, an outspoken critic of the BBC, as Minister for Culture, Media and Sports.[73] He had chaired a DCMS Select Committee that released the Green Paper *The Future of the BBC* in 2015, just before the election. This report had been highly critical of the BBC's governance and accountability structures, the "anachronistic" license fee funding system, and overly broad, unambitious programming which, it argued, threatened to crowd out smaller commercial media.[74] The report noted:

> Over the last few years the BBC has suffered from a succession of disasters of its own making, yet it remains a widely admired and trusted institution, and fulfils many important functions both at home and abroad. However, when an organisation is in receipt of nearly £4 billion of public money, very big questions have to be asked about how that money is provided and spent, and how that organisation is governed and made accountable.

The report led to the establishment of an independent review panel headed by Sir David Clementi, a financier and former deputy-general of the Bank of England. Clementi argued that events such as the Savile and McAlpine scandals showed the need for fundamental reform of the system of governance and regulation of the BBC:

> The BBC Trust model is flawed. It conflates governance and regulatory functions within the Trust . . . the BBC should have a single unitary Board, clearly responsible for governing its activities; and that regulatory functions in respect of the BBC should be in a separate body from the BBC [*i.e.* Ofcom].[75]

The 2016 Charter adopted Clementi's proposals, replacing the BBC Trust with a reconstituted Board of Governors. Oversight responsibilities were transferred to Ofcom, meaning that for the first time in its history, the BBC was being regulated by an external body. Some saw the abolition of the Trust as designed to make it harder to defend for the BBC to defend itself from subsequent attempts to diminish its reach and influence.[76]

Notwithstanding such objections, the 2016 Charter was kinder to the BBC than many had feared, not least in keeping the license fee system until the next Charter review in 2027. Responses to the 2015 Green Paper from the general public as well as various parliamentary and DCMS committees had been very supportive of the BBC, and Whittingdale did not press his desire for a radically smaller BBC.[77] The DCMS had considered Conservative proposals to decriminalize non-payment of the license fee but dismissed them, concluding that such a reform would lead to non-compliance.[78] However, just as the Charter negotiations were in full swing, the BBC's impartiality was tested by one of the most divisive issues in recent British politics: Brexit.

Prime Minister David Cameron's decision to hold a referendum on Britain's continued membership of the European Union revealed and exacerbated deep political and social divisions, and the rancorous campaign was as much a struggle over national identity as a debate about trade. The major newspapers were highly partisan, mostly in favor of Leave. With the Charter negotiations in full swing, the BBC was particularly vulnerable to accusations of bias. DCMS Minister Whittingdale delayed publication of his White Paper until after the referendum but had already publicly criticized the BBC's EU coverage. Labour Party shadow secretary Maria Eagle said his vocal support for Leave created a conflict of interest that put the BBC in an "intolerable" position.[79]

Opinions both popular and scholarly vary widely about how successfully the BBC covered the referendum, described by Director of Editorial Policy and Standards David Jordan as perhaps "the greatest impartiality challenge the Corporation had ever faced."[80] Jordan argues that the Corporation generally achieved the "due impartiality and broad balance" required by the editorial guidelines they had drawn up specifically for the vote.[81] On the other hand, Leave campaigners cast the BBC as anti-Brexit, a view shared by a large minority of their supporters. A YouGov survey found that BBC was seen as anti-Brexit by 45% of Leave voters and 27% of all voters, making it second only to the *Guardian* in terms of public perceptions of being anti-Brexit. Much smaller numbers of Remain supporters (13%) and all voters (5%) thought the BBC was pro-Brexit. However, the BBC was the news organization with the joint highest number of people saying it was neither pro- nor anti-Brexit (24%), while a large number (41%) didn't know its stance.[82]

However, these popular views are not necessarily born out on closer inspection. A 2016 study of BBC news by European analysts Media Tenor found a preponderance of BBC news cast the EU in a negative light.[83] Previous content analysis by scholars at Cardiff School of Journalism had found that the BBC's pre-referendum treatment of the EU tended to frame issues purely in terms of British party politics, failing to contextualize the meaning, costs, and benefits of membership.[84]

Some scholars find that in the highly partisan world of British media, the BBC was exceptional in its commitment to impartiality and fairness, and its presentation of fact.[85] However, a view seemingly more common among sympathetic observers, including many BBC-connected friends I spoke with, is that, in an admittedly horrendous position, the BBC failed to live up to its best reporting traditions. Jean Seaton writes:

> Historically, the BBC has had a much stronger understanding of the subordinate role of balance in impartiality. Impartiality has never been seen as a passive, arithmetical task, but as something difficult and far more testing.

But, she argues, fearful of the accusations of bias flying in from all sides, too much of the BBC's Brexit reporting lacked appropriate proportionality: "Claims were 'balanced' not interrogated or explored . . . the whole exercise became politicised."[86] Ivor Gaber, while dismissing claims of anti-Brexit bias, also deplores the "phony balance" of, for example, balancing the analysis of over 1,000 pro-Remain economists with the dissent of a single pro-Leaver.[87] In any event, the ugly debate proved yet again the truth of the words of Michael Swann, former chair of the BBC Governors: "a nation divided always has the BBC on the rack."[88]

Culture Wars

Leaver hostility to the BBC was bound up in larger cultural wars about multiculturalism and social liberalism.[89] Especially since Greg Dyke's time, the BBC had been struggling to properly reach and reflect a Britain whose demographics were changing rapidly: the ethnically non-white proportion of the population had doubled from about 6% to about 14% between 1991 and 2011.[90] Social attitudes over issues such as religion, race, and gender were also in flux: public support for same-sex marriages, for example, rose from 10% in 1987 to 70% in 2017.[91] Director-General Tony Hall had announced measures to improve diversity in 2013 and in April 2016 the BBC launched a major Diversity and Inclusion Strategy.[92] The goal was to have a workforce more diverse than any other in the industry and improve portrayal targets for marginalized groups, including ethnic minorities and the disabled.[93] In 2018, the 50:50 project set the goal of having at least half of the contributors to news programs be women.[94] At the time, BBC television staff were 82% white and 55% male compared to a UK industry average of 83% and 53%, respectively.[95] Meanwhile, programs such as *Goodness Gracious Me* (1996–2001), *The Kumars at No. 42* (2001–2006), *White Teeth* (2002), and *I May Destroy You* (2020) gave voice to groups previously underrepresented both on- and off-screen.

The BBC's embrace of diversity gave ammunition to existing critics on the cultural right. Charles Moore, editor of the conservative *Spectator*, said this as a guest on BBC Radio 4's flagship Today program:

> The BBC has decided to be a secular church and it preaches and tells us what we ought to think about things. So it tells us we shouldn't support Brexit and we should accept climate change alarmism and we have to all kowtow to the doctrines of diversity.[96]

Thus, when a second-generation Muslim Nadiya Hussein won *The Great British Bake-Off*, the BBC attracted criticism such as this from the Daily Mail:

> When this series of The Great British Bake Off began, the BBC was proud it was the most inclusive, multi-cultural line-up ever. Now we're down to the final three, it's certainly a PC triumph. We are left with Muslim mum Nadiya Hussain, gay doctor Tamal Ray, and New Man Ian Cumming. Poor Flora Shedden never stood a chance. She was far too middle class – and was booted off this week after her chocolate carousel was deemed sub-standard. Perhaps if she'd made a chocolate mosque, she'd have stood a better chance.[97]

Conservative attacks on the BBC for being too progressive are as old as the BBC itself, as we have seen, but so too are accusations that it is too conservative. Left-wing critics note the high number of senior managers and reporters associated directly or indirectly with the Conservative Party.[98] Director-General Tim Davie was a Conservative candidate for his local council. Chairman Richard Sharp was former boss and unpaid economic advisor to Conservative Chancellor of the Exchequer Rishi Sunak as well as serving as Director of the Thatcherite think-tank at the Center for Policy Studies. Robbie Gibb, appointed to the Board in 2021, was Theresa May's Director of Communications who had earlier described the BBC as "culturally captured by the woke-dominated group-think of some of its staff."[99] Global News controller Craig Oliver left the BBC to become David Cameron's Director of Communication. Chris Patten, Chair of the BBC Trust from 2011 to 2014, was a former Conservative Cabinet Minister. Nick Robinson, political editor during 2005–2015 was former head of the Oxford University Conservative Association. The list, and the argument about impartiality, goes on and on.

Boris Johnson's accession as Prime Minister in 2019 heightened the threat to the BBC. During the election campaign, he had said that the license fee was unfair and hinted at decriminalizing non-payment: "The system of funding out of what is a general tax bears reflection."[100] Johnson's attack on the BBC was part of a broader "war on woke" campaign that included defending slave–trader statues and an official report concluding there was no systemic racism in the United Kingdom.[101] In one fairly typical episode, Conservative MPs criticized the BBC for its unpatriotic coverage of the jingoistic anthem "Rule Britannia" during the *Last Night at the Proms*, and demanded more union jacks in the BBC Annual Report.[102] In 2021, Johnson appointed Nadine Dorries, an outspoken critic of the BBC, as Secretary of State for Digital, Culture, Media and Sport. Dorries promptly accused the BBC of being elitist and lacking impartiality.[103] Some suggested that Johnson and his Conservative allies simply wanted a new fight in the culture wars to detract from their numerous corruption scandals, failures in tackling COVID-19, and Brexit's economic damage.[104] Nonetheless, these broader attacks on the BBC as a national institution, and the attempts to place it on one side of a deepening cultural divide, represent a potentially profound new threat.

The COVID-19 pandemic of 2020–2021, however, highlighted the BBC's ongoing value to the nation. Amidst shock at the rising death count and bewildering uncertainties about proper precautions, the BBC upheld its role as the United Kingdom's most trusted news source.[105] Audiences rose by 70% compared with 2019.[106] Educational programming, especially on topics related to the national curriculum, was stepped up.[107] Using free-to-air television channels for remote learning even proved an effective way to lessen the digital divide because many poorer families lacked reliable internet access.[108] However, the BBC faced once again the dilemma of simultaneously supporting government efforts to convey vital information while holding the same government to account for mistakes, all along with helping maintain morale and assisting with the new demands for remote education. Scholars Stephen Cushion and Richard Sambrook argue that at the beginning of the crisis, the BBC did better at covering developments rather than uncovering their causes.[109] On the other hand, they note the immense potential for the pandemic to cement the BBC's reputation. Time will tell.

Notes

1 Des Freedman, *Television Policies of the Labour Party 1951–2001* (London: Frank Cass, 2003), 155–196.
2 Department of Culture, Media and Sport, *Creative Industries Mapping Document* (London: HMO Stationery Office, 1998).

3 Greg Dyke, *Inside Story* (London: HarperCollins, 2004), 135. For a flavor of the reaction in the conservative press, see Alison Boschoff, "Tony's Crony in BBC Storm," *Daily Mail*, June 25, 1999.

4 DCMS, "Attitude Survey," in *Review of the Future Funding of the BBC* (London: DCMS, April 1999), 176–178.

5 Jane Robbins, "Not a Moist Eye in the House as Birt Says a Cool Farewell to the BBC Staff," *Independent*, January 29, 2000.

6 Dyke, *Inside Story*, 155.

7 "Report of the Independent Review Panel," in *The Future Funding of the BBC* (London: DCMS, July 1999), http://news.bbc.co.uk/hi/english/static/bbc_funding_review/reviewco.pdf.

8 "When £2 Billion Is Not Enough," *The Economist*, August 7, 1999.

9 Jamie Doward, "Commons Probe for BBC Web Ads," *Observer*, January 28, 2001.

10 "Free TV," *The Economist*, May 11, 2002.

11 Tom Mills, *The BBC: Myth of a Public Service* (London: Verso Books, 2016), 164–165.

12 Alan Cowell, "Death of an Expert Witness," *The New York Times*, August 17, 2003.

13 Warren Hoge, "Reporter Admits BBC Report on Iraqi Arms Had Errors," *The New York Times*, September 17, 2003.

14 "Executive Summary HC 264," *The Report of the Iraq Inquiry*, June 6, 2016, para 330, accessed October 30, 2021, https://assets.publishing.service.gov.uk/government/uploads/system/uploads/attachment_data/file/535406/The_Report_of_the_Iraq_Inquiry_-_Executive_Summary_Cover_9mm_Spine.pdf.

15 www.the-hutton-inquiry.org.uk/index.htm.

16 Author's own interviews with BBC staff in London, March 2008.

17 This at least was the argument found in the normally conservative, BBC-skeptical *Sunday Telegraph*: Alisdair Palmer, "Panorama Blasts Its Bosses in Kelly Affair," *Sunday Telegraph*, January, 18, 2004. Video and transcript of *A Fight to the Death*: http://news.bbc.co.uk/2/hi/programmes/panorama/3357005.stm.

18 "Hutton Wrong on Kelly Verdict Says First Poll," *Evening Standard*, January 29, 2004.

19 Nigel Morris, "Opinion Polls Show Backlash against Blair after Whitewash of Report," *Independent*, February 2, 2004.

20 George Jones, Tom Leonard, and Matt Born, "Hutton a Whitewash Say 56%," *Daily Telegraph*, January 30, 2004.

21 Jones et al., "Hutton a Whitewash."

22 Max Hastings, "Hutton Report Does Great Disservice to the British People," *Daily Mail*, January 29, 2004.

23 "No Hasty Decisions about the Future of the BBC," *Daily Telegraph*, January 30, 2004.

24 "The Hutton Verdict: A Serious Inquiry Demands an Appropriate Response," *The Times*, January 29, 2004.

25 Des Freedman, *The Politics of Media Policy* (Cambridge: Polity Press, 2008), 147–171.

26 Marie Woolf, "Row over Dossier Will Not Affect Renewal of Charter Insists Jowell," *The Independent*, July 28, 2003.

27 Ofcom, "Review of Public Service Television Broadcasting," November 2004, www.ofcom.org.uk/__data/assets/pdf_file/0030/36669/psb_phase2.pdf.

28 DCMS, *The Funding of the BBC*, 10.

29 Mark Thompson, "Preface," in *From Public Service Broadcasting to Public Service Communications*, eds. Damian Tambini and Jamie Cowling (London: IPPR, 2004).

30 Ofcom, *Review of Public Service Television Broadcasting Phase 1: Competition for Quality* (London: Ofcom, 2004).

31 Freedman, *The Politics of Media Policy*, 154.

32 Richard Fletcher and Rasmus Kleis Nielson, "Paying for Online News: A Comparative Study of Six Countries," *Digital Journalism* 5, no. 9 (2017).

33 Ofcom, *Review of Public Service Television Broadcasting*.

34 DCMS, *Royal Charter for the Continuance of the British Broadcasting Corporation* (London: HMSO, 2006) Cmnd. 6925, 4(a)- 4 (f).
35 *Royal Charter*, 2006, 5.1.
36 Jane Robbins, "Smith Prepares to Scrap Role of BBC Governors," *The Independent*, July 10, 2000. The specific issue Smith disliked was Dyke's proposal for "genre channels" with all the popular entertainment moved to one channel (BBC 1) and all the high-quality information to another (BBC 2).
37 *Royal Charter 2006*, 22 (a) – 22 (c).
38 Janet Martinson, "BBC Cutbacks: Why No Mention of the Lonely Planet?" *The Guardian*, March 10, 2010.
39 Ofcom, *Second Public Service Broadcasting Review: Putting Viewers First* (London: Ofcom, 2009), http://stakeholders.ofcom.org.uk/consultations/psb2_phase2/statement/.
40 BBC, "Putting Quality First: BBC Strategy Review," December 2010, accessed October 30, 2021, http://downloads.bbc.co.uk/bbctrust/assets/files/pdf/review_report_research/strategic_review/final_conclusions.pdf.
41 Ian Burrell, "BBC's Flight to Quality in Bid to Satisfy Tory Critics," *The Independent*, March 3, 2010.
42 James Robinson, "6 Music Saved from Closure," *The Guardian*, July 7, 2010.
43 Mark Thompson, "Putting Quality First," *About The BBC Blog*, March 2, 2010, www.bbc.co.uk/blogs/aboutthebbc/2010/03/putting-quality-first.shtml.
44 "No Surrender," *The Economist*, March 6, 2010.
45 "Culture Secretary Warns BBC over Spending Commitments," *Herald Scotland*, July 27, 2010.
46 Nicole Martin, "BBC's Licence Fee Not for Sharing," *Daily Telegraph*, May 13, 2008.
47 Rosa Price, "Licence Fee on Death Row," *Daily Telegraph*, July 9, 2008.
48 Patrick Foster, "BBC Hints at Licence Fee Freeze," *The Times*, March 3, 2010.
49 Foster, "BBC Hints at Licence Freeze."
50 Dan Sabbagh, "A Tory Dilemma: How to Tame the BBC," *The Times*, September 11, 2009.
51 David Cameron, "Bloated BBC Out of Touch with the Viewers," *The Sun*, August 12, 2010.
52 Ross and Russell Brand, another highly paid BBC star, had made insulting comments about a woman who was the granddaughter of a well-known actor.
53 Cameron, "Bloated BBC."
54 Owen Gibson, "BBC1 Chief Forced to Resign over Crowngate," *The Guardian*, October 6, 2007.
55 The most popular name, Cookie, was deemed inappropriate for some reason, so production staff voted to ensure that the apparently more suitable name Socks won. "BBC Deceived Children over Socks the Kitten," *Reuters*, September 20, 2007.
56 Anita Singh, "Jonathan Ross Apologizes for Prank Calls to Andrew Sachs," *Daily Telegraph*, October 29, 2008.
57 "Pressure on BBC in Gaza Row," *BBC*, January 25, 2009, http://news.bbc.co.uk/2/hi/uk_news/7848673.stm.
58 The full story of his career and abuses can be found at "Profile: Jimmy Savile," *BBC*, February 214, 2016, www.bbc.com/news/entertainment-arts-19984684.
59 "Jimmy Savile Sexual Abuse Scandal: A Timeline of Events," *The Independent*, October 23, 2012.
60 Daniel Boffey, "Revealed: How Jimmy Savile Abused 1000s on BBC Premises," *The Observer*, January 18, 2014.
61 Janet Smith, "Opening Statement," *The Dame Janet Smith Review*, 2016, accessed 30, October 2021, http://downloads.bbci.co.uk/bbctrust/assets/files/pdf/our_work/dame_janet_smith_review/conclusions_summaries.pdf.
62 The story is compellingly told by Poppy Sebag-Montifiore "How Two BBC Journalists Risked Their Jobs to Reveal the Truth about Jimmy Savile," *The Guardian*, November 2, 2021.

63 Sam Marsden, "Jimmy Savile: Questions about Why the BBC Dropped Newsnight Investigation," *Daily Telegraph*, October 1, 2012.
64 Mark Lawrenson, "Exposure: The Other Side of Jimmy Savile – Review," *The Guardian*, October 3, 2012.
65 "The Pollard Review: Report" (London: ReedSmith, 2012), accessed January 4, 2022, http://downloads.bbc.co.uk/bbctrust/assets/files/pdf/our_work/pollard_review/pollard_review.pdf.
66 Interview with former BBC producer, London, May 2016.
67 "Pollard Review," 23.
68 Interview with former BBC producer, London May 2016.
69 Panorama, "Jimmy Savile: What the BBC Knew" aired *BBC* 1, October 22, 2012, accessed January 4, 2022, www.bbc.co.uk/programmes/b01nspvr.
70 The suggestion has been made that these procedural oversights in the second documentary happened at least in part because the program's normally cautious editor Peter Rippon, along with the most experienced reporter, were both sidelined dealing with the inquiry into the canceled earlier episode. Interview with BBC staff, London March 2015.
71 John Burns and Ravi Somaiya, "BBC Director Quits in Furor over Coverage of Sexual Abuse," *The New York Times*, November 10, 2012. Thompson went on to become CEO of the *New York Times*.
72 "Staring into the Abyss: The BBC, Trust and Jimmy Savile," *Conquest Research and Consultancy Group*, 2012, www.scribd.com/document/117119644/BBC-Trust-and-Jimmy-Savile5.
73 Steven Swinford, "Tories Go to War with the BBC," *Daily Telegraph*, May 11, 2015.
74 DCMS, *The Future of the BBC*, February 2015, https://publications.parliament.uk/pa/cm201415/cmselect/cmcumeds/315/31502.htm.
75 David Clementi, *A Review of the Governance and Regulation of the BBC* (London: DCMS, March 2016), 17.
76 Steve Barnett, "Why the BBC Trust Must Not be Abolished," *The Conversation*, August 25, 2015.
77 Patrick Barwise and Peter York, *The War against the BBC* (London: Penguin Books, 2020).
78 "TV Licence Fee Enforcement Review" (London: DCMS, July 2015), https://assets.publishing.service.gov.uk/government/uploads/system/uploads/attachment_data/file/445212/166926_Perry_Review_Text-L-PB.pdf.
79 John Plunkett, "John Whittingdale's Support for Brexit a Distraction from BBC, says Labour," *The Guardian*, March 10, 2016.
80 David Jordan and Ric Bailey, "Impartiality and the BBC – 'Broad Balance' in a Two-horse Race," in *Brexit, Trump and the Media*, eds. Richard Tait et al. (Bury St. Edmunds: Abramis Publishing, 2017), 254–261.
81 "Guidelines – Referendum Campaign on the UK's Membership in the European Union," *BBC Trust*, accessed March 14, 2016, www.bbc.co.uk/bbctrust/our_work/editorial_standards/eu_referendum.html.
82 YouGov, "Is BBC News Pro-Brexit or Anti-Brexit?," February 22, 2018, https://yougov.co.uk/topics/politics/articles-reports/2018/02/22/bbc-news-pro-brexit-or-anti-brexit.
83 Jasper Jackson, "BBC's EU Coverage More Negative than Its Putin Coverage," *The Guardian*, April 21, 2016.
84 Mike Berry, "Hard Evidence: How Biased Is the BBC?," *The Conversation*, August 23, 2013; Karin Wahl-Jorgensen et al., "BBC Breadth of Opinion Review," *Cardiff School of Journalism Working Paper*, accessed March 31, 2021, https://downloads.bbc.co.uk/bbctrust/assets/files/pdf/our_work/breadth_opinion/content_analysis.pdf.
85 Rita Payne, "Brexit and the British Media," *The Round Table* 107, no. 1 (2018): 109–110.

86 Jean Seaton, "Brexit and the Media," *Political Quarterly* 87, no. 3 (July–September 2016): 333–337, 335. See also Stephen Cushion and Justin Lewis, who find that across UK media, "journalists were reluctant to challenge or contextualize claims and counter-claims." "Impartiality, Statistical Tit-for-Tats and the Construction of Balance: UK Television News Reporting in the 2016 EU Referendum Campaign," *European Journal of Communication* (2017): 1–16, 1.

87 Ivor Gaber, "Did the BBC Fail Its Brexit Balancing Act?," in Brexit, Trump and the Media, 45–48.

88 Michael Swan (Chairman of the BBC Board of Governors, 1973–1980) quoted in James Butler, "The BBC on the Rack," London Review of Books 42, no. 6 (March 19, 2020).

89 Maria Sobolewska and Robert Ford, Brexitland: Identity, Diversity and the Reshaping of British Politics (Cambridge: Cambridge University Press, 2020).

90 Ethnicity and National Identity in England and Wales 2011, Office of National Statistics, December 11, 2012, www.ons.gov.uk/peoplepopulationandcommunity/culturalidentity/ethnicity/articles/ethnicityandnationalidentityinenglandandwales/2012-12-11.

91 Nancy Kelley, "Key Findings," in British Social Attitudes: The 36th Report, eds. J. Curtice et al. (London: The National Centre for Social Research, 2019), 6. www.bsa.natcen.ac.uk/media/39287/0_bsa36_keyfindings.pdf.

92 "BBC Launches Ambitious New Diversity and Inclusion Strategy," BBC Media Centre, April 28, 2016, www.bbc.co.uk/mediacentre/latestnews/2016/diversity.

93 "Diversity & Inclusion Plan," BBC, accessed March 31, 2021, www.bbc.co.uk/diversity/plan.

94 Laura Hazard Owen, "The BBC's 50:50 Project Shows Equal Gender Representations in News Is Achievable Even in Traditionally Male Areas," Nieman Lab, May 16, 2019.

95 Ofcom, "Diversity and Equal Opportunities in Television and Radio 2019/20," November 25, 2020, www.ofcom.org.uk/__data/assets/pdf_file/0022/207229/2019-20-report-diversity-equal-opportunities-tv-and-radio.pdf.

96 Amelia Wynne, "BBC Accused of Bias," Daily Mail, December 28, 2019.

97 Amanda Platell, "Why Womb Transplants Make Me Shudder," Daily Mail, October 2, 2015.

98 For example Tom Mills, "Richard Sharp's Arrival at the BBC will Entrench Conservative Influence," The Guardian, January 14, 2021.

99 Ashley Cowburn, "Theresa May's Former Director of Communications Appointed to BBC Board," The Independent, April 29, 2021.

100 "BBC: TV Licence Fee Decriminalization Being Considered," BBC, December 15, 2019, www.bbc.com/news/election-2019-50800128.

101 Mark Landler and Steven Castle, "Upbeat Official Report on Race in Britain Draws Swift Backlash," The New York Times, March 31, 2021.

102 Rajeev Syal, "BBC Chief Told to Use More than One Union Jack," The Guardian, March 23, 2021.

103 Adam Forest, "BBC May Not Exist in 10 Years Says Nadine Dorries in Attack on 'Elitist' Broadcaster," The Independent, October 4, 2021.

104 "The Guardian View on Boris Johnson and the BBC: It's Our Fight Too," The Guardian, September 3, 2020, www.theguardian.com/commentisfree/2020/sep/03/the-guardian-view-on-boris-johnson-and-the-bbc-its-our-fight-too.

105 Ben Bold, "BBC, Sky and Guardian Most-trusted News Brands, Thanks to Coronavirus Coverage," Campaign, March 20, 2020, www.campaignlive.co.uk/article/bbc-sky-guardian-most-trusted-news-brands-thanks-coronavirus-coverage/1677837.

106 Charlotte Tobitt, "Coronavirus Leads to 'Staggering Demand' for TV News," Press Gazette, March 17, 2020, https://pressgazette.co.uk/coronavirus-leads-to-staggering-demand-for-trusted-tv-news/.

107 "Lockdown Learning: What Educational Resources Are on TV, iPlayer and Online?," BBC, March 16, 2020, www.bbc.com/news/education-55591821.
108 Vanessa Jackson, "The BBC's Lockdown Educational Programming," The Conversation, January 13, 2021, https://theconversation.com/bbcs-lockdown-educational-programming-is-way-better-than-the-dull-fare-of-yesteryear-153139.
109 Stephen Cushion and Richard Sambrook, "Coronavirus: The BBC Is Uniquely Placed to Serve the Nation," The Conversation, April 1, 2020, https://theconversation.com/coronavirus-bbc-news-is-uniquely-placed-to-serve-the-nation-how-it-does-so-will-define-its-future-135265.

References

Barnett, Steve, "Why the BBC Trust Must Not be Abolished," *The Conversation*, August 25, 2015.

Barwise, Patrick, and Peter York, *The War Against the BBC* (London: Penguin Books, 2020).

"BBC Deceived Children Over Socks the Kitten," *Reuters*, September 20, 2007.

"BBC Launches Ambitious New Diversity and Inclusion Strategy," *BBC Media Centre*, April 28, 2016, www.bbc.co.uk/mediacentre/latestnews/2016/diversity.

"BBC: TV Licence fee Decriminalization being Considered," *BBC*, December 15, 2019, www.bbc.com/news/election-2019-50800128.

Berry, Mike, "Hard Evidence: How Biased Is the BBC?" *The Conversation*, August 23, 2013.

Boffey, Daniel, "Revealed: How Jimmy Savile Abused 1000s on BBC Premises," *The Observer*, January 18, 2014.

Bold, Ben, "BBC, Sky and Guardian Most-trusted News Brands, Thanks to Coronavirus Coverage," *Campaign*, March 20, 2020, www.campaignlive.co.uk/article/bbc-sky-guardian-most-trusted-news-brands-thanks-coronavirus-coverage/1677837.

Boschoff, Alison, "Tony's Crony in BBC Storm," *Daily Mail*, June 25, 1999.

Burns, John, and Ravi Somaiya, "BBC Director Quits in Furor over Coverage of Sexual Abuse," *The New York Times*, November 10, 2012. Thompson went on to become CEO of the *New York Times*.

Burrell, Ian, "BBC's Flight to Quality in Bid to Satisfy Tory Critics," *The Independent*, March 3, 2010.

Butler, James, "The BBC on the Rack," *London Review of Books* 42, no. 6 (March 19, 2020).

Cameron, David, "Bloated BBC Out of Touch with the Viewers," *The Sun*, August 12, 2010.

Clementi, David, *A Review of the Governance and Regulation of the BBC* (London: DCMS, March 2016).

Cowell, Alan, "Death of an Expert Witness," *The New York Times*, August 17, 2003.

"Culture Secretary Warns BBC over Spending Commitments," *Herald Scotland*, July 27, 2010.

Cushion, Stephen, and Justin Lewis, "Impartiality, Statistical Tit-for-Tats and the Construction of Balance: UK Television News Reporting in the 2016 EU Referendum Campaign," *European Journal of Communication* (2017): 1–16, 1.

Cushion, Stephen, and Richard Sambrook, "Coronavirus: The BBC is Uniquely Placed to Serve the Nation," *The Conversation*, April 1, 2020, https://theconversation.com/coronavirus-bbc-news-is-uniquely-placed-to-serve-the-nation-how-it-does-so-will-define-its-future-135265.

DCMS, "Attitude Survey," in *Review of the Future Funding of the BBC* (London: DCMS, April 1999).

DCMS, "The Future of the BBC," February 2015, https://publications.parliament.uk/pa/cm201415/cmselect/cmcumeds/315/31502.htm.

DCMS, *Royal Charter for the Continuance of the British Broadcasting Corporation* (London: HMSO, 2006).

"Diversity & Inclusion Plan," *BBC*, accessed March 31, 2021, www.bbc.co.uk/diversity/plan.

Doward, Jamie, "Commons Probe for BBC Web Ads," *Observer*, January 28, 2001.

Dyke, Greg, *Inside Story* (London: HarperCollins, 2004).

Ethnicity and National Identity in England and Wales 2011, Office of National Statistics, December 11, 2012, www.ons.gov.uk/peoplepopulationandcommunity/culturalidentity/ethnicity/articles/ethnicityandnationalidentityinenglandandwales/2012-12-11.

"Executive Summary HC 264," *The Report of the Iraq Inquiry*, June 6, 2016.

Fletcher, Richard, and Rasmus Kleis Nielson, "Paying for Online News: A Comparative Study of Six Countries," *Digital Journalism* 5, no. 9 (2017).

Foster, Patrick, "BBC Hints at Licence Fee Freeze," *The Times*, March 3, 2010.

Freedman, Des, *Television Policies of the Labour Party 1951–2001* (London: Frank Cass, 2003).

"Free TV," *The Economist*, May 11, 2002.

Gaber, Ivor, "Did the BBC Fail Its Brexit Balancing Act?" in *Brexit, Trump and the Media*, eds. Richard Tait et al. (Bury St. Edmunds: Abramis Publishing, 2017).

Gibson, Owen, "BBC1 Chief Forced to Resign Over Crowngate," *The Guardian*, October 6, 2007.

"The Guardian view on Boris Johnson and the BBC: It's Our Fight Too," *The Guardian*, September 3, 2020, www.theguardian.com/commentisfree/2020/sep/03/the-guardian-view-on-boris-johnson-and-the-bbc-its-our-fight-too.

"Guidelines – Referendum Campaign on the UK's Membership in the European Union," *BBC Trust*, accessed March 14, 2016, www.bbc.co.uk/bbctrust/our_work/editorial_standards/eu_referendum.html.

Hastings, Max, "Hutton Report Does Great Disservice to the British People," *Daily Mail*, January 29, 2004.

Hoge, Warren, "Reporter Admits BBC Report on Iraqi Arms Had Errors," *The New York Times*, September 17, 2003.

"The Hutton Verdict: A Serious Inquiry Demands an Appropriate Response," *The Times*, January 29, 2004.

"Hutton Wrong on Kelly Verdict Says First Poll," *Evening Standard*, January 29, 2004.

Jackson, Jasper, "BBC's EU Coverage More Negative than its Putin Coverage," *The Guardian*, April 21, 2016.

Jackson, Vanessa, "The BBC's Lockdown Educational Programming," *The Conversation*, January 13, 2021, https://theconversation.com/bbcs-lockdown-educational-programming-is-way-better-than-the-dull-fare-of-yesteryear-153139.

"Jimmy Savile Sexual Abuse Scandal: A Timeline of Events," *The Independent*, October 23, 2012.

Jones, George, Tom Leonard, and Matt Born, "Hutton a Whitewash Say 56%," *Daily Telegraph*, January 30, 2004.

Jordan, David, and Ric Bailey, "Impartiality and the BBC – 'Broad Balance' in a Two-horse Race," in *Brexit, Trump and the Media*, eds. Richard Tait et. al (Bury St. Edmunds: Abramis Publishing, 2017).

Kelley, Nancy, "Key Findings," in *British Social Attitudes: The 36th Report*, eds. J. Curtice et al. (London: The National Centre for Social Research, 2019), 6, www.bsa.natcen. ac.uk/media/39287/0_bsa36_keyfindings.pdf.

Landler, Mark, and Steven Castle, "Upbeat Official Report on Race in Britain Draws Swift Backlash," *The New York Times*, March 31, 2021.

Lawrenson, Mark, "Exposure: The Other Side of Jimmy Savile – Review," *The Guardian*, October 3, 2012.

"Lockdown Learning: What Educational Resources are on TV, iPlayer and Online?" *BBC*, March 16, 2020, www.bbc.com/news/education-55591821.

Marsden, Sam, "Jimmy Savile: Questions about Why the BBC Dropped Newsnight Investigation," *Daily Telegraph*, October 1, 2012.

Martin, Nicole, "BBC's Licence Fee Not for Sharing," *Daily Telegraph*, May 13, 2008.

Martinson, Janet, "BBC Cutbacks: Why No Mention of the Lonely Planet?" *The Guardian*, March 10, 2010.

Mills, Tom, *The BBC: Myth of a Public Service* (London: Verso Books, 2016).

Morris, Nigel, "Opinion Polls Show Backlash against Blair after Whitewash of Report," *Independent*, February 2, 2004.

"No Hasty Decisions about the Future of the BBC," *Daily Telegraph*, January 30, 2004.

"No Surrender," *The Economist*, March 6, 2010.

Ofcom, "Diversity and Equal Opportunities in Television and Radio 2019/20," November 25, 2020, www.ofcom.org.uk/__data/assets/pdf_file/0022/207229/2019-20-report-diversity-equal-opportunities-tv-and-radio.pdf.

Ofcom, "Review of Public Service Television Broadcasting," November 2004, www. ofcom.org.uk/__data/assets/pdf_file/0030/36669/psb_phase2.pdf.

Ofcom, *Review of Public Service Television Broadcasting Phase 1: Competition for Quality* (London: Ofcom, 2004).

Ofcom, *Second Public Service Broadcasting Review: Putting Viewers First* (London: Ofcom, 2009), http://stakeholders.ofcom.org.uk/consultations/psb2_phase2/statement/.

Owen, Laura Hazard, "The BBC's 50:50 Project Shows Equal Gender Representations in News is Achievable Even in Traditionally Male Areas," *Nieman Lab*, May 16, 2019.

Palmer, Alisdair, "Panorama Blasts its Bosses in Kelly Affair," *Sunday Telegraph*, January, 18, 2004.

Payne, Rita, "Brexit and the British Media," *The Round Table* 107, no. 1 (2018): 109–110.

Platell, Amanda, "Why Womb Transplants Make Me Shudder," *Daily Mail*, October 2, 2015.

Plunkett, John, "John Whittingdale's Support for Brexit a Distraction from BBC, Says Labour," *The Guardian*, March 10, 2016.

"The Pollard Review: Report" (*ReedSmith*, 2012).

Polls, Lord Ashcroft, "How the UK Voted on Thursday . . . and Why," June 24, 2016, http://lordashcroftpolls.com/2016/06/how-the-united-kingdom-voted-and-why/.

"Pressure on BBC in Gaza Row," *BBC*, January 25, 2009, http://news.bbc.co.uk/2/hi/uk_news/7848673.stm.

Price, Rosa, "Licence Fee on Death Row," *Daily Telegraph*, July 9, 2008.

"Profile: Jimmy Savile," *BBC*, February 24, 2016, www.bbc.com/news/entertainment-arts-19984684.

"Report of the Independent Review Panel," in *The Future Funding of the BBC* (London: DCMS, July 1999), http://news.bbc.co.uk/hi/english/static/bbc_funding_review/reviewco.pdf.

Robbins, Jane, "Not a Moist Eye in the House as Birt Says a Cool Farewell to the BBC Staff," *Independent*, January 29, 2000.

Robbins, Jane, "Smith Prepares to Scrap Role of BBC Governors," *The Independent*, July 10, 2000.

Robinson, James, "6 Music Saved from Closure," *The Guardian*, July 7, 2010.

Sabbagh, Dan, "A Tory Dilemma: How to Tame the BBC," *The Times*, September 11, 2009.

Seaton, Jean, "Brexit and the Media," *Political Quarterly* 87, no. 3 (July–September 2016): 333–337, 335.

Singh, Anita, "Jonathan Ross Apologizes for Prank Calls to Andrew Sachs," *Daily Telegraph*, October 29, 2008.

"Staring into the Abyss: The BBC, Trust and Jimmy Savile," *Conquest Research and Consultancy Group*, 2012, www.scribd.com/document/117119644/BBC-Trust-and-Jimmy-Savile5.

Swinford, Steven, "Tories Go to War with the BBC," *Daily Telegraph*, May 11, 2015.

Syal, Rajeev, "BBC Chief Told to Use More than one Union Jack," *The Guardian*, March 23, 2021.

Thompson, Mark, "Preface," in *From Public Service Broadcasting to Public Service Communications*, eds. Damian Tambini and Jamie Cowling (London: IPPR, 2004).

Thompson, Mark, "Putting Quality First," *About The BBC Blog*, March 2, 2010, www.bbc.co.uk/blogs/aboutthebbc/2010/03/putting-quality-first.shtml.

Tobitt, Charlotte, "Coronavirus Leads to 'Staggering Demand' for TV News," *Press Gazette*, March 17, 2020, https://pressgazette.co.uk/coronavirus-leads-to-staggering-demand-for-trusted-tv-news/.

"TV Licence Fee Enforcement Review" (London: DCMS, July 2015), https://assets.publishing.service.gov.uk/government/uploads/system/uploads/attachment_data/file/445212/166926_Perry_Review_Text-L-PB.pdf.

Wahl-Jorgensen, Karin, et al., "BBC Breadth of Opinion Review," *Cardiff School of Journalism Working Paper*, accessed March 31, 2021, https://downloads.bbc.co.uk/bbctrust/assets/files/pdf/our_work/breadth_opinion/content_analysis.pdf.

"When £2 Billion is Not Enough," *The Economist*, August 7, 1999.

Woolf, Marie, "Row over Dossier will Not Affect Renewal of Charter Insists Jowell," *The Independent*, July 28, 2003.

Wynne, Amelia, "BBC Accused of Bias," *Daily Mail*, December 28, 2019.

YouGov, "Is BBC News pro-Brexit or anti-Brexit?" February 22, 2018, https://yougov.co.uk/topics/politics/articles-reports/2018/02/22/bbc-news-pro-brexit-or-anti-brexit.

10 NHK and Politics 2000–2021

Abe, Memory, and Nostalgia

NHK entered the new millennium in what seemed to be a much more secure position than the BBC. It enjoyed warm relations with the electorally dominant LDP, helped greatly by an organizational culture that avoided controversy and confrontation and which hence tended to favor the conservative status quo. Scrupulous even-handedness in terms of giving airtime to all political parties kept opposition parties relatively happy, while the commercial television stations were usually content to coexist with their publicly funded rival as long as NHK did not try to encroach too hard on their ratings. NHK was still a central part of the broadcasting landscape, a reliable source of official information and education, thorough documentaries, lavish costume dramas, and time-honored national rituals such as the annual New Year's Eve show. For many, especially older Japanese, NHK was a loved and trusted part of their daily lives. Beneath the surface, though, problems were looming, and scandals would strain NHK's relationships with both political elites and audiences.

However, the broadcasters had to reckon with profound social and economic transformations. The country was coming to terms with seemingly permanent economic stagnation. Precarity and inequality were starkly visible.[1] The birthrate was falling and the population was aging. Previously marginalized groups such as women and second- and third-generation resident Koreans were becoming more outspoken. Immigration was becoming a salient political issue as the country struggled to integrate the non-Japanese workers needed to fill labor shortages. Nationalists grew more vocal, and historical revisionism was encouraged by hawkish Prime Ministers Koizumi and Abe. Amidst the malaise, as David Leheney brilliantly argues, hope for the future was often found in the form of nostalgia for the glory of the high-growth postwar era.

NHK responded to the challenges while avoiding where possible confrontation with ruling elites. When a documentary that questioned Japan's wartime human rights record was met with conservative pushback, NHK's management immediately surrendered to political intervention. Since then, news and current events programming have been more careful than before to avoid offending the government, becoming even more quiescent in the face of Prime Minister Abe's aggressive campaign to ensure sympathetic coverage and marginalize hostile media. NHK's coverage of the 3.11 catastrophe was exemplary at one level, a

DOI: 10.4324/b23015-10

vivid demonstration of the value of thorough, properly resourced, professional, and unsensational public broadcasting. Yet the broadcaster's willingness to accept official versions of events, and its deeper reluctance to challenge elite consensus about issues such as nuclear safety, demonstrated once again NHK's shortcomings as a watchdog. Entertainment programming such as *Project-X* and *Kōhaku Uta Gassen*, the New Year's Eve Song Contest, tended toward the safe and comforting, fueled and fueling nostalgic national narratives and traditional interpretations of national identity. NHK labs continue their role in industrial policy, working with the private sector to develop sophisticated media technologies such as Super Hi-Vision Television. Finally, NHK World became a willing partner in the Abe administration's public diplomacy offensive, a key tool in promoting soft power and what Prime Minister Koizumi called "the correct image of Japan" to the outside world.

In short, this chapter shows how NHK does well in performing many of the tasks that public broadcasters are expected to do. Equally, NHK does poorly at performing other tasks often thought essential to the public broadcasting mission. NHK's strategy has paid off in that it has retained the support of the conservative political establishment, support that had in the early 2000s seemed uncertain. But NHK has often been divided, with management and staff in frequent conflict over questions of editorial autonomy. The programming strategies have done little to entice younger viewers, who continue to shun NHK. Thus, while NHK's survival may not be in doubt, its continued relevance to all but a section of Japanese society may be.

Declining Audiences

By the early 2000s, Japan was entering a second decade of low economic growth, threatening NHK in several ways. A recession was fueling demands for liberalization of Japan's statist political economy and its insular, protected socioeconomic institutions, of which NHK was very much part. Pressure on public finances and household budgets clearly had implications for NHK's generous funding, undermining people's willingness and ability to pay viewer fees. Meanwhile, globalization and liberalization of media markets were rapidly expanding the number and quality of alternative sources of news and entertainment. NHK's programming, which still tended toward the traditional, worthy, and often dull, was becoming less appealing. Viewership was decreasing, while non-payment of fees was rapidly increasing.

Publicly, NHK claimed that voluntary compliance rates for viewer fees were still higher than those for the BBC, despite the criminal penalties for non-compliant Britons. In private, NHK managers were acutely aware that rates of non-payment were increasing sharply. A 1998 poll showed that around one-third of the public did not believe they should have to pay the viewer fee.[2] Young people in particular were abandoning NHK. In 2000, NHK was the most watched television broadcaster among elderly people, but was the most popular choice for less than 10% of people in their 20s.[3] A confidential internal survey revealed in 1999 that around 70% of people in their 20s said they did not watch NHK and did not want to pay the subscription fee.[4]

Declining audiences and rising non-payments posed a serious long-term threat because NHK's revenues were almost entirely dependent (97%) on viewer fees.[5] Moreover, NHK was still spending heavily on new technologies, most notably the ill-fated analog HDTV. Furthermore, fees had not been raised since 1990. This was partly because revenues from new satellite subscribers were being used to cross-subsidize the basic fee. A more important reason was that increases had to be approved by the Diet, which was extremely reluctant to do so in the face of rapidly deteriorating public finances. Management was attempting to cut costs, but its efforts were often clumsily executed and unpopular. For example, the fee exemption for schools was scrapped in 1998. The money saved was negligible but the symbolic retreat from NHK's core educational mission was deeply unpopular, not least with NHK's own staff.[6] Outside, the cut was interpreted as a sign of desperation and a lack of economic and political savvy on the part of senior management.[7] Against this background, a series of scandals plunged NHK into crisis.

The biggest crisis was the fall-out from *Sensō o dō sabaku ka: towareru senji seibōryoku* ("How to Judge War? Considering Wartime Sexual Violence"), a 2001 documentary about the movement for redress for surviving "comfort women." The documentary focused on a "People's Tribunal" organized by various Asian women's groups led by a Japanese NGO, VAWW-Net Japan in December 2000. Shortly after the documentary aired, the *Asahi Shimbun* revealed that the documentary had been substantially altered immediately prior to broadcast, seemingly at the behest of senior LDP politicians.[8] Last-minute revisions had fundamentally changed its tone, which had gone from being broadly critical of state policy toward war crime victims and sympathetic to the redress movement to being broadly sympathetic to the government and critical of the redress movement.[9]

What makes the case unusual is that the documentary in question got so close to broadcast that the LDP itself intervened before management at NHK censored it for them. It was also one of the very rare cases in Japan where a case of political interference in the media was taken to court. As such, the episode is worth exploring in depth in the following chapter, allowing a rare glimpse at how Japan's conservative elites define and police the boundaries of acceptable speech, and how NHK's organizational tendency toward self-censorship, itself reflecting divisions between management and journalists, was reinforced by active political interference.

NHK escaped legal culpability and political reprisal for the affair, thanks in large part to the support of the LDP and Japan's traditionally conservative courts. The impact on NHK's reputation was more damaging. Trust in NHK was further hurt by a widely publicized embezzlement case begun in 2004 when an NHK producer admitted to stealing fee income by claiming expenses for fake program scripts in order to finance an extra-marital affair.[10] The two scandals together stoked public anger with NHK, while morale within the organization sunk lower.[11] NHK's labor union *Nippōrō* called for Ebisawa's resignation, while over 100,000 households began boycotting the viewer fee in protest. Such protests demonstrate once again that differences in ethical standards between staff and management or audiences and broadcasters can cut straight across national and cultural lines.

President Ebisawa faced down the public outrage for a while, and even launched a court case against the Asahi Shimbun, who had first made the allegations of censorship. Late in 2004, though, Ebisawa agreed to demands from *Nippōrō* to appear on a two-hour special live program apologizing for damaging public trust.[12] The program *NHK ni iitai* ("I want to say to NHK . . .") invited viewer responses, and certainly got them, but not perhaps in the way Ebisawa envisaged. The program allowed viewers to direct their ire directly at NHK leadership, with one radio host claiming 90% of his call-in listeners would refuse to pay their fees unless Ebisawa resigned.[13] The number of fee-refusers continued to rise, and Ebisawa resigned a few weeks later to take responsibility for the scandals. In keeping with corporate tradition, he was kept on as a well-paid senior advisor. The Management Committee moved to restore trust by appointing as President Chief Engineer Hashimoto Genichi, considered less political and hence more publicly acceptable.

Battle for Reform

By 2005, NHK faced a three-pronged threat of collapsing audience trust, increasingly fragile support in the Diet, and a political climate in which liberalization and even privatization were on the agenda. The audience crisis continued. Commercial broadcasters had always had the upper hand in entertainment, but as Krauss describes, they began to challenge NHK's unquestioned primacy in news in the late 1990s. The commercial stations had the advantage of a greater willingness to take risks, as when NTV aired *Retsu Gō! Nagatacho* ("Let's Go Nagata-Cho!") in 2001. The show became the first regular prime-time comedy to satirize currently serving politicians, in this case Prime Minister Koizumi and Foreign Minister Tanaka Makiko.[14]

By mid-2006, the total number of households not paying NHK's viewer fees was estimated at 13 million out of a total of about 46 million, or a 30% non-payment rate.[15] These included around 1.3 million who were formally boycotting the fee to protest NHK's perceived misconduct during the scandals, and a further 9.6 million who were in arrears of payments or had not signed a contract.[16]

The crisis drew the attention of the LDP, who were already in the middle of an ambitious program of economic liberalization under Prime Minister Koizumi Jun'Ichiro's famous slogan "Reform With No Sacred Cows." Koizumi now asked, "What can be done to regain the public trust in NHK?"[17] Privatization was an obvious answer, one that was by now being actively debated in intellectual and media circles. Proponents came from different ends of the political spectrum, though. Conservatives envisaged marketization, while for many on the left privatization meant wresting control from elitist bureaucrats and placing it in the hands of progressive NGOs and other citizens' groups.[18]

The LDP were divided about NHK reform along some of the same lines as they were over many other of Koizumi's liberalizing initiatives such as postal privatization. Younger Diet members generally favored reform and older, more entrenched leaders were keener to defend the status quo. In 2005, Takenaka Heizo, the reformist, pro-market economist serving as Minister for Internal Affairs and Communications, established an advisory panel on NHK reform with privatization very much on the agenda.[19] However, privatization was fiercely resisted by an old guard of policy heavyweights in key positions such as Katayama Toranosuke, a former MPT Minister and Chair of the LDP's Telecommunications and Broadcasting Subcommittee, and Kawamura Takeo, Chair of the LDP Subcommittee on Broadcasting Reform.[20]

Koizumi came down firmly against privatization. His reformist instincts may have been tempered by the easy ride that NHK gave him compared with the commercial broadcasters over such controversial policies as his visits to the notorious Yasukuni Shrine. His final visit, in August 2005, had attracted widespread criticisms, which were well covered by TBS and TV Asahi, but given a bland, neutral coverage by NHK.[21] Not unrelatedly, Koizumi was supportive of moves to boost NHK's international operations to help improve Japan's tarnished global reputation, to be discussed subsequently. Whatever the reason, he announced that his Cabinet had decided that "NHK would remain a special private corporation. Instead of privatization, I believe other measures to reform NHK should be discussed."[22] Despite widespread feeling among the general public and even within the LDP that NHK needed some sort of reform, the eventual changes were modest. Proposed reforms centered around two issues: reforming the voluntary viewer fee system and cutting costs.

The most contentious reform proposal concerned viewer fees.[23] NHK management wanted legislation to impose fines or other penalties against non-payers and had been lobbying to that effect for a number of years. The door-to-door collection system was subject to extensive abuse, not least by allowing free-riders to cast themselves as principled objectors to NHK content. In addition, collection costs were extremely high, estimated at 12% of total revenues, compared with about 1–2% for European public broadcasters.[24] In 2006, NHK managers took the unprecedented step of bringing a group of non-paying viewers to Tokyo District Court to enforce payment of fees.[25] This move was extremely unpopular with viewers, of course. It was also resisted by NHK staff, many of whom opposed penalties for non-payment on the grounds that this would effectively make the fee a tax rather than a voluntary expression of goodwill. This would alienate audiences and bind NHK under even closer government control.[26]

The LDP sided with management's proposal. Katayama and other opponents of privatization believed that NHK could be kept in its publicly funded form only by following the BBC in having criminal penalties for non-payment of fees, and MIAC Minister Aso Taro proposed fines in 2005.[27] However, the LDP's agreement to impose legal penalties for non-payment was conditional on NHK, making the unpopular move slightly more palatable to the public by lowering the cost of viewer fees.[28] NHK management hated the prospect of losing revenue and stalled. When MIAC Minister Suga Yoshihide proposed a 20% cut, NHK refused to cut more than 10% and both the fee cuts and proposed sanctions were abandoned by 2007. The LDP evidently had no real desire to reform NHK.

NHK's problems continued, hit in 2008 by an insider trading scandal in which producers had traded shares based on confidential information gleaned while making a documentary.[29] President Hashimoto resigned to take responsibility. The Board of Governors replaced Hashimoto with Fukuchi Shigeo, an outsider with extensive business experience as CEO of Asahi Breweries. Fukuchi's appointment was a statement by the increasingly worried Board of Governors that NHK should follow the BBC's lead in becoming more commercially minded and entrepreneurial.[30] His public statements further reflected the extent to which senior management had recognized the depth of the crisis NHK was in. Reforms were clearly needed to connect with lost audiences, and this would involve a long process of regaining public trust and the Governors taking more seriously their watchdog role. The 2008 three-year corporate plan began: "Fully reflecting on a succession of unfortunate episodes involving NHK, we will make all efforts to regain the public's trust." Among the means of doing that was the policy that "NHK will directly address global-scale problems like global warming as well as problems and issues Japan is struggling with such as social security, income disparities, and regional revitalization, and we will attempt to show means to solve these problems."[31] By the end of the decade, the number of boycotters had fallen somewhat, and the calls for further reform had lessened. NHK had weathered the most serious reform debate of its postwar history with its institutional form intact, albeit with its reputation battered.

As the crises unfolded, traditional programming continued as normal. Two programs in particular continued to draw large audiences. Both illustrate the ways in which NHK programming can help bind the nation together, while also reinforcing essentially conservative national narratives. They certainly won the loyalty of certain audiences and, one might speculate, the sympathy of political elites. *Project X* and *Kōhaku Uta Gassen* are therefore worth examining in closer detail.

Project X and Kōhaku: Nostalgia and Tradition

Project X: Challengers (*Purojekuto X: Chōsenshatachi*) first aired in 2000. The documentary series is an unabashedly nostalgic celebration of postwar Japanese triumphs told through stories of ordinary people, often engineers or scientists, struggling against adversity and in obscurity to solve some important social problem.[32] In the words of the program's website, the series tells the stories "of anonymous Japanese individuals who, fired with enthusiasm and a burning sense of mission, worked to create the landmark achievements of the postwar period."[33]

The first episode told of early 1960s engineers working in appalling, dangerous conditions to install a radar at the summit of Mount Fuji to create the world's highest and most sophisticated weather-monitoring system. The second episode recounted how three employees at Japan's Victor Company (JVC) secretly and against all odds developed the VHS video format.[34] Other topics included the Shinkansen, the transistor radio, LCD displays, the world's longest tunnel beneath the treacherous Tsugaru Strait, and the activities of Japanese volunteers cleaning up the coastline after an oil spill from a Russian tanker. While the earlier episodes tended to focus on the postwar technological and engineering triumphs, later topics included a broader variety of Japanese accomplishments, for example, the Cup Noodle, the entrepreneurs behind the 7–11 convenience store chain, and a

2005 episode about the iconic all-female Takarazuka theater company's success-ful attempt to stave off bankruptcy in 1974.[35]

Umai kome ga tabetai! ("We Want Tasty Rice!") is a typical episode. It tells the story of a bright young agricultural scientist and his small team of researchers as they struggled to find a better, more commercially viable strain of rice in the poverty of the immediate postwar era. Two presenters, an older man and a younger woman, beam into the steaming contents of a rice cooker. It looks delicious, they agree. An elderly man dressed soberly in a dark suit and light tie, enters with quiet dignity. The presenters treat him with great respect, listening earnestly as he explains how important it is that rice plants be the right height, and explains how his team figured a way to make the rice stem shorter, and therefore less vulnerable to collapsing under its own weight.

The story begins in the bleak postwar years, narrated over newspaper headlines announcing grim economic news and black-and-white footage of poverty-stricken farmlands. Rice from Niigata prefecture was deemed *mazui* (unappetizing) because it was too long and drooped in the floods. Professor Sugita Hideo and his team of eager young scientists from the Ministry of Agriculture head to Niigata to study rice-farming methods. The music swells as the team overcomes hardship, then briefly drops to a menacing minor key when a senior bureaucrat threatens to axe the project. New age music backgrounds the problem of finding the right shade of green for the rice, then crescendos as the right hue is finally found, in the face of great hardship. Three of the old team are ushered in and the music swells again as a team member explains that it was *gaman* (perseverance) that saw them through the bad times, and *gaman* that Sugita inspired in his young team. We hear effusive praise for Sugita from various quarters, then the music switches to uplift-ing, minor key Enka as we learn how, on his hospital deathbed in 1985, his dying words were about the rice. It ends with a picture of a mechanized planter, patiently harvesting rice under a clear blue sky.

Whatever the topic, *Project X* episodes all carry the message that, with enough *gaman*, ordinary Japanese people could achieve extraordinary results. Chief Pro-ducer Imai Akira designed the series deliberately to help lift the low morale of the country after the "lost decade" of economic stagnation, relentlessly presenting a model of dogged citizenship that would, in the words of the NHK archives, dem-onstrate "the latent power of the Japanese people" ("*Nihonjin no sokojikara*"). And when accused by the *Shukan Asahi* news magazine of being too one-sidedly positive about their subjects, NHK responded that the purpose of the show was "to instill courage and the spirit of challenge" to Japanese "who are losing their confidence in the prolonged economic slump."[36]

The Japaneseness being celebrated is interestingly nuanced. At one level, the series seems to function as a somewhat crude techno-nationalism, although of course it should also be noted that such national pride is by no means unique to Japanese programming. Of greater interest is that Japanese accomplishments are trumpeted by dwelling nostalgically in the sepia tones of the high-growth era. Often the story is framed as a contest against bigger, better funded American rivals, as in the episodes on the LCD and the Yamaha Grand Piano, apparently dismissed by Westerners for its "feeble sound."[37] National pride in Rikidōzan's heroic under-dog battles against the Sharp brothers comes to mind. As such, Project X serves as an example of the politics of hope so convincingly articulated by David Leheny, who argues that a powerful emotional response to the lost decades was to construct a highly idealized, hope-inspiring nostalgia for the recent past.[38] Iwona Merkljn argues that "Shōwa Nostalgia" also ran through much of NHK's early 2000s-era representation of the Japanese women's volleyball team in the 1964 Tokyo Olympics. Portrayals of the Gold-medal winning team were seemingly non-gendered but in fact "provide normative notions of gender roles with which 'proper' Japanese women were supposed to conform in the idealized Shōwa era."[39]

At the same time, though, the emphasis in *Project X* is on individuals rather than either the state or corporations as such. True, many of the engineers or scientists are working for big companies or government labs, but they often succeed in the face of hostility or indifference from more senior management. *Project X* thus simultaneously combines a celebration of traditional Japanese notions of teamwork and perseverance with an explicit endorsement of the sort of maverick individuality Japan was said to be lacking. The philosophy was spelled out by Imai:

> People say that the Japanese tend to be middle-of-the-road or lack individuality, but that is simply not the case. The people featured in *Project X* achieved incredible things. Many Japanese are bold and fearless and ready to take on new challenges. . . . Rather than living with a defeatist attitude, you have to go out there, face the future and find something worth living for.[40]

Whatever the causes, *Project X* clearly struck deep emotional chords. The series found great popularity, achieving up to 20% ratings – remarkably high for a documentary series – and a cult following going beyond the middle-aged white collar salarymen who were the original targets.[41] The theme song, Nakajima Miyuki's soaring ballad *Chijiyo no Hoshi* ("Stars of Earth"), stayed in the music charts longer than any other single in Japanese history.[42] The episode about Sony's development of VHS was made into a major movie *Hi wa Mata Noboru* ("Dawn of a New Day") featuring superstars Ken Watanabe as a mild-mannered accountant and Toshiyuki Nishida as the maverick engineer ignoring orders to downsize while secretly working on his videotape system. The Japanese Government helped pay for episodes to be aired abroad in order to demonstrate "how Japan achieved modernization while keeping its traditions at the same time."[43]

Kōhaku Uta Gassen

Few programs epitomize NHK's influence on national life more than *Kōhaku Uta Gassen*, the New Year's Eve Song Contest. Its story carries almost allegorical significance in matching NHK's own trajectory. As we saw in Chapter 3, it was created after the war under SCAP guidance as part of the attempt both to democratize programming and to provide an inoffensive means to unify the country.[44] In this, it succeeded wildly, and as a national ritual, the Kōhaku came to have no peer. In its heyday in 1963, viewership was 81%, the highest ratings ever for any program in Japanese television history. Performers for the rival red (all-female) and white (all-male) teams are drawn from both popular and more traditional musical forms, with the most popular artists of the day the headline contestants. But as well as the J-Pop stars, Christine Yano argues, NHK was a strong supporter of *enka*, a traditional and sentimental ballad form of popular music. Enka, Yano suggests, epitomizes for many, especially elderly Japanese, the heart of Japan (*Nihonjin no kokoro*) and it is no surprise that NHK is the primary producer of enka on both radio and television.[45] Of all enka programming, the Kōkahu had become especially important, keeping *enka* "in the limelight of Japanese popular music, where it plays a central role." The Kōhaku is, Yano argues, "the most important event in the enka world."[46] And, she continues, it became "increasingly focused on themes of nostalgia and cultural nationalism – in 1992, family and childhood; in 1993, unchanging Japan ('*Kawaranu Nippon*'). Such nationally broadcast mass media programs inextricably link song and emotion to nationhood."[47]

But audiences for Kōhaku have been declining, with urban and younger viewers less enamored of the very traditional style. In 2016, viewership was 39.2%, still high by the standards of other programs, but a far cry from its peak.[48] Part of the decline in popularity seems to have been NHK's use of the show as a political tool to register solidarity with government policy goals. Most notably, Korean singers were not invited to appear on the show from 2012 to 2017. This decision by NHK was highly controversial since K-Pop, part of the *hallyu* "wave" of Korean pop culture, had achieved great popularity in Japan and acts such as *TVXQ* and *Girls' Generation* had been appearing annually on Kōhaku since at least 2001.[49] The ban was generally seen as a gesture of solidarity from NHK to Prime Minister Abe's hawkish foreign policy at a time when Korea–Japan relations had deteriorated sharply over territorial disputes and war history. NHK denied any such connection, claiming that the decision had been based on artistic considerations only, but given the continued success of Korean acts in the Japanese pop charts, it was difficult for many to believe that explanation.[50]

By the later 2000s, Japan was undergoing a growing reckoning with the realities of immigration and ethnic diversity. Yet scholars such as Satako Suzuki argue that NHK's programming has not fully embraced the changes, paying lip service to inclusion while in reality extolling more traditional views of Japaneseness. Suzuki examines the 2014 *asadora Massan*, which reflected growing awareness of the rising number of non-Japanese living in Japan. Set in the 1920s and based on a true story, it seemed to embrace multiculturalism with its sympathetic portrayal of Ellie and Masaharu Kameyama, a Scottish woman married to a Japanese man. NHK made fanfare of the fact that this was the first morning drama to feature a non-Japanese lead character, and photos of present-day international couples aired during the closing credits. However, Satoko Suzuki argues that the show in fact reinforced tropes of traditional gender roles, Ellie embraces her role as a supportive wife, and cultural nationalism. Ellie is portrayed as conspicuously foreign, to the extent that the lead actress was required to dye her brunette hair blonde. Moreover, she is never able to master the nuances of Japanese language.

Hence, Suzuki argues, "NHK successfully highlighted Ellie's role as an outsider and underscored the idea that only ethnic Japanese can know the Japanese language and culture, a crucial element of cultural nationalism in Japan."[51] Suzuki underscores the show's purpose in celebrating a traditional view of Japanese cultural identity by quoting comments from its makers. The scriptwriter said, "What I am rediscovering is that the Japanese from those days were really good people," while the director added, "This is a drama in which Ellie discovers the splendor of Japan and the Japanese."[52]

Industrial Policy

NHK's central role in technology development and industrial policy, now including digitization and "new media" industries, also helped secure political support from the regulatory authorities and the electronics industry.[53] In 2003, the Science and Technical Research Laboratories began work on Super-Hi Definition Television, with resolution planned to be 16 times greater than regular HDTV.[54] Critics claimed that the difference in resolution was undetectable by the human eye, with one American engineer calling Super Hi-Vision "beyond silly."[55] NHK continued development regardless, and Super-Hi Vision was triumphantly unveiled at the London Olympics, with NHK technicians cooperating closely with the BBC's Research and Development division.[56] Observers at the special screenings enthused that the experience made regular HDTV look blurry, and was "like being there," although staff at both broadcasters noted that regular Super-Hi Vision broadcasts were unlikely before 2020 at the earliest.[57] Once again, the Olympics had served as the site for NHK to unveil to the world its pathbreaking contributions to broadcasting technology, as at Tokyo in 1964 (color) and Los Angeles in 1984 (HD). NHK continued working closely with Japan's consumer electronics industry, notably Panasonic and Sony, in order to develop and promote Super Hi-Vision sufficiently to stream the entire 2020 Olympics.[58]

NHK World

During the debates over institutional reform in the mid-2000s, we have seen that the LDP were ultimately very protective of the status quo concerning NHK. One reason mooted for this was the LDP's continued desire to use the broadcaster for its own political purposes. For instance, at the time, one of the most pressing political issues was that of the DPRK abductees, that is, Japanese citizens who had been kidnapped and were believed still alive within North Korea. In 2006, Minister of Internal Affairs and Communications Suga Yoshihide demanded that the radio regulatory panel discuss ordering NHK to carry more news of the DPRK abductions.[59] In addition, one of the few reform proposals of the mid-2000s to come to fruition was the LDP's insistence that NHK cut a number of its domestic satellite channels. This was presented as a cost-cutting measure and a gesture toward greater entrepreneurialism, but the real reason seems to have been a redirection of resources. The LPD concurrently proposed that NHK launch an international English-language satellite TV channel with the money saved on the domestic services.[60] This global news channel was conceived unabashedly as to be a tool of state policy, to better present Japan to the world. Prime Minister Koizuimi was said to be concerned by the expansion of South Korean and Chinese overseas broadcasting and saw NHK World as a counter. "It's important to send a message regarding what country Japan is," Koizumi declared in proposing the new channel.[61] Komori Shigetaka, the then chair of the Board of Governors, agreed, noting that Japan's international broadcasts should be more assertive in promoting "Japan's national interest."[62] The English-language NHK World was duly launched in 2009, offering a radio channel and two TV channels, free-to-air and premium. NHK World's stated purpose was summed up as follows:

> To encourage the correct understanding of Japan with accurate information, we will strengthen international broadcasting and actively disseminate Japan to the world.[63]

It is worth highlighting the phrase "the *correct* understanding of Japan" because that seems to be a step further than the often self-congratulatory pride in Britishness evidenced by the BBC. The notion that there is a single right way to understand any nation is at odds with the celebration of diverse perspectives ostensibly served by truly public broadcasters. There seems to be no equivalent language at the BBC, although of course belief in a single correct view of national identity is one shared by many in Britain.

NHK World has become a central player in a broader effort at public diplomacy.[64] In addition to news, NHK World's main program offerings are essentially celebrations of Japanese culture and lifestyle such as *Cool Japan* and *Selfie Japan*, in which foreigners expressed delight at cool aspects of Japanese life.[65] Programs such as *Ceramic Treasures*, *Japanolgy Plus*, and *Kabuki Cool* often carry the air of marketing videos.[66] Yoshitaka Mōri notes the role of NHK World's J-MELO, the only English-language program devoted to J-Pop, as an important component of the "Cool Japan" strategy to promote creative industry exports.[67] Prime Minister Abe has been especially enthusiastic about these efforts at national branding, and is particularly concerned with improving Japan's international reputation ahead of the 2020 Olympic and Paralympic games, in which he has invested much political capital. NHK is playing an energetic role in tying Japanese culture to the Games through such fusions of sort-of traditional and modern culture as a concert starring virtual icon *Hatsune Miku* and *Kodo* drummers.[68] In short, NHK World has become what Koizumi intended, a tool to serve often specific state goals.

Covering the 3.11 Disaster

NHK's coverage of the "3.11 Triple Disaster" – the earthquake, tsunami, and nuclear meltdown of March 2011 – illustrated both its undoubted strengths and some of its worst weaknesses as a national public broadcaster.[69] The emergency coverage and disaster reporting during the weeks of the crisis itself, monumentally difficult and dangerous tasks, were extensive, thorough, and widely praised.[70] Of all Japan's news organizations, only NHK had anything like enough resources to cover the entire disaster fully. Their reporters, too, were trained to provide the gravitas and solemn tone appropriate for the tragedy.[71] NHK's footage, aired 24 hours a day over the English-language cable channel and website, won international acclaim.[72] Media scholars Tanaka Takanobu and Sato Toshiyuki praised NHK's coverage, arguing that it showed greater focus on public safety than all other commercial news organizations, thereby proving the higher social value of public broadcasting.[73] But NHK's reporting was also criticized for being too complacent, and for almost exclusively repeating rather than challenging the official version of events from the Government and power company TEPCO.[74]

The bigger issue is that in the years before the accident, NHK, like the rest of Japan's mainstream media, had done little to question the collusive relationships between LDP politicians, regulators, and power companies in the so-called nuclear village. The consequences of the disaster had been significantly worsened as a result of structural corruption "made in Japan," according to an official report, but neither NHK nor the commercial broadcast media had engaged in much investigative journalism to probe the open secret. This reluctance to challenge pro-nuclear attitudes among conservative elites was further illustrated during the Tokyo Mayoral election of 2014. The election was contested by an LDP-supported pro-nuclear candidate and two candidates running on anti-nuclear platforms. NHK managers instructed news teams to avoid any discussion of nuclear energy, ostensibly in the aim of neutrality. But in practice, not having nuclear issues on the agenda benefitted the pro-nuclear status quo. A prominent radio contributor to NHK resigned in protest.[75]

By contrast, social media grew enormously during the disaster as an alternative universe of real-time news and information (and, of course, rumor and misinformation). Many activists used blogs and other social media to portray realities often missing from official coverage.[76] Yet NHK, rather than seeking to reach out to alienated audiences, became even more cautious and conservative.

PM Abe's Media Strategy

Recent incidents suggest that Prime Minister Abe Shinzō successfully influenced NHK to surrender even further its editorial autonomy and more closely reflect his conservative views. An important weapon was his active use of the power to appoint the Governors and hence influence their choice of Chairman. In 2010, Chairman Fukuchi stepped down, citing ill health. Amidst much confusion, not least due to the inexperience of the recently elected DPJ government, the Board of Governors selected as replacement Matsumoto Masayuki, another outsider businessman from JR Tokai, underlining the degree to which NHK were concerned to bring commercial experience into the organization. Under Matsumoto and with the DPJ struggling in power, NHK staff enjoyed a period in which they were less subject to pressure to self-censor. This period ended when Abe won the Prime Ministership again in 2013. He appointed to the Board of Governors four political allies who shared his conservative views. Such views were often highly controversial, such as novelist Hyakuta Naoki's claim that the Nanjing Massacre never happened.[77] Matsumoto abruptly announced he would not serve a second term when his first term ended in 2013, a decision reportedly prompted by anger at these appointments. The new governors, in turn, were happy to see him go, sympathetic to right-wing complaints that NHK's coverage of issues such as nuclear energy, Okinawa and the territorial disputes were insufficiently supportive of conservative policies. The governors approved Momii Katsuto, a personal Abe recommendation, as the new Chairman.[78]

Momii was yet another outsider from the business world, formerly an executive at Mitsui Trading and Chairman of Nihon Unisys. He had no previous experience in broadcasting but shared Abe's political views and immediately provoked controversy. In his first press conference, Momii made statements dismissive of the comfort women and stated that, whereas NHK would be impartial in domestic reporting, its international broadcasts would naturally take the government's side in disputes over issues like the Senkaku/Daioyu Islands. "When the government is saying 'Right' we can't say 'Left,'" he announced.[79] There was international as well as domestic outcry, and a renewed fee boycott. The LDP government and the Board of Governors stood by their man, with an LDP spokesman declaring that Momii was merely expressing private opinions, as was his right as a private citizen.

Many observers within the scholarly community have been critical of NHK's increasing willingness to defer to the government.[80] Considerable anecdotal evidence suggests that assertive conservatism among the governors and senior management is having a powerful influence throughout the organization. Richard Lloyd Parry of the *Times* broke what was essentially an open secret about NHK's confidential internal guidelines to reporters, known as the "Orange Book." Reportedly, NHK staff were ordered to avoid certain politically loaded words or phrases. While such guidelines are in principle reasonable, in practice, the instructions seemed to require adherence to conservative sensibilities. For example, reporters were explicitly instructed not to use certain terms such as "controversial" or "wartime" in connection with the Yasukuni Shrine, or "forced to," "brothels," or "sex slaves" when referring to victims of the "comfort women" system.[81]

To give another example, President Momii instructed senior executives that reports on vulnerable nuclear reactors during a spate of earthquakes in Kumamoto in 2016 should be based only on official announcements. He also reportedly told staff to avoid including the views of outside experts in case that confused the public. When a member of the DPJ questioned him in the Diet about whether this amounted to propaganda, Momii replied "keeping our coverage fact-based is what gives locals a sense of reassurance."[82]

Other examples of government interference abound. In April 2015, an LDP committee questioned NHK about a 2014 report despite having no authority to do so, but NHK complied with the request. Then, MIAC minister Sanae Takaichi gave a stern warning to NHK about violating the Broadcast Law, claiming that criticism of the LDP was tantamount to giving unfair coverage.[83] In 2016, Kuniya Hiroko resigned as long-time host of *Close-up Gendai*, NHK's flagship investigative current events program. Her resignation followed reports that management was considering removing her after LDP representative Suga Yoshide had complained to them about probing interview questions she had put to him about the implications of revising the Constitution. Kuniya spoke of growing "pressure to conform" within the organization.[84]

NHK journalists and staff, it is important to emphasize, are often dismayed by both LDP pressure and senior management's acquiescence in such manipulation. In response to Momii's comments about the Kumamoto reporting, Nakamura Masatoshi, chairman of the Japan Broadcasting Labor Union (*Nippōren*) said: "The confirmation of facts does not come from announcements or acknowledgements from Administrative bodies. The facts are unveiled through NHK's independent research efforts."[85] Yasuo Onuki, a former NHK reporter, noted that the LDP had become "very good at constant, behind-the-scene pressure" and attributed this pressure to Kuniya's decision to quit NHK.[86]

Momii was not reappointed when his first term as Chairman expired. The governors were said to be troubled by the controversy he raised, as well as by his proposal to win back viewer support by lowering viewer fees, a proposal they rejected.[87] In his place, the Governors appointed another businessman with no broadcasting experience. Ueda Ryuichi was a former executive at Mitsubishi Corporation who was serving on NHK's board at the time of his appointment. Top-down editorial pressure on reporters has continued, however. In 2018, *Close-Up Gendai* reported on Japan's public postal service using illegal methods to sell insurance to the elderly. Japan Post complained to NHK's Board of Governors whose acting chair, Morishita Shuzo, then publicly reprimanded Chairman Ueda. Morishita was reelected Chairman of the Board in 2021 despite widespread criticism of his editorial interference, and NHK refused to release details of the Japan Post discussions.[88] Ueda left at the end of his first term in 2020 and was replaced by Maeda Teranobu, a former banker and President of Mizuho Financial Groups. The Governors, in short, continued their practice of appointing as Editor-in-Chief former businessmen with no relevant media experience whatsoever. It remains to be seen whether future NHK leaders will offer more resistance to political pressure. As long as the most senior staff continue to be drawn exclusively from the conservative establishment, NHK's political position seems secure.

Notes

1 Anne Allison, *Precarious Japan* (Durham, NC: Duke University Press, 2015).
2 *The Annual Bulletin of NHK Broadcasting Culture Research Institute*, May 1998.
3 Kamimura Shuichi, Ikoma Chiho, and Nakano Sachiko, "The Japanese and Television, 2000," *The Annual Bulletin of NHK Broadcasting Culture Research Institute* 13 (Summer 2000): 10.
4 Author's own interview with an NHK staff member in Tokyo, November 2000.
5 *Annual Report 1999* (Tokyo: NHK, 1999), 35.
6 Author's own interview with an NHK staff member in Tokyo, October 2000.
7 "NHK, Ministry at Odds over Fees," *Asahi Evening News*, November 30, 1998.
8 Takahashi Tetsuya, "Nani ga Chokuzen ni Kesareta [What Was Cut at the Last Minute?]," *Sekai* 688 (May 2001): 209–219.

9 "NHK, Chokuzen ni Okaihen [NHK: Big Change at the Last Minute]," *Asahi Shimbun*, March 3, 2001.
10 "Former NHK Producers Pleads Guilty," *Japan Times*, March 10, 2005.
11 Author's own interviews with NHK staff members in Tokyo, August 2005.
12 "NHK Airs Show Aimed at Restoring Public Trust," *Japan Times*, December 20, 2004.
13 "Flurry of NHK Scandals," *Asahi Shimbun*, December 24, 2004.
14 Irene Prusher, "Japan Finally Gets Politicians Worth a TV Satire," *Christian Science Monitor*, November 11, 2001.
15 "Role of Public Broadcaster under Scrutiny," *Nikkei Weekly*, March 27, 2006.
16 Tad Osaki, "Public Broadcaster under Siege," *onscreenasia.com*, June 1, 2006.
17 "Role of Public Broadcaster under Scrutiny," *Nikkei Weekly*.
18 Takayuki Awazu, *NHK Mineikaron* [NHK Privatization Debate] (Tokyo: Nikkan Kōgyō Shimbunsha, 2000).
19 "Govt Panel to Rethink NHK Ops," *Nikkei Weekly*, December 12, 2005. As with so many conservative critics of public broadcasting in the UK, Takenaka's favorable personal attitude toward NHK clashed with his ideological leanings.
20 Suzuki Yoshikazu and Hidaka Tetsuo, "NHK Reform Plans Vex Lawmakers," *Daily Yomiuri*, March 21, 2006.
21 Philip Seaton, "Pledge Fulfilled," in *Yasukuni: The War Dead and the Struggle for Japan's Past*, ed. John Breen (London: Hurst and Company, 2007), 163–188.
22 Yoshikazu and Tetsuo, "NHK Reform Plans Vex Lawmakers."
23 Naotake Katori and Koji Hatamoto, "NHK Fee Tug-of-war Begins," *Daily Yomiuri*, February 9, 2007.
24 Waichi Sekiguchi, "Will NHK Capitalize on Scandals," *Nikkei Weekly*, February 13, 2007.
25 "NHK Takes Legal Action against Non-payers," *Japan Times*, November 30, 2006.
26 Kaori Hayashi, "The Dilemmas of Reforming Japan's Broadcasting System: Ambivalent Implications of Its Liberalization," in *Television and Public Policy: Change and Continuity in an Era of Global Liberalization*, ed. David Ward (New York: Taylor and Francis, 2008).
27 "Aso Proposes Fines for NHK Fee Dodgers," *Daily Yomiuri*, March 11, 2005; Suzuki and Hidaka, "NHK Reform Plans Vex Lawmakers."
28 "Panel Urges Retooling NHK," *Nikkei Weekly*, June 12, 2006.
29 "Hashimoto Resigns over Insider Trading Scandal," *Japan Economic Newswire*, January 24, 2008.
30 "Public Broadcaster's Next President Comes from Outside," *Daily Yomiuri*, December 27, 2007.
31 NHK, *Wherever You Are, NHK: Corporate Plan for 2009–2011* (Tokyo: NHK, 2009), 1.
32 Hitoshi Chiba, "Project X Hits the Spot," *Look Japan*, April 2003.
33 Quoted in: Mamoru Ito, "Television and Violence in the Economy of Memory," *International Journal of Japanese Sociology*, no. 11 (November 2002): 23.
34 Shizuka Saeki, "Project X Inspires Generation Y," *Look Japan* 47 (October 2001).
35 "NHK's Project X on the Takarazuka Production of Rose of Versailles," *Japan Times*, December 4, 2005.
36 Philip Brasor, "Not Letting Facts Get in the Way of a Good Documentary," *Japan Times*, December 14, 2003. On the politics of hope, see David Leheney, *Empire of Hope* (Ithaca, NY: Cornell University Press, 2018).
37 Ito, "Television and Violence in the Economy of Memory," 26.
38 For a full and much better discussion of the political uses of nostalgia with reference to *Project X*, see Leheney, *Empire of Hope*.
39 Iwona Merklejn, "Remembering the Oriental Witches: Sports, Gender and Shōwa Nostalgia in the NHK Narratives of the Tokyo Olympics," *Social Science Japan Journal* 16, no. 2 (2013): 235–250, 237.
40 Shizuka Saeki, "Project X Inspires Generation Y," *Look Japan* 47 (October 2001): 35.
41 Akiko Kashiwagi, "TV Show Hooks Recession-weary Japanese: Series Lauds Traditional Values of Devotion, Teamwork," *The Washington Post*, January 13, 2002.

42 Shihoko Goto, "Salaryman's Anthem Hits No. 1," *United Press International*, January 14, 2003.
43 "Documentaries on Japan's 'Economic Miracle' to be Aired in the Middle East," *Japan Economic Newswire*, April 6, 2004.
44 Shelley D. Brunt, "The Infinite Power of Song: Uniting Japan at the 60th Annual Kōhaku Song Contest," in *Made in Japan: Studies in Popular Music*, ed. Tōru Mitsui (New York: Routledge, 2014), 37–51.
45 Christine R. Yano, *Tears of Longing: Nostalgia and the Nation in Japanese Popular Song* (Cambridge, MA: Harvard University Press, 2002), 217, n9.
46 Yano, *Tears of Longing*, 50.
47 Yano, *Tears of Longing*, 89.
48 "Ratings of NHK's 'Kōhaku Show Drop to Record Low," *Japan Economic Newswire*, January 2, 2016.
49 "K-pop's Female Stars Wow Japanese Music Lovers," *Nikkei Weekly*, November 29, 2010; "Top of the K-Pops," *The Economist*, August 18, 2012.
50 "Korean Singers Dropped from NHK Yearend Show," *Japan Times*, November 28, 2012.
51 Satoko Suzuki, "Multiculturalism or Cultural Nationalism? Representation of Ellie Kameyama as a Conduit and the Other in the NHK Morning Drama Massan," *Japanese Studies* 40, no. 2 (2020): 121–140.
52 Quoted in Suzuki, "Multiculturalism or Cultural Nationalism?," 125.
53 Author's own interview with a media analyst, July 2005.
54 Yoshiko Hara, "NHK Gives Reality TV a New Twist," *Electronic Engineering Times*, June 9, 2003. See also Douglas Heingartner, "What's Next: Just Like High-definition TV, but with Higher Definition," *The New York Times*, June 3, 2004. Note that HDTV is sometimes referred to as UHDTV (Ultra-High Definition Television).
55 Junko Yoshida, "Broadcasters Look for New Hits among Golden Oldies," *Electronic Engineering Times*, September 22, 2008.
56 Eric Pfanner, "With Live Streaming and New Technology, the BBC Tries to be Everywhere at the Olympics," *The New York Times*, August 5, 2012.
57 Dan Grabham, "Super-Hi Vision: The Future of TV that's 16x HD," accessed August 13, 2012, www.techradar.com/news/television/tv/super-hi-vision-the-future-of-tv-thats-16x-hd-1091821.
58 "Panasonic, Sony and NHK: Alliance Japanese to Promote Technology before 2020 Olympics," *Digital TV Magazine*, August 29, 2016, www.digitalavmagazine.com/en/2016/08/29/panasonic-sony-y-nhk-alianza-japonesa-para-fomentar-la-tecnologia-8k-antes-de-tokio-2020/; Martyn Williams, "Why Japan's 2020 Olympics Will Revolutionize Tech," *PCWorld*, October 3, 2013, www.pcworld.com/article/2051900/why-japans-2020-olympics-will-revolutionize-tech.html.
59 "Government to Order NHK Radio to Broadcast More on Abductions," *Japan Today*, October 25, 2006.
60 "Ruling Party Urges NHK to Launch New Global TV Channel," *Kyodo News Service*, May 17, 2006.
61 "NHK Says Consensus Is Needed to Use Viewers Fees for Overseas Service," *Kyodo News Service*, March 2, 2006; Kwan Weng Kim, "New Channel to Lift Japan's Profile Abroad," *The Straits Times*, February 13, 2009.
62 Masahiki Ishizuka, "Can NHK Help Japan Speak Its Mind to the World?," *Nikkei Weekly*, April 28, 2008.
63 NHK, *Keiei Keikaku* [Corporate Plan] 2015–2017, www.nhk.or.jp/pr/keiei/plan/pdf/25-27keikaku.pdf.
64 Craig Hayden, *The Rhetoric of Soft Power: Public Diplomacy in Global Contexts* (Plymouth: Lexington Books, 2012), 94–97.
65 Accessed August 15, 2018, https://www3.nhk.or.jp/nhkworld/en/vod/selfiejapan/3004507/.
66 "Kabuki Kool," *NHK*, accessed August 15, 2018, https://www3.nhk.or.jp/nhkworld/en/tv/kabukikool/.

67 Yoshitaka Mōri, "J-Pop Goes the World: A New Global Fandom in the Age of Digital Media," in *Made in Japan: Mitsui*, 211–224.
68 Patrick St. Michel, "NHK Pushes to Define Culture Ahead of 2020 with Some Help from Perfume," *Japan Times*, April 25, 2018.
69 David McNeill, "Truth to Power: Japanese Media, International Media and 3.11," *Asia-Pacific Journal* 11, no. 10 (March 5, 2013).
70 Gavin Blair, "How Japan's NHK Adapted to Cover the Earthquake and Tsunami," *The Hollywood Reporter*, May 10, 2011.
71 Shuzo Yamakoshi, "Reexamining the Journalistic Function of Public Service Broadcasting in Japan: A Discourse of Television News Coverage on the Fukushima Nuclear Crisis," *Keio Communication Review*, no. 37 (2015).
72 Gavin Blair, "Japan's NHK World Wins Broadcaster of the Year in New Internet TV Awards for Disaster Reporting," *The Hollywood Reporter*, September 14, 2011.
73 Takanobu Tanaka and Toshiyuki Sato, "Disaster Coverage and Public Value from Below: Analysing the NHK's Reporting on the Great East Japan Disaster," in *The Value of Public Service Media*, eds. Gregory Ferrell Lowe and Fiona Martin (Gothenburg: Nordicom, 2014).
74 Eriko Arita, "Keeping an Eye on TV News Coverage of the Nuke Crisis," *Japan Times*, July 3, 2012.
75 McNeill, "Truth to Power," *Japan Times*, February 9, 2014.
76 D. Slater, K. Nishimura, and L. Kinstrand, "Social Media and Nuclear Crisis in Japan," in *Nuclear Disaster and Nuclear Crisis in Japan*, ed. Jefffrey Kingston (London: Routledge, 2012).
77 Ayako Mie, "NHK Governors' Impartiality Doubted," *Japan Times*, February 7, 2014.
78 "All Eyes on NHK's New Chief," *Japan Times*, December 26, 2013; Martin Fackler, "News Giant in Japan Seen as Being Compromised," *The New York Times*, February 3, 2014.
79 R. Yoshida, A. Mie, and E. Johnston, "Momii's Rise Tests NHK's Reputation," *Japan Times*, February 2, 2014.
80 Katsuhiko Iimuro, *NHK to seiji shihai: Jānarizumu wa dare no mono ka* [NHK and Political Rule: Who Does Journalism Belong to?] (Tokyo: Gendai Shokan, 2014).
81 Richard Lloyd Parry, "Japan's BBC Bans Any Reference to Wartime 'Sex Slaves'," *The Times*, October 17, 2018.
82 Tomohiko Osaki, "NHK Chairman's Orders to Follow Government Line on Kyushu Nuclear Reactors Sparks Outcry," *Japan Times*, April 27, 2016.
83 Nobuyki Okamura, "Abe seiken ni kontorōru sa reru Nihon media no 'futsugōnashinjitsu' [The Inconvenient Truth of Japan's Abe-controlled Media]," *Nippon.com*, April 2016.
84 Martin Fackler, "The Silencing of Japan's Free Press," *Foreign Policy*, May 27, 2016.
85 "NHK President Rapped over Remarks on Nuclear Power Reporting," *Mainichi Shimbun*, May 2, 2016.
86 Steven Borowiec, "Writers of Wrongs," *Index of Censorship* 45, no. 2 (June/July 2016): 48–50.
87 "Momii NHK Kaichō Sainin Konnan [NHK Chairman Momii's Reappointment Trouble]," *Asahi Shimun*, December 2, 2016.
88 "Controversial Chair of NHK's Governing Board Re-elected," *Asahi Shimbun*, March 10, 2021.

References

"All Eyes on NHK's New Chief," *Japan Times*, December 26, 2013.
Allison, Anne, *Precarious Japan* (Durham, NC: Duke University Press, 2015).
The Annual Bulletin of NHK Broadcasting Culture Research Institute, May 1998.
Annual Report 1999 (Tokyo: NHK, 1999).

Arita, Eriko, "Keeping an Eye on TV News Coverage of the Nuke Crisis," *Japan Times*, July 3, 2012.

"Aso Proposes Fines for NHK Fee Dodgers," *Daily Yomiuri*, March 11, 2005.

Awazu, Takayuki, *NHK Mineikaron* [NHK Privatization Debate] (Tokyo: Nikkan Kōgyō Shimbunsha, 2000).

Blair, Gavin, "How Japan's NHK Adapted to Cover the Earthquake and Tsunami," *The Hollywood Reporter*, May 10, 2011.

Blair, Gavin, "Japan's NHK World Wins Broadcaster of the Year in New Internet TV Awards for Disaster Reporting," *The Hollywood Reporter*, September 14, 2011.

Borowiec, Steven, "Writers of Wrongs," *Index of Censorship* 45, no. 2 (June/July 2016): 48–50.

Brasor, Philip, "Not Letting Facts Get in the Way of a Good Documentary," *Japan Times*, December 14, 2003.

Brunt, Shelley D., "The Infinite Power of Song: Uniting Japan at the 60th Annual Kōhaku Song Contest," in *Made in Japan: Studies in Popular Music*, ed. Tōru Mitsui (New York: Routledge, 2014), 37–51.

Chiba, Hitoshi, "Project X Hits the Spot," *Look Japan*, April 2003.

"Controversial Chair of NHK's Governing Board Re-elected," *Asahi Shimbun*, March 10, 2021.

"Documentaries on Japan's 'Economic Miracle' to be Aired in the Middle East," *Japan Economic Newswire*, April 6, 2004.

Fackler, Martin, "News Giant in Japan Seen as Being Compromised," *The New York Times*, February 3, 2014.

Fackler, Martin, "The Silencing of Japan's Free Press," *Foreign Policy*, May 27, 2016.

"Flurry of NHK Scandals," *Asahi Shimbun*, December 24, 2004.

"Former NHK Producers Pleads Guilty," *Japan Times*, March 10, 2005.

Goto, Shihoko, "Salaryman's Anthem Hits No. 1," *United Press International*, January 14, 2003.

"Govt Panel to Rethink NHK Ops," *Nikkei Weekly*, December 12, 2005.

Hara, Yoshiko, "NHK Gives Reality TV a New Twist," *Electronic Engineering Times*, June 9, 2003.

"Hashimoto Resigns Over Insider Trading Scandal," *Japan Economic Newswire*, January 24, 2008.

Hayashi, Kaori, "The Dilemmas of Reforming Japan's Broadcasting System: Ambivalent Implications of its Liberalization," in *Television and Public Policy: Change and Continuity in an Era of Global Liberalization*, ed. David Ward (New York: Taylor and Francis, 2008).

Hayden, Craig, *The Rhetoric of Soft Power: Public Diplomacy in Global Contexts* (Plymouth: Lexington Books, 2012).

Heingartner, Douglas, "What's Next: Just like High-Definition TV, But with Higher Definition," *The New York Times*, June 3, 2004.

Iimuro, Katsuhiko, *NHK to seiji shihai: Jānarizumu wa dare no mono ka* [NHK and Political Rule: Who Does Journalism Belong to?] (Tokyo: Gendai Shokan, 2014).

Ishizuka, Masahiki, "Can NHK Help Japan Speak its Mind to the World?" *Nikkei Weekly*, April 28, 2008.

Ito, Mamoru, "Television and Violence in the Economy of Memory," *International Journal of Japanese Sociology* no. 11 (November 2002).

"Kabuki Kool," *NHK*, accessed August 15, 2018, https://www3.nhk.or.jp/nhkworld/en/tv/kabukikool/.

Kashiwagi, Akiko, "TV Show Hooks Recession-Weary Japanese: Series Lauds Traditional Values of Devotion, Teamwork," *The Washington Post*, January 13, 2002.

Katori, Naotake, and Koji Hatamoto, "NHK Fee Tug-of-War Begins," *Daily Yomiuri*, February 9, 2007.

"Korean Singers Dropped From NHK Yearend Show," *Japan Times*, November 28, 2012.

"K-pop's Female Stars Wow Japanese Music Lovers," *Nikkei Weekly*, November 29, 2010.

Leheney, David, *Empire of Hope* (Ithaca, NY: Cornell University Press, 2018).

McNeill, David, "Truth to Power: Japanese Media, International Media and 3.11," *Asia-Pacific Journal* 11, no. 10 (March 5, 2013).

Merklejn, Iwona, "Remembering the Oriental Witches: Sports, Gender and Shōwa Nostalgia in the NHK Narratives of the Tokyo Olympics," *Social Science Japan Journal* 16, no. 2 (2013): 235–250.

Michel, Patrick St., "NHK Pushes to Define Culture Ahead of 2020 with Some Help from Perfume," *Japan Times*, April 25, 2018.

Mie, Ayako, "NHK Governors' Impartiality Doubted," *Japan Times*, February 7, 2014.

"Momii NHK Kaichō Sainin Konnan [NHK Chairman Momii's Reappointment Trouble]," *Asahi Shimbun*, December 2, 2016.

Mōri, Yoshitaka, "J-Pop Goes the World: A New Global Fandom in the Age of Digital Media," in *Made in Japan: Studies in Popular Music*, ed. Tōru Mitsui (New York: Routledge, 2014), 211–224.

"NHK Airs Show Aimed at Restoring Public Trust," *Japan Times*, December 20, 2004.

"NHK, Chokuzen ni Okaihen [NHK: Big Change at the Last Minute]," *Asahi Shimbun*, March 3, 2001.

"NHK, Ministry at Odds over Fees," *Asahi Evening News*, November 30, 1998.

"NHK President Rapped Over Remarks on Nuclear Power Reporting," *Mainichi Shimbun*, May 2, 2016.

"NHK's Project X on the Takarazuka Production of Rose of Versailles," *Japan Times*, December 4, 2005.

"NHK Says Consensus is Needed to Use Viewers Fees for Overseas Service," *Kyodo News Service*, March 2, 2006.

"NHK Takes Legal Action Against Non-payers," *Japan Times*, November 30, 2006.

NHK, "Wherever You Are, NHK," Corporate Plan for 2009–2011.

Okamura, Nobuyuki, "Abe seiken ni kontorōru sa reru Nihon media no 'futsugōnashinjitsu' [The Inconvenient Truth of Japan's Abe-controlled Media]," *Nippon.com*, April 2016.

Osaki, Tad, "Public Broadcaster Under Siege," *onscreenasia.com*, June 1, 2006.

Osaki, Tomohiko, "NHK Chairman's Orders to Follow Government Line on Kyushu Nuclear Reactors Sparks Outcry," *Japan Times*, April 27, 2016.

"Panasonic, Sony and NHK: Alliance Japanese to Promote Technology Before 2020 Olympics," *Digital TV Magazine*, August 29, 2016, www.digitalavmagazine.com/en/2016/08/29/panasonic-sony-y-nhk-alianza-japonesa-para-fomentar-la-tecnologia-8k-antes-de-tokio-2020/.

"Panel Urges Retooling NHK," *Nikkei Weekly*, June 12, 2006.

Parry, Richard Lloyd, "Japan's BBC Bans Any Reference to Wartime 'Sex Slaves'," *The Times*, October 17, 2018.

Pfanner, Eric, "With Live Streaming and New Technology, the BBC Tries to be Everywhere at the Olympics," *The New York Times*, August 5, 2012.

Prusher, Irene, "Japan Finally gets Politicians Worth a TV Satire," *Christian Science Monitor*, November 11, 2001.

"Public Broadcaster's Next President Comes from Outside," *Daily Yomiuri*, December 27, 2007.

"Ratings of NHK's 'Kōhaku Show Drop to Record Low," *Japan Economic Newswire*, January 2, 2016.

"Role of Public Broadcaster Under Scrutiny," *Nikkei Weekly*, March 27, 2006.

Saeki, Shizuka, "Project X Inspires Generation Y," *Look Japan* 47 (October 2001).

Seaton, Philip, "Pledge Fulfilled," in *Yasukuni: The War Dead and the Struggle for Japan's Past*, ed. John Breen (London: Hurst and Company, 2007), 163–188.

Sekiguchi, Waichi, "Will NHK Capitalize on Scandals," *Nikkei Weekly*, February 13, 2007.

Shuichi, Kamimura, Ikoma Chiho, and Nakano Sachiko, "The Japanese and Television, 2000," *The Annual Bulletin of NHK Broadcasting Culture Research Institute* 13 (Summer 2000): 10.

Slater, D., K. Nishimura, and L. Kinstrand, "Social Media and Nuclear Crisis in Japan," in *Nuclear Disaster and Nuclear Crisis in Japan*, ed. Jefffrey Kingston (London: Routledge, 2012).

Suzuki, Satoko, "Multiculturalism or Cultural Nationalism? Representation of Ellie Kameyama as a Conduit and the Other in the NHK Morning Drama Massan," *Japanese Studies* 40, no. 2 (2020): 121–140.

Tanaka, Takanobu, and Toshiyuki Sato, "Disaster Coverage and Public value from below: Analysing the NHK's Reporting on The Great East Japan Disaster," in *The Value of Public Service Media*, eds. Gregory Ferrell Lowe and Fiona Martin (Gothenburg: Nordicom, 2014).

Tetsuya, Takahashi, "Nani ga Chokuzen ni Kesareta [What Was Cut at the Last Minute?]," *Sekai* 688 (May 2001): 209–219.

"Top of the K-Pops," *The Economist*, August 18, 2012.

Weng Kim, Kwan, "New Channel to Lift Japan's Profile Abroad," *The Straits Times*, February 13, 2009.

Williams, Martyn, "Why Japan's 2020 Olympics will Revolutionize Tech," *PCWorld*, October 3, 2013, www.pcworld.com/article/2051900/why-japans-2020-olympics-will-revolutionize-tech.html.

Yamakoshi, Shuzo, "Reexamining the Journalistic Function of Public Service Broadcasting in Japan: A Discourse of Television News Coverage on the Fukushima Nuclear Crisis," *Keio Communication Review*, no. 37 (2015).

Yano, Christine R., *Tears of Longing: Nostalgia and the Nation in Japanese Popular Song* (Cambridge, MA: Harvard University Press, 2002).

Yoshida, Junko, "Broadcasters Look for New Hits among Golden Oldies," *Electronic Engineering Times*, September 22, 2008.

Yoshida, R., A. Mie, and E. Johnston, "Momii's Rise Tests NHK's Reputation," *Japan Times*, February 2, 2014.

Yoshikazu, Suzuki, and Hidaka Tetsuo, "NHK Reform Plans Vex Lawmakers," *Daily Yomiuri*, March 21, 2006.

11 NHK and the Comfort Women

One of the most controversial subjects in contemporary Japan is the issue of war guilt. Nationalists, conservatives, and progressives are bitterly divided about how the nation should portray, remember, and take responsibility for the activities of the Imperial Army during the Second World War. Especially controversial is the issue of the so-called comfort women, the 200,000 or so Asian women forced into sexual slavery by the Japanese Army between 1932 and 1945. This chapter takes a closer look at the events surrounding the drastic last-minute revisions to an NHK documentary about the issue. The case was one of the rare instances where political pressure on NHK's editorial process was so blatant that it resulted in overt pushback from junior staff and legal action. As such, the case clearly illustrates the dynamic interactions between politicians, senior managers, editors, and program makers, which help produce the organizational culture of self-censorship identified by so many observers.

The comfort women "problem" (*jugen ianfu mondai*) had become a salient issue in Japanese political discourse only in the 1990s, when survivors first started speaking openly about their ordeals and demanding apology and compensation from the Japanese Government. A rare break in LDP rule in 1995 resulted in Socialist Prime Minister Murayama Tomiichi issuing an apology for Japan's war crimes and establishing the Asian Women's Fund, a controversial, publicly administered, privately funded compensation pool. Further efforts to redress the atrocities were blocked by conservatives within the LDP who opposed what they called "the masochistic view of history." Some even denied the existence of a system of sexual slavery. The group's leaders included Nakagawa Shoichi and rising star (and later Prime Minister) Abe Shinzō, grandson of convicted war criminal and former Prime Minister Kishi Nobusuke. Their views were endorsed by revisionists of the Society for History Textbook Reform (*Atarashii rekishi kyōkai o tsukuru kai* or *tsukuru kai*) led by Professor Hata Ikuo. Supporters of the survivors' claims for redress included left-leaning journalists, lawyers, academics, women's groups, and politicians from the Socialist and Communist parties, led by the umbrella organization VAWW-Net Japan (Violence against Women in War).

NHK, along with most mainstream media, tended to avoid such a politically charged subject. In 1996, NHK made a documentary based on a Dutch war-tribunal document, titled "The Comfort Women Problem" (*Ianfu Mondai*). However,

DOI: 10.4324/b23015-11

the Ministry of Justice put so much pressure on NHK that the program was never aired. According to one producer, "senior staff at NHK gave in to political pressure."[1] Kano Tomoka worked for eight years as a director at NHK and made a number of requests to make a documentary on the subject, all of which were rejected by senior management.[2]

In December 2000, in a bid to raise public awareness of the issue, VAWW-Net convened a "People's Tribunal" to examine the legal aspects of the wartime government's responsibility for the system, and highlight the current government's responsibilities to surviving victims. The Tribunal took the form of a trial presided over by leading experts in international law, including Gabrielle Kirk MacDonald, Chief Justice for the UN War Crimes Trials for the former Yugoslavia.[3] The LDP were invited repeatedly to attend as either advocates or observers, but declined to participate.[4]

The Tribunal was filmed by Documentary Japan, an independent production company making a documentary about the Comfort Women's reparations movement under a commission from the NHK via a subsidiary in the education division, NHK Enterprises 21. The documentary was one of a four-part series on war guilt, "How Should War be Judged?" Filming began during the four days of the Tribunal and later in December. Documentary Japan recorded comments from experts, including Lisa Yoneyama of the University of California San Diego and Takahashi Tetsuya of the University of Tokyo.[5]

Senior NHK management had become increasingly worried about the likely political fallout from a program bound to provoke intense controversy. Indeed, since mid-December, NHK had been receiving angry calls from nationalist groups demanding the cancelation of the program. Sakagami Kaoru, producer of the third program in the series, claims that the section chief of Educational Programming pressed her repeatedly to change the tone of the script, an account corroborated by producer Nagai Satoru.[6]

On January 15, a copy of the 45-minute script was sent to VAWW-Net Japan, titled "Sexual Violence by the Japanese Military in World War Two" (*Daini daisen Nihongun ni yoru seibōryoku*). On January 20, a slightly amended title, "Japanese Military's Wartime Sexual Violence" (*Nihongun senji seibōryoku)*, was released to the media for advanced publicity and TV listings. After the title became public, outrage from conservatives grew, culminating in a noisy and intimidating seven-hour protest in NHK headquarters by ultranationalists in paramilitary dress from the Greater Japan Patriotic Party.[7] Management pressure for changes appears to have grown in response.

On January 26, revisionist historian Hata Ikuo was asked by Nagai to record an interview about the Tribunal as soon as possible. Hata was so struck by the short notice and Nagai's obvious reluctance that he concluded the producer must have been ordered to conduct the interview against his will.[8] On January 28, Takahashi was sent a revised script and called to tape additional comments.[9] Although the script was shorter and had changed significantly, Takahashi thought it still assessed the Tribunal impartially, and agreed to the interview.[10] Nagai believed the program "almost complete" by the evening of January 28.[11]

The next day, the LDP stepped in. A meeting took place between Deputy Chief Cabinet Secretary Abe Shinzō and NHK officials, including Matuso Takeshi, NHK's Director-General of Broadcasting.[12] LDP Representative Nakagawa Shoichi may or may not have attended. Questioned by the Asahi Shimbun in 2005, Nakagawa claimed to have been present, but quickly retracted his statement following the subsequent media uproar about political interference. Details of the meeting and what happened next are contested, but the overall account has become clear. Abe originally said he had requested the meeting specifically to discuss the program, but later reversed course, claiming instead that the subject had come up coincidentally during other discussions about NHK's budget.[13] Either way, Abe admitted to expressing the view that "the contents were clearly biased, and I told [NHK] that it should broadcast from a fair and neutral viewpoint, as it is expected to."[14] Following the meeting with Abe, Matsuo instructed Nagai: "We're going to change the program: show it to me."[15] There followed a screening for senior NHK executives, including Matsuo and the director of the Corporate Planning Bureau responsible for Diet relations. The executives recommended major changes, including cuts and additional comments by Hata. On January 30, just hours before the show aired, Matsuo demanded further cuts and changes.

The aired version was dramatically different from the script completed three days earlier. The title had been changed from "Japanese Military's Wartime Sexual Violence (*Nihongun senji seibōryoku*) to "Questioning Wartime Sexual Violence" (*Towareru senji seibōryoku*), deleting references to Japan.[16] Deleted scenes included dramatic footage of testimony by Japanese veterans confessing to having raped women; accounts by Chinese victims of their ordeals; a statement by the Tribunal's judge that Emperor Hirohito was guilty of crimes against humanity; an opinion offered by a scholar of international law that the Japanese government was liable to pay compensation to survivors; and Takahashi's comment questioning the government's defense of its inaction:

> The Japanese Government's position that its responsibility for crimes against humanity were absolved by the San Francisco Peace Treaty and other bilateral treaties has been dismissed in the judgement of the international legal community including, among others, the [United Nations] MacDougall Report.

Newly added to the original script was extensive footage of Hata's last-minute interview. Hata, falsely introduced as having attended the Tribunal, makes a number of inaccurate or highly debatable claims about the Tribunal, for example, fabricating an argument between Japanese and Korean participants and insisting that there had never been a "comfort woman system," merely a series of private business transactions. These claims all went unchallenged. Other last-minute inclusions included irrelevant footage of US bombers in action over Vietnam and an equally irrelevant statement by Takahashi that the US atomic bombings were war crimes, a response to a question put to him during his last-minute follow-up interview. In addition, the studio commentators' remarks had been extensively edited to the point of distortion.[17] Takahashi's comments on the compensation issue, for example, were changed from this:

> The victims are asking for reparations to be made from the state to individuals. Unless this happens, words of apology will be considered superficial. As for the Asian Women's Fund, since the money comes from the private sector and not from the government of Japan, the victims feel that the foundation was established by the government to evade its responsibility. Unless compensation is made by the government, the victims will not be satisfied.[18]

To this: "The victims are asking for reparations to be made from the state to individuals."[19] Several of the studio commentators complained to NHK about the distortions and Yoneyama filed a complaint with the Broadcasting Regulatory Organization. In 2003, the BRO found in favor of Yoneyama that NHK was guilty of a violation of broadcasting ethics, and had violated her rights by editing her remarks without permission.[20]

In short, the theme had changed from a presentation of the Tribunal and its findings to one that was critical of the Tribunal, without mentioning its most important conclusions. Criticism of the old Emperor and the present government had all been removed.

Government intervention in NHK's editorial policy is illegal under the Broadcast Law. A few opposition Diet members took up the case, but most were reluctant to do so. On March 16, 2001, the House of Representatives General Affairs Committee questioned Chairman Ebisawa and Matsuo.[21] Oide Akira of Minshutō (Democratic Party of Japan) spoke of the "chilling effect" on broadcasting of political interference and asked the reasons for the cutting of the perpetrators' testimony and other missing footage. Ebisawa and Matusuo denied external pressure and claimed any alterations were the result of the legitimate editorial process. Oide did not accept the defense, remarking, "We cannot say that Chairman Ebisawa took responsibility for explaining the truth to the people. Public broadcasting cannot exist without respecting the rights of project planners."[22]

Ebisawa was questioned again on March 29 at the House of Councilors General Affairs Committee. Councilor Hata Hiroko of the Japan Communist Party asked:

> Newspapers recently carried a letter to NHK's Chairman signed by 360 academics and scholars of Japan, including from Harvard's Reischaeur Institute, protesting the last-minute editorial changes to a program. As the Chairman certainly knows, this was about an NHK Educational TV documentary about the People's Tribunal discussing responsibility for the Japanese Army's comfort woman system. The program that was aired was completely different from the one that the participants had made. It was based on a very distorted view of the Women's International Tribunal on Wartime Sex Crimes, and presented this Tribunal to viewers in a very negative light. From the point of view of making fair and impartial programs, how do you respond? I also

attended the Tribunal and in the program neither the title nor the judgement were broadcast, which was very surprising. What do you think about that?

Chairman Ebisawa replied, "I have also read the newspaper and magazine reports. In all broadcasting, there is a lot of give-and-take during the editing process and so I think it's only natural."[23] He noted that they had received many opinions to which they were listening very carefully, but he did not comment specifically on either the program or any of the allegations.

With the exception of the Asahi Shimbun, Japan's media were reluctant to cover the issue, and the case went quiet until January 2005, when the program's chief producer, Nagai Satoru, had requested that NHK's compliance commission conduct an investigation into the incident.[24] Receiving no response, he went public with allegations of censorship and held a press conference, stating:

> We were ordered to alter the program before it was aired. I would have to say that the alteration was made against the backdrop of political pressure. . . . Outspoken cases of political intervention like this are rare, but since the establishment of the system under President Ebisawa Katsuji, political intervention has been constant. . . . In response to the second revision order, in particular, everyone there at the time was opposed, including the section chief.[25]

Abe, by then acting Secretary-General of the LDP, and Nakagawa, now Minister of Economy, Trade and Industry, both initially told the Asahi Shimbun that the revisions had indeed been made at their insistence. These admissions generated considerable attention, which apparently caught both men by surprise. They quickly retracted their claims and sought to distance themselves from charges of political interference. Abe next claimed:

> I spared some time because the NHK side told me they wanted to discuss the broadcaster's budget. On that occasion, [NHK] gave me an explanation about the program, which had become a topic of discussion within [the LDP], and I told them that I want them to report on the matter from a fair and neutral viewpoint.[26]

Abe then went on the television talk show circuit, denying that he had pressured NHK, denouncing the Tribunal as biased, and claiming without evidence that it had been infiltrated by North Korean spies. Meanwhile, LDP Chief Cabinet Secretary Hiroyuki Hosoda bizarrely argued that Abe's intervention was not government intervention because he was not acting in his capacity as deputy Chief Cabinet Secretary, the office he held at the time of the intervention.[27]

NHK's management continued to deny external interference, maintaining that all changes were the result of the internal editing process. They admitted that the program had been a topic for discussion when they were "explaining NHK's activities to members of the Diet" during the course of the Diet budget deliberations, but insisted "that did not spoil the fairness or impartiality of the program. We aired it after our editor in charge edited the program to his own judgement."[28] Many observers, including at least several junior NHK staff I spoke with, did not believe the claim that budget discussions in a time of austerity were entirely unrelated to editorial decisions. NHK's Director of Broadcasting seemed to say as much, perhaps unwittingly, when he remarked that it was "normal practice" for NHK to explain the content of specific programs to interested politicians ahead of broadcast. "The NHK budget has to be approved by the Diet, so it's necessary to gain the clear understanding of Diet members concerning our business plans and specific programs."[29]

Meanwhile, the affair had been working its way through the courts, highlighting the tensions between government-approved funding and editorial autonomy, as well as between editorial freedom and broadcasters' obligations to the subjects of their reporting.[30] In 2001, VAWW-Net Japan filed a damages suit in the Tokyo District Court against NHK, NHK Education TV, and the production company Documentary Japan.[31] The basis of the plaintiff's case was that the defendants had breached trust by making substantive alterations to the program without informing or consulting them, in breach of agreements that had been made as the basis for VAWW-Net's full cooperation in the filming of the documentary. In so doing, VAWW-Net argued that NHK and the other defendant had breached the "expectation rights" of participants in a documentary, as well as failing in their "duty to disclose" as broadcasters.[32] NHK continued to claim they had editorial rights to make any alterations they saw fit.

In March 2004, the Tokyo District Court found narrowly in favor of VAWW-Net Japan against Documentary Japan because the production company had given "wrong expectations about the program to the NGO."[33] However, the District Court cleared NHK of censorship on the grounds that Article 3 of the Broadcast Law guarantees "freedom to edit" (*Henshu no jiyu*) and "freedom to compile a broadcast program" (*hōsō bangumi hensei no jiyu*). Nagai testified that he had been forced against his own editorial judgment to cut the veterans' confessions and shorten victims' testimonies, but as long as the revisions had been made following instructions from NHK management and not directly from outside sources, they were legal.[34] All sides appealed and the case went to the Tokyo High Court.[35]

In January 2007, the Tokyo High Court ruled in ways that allowed both sides to claim victory. It sided with VAWW-Net Japan in concurring that the defendants had indeed breached promises made to VAWW-Net Japan, on the basis of which the latter had participated in the program.[36] The defendants were fined. On the other hand, the Court did not find sufficient evidence to prove that there had been political interference, which seemed to exonerate Abe and Ebisawa. However, the Court criticized NHK for self-censorship, dismissing many of NHK management's explanations for why the drastic changes had been made. For example, NHK claimed the guilty verdict on Hirohito was cut because opinion was divided about it. The High Court rejected this argument, noting that NHK could easily have made such caveats clear.[37]

The High Court summary made clear that NHK's senior management had not shown appropriate editorial independence, giving in too easily to the LDP's implied threats:

The NHK officials met with the lawmakers in order to prevent the program from negatively affecting the outcome of Diet deliberations on NHK's budget. During the meeting, the officials were told by the lawmakers to be "fair and unbiased in the production of programs." The officials overreacted to this "advice" and had the program altered. The officials must have sensed the lawmakers' deep displeasure with the program. And as NHK's budget is controlled by the Diet, this understanding made the officials decide to change the contents of the program. A news organization is as good as dead if it relinquishes its right to independent editing. No public broadcaster can fulfill its mission if it is incapable of standing up to politicians.[38]

On appeal in 2008, the Supreme Court overturned the ruling against NHK, concluding that NHK and the other production companies had no legal obligation to make programs according to the wishes of participants. Essentially, the Court ruled, editorial freedom trumped expectation rights or duty to disclose.[39] However, the Supreme Court said nothing to contradict the lower courts' conclusion that NHK's managers were both vulnerable to political threats over the budget and reactive, even over-reactive, to political intervention.

Abe's defense of his interjection, echoed by many conservatives, is that that NHK's Charter requires programs to be "fair and neutral." The documentary as envisioned by both producers and subjects was critical of both current Government policy and Emperor Hirohito, and as such could certainly be construed as lacking neutrality, and arguably, fairness. One might respond immediately that any documentary about the Tribunal could hardly have presented the LDP's side, because the LDP had refused to participate. Abe's justification fails, though, even on its own terms. First, because of the selectivity with which the LDP insists on the "fairness and neutrality" standard. NHK documentaries and other programs that reflect conservative priorities are routinely aired, yet are never subjected to the fairness standard. For example, there was no consideration of US justifications for the atomic bombings in the NHK Special "A-Bomb Victims." Whether or not one regards such justifications as valid, the fairness doctrine as interpreted by Abe and NHK management would seem to demand they at least be aired. Second, Abe's conclusion that the program would not be fair or neutral was evidently made before he had even seen the program, suggesting he believes that NHK should regard entire topics such as war crimes as off-limits. Finally, the program was not altered to be fair and neutral. Content damaging to the LDP's position was not balanced with different perspectives, it was simply cut out.

Supporters of NHK argued that it was inappropriate for a supposedly impartial public broadcaster to air a program produced clearly from the perspective of an activist NGO group with a political agenda. The argument seems reasonable, but as Tessa Morris-Suzuki argues, NHK routinely airs such content from other, more politically acceptable NGOs. Most notably, NHK devotes frequent, uncritical, and completely one-sided attention to NGOs devoted to lobbying for the families of those abducted by North Korea (the *Kazokukai*).[40]

As always, the boundaries of inclusivity and social acceptance are subjective. In this case, more clearly than most, the lines between impartiality, the watchdog role, and the requirements of inclusivity were drawn explicitly to suit the purposes of the conservative elite. As an instance of NHK's organizational self-censorship, the episode tells us much about the internal conflict between management and staff about these boundaries, as well as the conflict between government and broadcaster. The unusually bitter and public nature of the case is also instructive about the culture of self-censorship. It was suggested to me by a number of those connected with the affair that the case became so big and ugly in large part because the makers of the offending program, Documentary Japan, were an outside production company. As such, they were much less familiar with what material would or what not be acceptable to senior management and the government, and unwittingly went too far, as it turned out, in pushing the boundaries of controversy. Regular NHK staff, I was told repeatedly, would have known better than to even try to get such a documentary aired in its original form.[41]

Notes

1 Sakamaki Sachiko, "Remote Control: Broadcaster Kills Program on Comfort Women," *Far East Economic Review* (July 1996): 27.
2 Hera Diani, "Turning a Lens on the Past," *Jakarta Post*, November 4, 2001.
3 Tessa Morris-Suzuki, "Free Speech and Silenced Voices – The Japanese Media, the Comfort Women Tribunal and the NHK Affair," *Asia-Pacific Journal: Japan Focus* 4, no. 12 (December 2006).
4 Author's own interview with VAWW-Net Japan staff in Tokyo, January 2001.
5 Lisa Yoneyama, "Media no kōkyōsei to hyōsho no bōryoku: NHK "towareru senji seibōryoku" kaihen o megutte [Media Publicity and Violence of Representation: On the Alteration of the NHK Program 'Problematizing Wartime Sexual Violence']," *Sekai* (July 2001): 209–219; Kozo Nagata, *NHK to seiji Kenryoku: Bangumi Kaihen Jiken Tōjisha no Shōgen* [NHK and Political Power: The Testimony of a Person Directly Impacted by the Incident of Forced Revision of the Documentary] (Tokyo: Iwanami Shoten, 2014).
6 Lisa Yoneyama, "NHK's Censorship of Japanese Crimes against Humanity," *Harvard Asia Quarterly* 6, no. 1 (Winter 2002): 15–19; "NHK Producer Says Political Intervention Was 'Constant'," *Mainichi Daily News*, January 13, 2005.
7 "NHK, Chokzen ni okaihen [NHK: Big Change at the Last Minute]," *Asahi Shimbun*, March 3, 2001.
8 Takeuchi Kazuharu, "NHK 'Sensō o dō sabakuka' ni nani ga okita? [What Happened to NHK's 'How Should War Be Judged?']," *Shukan Kinyobi*, March 2, 2001, 66–67.
9 For the sake of continuity, he was asked to wear the same clothes again, but in the month between comments his hair has clearly grown longer, belying the impression that the commentary was one smooth take. See Kitahara Megumi, "Aato Akutebizumu [Art Activism]," *Impakushon* no. 124 (April 2001): 26–131.
10 Takahashi Tetsuya, "Nani ga Chokuzen ni Kesareta," *Sekai* no. 688 (May 2001): 209–219.
11 "NHK Producer," *Mainichi Daily News*.
12 "NHK Producer," *Mainichi Daily News*.
13 "NHK Censored TV Show Due to Political Pressure," *Japan Times*, January 14, 2005.
14 "Abe Admits Telling NHK to Censor TV Program," *Japan Times*, January 13, 2005.
15 "NHK Producer," *Mainichi Daily News*.

214 NHK and the Comfort Women

16 "NHK, Chokzen ni okaihen [NHK: Big Change at the Last Minute]," *Asahi Shimbun*, March 3, 2001.
17 Yoneyama, "NHK's Censorship of Japanese Crimes against Humanity."
18 Unpublished transcript of "Japanese Military's Wartime Sexual Violence (*Dainni Daisen Nihongun ni yoru seiboryoku.*" Draft copy, January 27, 2001.
19 NHK, "Questioning Wartime Sexual Violence [Towareru senji seiboryoku]," *Aired*, January 30, 2001.
20 "Panel Raps NHK for Editing Remarks without Permission," *Kyodo News Service*, March 31, 2003.
21 *Shugiin sōmu iinkai* [House of Representatives], transcript of proceedings, March 16, 2001.
22 Takeuchi, "*NHK: Sensō o dō sabakuka.*"
23 *Shugiin sōmu iinkai*, transcript.
24 "NHK Censored TV Show Due to Political Pressure," *Japan Times*, January 14, 2005.
25 "NHK Producer," *Mainichi Daily News*.
26 "Abe Admits Telling NHK to Censor TV Program," *Japan Times*, January 13, 2005.
27 "Abe Admits Telling NHK to Censor TV Program," *Japan Times*.
28 "NHK Censored TV Show Due to Political Pressure," *Japan Times*.
29 "Asahi Refutes NHK Official's Claim," *Asahi Shimbun*, January 21, 2005.
30 The legal proceedings are thoroughly discussed in Norma Field, "The Courts, Japan's 'Military Comfort Women,' and the Conscience of Humanity: The Ruling in VAWW-Net Japan v. NHK," *Asia Pacific Journal: Japan Focus* 5, no. 2 (February 2007).
31 "Civic Group Sues NHK over Aired Program on Sexual Slavery," *Kyodo News Agency*, July 24, 2001.
32 Field, "The Courts," 3.
33 "NHK Stung by Censorship Suit Appeal," *Japan Times*, January 30, 2007.
34 Japan Press Service, "Producer Testified He Was Pressured by Japanese Public Broadcaster," *Japan Press Weekly*, July 16–22, 2003.
35 "NHK Off Hook for Sex-slave Trial Editing," *Japan Times*, March 25, 2004.
36 The legal issues are discussed in more detail in Field, "The Courts."
37 Field, "The Courts," 3.
38 "Tokyo High Court in Ruling on NHK Program on Sexual Violence by the Former Imperial Army Said 'Surmising the Wishes of Certain Individuals, Including Diet Members, NHK Altered the Contents of the Program'," *Asahi Shimbun*, January 31, 2007.
39 Akemi Nakamura, "NHK Censorship Ruling Reversed," *Japan Times*, June 13, 2008.
40 Morris-Suzuki, "Free Speech, Silenced Voices," 8.
41 Author's own interview with a former NHK employee, Tokyo, August 2005.

References

"Abe Admits Telling NHK to Censor TV Program," *Japan Times*, January 13, 2005.
"Asahi Refutes NHK Official's Claim," *Asahi Shimbun*, January 21, 2005.
"Civic Group Sues NHK Over Aired Program on Sexual Slavery," *Kyodo News Agency*, July 24, 2001.
Diani, Hera, "Turning a Lens on the Past," *Jakarta Post*, November 4, 2001.
Field, Norma, "The Courts, Japan's 'Military Comfort Women,' and the Conscience of Humanity: The Ruling in VAWW-Net Japan v. NHK," *Asia Pacific Journal: Japan Focus* 5, no. 2 (February 2007).
Japan Press Service, "Producer Testified He Was Pressured by Japanese Public Broadcaster," *Japan Press Weekly*, July 16–22, 2003.
Kazuharu, Takeuchi, "NHK 'Sensō o dō sabakuka' ni nani ga okita? [What Happened to NHK's 'How Should War be Judged?']," *Shukan Kinyobi*, March 2, 2001, 66–67.

Megumi, Kitahara, "Aato Akutebizumu [Art Activism]," *Impakushon*, no. 124 (April 2001): 26–131.

Morris-Suzuki, Tessa, "Free Speech and Silenced Voices- The Japanese Media, the Comfort Women Tribunal and the NHK Affair," *Asia-Pacific Journal: Japan Focus* 4, no. 12 (December 2006).

Nagata, Kozo, *NHK to seiji Kenryoku: Bangumi Kaihen Jiken Tōjisha no Shōgen* [NHK and Political Power: The Testimony of a Person Directly Impacted by the Incident of Forced Revision of the Documentary] (Tokyo: Iwanami Shoten, 2014).

Nakamura, Akemi, "NHK Censorship Ruling Reversed," *Japan Times*, June 13, 2008.

"NHK Censored TV Show Due to Political Pressure," *Japan Times*, January 14, 2005.

"NHK, Chokzen ni okaihen [NHK: Big Change at the Last Minute]," *Asahi Shimbun*, March 3, 2001.

"NHK Off Hook for Sex-slave Trial Editing," *Japan Times*, March 25, 2004.

"NHK Producer Says Political Intervention Was 'Constant'," *Mainichi Daily News*, January 13, 2005.

"NHK Stung by Censorship Suit Appeal," *Japan Times*, January 30, 2007.

"Panel Raps NHK for Editing Remarks Without Permission," *Kyodo News Service*, March 31, 2003.

Sachiko, Sakamaki, "Remote Control: Broadcaster Kills Program on Comfort Women," *Far East Economic Review*, July 1996.

Shugiin sōmu iinkai [House of Representatives], Transcript of Proceedings, March 16, 2001.

Tetsuya, Takahashi, "Nani ga Chokuzen ni Kesareta," *Sekai*, no. 688 (May 2001): 209–219.

"Tokyo High Court in Ruling on NHK Program on Sexual Violence by the Former Imperial Army Said 'Surmising the Wishes of Certain Individuals, Including Diet Members, NHK Altered the Contents of the Program'," *Asahi Shimbun*, January 31, 2007.

Yoneyama, Lisa, "Media no kōkyōsei to hyōsho no bōryoku: NHK "towareru senji seibōryoku" kaihen o megutte [Media Publicity and Violence of Representation: On the Alteration of the NHK Program 'Problematizing Wartime Sexual Violence']," *Sekai* (July 2001): 209–219.

Yoneyama, Lisa, "NHK's Censorship of Japanese Crimes Against Humanity," *Harvard Asia Quarterly* 6, no. 1 (Winter 2002): 15–19.

12 Not Dead Yet! The Future of Public Service Media

This book has asked how and why two public broadcasters that share almost identical governance structures, funding sources, and remits vary so much in the political and social roles they seek to play. The BBC is more independent, confrontational, progressive, and entrepreneurial. NHK tends to be more cooperative with both the government and commercial media and more traditional and less controversial in its content. I have argued that their differences can be best understood as a result of the evolution of distinctive responses to a century's worth of momentous political, economic, and technological challenges. Differences in organizational culture between the BBC and NHK today reflect the outcomes of political choices and distributional battles first fought over a century ago, and refought periodically ever since. The BBC developed an audience-centric philosophy, securing political support by generating wide, deep listener and viewer loyalty. NHK developed a government-centric strategy, faithfully serving public goals set, or at least strongly influenced, by state interests.

Editorially, NHK observes strict neutrality in allocating airtime to different parties. But Ellis Krauss has amply demonstrated that NHK portrays the state, in particular the bureaucracy, extensively and favorably. He also makes clear that the price of neutrality has often been a form of self-censorship as managers seek to avoid confrontation or controversy. More broadly, too, NHK programming tends to reflect traditional understandings of Japanese society and culture. Well-produced dramas reflecting morally wholesome traditional values have been a staple since the 1960s, while lavish attention is paid to nationally unifying events such as Royal Ceremonies and the Olympics. It was the commercial stations who were first to air dramas about homosexuals, first to use exit polls for elections (for in the 1992 Upper House Elections), and first to bring down a government with a hostile on-air interview.

The BBC is far more willing to tackle controversial issues or confront the government of the day, happy to act as an agent of change, while NHK is content to serve as an agent of stability. In the 1960s, where the BBC embraced sweeping social change, NHK chose to uphold traditional values, looking back nostalgically and serving as an agent of stability rather than change. Since the 1960s, the BBC has become more likely to serve as a progressive agent for social change across all genres from news and documentaries to entertainment. The enormous popularity

DOI: 10.4324/b23015-12

of its programs has in turn imbued the BBC with a degree of protection against political backlash. At its best, public broadcasting can be a powerful vehicle for social inclusion. But it is not necessarily so, and often in the past the demands of building national identity and reinforcing existing social norms came at the price of inclusivity. Nation-building does not always, or even usually, accommodate diversity or dissent, and as we have seen, both the BBC and NHK have been guilty of marginalizing entire groups or opinions that fell outside the social mainstream, especially in the early decades of their existence. The BBC's early refusal to air Jewish or Muslim religious services shows the dangers of identifying the public interest too exclusively. Similarly, it was not until the 1960s that programming began to reflect interests much beyond those of the white English middle class. Progress toward inclusivity has been fraught, contentious, and liable to backlash.

Why did the BBC develop into an assertively independent broadcaster, while NHK is less confrontational and succumbs more readily to political bullying? Some of the explanations seeking to explain such differences fall short. Explanations for NHK's timidity have referenced governance structures such as political control over the appointment of the governing bodies or the power of the Prime Minister over the choice of President. Similarly, the need for parliamentary approval for viewer fee increases or business expansion are said to constrain NHK. Yet the BBC has similar mechanisms and behaves differently. Some might invoke differences in political culture between Britain and Japan. Perhaps NHK's reluctance to confront the government is a reflection of a more hierarchically organized, deferential national culture? But such explanations would not explain why there are such profound differences in attitudes between management and staff, especially in Japan. NHK's reporters and producers are not averse to questioning authority and challenging the status quo. It is their bosses who prefer to avoid offending politicians or outraging public sentiment.

The postwar electoral dominance of the LDP surely explains much of NHK's conservatism, although the two reinforce each other. Krauss argues that the likelihood that the LDP would remain in power gave LDP politicians more incentive to try to exercise influence over NHK. The broadcaster, in turn, had more incentive to acquiesce to the pressure, generating an organizational culture of self-censorship.[1] Media scholars Hallin and Mancini make a similar point, noting that alteration in power means that "major political parties accept the inevitability of losing power and are therefore willing to give up trying to control broadcasting."[2] But this line of explanation does not tell the whole story. History matters.

Different organizational cultures still reflect, in part, the different political climates in the early days of the 1920s and especially the 1930s when Japan's increasingly authoritarian governments took firm control over all aspects of national life. The BBC's relative editorial independence does not come from the absence of government pressure. On the contrary, politicians from Winston Churchill to Margaret Thatcher, Tony Blair, and most recently Boris Johnson all have attempted to influence the broadcaster, either directly or through political appointments of the Director-General and the Governing board. However, the

BBC's management have more often chosen to resist the pressure, developing over the decades a powerful internal culture of journalistic autonomy. Reith made the decision to defend editorial independence against political intervention early, and this approach became ingrained, heightened even during the Second World War. In the 1960s, the BBC even became confrontational toward those in power, calculating correctly that this made politicians less rather than more likely to seek to dismantle the organization. Fiercely independent journalism became seen as not only desirable in its own right, but a survival strategy to win loyalty over audiences. NHK, by contrast, sought protection from government pressure by a policy of studied editorial neutrality and non-confrontation toward those in power.

After the Second World War, the SCAP occupiers also treated NHK as a mouthpiece rather than an independent news source, even as they laid the groundwork for a free press. NHK's reporters and program makers proved during the Occupation that they could be as outspoken and fearless as any, but these impulses were never given a chance to develop into a sustained organizational culture. As soon as SCAP left, NHK's management began to demand journalism and entertainment, which was less provocative and more sympathetic to the state.

Now, BBC writers and journalists wear their editorial independence as a badge of honor, as the cases of *The War Game*, *Real Lives*, and the Gilligan Affair demonstrate. Over time, the cultures become self-sustaining. BBC reporters can take risks in relative confidence that management will back them. Conversely, when BBC management seem to give in to pressure or succumb to timidity, BBC journalists are among the first to call them out. For example, editorial timidity concerning *Newsnight*'s canceled Jimmy Savile documentary was thoroughly examined and publicly criticized across the organization. By contrast, NHK's journalists can be less confident of managerial support, and less likely to demand that managers show backbone in the face of government interference. In this regard, the events of the Jimmy Savile scandal are instructive. Director-General George Entwhistle resigned in November 2011 following the revelations of child abuse by Savile. The precipitating factor in Entwistle's resignation was generally agreed to be his hapless performance in the face of a fiercely penetrating interview by one of his own journalists, John Humphreys of Radio 4's *Today*.[3] Such moments of public self-criticism are rare at NHK.

Is Public Broadcasting Doomed?

What does the future hold? Many argued that neoliberalism and globalization would render public broadcasting obsolete.[4] As Hallin and Mancini put it, the highly commercialized US media model "has clearly become increasingly dominant across Europe as well as North America – as it has, no doubt, across much of the world."[5] Digitization, too, has utterly altered the media landscape.[6] On top of these broader challenges, both broadcasters are facing immediate threats from political hostility and eroding public trust to competition from vastly wealthier streaming services and indifference from younger audiences. In the United Kingdom, populists on the right are once again seeking to drag the BBC into the front lines of the culture wars. Boris Johnson, angered like many Brexiteers by what he claimed was the BBC's pro-EU bias, boycotted *Today*, the BBC's flagship current affairs show.[7] Johnson also hinted at decriminalizing the license fee, which would represent a significant step up in what some observers have seen as a longer conservative strategy of weakening the BBC through financial strangulation.[8] The Conservative government also appointed or discussed appointing critics of the BBC to prominent oversight positions on the Board of Governors or Ofcom.[9] Some observers see the BBC as succumbing to its own forms of self-censorship and timidity in the face of this constant pressure.[10] In Japan, the resignation of Prime Minister Abe reduced what had been near-constant political interference, but his successor, Suga Yoshihide, showed little interest in cultivating better relationships with the media he was wont to stonewall during his notoriously tight-lipped conferences as Chief Cabinet Secretary.[11] Declining interest by younger audiences remains an ongoing headache for both broadcasters, although the problem is more acute at NHK.[12]

Yet the BBC and NHK have survived for a century in the face of daunting obstacles. They have kept faith in the public service ethos and rejected the dogma that market forces alone will suffice to provide all the information, education, and entertainment that democratic society needs. Both broadcasters have survived also because of their capacity to adapt to new political and technological realities. Will they be able to continue to do so? There are reasons for guarded optimism.

The first reason for optimism is that new media technologies have never yet had as far-reaching or transformative effects as their fans or naysayers claim. At the turn of the last century, radio was predicted to replace newspapers, theater, live music, and professional sports. Yet, as sociologist Marshall Beuick argued in 1927, the social effects of radio broadcasting would be far less than popularly believed. He caricatured the breathless predictions of radio's supporters in terms eerily echoed by today's new media enthusiasts:

> These programs have stimulated the conclusions that we shall have a greater religious consciousness, that we shall take a greater interest in politics than we are wont to, that we shall find less apathy for education, and that we shall wake up one bright morning with an international consciousness, the result of world-wide broadcast programs, and the dawn of mutual understanding and world peace will have come.[13]

Similar predictions had been made for commercial printing presses, Beuick noted, and they had been equally wrong. In the 1950s, television was said to spell doom for radio as well as for newspapers, theater, live music, and professional sports, which, far from being killed off, had thrived as radio brought in new audiences and greater national attention. Cinema, too, was meant to be shoved aside. Sam Goldwyn wondered, "Who's going to go out and pay to see bad films when they could stay at home and see bad television for nothing?" In the 1970s, cable and satellite apparently meant death for network television. In the 1980s, famously, video was going to kill the radio star. The internet was billed to destroy television. Now the debate has become how great a threat social media poses to democracy itself.[14]

Popular attitudes toward new media have always gone through a cycle of utopian optimism followed by panic-stricken pessimism, and finally pragmatic acceptance. Each new technology has been hailed and then cursed for its likely social influence. Boosters predicted each new device would democratize knowledge, spread culture to the masses, bind families and nations together, even bring world peace through greater global understanding. Indeed, the BBC's first official motto was "Peace Shall Speak Peace Unto Nations." In 1926, John Reith wrote that radio would mean:

> People may have an opportunity of listening to outstanding opinions on the great questions political and social which are today understood by a mere fraction of the electorate. I have heard it said that in the old days of limited suffrage, two-thirds of the voters were students of politics whereas today not five percent have any real knowledge of the principles on which they cast their vote. Extension of the scope of broadcasting will mean a more intelligent and enlightened electorate.[15]

Reith's assumption that people were better informed back in the day seems ironic in light of contemporary concerns about dumbing down. His faith that new media would make everyone smarter is an equally ironic but not uncommon misconception. Orrin Dunlap, first television correspondent for *The New York Times*, claimed with breathtaking lack of foresight that, thanks to television, "we are approaching the dawn of clear, intelligent politics."[16] Theodore Roosevelt Jr. wrote that television would "stir the nation to a lively interest in those who are directing its policies" and result in "more intelligent, more concerted action from an electorate; the people will think more for themselves."[17] Metta Spencer argues that by cheering us up and encouraging empathy for its fictional characters, television enhances our physical and mental health and "contributes to a culture of peace and compassion."[18] Rupert Murdoch announced in 1993 that satellite television represented "an unambiguous threat to totalitarian regimes everywhere."[19]

Detractors, on the other hand, denounced each new technology as liable to destroy families, vulgarize high art, erode traditional culture, dumb down civic discourse, and generally undermine the moral fabric of society. In 1952, Lord Reith likened the introduction of commercial television to the introduction of smallpox and the Black Death, while five years later, Oya Shoichi predicted that television would turn Japan into a nation of 100 million idiots.

The social and political effects of each new technology were usually smaller than many of the wild predictions. This is not to say that new technologies have had no effect, especially on the fortunes of media organizations who either adapted successfully or failed. Invariably, though, the uses of every technology are shaped by the values and political realities of the societies in which they emerge rather than vice versa. In the 1930s, radio was used to drum up nationalistic pride in Japan, play opera in Britain, and sell soap in America. In an earlier era, demagogues, artists, and salesmen used newspapers or mass meetings – now they can use Twitter, but the message has always been more important than the medium.

The second reason for optimism is that the new media revolution is providing opportunities as well as challenges for the broadcasters. In the words of one BBC editor, "Interactivity allows us to put 'the public' in public broadcasting."[20] This is especially true for the BBC, which moved more quickly, innovatively, and effectively to adopt new technologies. Some in NHK also see social media tools such as Twitter as a way of engaging the younger audiences they are in danger of losing.[21] These efforts have not yet been particularly thorough, perhaps because NHK has a clear sense of its existing mission and has prioritized continuing to do what it already does well. The gamble is that as the Japanese population ages, audience tastes will change.

Most importantly, the multiplication, fragmentation, and increasingly partisan nature of news sources are generating more rather than less need for the serious, trustworthy, and dispassionate content, which public, non-commercial broadcasting is well-equipped to provide.[22] New media are destroying old business models, resulting in what many see as a journalism crisis.[23] The collapse of local and regional newspapers, as well as the retreat from serious news by network television, demonstrates the degree to which high-quality journalism has so often been subsidized in one form or another. However, as media analyst Clay Shirkey puts it, "Society doesn't need newspapers. What we need is journalism."[24] The BBC and NHK continue to provide such journalism, slow news for bewildering times.

And this is the final, best reason for optimism: the BBC and NHK do their jobs. Public broadcasters can serve many roles: reporter of reliable news and information; educator; forum for democratic debate; vehicle for social cohesion; voice for minority or marginalized interests; and watchdog on the powerful.[25] There is no question that both the BBC and NHK have performed many of their duties exceptionally.

Both broadcasters are their nation's primary source of thorough, accurate news. They take seriously their mandates to be impartial and even-handed, although they differ in how they interpret those concepts and are not always successful. The requirement to air all politically relevant sides of contentious issues is often at odds with the civic imperative not to give publicity to inaccurate or bad-faith views. Recently, many observers, including their own journalists, have criticized the BBC's decision to include discredited or unqualified sources such as climate change deniers purely for the appearance of balance.[26] Both are also criticized from left and right for partisan bias. Yet they remain their nations' most trusted news sources.[27] In 2017, Ipsos MORI found the BBC to be the most trusted news source for 57% of the respondents, compared to 10% for the next most trusted, ITV. No other news source, including the Guardian, Sky News, The Times, or Facebook, was trusted most by more than 5%. The BBC scored similarly highly when respondents were asked which news sources they regarded as most impartial.[28] Similar findings can be found in the Reuters Institute for Journalism survey on Digital News, which finds that BBC News was the highest-used UK news source (67% used it at least once a week), the most trusted for accuracy (70%

of respondents ranked it most accurate) and the most likely to be placed in the middle of the political spectrum.[29] The same report found that NHK news was most trusted for accuracy by 59% of respondents. NHK was the most used source of television news (56% used it at least once a week), but considerably less popular online (23% used it once a week).[30] The public's tendency to trust the public broadcasters only intensifies during times of confusion or crisis, as seen rising viewership for NHK news during the 3.11 Triple Crisis.[31] Similarly, both broadcasters were where viewers turned first for information about the COVID-19 pandemic. And while there are always questions of causality in surveys of political knowledge, the evidence is that regular consumers of public broadcasting news are better informed about political issues than those who relied on commercial media.[32]

Both broadcasters are also preeminent cultural institutions, at the heart of the national imagination and creators of many of the rhythms and routines that embed national consciousness. They, perhaps more than any other institutions, created and sustained such banal daily rituals as the evening news and such majestic national ceremonies such as the royal weddings and coronations. They continue to serve, albeit imperfectly, as familiar, unifying national institutions in the face of a public sphere being rapidly shredded from all sides.

Both also continue to play vital roles in national economic development. NHK Labs have played a vital role in research and development for technologies vital to the success of Japan's consumer electronics industry. The BBC has been vital to the development of Britain's increasingly important creative industries by producing and training actors, writers, editors, and technical staff as well as commissioning work from independent companies. Finally, both broadcasters continue to serve as national ambassadors, the most visible and multifaceted public face of their country, and an irreplaceable source of soft power in a troubled world.

As the BBC and NHK move into another new media age, old questions remain. Are they truly fulfilling public interests? How are they defining those interests? Could their services be provided cheaper or better by free markets? How will political control square with the demands of editorial autonomy? These are ongoing questions and legitimate concerns that will continue to be debated. For now, though, the belief remains strong that public broadcasters can and should serve the common good as well as private interest, and that they are worthy of public support.

Notes

1 Ellis Krauss, *Broadcasting Politics in Japan* (Ithaca, NY: Cornell University Press, 2000), 255–258.
2 Daniel C. Hallin and Paolo Mancini, *Comparing Media Systems: Three Models of Media and Politics* (Cambridge: Cambridge University Press, 2004), 53.
3 Gillian Reynolds, "BBC Crisis: John Humphreys Sealed George Entwistle's Fate," *Daily Telegraph*, November 12, 2012.
4 For example, Michael Tracey, *The Decline and Fall of Public Broadcasting* (Oxford: Oxford University Press, 2002).

5 Hallin and Mancini, *Comparing Media Systems*, 251.

6 On this debate, see: Clay Shirky, *Cognitive Surplus: Creativity and Generosity in a Connected Age* (Penguin Books, 2010); Nicolas Carr, *The Shallows: What the Internet Is Doing to Our Brains* (London: WW Norton, 2010); Malcolm Gladwell, "Small Change: Why the Revolution Will Not be Tweeted," *The New Yorker* 86, no. 30 (October 4, 2010); Clay Shirky, "The Political Power of Social Media" *Foreign Affairs* 90, no. 1 (January/February 2011).

7 Matthew Taylor and Jim Waterson, "Boris Johnson Threatens BBC with Two-pronged Attack," *The Guardian*, December 15, 2019, www.theguardian.com/media/2019/dec/15/boris-johnson-threatens-bbc-with-two-pronged-attack.

8 Patrick Barwise and Peter York, *The War against the BBC: How an Unprecedented Combination of Hostile Forces Is Destroying Britain's Greatest Cultural Institution . . . and Why You Should Care* (London: Penguin Books, 2020).

9 For example, former Conservative Communications Director Sir Robbie Gibb was appointed to the Board of Governors in April 2021. Paul Dacre, former editor of the *Daily Mail* and a prominent anti-BBC voice, was closely considered as Chair of Ofcom. Amol Rajan, "Sir Robbie Gibb: Former Downing Street Communications Director Joins BBC Board," *BBC*, April 29, 2021, www.bbc.com/news/entertainment-arts-56929982.

10 For example, Tom Mills, "Richard Sharp's Arrival at the BBC Will Entrench Conservative Influence," *The Guardian*, January 14, 2021.

11 Henry Laurence, "After Abe, Will Press Freedom Improve in Japan?," *The Diplomat*, October 10, 2020, https://thediplomat.com/2020/10/after-abe-will-press-freedom-improve-in-japan/.

12 Author's own interview with members of the NHK Planning Department, Tokyo, June 2017.

13 Marshall Beuick, "The Limited Social Effects of Radio Broadcasting," *The American Journal of Sociology* 32, no. 4 (January 1927): 617.

14 A concern shared from both left and right. For example, David Runciman, *How Democracy Ends* (London: Profile Books, 2018); Niall Ferguson, "Silicon Valley and the Threat to Democracy," *Daily Beast*, January 20, 2018.

15 J.C.W. Reith, *Broadcast over Britain* (London: Hodder and Staunton, 1924), 113.

16 Quoted in: Rick Shenkman, *Just How Stupid Are We? Facing the Truth about the American Voter* (New York: Basic Books, 2008), 82.

17 Shenkman, *Just How Stupid Are We?*, 2.

18 Metta Spencer, *Two Aspirins and a Comedy: How Television Can Enhance Health and Society* (Boulder, CO: Paradigm Publishers, 2006), 272.

19 "Murdoch and China," *The Guardian*, August 23, 2003. Ironically, a few months after this pronouncement, Murdoch dropped BBC World from his STAR TV satellite service because an unflattering documentary about Mao Tse-tung had upset the CCP, whose support Murdoch needed to expand his Chinese media operations.

20 Author's own interview with a BBC editor, London, March 2008.

21 Author's own interviews with members of the NHK planning department, Tokyo, August 2017.

22 Pew Research Center, "News Audiences Increasingly Politicized," June 8, 2004, http://people-press.org/report/215/news-audiences-increasingly-politicized.

23 Jeffrey Alexander, Elizabeth Butler Breese, and Maria Luenge, eds., *The Crisis of Journalism Reconsidered* (Cambridge: Cambridge University Press, 2016).

24 Clay Shirky, "Newspapers and Thinking the Unthinkable," in *Will the Last Reporter Please Turn Out the Lights*, eds. Robert W. McChesney and Victor Pickard (New York: The New Press, 2011), 43.

25 Karol Jakubowicz, "Public Service Broadcasting and Public Policy," in *The Handbook of Global Media and Communication*, eds. Robin Mansell and Marc Raboy (Oxford: Blackwell Publishing, 2011), 210–229.

26 The House of Commons Select Committee on Science and Technology's "Report on Communicating Climate Science" (2014) found that although the BBC's coverage of climate change was generally good, constituting the main source of information on climate change for most people in Britain, it was guilty of over-representing denialist viewpoints for the sake of balance: "The lack of distinction within BBC News between proven scientific facts and opinions or beliefs is problematic." See page 19, https://publications.parliament.uk/pa/cm201314/cmselect/cmsctech/254/254.pdf.

27 Daniel Marshall, "BBC Most Trusted News Source," *Ipsos MORI*, November 22, 2017, www.ipsos.com/ipsos-mori/en-uk/bbc-most-trusted-news-source; Yokoyama Shigeru and Yonekura Ritsu, "Structure of Trust in the Mass Media," NHK *Hōsōkenkyū chōsa* [Broadcast Research Survey] (Tokyo: NHK Broadcasting Culture Research Institute, 2009).

28 Marshall, "BBC the Most Trusted News Source."

29 Nic Newman, "Digital News Report: United Kingdom," Reuters Institute for the Study of Journalism at Oxford University, 2017, www.digitalnewsreport.org/survey/2017/united-kingdom-2017/.

30 Yasaomi Sawa, "Digital News Report: Japan," Reuters Institute for the Study of Journalism at Oxford University, 2017, www.digitalnewsreport.org/survey/2017/japan-2017/.

31 Mark Schilling, "NHK Up to Earthquake Challenge," *Variety*, April 2, 2011.

32 Christian Collett and Gento Kato, "Does NHK Make You Smarter (and Super News Make You 'softer')? An Examination of Political Knowledge and the Potential Influence of TV News," *Japanese Journal of Political Science* 15, no. 1 (2014): 25–50; Toril Aalberg and James Curran, eds., *How Media Inform Democracy: A Comparative Approach* (New York: Routledge, 2012). See also James Curran et al., "Media System, Public Knowledge and Democracy," *European Journal of Communication* 24, no. 1 (2009): 5–26; Pippa Norris and Christina Holz-Bacha, "To Entertain, Inform and Educate: Still the Role of Public Television," *Political Communication* 18, no. 2 (April–June 2001): 123–140.

References

Aalberg, Toril, and James Curran, eds., *How Media Inform Democracy: A Comparative Approach* (New York: Routledge, 2012).

Alexander, Jeffrey, Elizabeth Butler Breese, and Maria Luenge, eds., *The Crisis of Journalism Reconsidered* (Cambridge: Cambridge University Press, 2016).

Barwise, Patrick, and Peter York, *The War Against the BBC: How an Unprecedented Combination of Hostile Forces is Destroying Britain's Greatest Cultural Institution . . . and Why You Should Care* (London: Penguin Books, 2020).

Beuick, Marshall, "The Limited Social Effects of Radio Broadcasting," *The American Journal of Sociology* 32, no. 4 (Jan 1927): 617.

Carr, Nicolas, *The Shallows: What the Internet is Doing to Our Brains* (London: WW Norton, 2010).

Collett, Christian, and Gento Kato, "Does NHK Make You Smarter (and Super News Make You 'Softer')? An Examination of Political Knowledge and the Potential Influence of TV News," *Japanese Journal of Political Science* 15, no. 1 (2014): 25–50.

Curran, James, et al., "Media System, Public Knowledge and Democracy," *European Journal of Communication* 24, no. 1 (2009): 5–26.

Ferguson, Niall, "Silicon Valley and the Threat to Democracy," *Daily Beast*, January 20, 2018.

Gladwell, Malcolm, "Small Change: Why the Revolution Will Not be Tweeted," *The New Yorker* 86, no. 30 (October 4, 2010).

Hallin, Daniel C., and Paolo Mancini, *Comparing Media Systems: Three Models of Media and Politics* (Cambridge: Cambridge University Press, 2004).

Jakubowicz, Karol, "Public Service Broadcasting and Public Policy," in *The Handbook of Global Media and Communication*, eds. Robin Mansell and Marc Raboy (Oxford: Blackwell Publishing, 2011), 210–229.

Krauss, Ellis, *Broadcasting Politics in Japan* (Ithaca, NY: Cornell University Press, 2000).

Laurence, Henry, "After Abe, Will Press Freedom Improve in Japan?" *The Diplomat*, October 10, 2020, https://thediplomat.com/2020/10/after-abe-will-press-freedom-improve-in-japan/.

Marshall, Daniel, "BBC Most Trusted News Source," *Ipsos MORI*, November 22, 2017, www.ipsos.com/ipsos-mori/en-uk/bbc-most-trusted-news-source.

"Murdoch and China," *The Guardian*, August 23, 2003.

Newman, Nic, "Digital News Report: United Kingdom," Reuters Institute for the Study of Journalism at Oxford University, 2017, www.digitalnewsreport.org/survey/2017/united-kingdom-2017/.

Norris, Pippa, and Christina Holz-Bacha, "To Entertain, Inform and Educate: Still the Role of Public Television," *Political Communication* 18, no. 2 (April–June 2001): 123–140.

Pew Research Center, "News Audiences Increasingly Politicized," June 8, 2004, http://people-press.org/report/215/news-audiences-increasingly-politicized.

Rajan, Amol, "Sir Robbie Gibb: Former Downing Street Communications Director Joins BBC Board," *BBC*, April 29, 2021, www.bbc.com/news/entertainment-arts-56929982.

Reith, J.C.W., *Broadcast Over Britain* (London: Hodder and Staunton, 1924).

Reynolds, Gillian, "BBC Crisis: John Humphreys Sealed George Entwistle's Fate," *Daily Telegraph*, November 12, 2012.

Runciman, David, *How Democracy Ends* (London: Profile Books, 2018).

Schilling, Mark, "NHK Up to Earthquake Challenge," *Variety*, April 2, 2011.

Shenkman, Rick, *Just How Stupid Are We? Facing the Truth about the American Voter* (New York: Basic Books, 2008).

Shigeru, Yokoyama, and Yonekura Ritsu, "Structure of Trust in the Mass Media," *Hōsōkenkyū chōsa* [Broadcast Research Survey] (Tokyo: NHK Broadcasting Culture Research Institute, 2009).

Shirky, Clay, *Cognitive Surplus: Creativity and Generosity in a Connected Age* (London: Penguin Books, 2010).

Shirky, Clay, "Newspapers and Thinking the Unthinkable," in *Will the Last Reporter Please Turn Out the Lights*, eds. Robert W. McChesney and Victor Pickard (New York, NY: The New Press, 2011).

Shirky, Clay, "The Political Power of Social Media," *Foreign Affairs* 90, no. 1 (January/February 2011).

Spencer, Metta, *Two Aspirins and a Comedy: How Television Can Enhance Health and Society* (Boulder, CO: Paradigm Publishers, 2006).

Taylor, Matthew, and Jim Waterson, "Boris Johnson Threatens BBC with Two-Pronged Attack," *The Guardian*, December 15, 2019, www.theguardian.com/media/2019/dec/15/boris-johnson-threatens-bbc-with-two-pronged-attack.

Tracey, Michael, *The Decline and Fall of Public Broadcasting* (Oxford: Oxford University Press, 2002).

Appendix: Timelines

BBC Timeline

1895   Marconi sends wireless signal.

1920   Nellie Melba broadcasts for Marconi/Daily Mail.

1922   British Broadcasting Company founded.

           John Reith made General Manager.

1923   Sykes Report recommends license fee.

1927   British Broadcasting Company becomes British Broadcasting Corporation (BBC). John Reith becomes the Director-General.

1930   Number of radio licenses increases to 12 million.

1932   BBC Empire Service (later the World Service) launched. King George V delivers a Christmas Day message on the new Service.

1936   BBC begins TV broadcasts (the first broadcaster to do so).

1938   Reith resigns as Director-General of BBC. BBC begins foreign language service, first in Arabic, followed by French, German, and Italian.

1939   BBC Television Service suspended over concerns that bombers could target VHF transmissions.

1945   Regional radio programming resumes.

1946   Television broadcasts resume.

1954   Television Act creates ITV.

1955   The Wrotham transmitter allows radio service to broadcast on VHF (FM).

1962   Beginning of experimental stereo radio broadcasts.

1964   BBC 2 (TV) launched. Pirate radio stations grow in influence.

1967   Pirate radio stations forced off-air. BBC Radio 1 launched.

           BBC launches Local Radio, beginning in Leicester.

1978   Parliament begins regular radio broadcasts.

1982   Channel 4 (commercial public service TV broadcaster) launched.

1986   BSB begins satellite service.

1989   Sky TV launches direct-to-home (DBS) satellite service.

1990   Broadcasting Act. BSB and Sky TV form BSkyB.

1991   BBC World (TV) launched.

1996   Broadcasting Act. Radio 1 is available streaming live over the internet.

Director-General John Birt restructures the BBC. Under the new structure, BBC Broadcast commissions programs and BBC Production creates them.

1997   New corporate identity created at a cost of £5 million.

1998   Launch of terrestrial digital TV.

2004   Publication of the Hutton Inquiry results in the resignation of Chairman Gavyn Davies.

Resignation of the Director-General, Greg Dyke.

Appointment of Michael Grade as Chairman and Mark Thompson as Director-General.

2005   DG Thompson announces 14% of staff will be laid off and one-third of staff go on strike.

2006   BBC's first HD broadcast.

2007   BBC Trust replaces Board of Governors.

DG Thompson announces further cuts to budget, staffing, and programming.

BBC iPlayer allows viewers to watch previously aired shows.

2008   Red Button allows limited Video on Demand and interactivity.

2010   Conservative government freezes license fee until 2016.

Launch of BBC One HD.

2011   *Newsnight* report into Jimmy Savile's child sex abuse is canceled.

2012   Coverage of London Olympics breaks records for online and TV audiences.

Includes broadcasts in NHK's Super-Hi Vision.

ITV breaks Savile story.

Operation Yewtree (criminal investigation into Savile) uncovers extensive abuse.

Newsnight falsely implicates Lord MacAlpine as a sex offender.

Director-General George Entwhistle resigns.

2017   Royal Charter renewed for 10 years.

BBC Trust scrapped, replaced by BBC Board.

Ofcom assumes regulatory oversight.

NHK Timeline

1895   Marconi sends wireless signal from Italy.

1915   Wireless Telegraphy Law.

1925   Tokyo Broadcasting Station begins commercial services. Osaka Broadcasting Station and Nagoya Broadcasting Station follow.

1926   Takayanagi Kenjiro displays Japanese character on a cathode-ray tube.

1927   Ministry of Communications oversees formation of NHK through the merger of three commercial stations.

1928   First live sumo broadcast.
1931   Government bans news flashes in light of war in China. Launch of second radio station.
1935   School broadcasting begins. Launch of shortwave radio service for overseas listeners.
1941   Japanese Army nationalizes news networks for the duration of Second World War.
1945   Regular radio programs resume.
1946   NHK workers strike. Broadcasts put under control of Ministry of Communications.
1950   Under the Broadcast Law, NHK is recreated as a viewer-supported corporation. NHK launches General TV.
1951   Commercial radio broadcasts begin.
       National Association of Broadcasters (NAB) founded.
1953   NHK begins regular TV service. Commercial broadcasters follow.
1959   Revision to the Broadcast Law requires NHK and commercial broadcasters to balance TV programming between news, entertainment, educational, and cultural programming.
1960   NHK launches color TV. NHK begins to edit cut violent scenes.
1962   Number of TV sets in Japan reaches 10 million.
1965   NHK Broadcasting Center opens.
1971   All General TV broadcasts in color, but only 50% of households own color TVs.
1978   First experimental broadcasting satellite.
1984   NHK begins experimental satellite broadcasts
1989   NHK launches 24-hour satellite services. Beginning of Hi-Vision broadcasts.
1991   Commercial satellite service WOWOW launched.
1995   NHK creates an international arm, NHK World TV.
1997   Broadcast and Human Rights watchdog (BRC) founded.
1998   Hi-Vision broadcast of Earth from space on NHK World TV.
2000   Launch of internet news service and satellite digital TV.
2003   Digital Terrestrial TV launched.
2008   NHK Video on Demand launched.
2010   NHK offers an application for iPhone users to listen to NHK World TV live.
2011   NHK World TV starts broadcasting on cable TV due to demand for English programming following the major earthquake in April.
2012   NHK introduces a new application for Android OS that provides access to live streaming news, documentaries, and cultural programs. NHK also announces that World Radio Japan will be streamed live on the website.
2013   Momii Katsuto appointed President. Causes controversy with remarks about wartime "comfort women" and editorial independence.
2018   4k/8k Super-Hi Vision Broadcasting launched
2019   Anti-NHK Party wins Diet seat.

Index

Note: Page numbers in in **bold** indicate a table on the corresponding page.

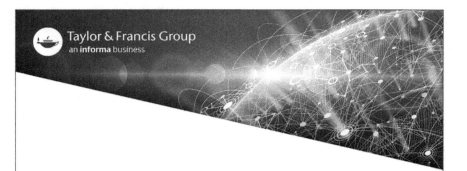

CPSIA information can be obtained
at www.ICGtesting.com
Printed in the USA
BVHW011656280722
643265BV00002B/13